THE

FEDERALIST ERA

1789 — 1801

THE
FEDERALIST ERA
1789 – 1801

By JOHN C. MILLER

WAVELAND
PRESS, INC.
Prospect Heights, Illinois

For information about this book, write or call:
Waveland Press, Inc.
P.O. Box 400
Prospect Heights, Illinois 60070
847/634-0081

Contents

Illustrations

Map

Editors' Introduction

THE ADMINISTRATIONS of George Washington and John Adams, the theme of this volume, constitute a record of extraordinary accomplishment. Assuming from the start a national role for the central government, the Federalists literally followed Alexander Hamilton's earlier counsel to "think continentally." In a scant dozen years the Constitution was demonstrated to be a workable instrument of government. During that time the Chief Executive determined the powers and traditions of his great office, the cabinet system evolved, a federal judiciary was established, the taxing power was wielded audaciously and effectively, a national debt was created to strengthen the national authority and stimulate the economy, American credit was fixed at home and abroad on a firm foundation and American territory cleared of British and Spanish interlopers.

If the record of the Federalists in the field of foreign affairs was less considerable than on the home front, it was noteworthy and equally controversial. Held in contempt by foreign powers during the years of the Confederation, the United States gained a measure of respect for its purpose and stability in the years that followed. Washington and Adams prudently steered a course of neutrality, however unpopular that policy might seem at one time or another to the opposing factions. This neutrality was achieved at the sacrifice of the French alliance and by making considerable concessions to Great Britain. Its objective was survival, and measured by that objective it was a stunning success.

Washington was the unanimous choice for the Presidency, but the principal measures of his administration and the program of his prime minister, Alexander Hamilton, were bitterly contested every inch of the way. Writing on the eve of his election to serve his first term in the

Presidency, Washington declared that "if the friends to the Constitution conceive that my administering the government will be a means of its acceleration and strength, is it not probable that the adversaries of it may entertain the same ideas, and of course make it an object of an opposition?" Washington may have been somewhat premature in his forecast of the precipitate rise of the party system, but by the end of his first term in office the party of the administration was confronted by a formidable opposition.

The opposition of Madison and Jefferson was not seriously embarrassed by a sense of restraint. Nor was their chief critic, Hamilton. Both sides fought fiercely and not always fairly. But the value of an opposition party was effectively demonstrated. The Jeffersonians sniffed at corruption and undue influence in high places. They served as watchdogs against encroachments upon civil liberties. They prepared the way for the more democratic state that was to be ushered in with John Adams' departure from office. Perhaps the Jeffersonians were uncritical in their enthusiasm for the French Revolution and overlooked the authoritarian cast of the revolutionary left. This enthusiasm affected their judgment in foreign affairs, which fortunately did not prevail during this period.

With pace, clarity, judiciousness and a sense of balance, Professor Miller recounts the story of the dramatic clashes over fundamental issues which marked the Federalist administrations, the classic contest between Hamilton and Jefferson for dominance in Washington's administration, and between John Adams and the Hamiltonians when the New Englander succeeded to the Presidency. He does not adopt the highly critical anti-Jeffersonian bias which marked such older nationalist historians as Hildreth and von Holst. At the same time, he does not follow some of the recent historians, who apotheosize Jefferson and all his actions and save for Hamilton nothing but partisan vilification. Both men get their due in these pages. Nor does Washington emerge as the decrepit, senile figure, pathetically dependent on his *éminence grise*, Hamilton, as some recent critics would depict the first President. True, the last years do not always show Washington at his best, but the author leaves us in no doubt that he remained in command of the ship until the end. The author shows how John Adams, after an inept start, rallied magnificently to override the warmongers in his cabinet and settle outstanding differences with France. Mr. Miller makes it perfectly clear that the Federalists were maladroit poli-

ticians who failed to recognize the democratic roots of American society. One can understand why the Federalists felt that the American
experiment in free government had failed when Jefferson was elected,
but, despite their shortsightedness, they had taken a parchment and
turned it into an effective instrument of government.

Preface

THE historian of the Federalist Era is at no loss to discern significant trends of development. This period was marked by the organization of the Federal government, the enactment of legislation of such far-reaching importance that the First Congress of the United States has been compared with the Constitutional Convention, and the laying down of a foreign policy which, for over a century, served as a guide to the statesmen of the Republic.

The passions engendered by the political disputes of the Federalist Era have not yet subsided. Historians fall easily into the ways of thinking of their favorite protagonists who held sway during this period. As a result, in the historical context, Hamilton is often seen through the eyes of Jefferson and Madison, and—more rarely—Jefferson and his colleagues are viewed from the perspective of Hamilton. The bias of the author of this book will be readily discernible to his readers: upon some issues, his sympathies are strongly inclined toward Hamilton; in other instances, he finds himself standing with Jefferson. The two criteria which have materially shaped the author's point of view are: what measures were necessary to promote the growth, prosperity, and cohesion of the United States; and what needed to be done to protect the individual in the exercise of his constitutional rights. In short, the dominant themes of this book are Union and Liberty.

In the course of my research I have been accorded by librarians all the privileges and amenities for which a scholar could ask. I owe a special debt to Professor Richard B. Morris, who has painstakingly read my manuscript and suggested many changes which have been incorporated in this volume.

JOHN C. MILLER

CHAPTER 1

The Launching of the "Great Experiment"

IN 1789, for the second time since the Declaration of Independence, the American people attempted to establish an efficient, durable national government, acceptable to all sections of the country. Their first effort, the Articles of Confederation, having failed to meet the urgent financial needs of the nation, uphold national rights abroad, and counteract the strong centrifugal forces at work in the United States, was supplanted in 1788 by the Federal Constitution. Because they had learned from experience the ephemerality of governments—in a little over a decade, Americans had subverted two governments, one of their own creation and the other the rule of Great Britain over the thirteen colonies—the Founding Fathers were wary of claiming their handiwork as eternal. Even though James Madison maintained that the Constitution was "intended to last for ages," he admitted that social and economic changes would in the foreseeable future subject the frame of government to severe strain. For the most part, the framers regarded the Constitution as an experiment which would go far toward determining "the long contested question whether men can govern themselves."[1] The outcome, it was generally agreed, depended upon the degree of wisdom, moderation, and self-restraint exhibited by the American people. As Washington said, "a good general government, without good morals and good habits, will not make us a happy People."[2]

[1] Charles C. Tansill (ed.), *Documents Illustrative of the Formation of the Union of the American States* (Washington, 1927), p. 811.
[2] J. C. Fitzpatrick (ed.), *The Writings of George Washington* (Washington, 1931–44), XXX, 32, 34, 493, 496.

Few of those who had participated in the drafting of the Federal Constitution felt more than a guarded optimism that their countrymen would prove equal to the heavy responsibilities thrust upon them. Benjamin Franklin, whose faith in the wisdom of the people was stronger than that of most of his colleagues, remarked in 1788 that Americans were prone to pay too much regard to their rights and too little to their duties as citizens.[3] They had amply demonstrated their proficiency in overthrowing governments, but now, said Franklin, something very different was required of them—the capacity of submitting to restraints upon their freedom and of yielding obedience to laws of their own making. In much the same vein, President Washington declared in his first annual message to Congress that the American people must learn "to distinguish between oppression and the necessary exercise of lawful authority . . . to discriminate the spirit of Liberty from that of licentiousness."[4]

The Federalists—the men responsible for the summoning of the Constitutional Convention, the drafting of the Constitution, and its ratification by the state conventions—were well aware of the magnitude of the undertaking upon which they had embarked. When Washington asserted that he was "determined the experiment should have a fair trial, and would lose the last drop of his blood in support of it," he knew that he was committing himself to a struggle almost as arduous and dubious as the effort to achieve the independence of the United States. And yet it was a venture he could not shirk, for, as Jefferson said in 1776, the establishment of a workable political system was "the whole object" of the American Revolution. "Should a bad government be instituted for us in future," Jefferson observed, "it had been as well to have accepted at first the bad one offered to us from beyond the water without the risk and expense of contest."[5]

With a population of approximately four million, including 700,000 Negro slaves, the American Republic consisted in 1789 of thirteen states which had been united for little more than a decade. Because of the inadequacy of the roads, the country depended chiefly upon water transportation for internal trade and communication. It was divided into three distinct sections, the economic and social institu-

[3] A. H. Smyth (ed.), *The Writings of Benjamin Franklin* (New York, 1905–7), X, 7.

[4] Fitzpatrick, *Washington*, XXX, 493.

[5] *Ibid.*, XXX, 119, 121, 148, 171; Henry Cabot Lodge (ed.), *The Works of Alexander Hamilton* (New York, 1904), IX, 441, 444–446, 453.

tions of which were so divergent that James Madison declared that the fundamental challenge to American statesmanship was to unite "the minds of men accustomed to think and act differently." Only seventy-five post offices existed in the entire country. Two states, Rhode Island and North Carolina, were still out of the Union: they complained that the other states had seceded from them! In 1789, Madison was rebuked in the House of Representatives for using the word "national"—a term so suspect that it was deliberately omitted from the Federal Constitution.[6] Plainly, the men who were chosen to administer the new government were well advised to walk with circumspection.

While the new government made ready to assume its duties, the old government was quietly slipping into limbo. At no time after October, 1788, was a quorum present in the Continental Congress, and although John Jay continued to serve as Secretary of Foreign Affairs, he could conduct no business—not even to the extent of giving Thomas Jefferson permission to return home from France, where he was serving as United States minister.[7]

Happily for the success of the great experiment, there were a goodly number of factors working in its favor. Washington fully grasped the situation when he remarked that "nothing but harmony, honesty, industry and frugality are necessary to make us a great and happy people. . . . We are surrounded by the blessings of nature."[8] In 1789, the country was rapidly recovering from the effects of the postwar depression; commerce and shipbuilding were reviving; and the demand for American agricultural products was increasing sharply as a result of poor harvests in Europe. Public and private enterprise was beginning to transform the face of the country; work had begun on the Potomac Canal, designed to link the eastern and western parts of the country; three large bridges were being erected in Massachusetts; the

[6] By way of answer to his critics, Madison pointed out that "the words 'no national religion shall be established by law' did not imply that the government was a national one." *Abridgment of the Debates of Congress* (New York, 1860), I, 138; see also Mathew Carey, *The American Museum,* VI, 1789 (Philadelphia, 1798), 459–460; John Marshall, *Life of George Washington* (Philadelphia, 1804–7), V, 178; Fitzpatrick, *Washington,* XXX, 442; J. C. Ballagh (ed.), *The Letters of Richard Henry Lee* (New York, 1911–14), II, 506–507; Ralph H. Brown, *Mirror for Americans* (New York, 1943), pp. 43–44, 50.

[7] Leonard D. White, *The Federalists* (New York, 1948), p. 1; Julian Boyd (ed.), *The Papers of Thomas Jefferson* (Princeton, 1950—), XIV, 628; John Spencer Bassett, *The Federalist System, 1789–1801* (New York, 1906), p. 4.

[8] Fitzpatrick, *Washington,* XXX, 186, 218.

first turnpike in the United States had been built near Alexandria, Virginia; and fast-sailing merchantmen were carrying the American flag to China and the East Indies. The conditions which had produced the stay laws, tender acts, and other invasions of property rights— stigmatized by the Founding Fathers as "democracy"—were disappearing with the advent of better times.

"Since the federal constitution has removed all danger of our having a paper tender," reported a Philadelphia newspaper in 1789, "our trade is advanced fifty per cent. . . . Our monied people can trust their cash abroad, and have brought their coin into circulation."[9] At the same time, several states, having passed under the control of Federalists, began to revise their constitutions along the lines laid down by the Federal Constitution. In 1790, Pennsylvania abolished its unicameral legislature, establishing in its stead a bicameral body. Equally important, the executive was empowered to check the activities of the legislators and the judiciary was given tenure during good behavior.[10]

The elections of 1788 had ensured that the Federal government would be administered by its friends. At the head stood a man whose renown, prestige, and ability offered the best guarantee of its success: President George Washington. The office of Vice-President was filled by John Adams of Massachusetts, a statesman whose long career had included service in the Continental Congress, the negotiation of the treaty of peace of 1782, and appointment as first United States minister to Great Britain. The elections had also resulted in the seating of a large majority of Federalists to the House and Senate. In

[9] *Pennsylvania Gazette,* December 16, 1789; Boyd, *Jefferson,* IX, 303; Robert L. Brunhouse, *The Counter-Revolution in Pennsylvania, 1776–1790* (Harrisburg, 1942), pp. 226–227; *Report on Canadian Archives* (Ottawa, 1890), p. 124; Fitzpatrick, *Washington,* XXX, 11, 72, 83; XXXI, 45, 92, 319, 328; *Report of the American Historical Association,* I (Washington, 1897), 628–629, 781; *American Political Science Review,* III (1908), 544; Brown, *Mirror for Americans,* p. 50; *Magazine of American History,* I (1877), 113; W. G. Sumner, *Financier and Finances of the American Revolution* (New York, 1891), II, 256; Tench Coxe, *View of the United States of America* (Philadelphia, 1794), p. 365; William Prescott to Nathan Dane, June 20, 1788, Nathan Dane MSS., LC.

[10] In 1789–90, Georgia and South Carolina adopted new constitutions which extended the franchise, eliminated religious tests for officeholders, and, in part, redressed the balance between the eastern and western sections of the state, hitherto heavily weighted in favor of the east. On the other hand, in both these states, the executive and the judges continued to be chosen by the legislature. But in South Carolina, the council, hitherto a check upon the governor, was abolished.

York County, Pennsylvania, 858 Federalist votes were cast against one Antifederalist vote. In the Boston district, Fisher Ames, a young man who had not been old enough to see military service during the War of Independence, was elected to Congress over Sam Adams, a signer of the Declaration of Independence whose devotion to the cause of Federalism was in doubt. Only Virginia returned Antifederalist senators. Of the eight Antifederalists in the House of Representatives it was said that they were "so lukewarm as scarcely to deserve the appellation."[11]

Manifestly, Washington's hope that "whatever there be of wisdom, and prudence, and patriotism on the Continent, should be concentrated in the public councils, at the first outset" had been largely attained. No less than forty-four members of the First Congress had taken part in the formation and adoption of the Federal Constitution, and over half the members of the Constitutional Convention of 1787 served the new government in the capacity of legislators, administrative officers, and judges.[12] With these circumstances in mind, Charles Beard observed that "one may say with a high degree of truth that the Constitutional Convention, although it adjourned on September 17, 1787, never dissolved until the great economic measures which were necessary to make the Constitution a living instrument were fully realized."[13]

When Washington delivered his inaugural address to the House and Senate, he appeared "agitated and embarrassed more than ever he was by the leveled cannon or pointed musket." He had good reason to be perturbed: even before he took office he was heard to complain of the "ten thousand embarrassments, perplexities and troubles of the

[11] James Hart, *The American Presidency in Action* (New York, 1948), pp. 70–72, 132; William Wirt Henry, *Patrick Henry: Life, Correspondence and Speeches* (New York, 1891), III, 301; Jared Sparks (ed.), *Correspondence of the Revolution* (Boston, 1853), IV, 298; Isaac Q. Leake, *General John Lamb* (Albany, 1850), p. 311; Fitzpatrick, *Washington,* XXX, 62–63, 185, 195; Gaillard Hunt (ed.), *The Writings of James Madison* (New York, 1900–1910), V, 309–310; C. R. King, *The Life and Correspondence of Rufus King* (New York, 1894–1900), V, December 21, 1788; Seth Ames (ed.), *The Works of Fisher Ames* (Boston, 1854), I, 31.
[12] Fitzpatrick, *Washington,* XXX, 413–414; XXXI, 51.
[13] Charles Beard, *Economic Origins of Jeffersonian Democracy* (New York, 1927), pp. 101, 104, 105–106; Hart, *American Presidency,* pp. 70–72, 132; H. L. McBain, *De Witt Clinton and the Origin of the Spoils System in New York* (New York, 1907), pp. 24–25; William S. Carpenter, *American Political Thought* (Princeton, 1930), pp. 92–93.

presidency."[14] Particularly disturbing to his peace of mind were the importunate office seekers by whom he was besieged: it seemed, he said in March, 1789, that there would be one hundred competitors for every office of importance at his disposal.[15]

The President's misgivings were fully justified: he was venturing his reputation and his tranquillity upon the dubious field of politics. How strenuous this battle was to be was soon revealed to him. Despite the urgency of the problems by which the country was beset in 1789, Congress fell to wrangling over titles and ceremonies, quite as though the answer to the question whether the President and other high officers of the government should be addressed in the high-flown language of courts or as plain "Mister" would determine if the United States remained a republic or lapsed into monarchism.[16]

Some Federalists, prone to hold up the British Constitution as an example to Americans, wished to hedge President Washington with a title and other insignia of royalty. The stronghold of this "monarchical faction" was the Senate, a body that prided itself upon its aloofness from the people and dedicated itself to maintaining a "steadying influence" upon the public councils. While the debates and proceedings of the House of Representatives were open to the public, the Senate, like the Continental Congress before it, preserved the rule of secrecy —and thereby incurred the charge of being a "divan" of aristocrats who sneered, from the safety of their chambers, at the "common herd."[17]

[14] Marcus Cunliffe, *George Washington, Man and Monument* (Boston, 1958), p. 151; Fitzpatrick, *Washington*, XXX, 40, 67, 173–174, 237–240, 268; Marshall, *Washington*, V, 135; Jared Sparks, *Life of Gouverneur Morris* (Boston, 1832), I, 290; *Pennsylvania Magazine of History and Biography*, XXXVIII (1914), 47.

[15] Hunt, *Madison*, V, 373, 385, 409–410 (footnote); *Publications of the Southern History Association* (Washington, 1903), VII, 183.

[16] Richard Hildreth, *The History of the United States* (New York, 1880–82), IV, 60–61; Joseph Charles, *The Origins of the American Party System* (Williamsburg, 1956), p. 52.

[17] Louise Burnham Dunbar, *A Study of 'Monarchical Tendencies' in the United States from 1776 to 1801*, University of Illinois Studies in the Social Sciences, X (1920), 125–127; Hart, *American Presidency*, p. 50; Fitzpatrick, *Washington*, XXIX, 190; W. C. Ford (ed.), *The Correspondence and Journals of Samuel P. Webb* (New York, 1894), III, 143; Lyon G. Tyler, *The Life and Times of the Tylers* (Richmond, 1884), I, 170; Alexander Biddle, *Old Family Letters* (Philadelphia, 1892), pp. 42–43, 46–47; *The Alexander Biddle Papers* (New York, 1943), p. 81; *Proceedings of the Massachusetts Historical Society*, 63 (1930), 497.

In this body it was proposed to address the President as "His Excellency" or "His Elective Highness," and a committee appointed for the purpose of devising a proper title reported in favor of "His Highness the President of the United States and Protector of the Rights of the Same." None supported this proposal more vehemently than did Vice-President John Adams and Senator Richard Henry Lee. These two men, the "radical" leaders of the Continental Congress in 1775–76, had parted company over the Federal Constitution and Lee had been elected to the Senate as an Antifederalist whereas Adams had been elevated to the Vice-Presidency as a Federalist. But Lee was already on the road that was to conduct him—together with many other Antifederalists—into the Federalist camp.[18] In 1789, throughout the whole of what a Senator called the "idolatrous business" of converting President Washington into a graven image, Adams and Lee worked together as closely as they had in the very different cause of promoting American independence of Great Britain.

Austere in his private life, Adams strove to surround the government with regal "dignity and splendor." A student of psychology and social institutions, Adams believed that society was held together by customs, prejudices, and superstitions, the "use and wont" of mankind. As he saw it, something more than the social compact was required to give permanency to the state: men did not live together peacefully and co-operatively merely because they or their ancestors had agreed to create a government and to yield obedience to its just commands. On the contrary, he contended that organized society was the creation of both rational and nonrational elements and that the nonrational was quite as important as the rational in giving strength and durability to the state. He concluded, therefore, that no government could long endure without awe and veneration on the part of its citizens. Least of all, in his opinion, could Americans ignore these indispensable adjuncts to government: there was "no people in the world," he roundly declared, "so much in favor of titles as the people of America. . . . This is all nonsense to the philosopher but so is all government whatever."[19]

Much as it ran against Adams's grain to exalt Washington higher than he already stood in the esteem of his countrymen—Adams had always been jealous of Washington's fame—he conceived that in this

[18] Hart, *American Presidency*, pp. 28–29, 31, 34.
[19] Hart, *American Presidency*, p. 45; *Biddle Papers*, p. 81.

instance he was doing honor to the office rather than to its temporary occupant. Moreover, Adams wished to see titles given to all the higher officers of the government, not merely to the President, and to make the President and Senate the fountain of honor in the United States. Finally, having sworn to uphold the Constitution of the United States, he believed that in promoting the cause of titles he was doing no more than his duty. In his opinion, a President without a title would be like the emperor without clothes. The spectacle promised to convulse the country: "What will the common people of foreign countries, what will the sailors and soldiers say, 'George Washington, President of the United States'? They will despise him to *all eternity.*" Bereft of a title, he predicted, the President might be mistaken for the president of a fire company or a cricket club.[20]

On the other hand, many members of Congress, much as they revered Washington, feared that a President tricked out in the trappings of royalty would make that "bold push for the American throne" predicted by Patrick Henry. There was good reason for apprehension: Americans had been under a republican form of government for only fourteen of the 180 years of their history; republicanism was still on trial in a world of enemies; and monarchism was almost universally accepted as the form of government best suited to the human condition. And so, whenever they saw monarchism rearing its head in the Republic, they rushed out to crush the horrid thing. When it was proposed that the coins of the United States be stamped with the head of the President, the "anti-monarchists" protested that some future Chief Magistrate, conceiving himself to be a Caesar, might emulate the example of "a NERO, CALIGULA, or a HELIOGABALUS." Congress therefore chose the safer course of placing an emblematical figure of liberty upon American coins.[21]

[20] John Adams referred to Washington's inaugural address as "His most gracious speech." When it was objected that these were the words applied to his Britannic Majesty's speech from the throne, Adams expressed astonishment that objections should be raised to following the practice of the government "under which we had lived so long and happily formerly." Hart, *American Presidency,* pp. 29, 34–36, 38 (footnote), 39, 46; Biddle, *Old Family Letters,* pp. 42–43; Charles Francis Adams (ed.), *The Works of John Adams* (Boston, 1850–56), IX, 566; *John P. Branch Historical Papers* (Richmond, 1905), II, 267.
[21] *Abridgment of Debates,* I, 372; *Gazette of the United States,* April 28, May 16, 1792; James Madison to William Short, April 6, 1792, Madison to Henry Lee, March, 1792, Madison MSS., LC; Hart, *American Presidency,* p. 37.

Meanwhile, the object of all this furor—the President himself—was lamenting that the question of titles had never been raised. It had been introduced, he complained, "without any privity of knowledge of it on my part, and urged after I was apprized of it contrary to my opinion." In 1787 he had dismissed monarchy as impossible of realization in the United States "without shaking the Peace of this Country to its foundation." To risk his popularity for the sake of a title seemed to him to be the height of folly and he did not thank his admirers for having created the impression that he would accept a crown if it were offered him.[22]

Since the House of Representatives refused to concur with the Senate in the matter of a title for the President—it even denied senators the title of "Honorable"—a joint committee was appointed. But the committee was unable to reach an agreement, and in the end the Senate was obliged to accept defeat. The Senate majority, however, made no pretense of having been converted to the representatives' way of thinking. On May 14, 1789, as a last gesture of defiance, the Senate put itself on record in favor of annexing a title to the office of President "from a decent respect for the opinion and practice of civilized nations."[23]

As the event proved, John Adams exaggerated the strength of his countrymen's devotion to monarchical forms and usages and their importance in buttressing the fabric of the Federal government. Americans might love a lord but they could not endure a king. The President lost none of his prestige or influence by being addressed in the style of an ordinary citizen of the Republic. And a title such as "His Elective Majesty" would have been wholly at variance with the democratic tendencies that were already reshaping American society and government.

The controversy over titles consumed virtually all of the Senate's time from April 23 to May 14—and all that came of it was that Vice-President John Adams was given the derisive title of "His Rotundity." Nevertheless, the significance of this dispute was far greater than appeared from its results. For this was a clash not between Federalists and Antifederalists but between Federalists themselves. "Monarchism" was one of the issues that later divided the Federalist party into Ham-

[22] Hart, *American Presidency*, p. 40; P. L. Ford (ed.), *The Writings of Thomas Jefferson* (New York, 1892–99), I, 231.
[23] Hart, *American Presidency*, pp. 34–35.

iltonian Federalists and Jeffersonian Republicans; its appearance in 1789 revealed the existence of a dangerous fissure within the Federalist party.[24]

Even though Washington was loath to take a monarchical title, he had no intention of making the President a "man of the people." Washington owed none of his popularity to his democratic tastes or manners; by nature he was reserved, aloof, and, particularly in large companies, solemn. There is a story that when Gouverneur Morris, acting on a wager, slapped Washington on the back, he was frozen in his tracks by the icy stare with which the great man responded to this familiarity. As President, Washington was disposed to keep people at arms' length, and this inclination was reinforced by the fact that his duties compelled him to ration strictly the time devoted to social intercourse. But before drawing up a system of presidential etiquette, he consulted, as was his settled habit, with the friends upon whose judgment he placed the greatest reliance. To these friends he made clear that in his opinion the President ought to maintain the dignity of his office "without subjecting himself to the imputation of super-ciliousness or unnecessary reserve." Above all, he determined to shun the example of the President of the Continental Congress, who, by making himself available to all comers, had ended by becoming a sort of maître d'hôtel. With the aid of his advisers, Washington formulated a set of rules which committed him to hold levees on certain days, to avoid displays of extravagance, to return no visits, and to entertain only "official persons." Until Jefferson assumed the Presidency in 1801, this system governed the social conduct of the Chief Executive.[25]

Nor did Washington object to giving Republican institutions a monarchical gloss. After he delivered his address personally to Congress in April, 1789, both houses made addresses in reply and the President formally responded. Thereupon the members of both House and Senate waited upon the President at his residence. These vestiges of monarchism were derived from the practice of the English government

---

[24] Sparks, *Correspondence of the Revolution,* IV, 265–266; Fitzpatrick, *Washington,* XXX, 319–321; Hart, *American Presidency,* p. 39; Nathan Schachner, *The Founding Fathers* (New York, 1954), pp. 54–55.

[25] Lodge, *Hamilton,* VIII, 83–84; *Proceedings of the Massachusetts Historical Society,* LII (1928), 128–129; Hart, *American Presidency,* pp. 28–29; I. N. P. Stokes, *Iconography of Manhattan Island* (New York, 1895–1928), V, 1263; Ford, *Jefferson,* VI, 293; Rufus Wilmot Griswold, *The Republican Court* (New York, 1867), pp. 149–152.

by which, after the speech from the throne, the two Houses of Parliament made addresses in reply; and they persisted until 1801, when President Jefferson, discarding "the rags of royalty," sent his messages to Congress rather than delivering them in person.[26] Mrs. Knox, Mrs. Hamilton, Mrs. Washington, and other women prominent in the "Republican Court" held levees, but Jefferson, having no wife, spared the country "the burlesque of a female levee."[27]

During the Federalist era, the highlight of the social season was the celebration of the President's birthday. Parades, balls, banquets, firing of cannon, and drinking of toasts commemorated the happy event. The Duc de la Rochefoucauld-Liancourt reported that in Philadelphia "the splendor of the rooms, and the variety and richness of the dresses did not suffer in comparison with Europe; and it must be acknowledged that the beauty of the American ladies has the advantage in the comparison." Chief Justice John Jay appeared on the bench garbed in "parti-colored silken robes, as flashy as any Roman Bishop ever wore when performing the ceremony of high mass on an Easter holiday." The Duc de la Rochefoucauld-Liancourt had no reason to fear that he was demeaning himself by consorting with republicans.[28]

Despite Washington's conviction that ceremony was compatible with republicanism, his actions did not escape the censure of anti-monarchists. When they beheld the President driving through the streets of New York in a carriage drawn by six horses and escorted by uniformed outriders, they groaned that George Rex rode again. And when they observed the elaborate etiquette at the President's levees, they exclaimed that monarchical pomp and ostentation had crossed the Atlantic and firmly embedded themselves in the American Republic—and all this before the new government was a year old. James Madison lamented that "the satellites & sycophants which surrounded

[26] Ford, *Jefferson*, VI, 293; *Pennsylvania Magazine of History and Biography*, IX, 217; Stewart Mitchell (ed.), *New Letters of Abigail Adams* (Boston, 1947), p. 30; E. S. Maclay (ed.), *The Journal of William Maclay, 1789-1791* (New York, 1890), p. 351; Fitzpatrick, *Washington*, XXX, 360-362; XXXI, 55.

[27] James Callender, *American Annual Register* (Philadelphia, 1796), p. 180; Edward Channing, *A History of the United States* (New York, 1905-25), IV, 152-153; Mitchell, *Letters of Abigail Adams*, p. 35.

[28] *Pennsylvania Magazine of History and Biography*, IX, 217; François, Duc de La Rochefoucauld-Liancourt, *Voyage to the United States* (London, 1799), II, 385-387; Tom Callender (pseud.), *Letters to Alexander Hamilton, King of the Feds* (New York, 1802), p. 74.

him [Washington] had wound up the ceremonials of the government to such a pitch of stateliness which nothing but his personal character could have supported, & which no character him could ever maintain."[29] Above the shrill cries of these outraged republicans, Washington was heard protesting that he hated ceremony, that he wished he had never held a levee, that he was happiest at home, and that he could not wait to get back to Mount Vernon.[30]

Washington might reign in his own drawing room, but at least one state governor was unwilling to accord the Chief Executive precedence outside the presidential precincts. In 1789, when Washington made a tour of New England, Governor John Hancock of Massachusetts, soured by his failure to attain the Vice-Presidency, attempted to assert his superiority over the President by refusing to pay the first call upon Washington after his arrival in Boston. Angered by this slight, Washington refused to attend the dinner to which he had been invited by Hancock. The Governor and the President stood rigidly upon protocol, each remaining in his own quarters, until Hancock, realizing that he was certain to lose popularity by trying to humiliate Washington, decided to pay his respects to the President. Swathed in bandages and lying prone in a litter—Hancock alleged that it was a sudden seizure of gout that had kept him at home—he was carried into Washington's presence. Hancock's health never ceased to afford him pretexts for escaping from awkward situations, but in this instance even his bandages could not conceal the fact that Washington had scored his point that a President takes precedence over a state governor.[31]

Much more than the semblance of power was at stake in these encounters, but it was especially in the field of foreign affairs that President Washington most firmly asserted his authority. From the beginning to the end of his tenure of the Presidency, Washington kept a steady hand upon the Republic's relations with foreign powers.[32]

[29] Ford, Jefferson, VI, 293.
[30] James Hutton (ed.), Correspondence of Sir James Bland Burges (London, 1885), p. 223; Mitchell, Letters of Abigail Adams, p. 26; Ford, Jefferson, I, 203–204, 216; Fitzpatrick, Washington, XXXI, 55; Maclay, Journal, pp. 122–123, 351; Stephen Decatur, Jr., Private Affairs of George Washington (Boston, 1933), p. 12; Henry, Patrick Henry, III, 406; Hildreth, History, IV, 60–61.
[31] Hart, American Presidency, pp. 18–20.
[32] Alexander DeConde, Entangling Alliance: Politics and Diplomacy under George Washington (Durham, N.C., 1958), asserts that Hamilton, not Washington, was the guiding spirit in the administration as regards the formulation of foreign policy. The weight of evidence, however, seems to support the con-

Even though he permitted the Secretary of State to become the normal channel of communication between the United States and the European powers, he never excluded the possibility of personal negotiations and, in time of crisis, he made the final and meaningful decisions. As early as October, 1789, he appointed Gouverneur Morris as a "special agent" to explore the possibility of a commercial treaty with Great Britain—thereby establishing a precedent which has played an increasingly important part in the conduct of foreign affairs.[33]

The dominance won by the President in this department was not altogether the result of a policy consciously and unremittingly pursued. Washington scrupulously avoided exceeding his constitutional mandate, and at the beginning of his administration he was willing to concede the Senate a larger measure of co-ordinate authority than that body was prepared to exercise. With regard to the making of treaties the Constitution directs the President to act with "the advice and consent" of the Senate. Washington interpreted that directive in its most literal sense. In August, 1789, while negotiations with the southern Indians were still pending, the President, accompanied by Secretary of War Henry Knox, went to the Senate Chamber, took the Vice-President's chair, and informed the senators that he had come to ask their advice and consent regarding the instructions to be given the American commissioners. Thereupon he submitted seven questions to the Senate. Vice-President Adams read the questions to the senators, asking at the end of each question: "Do you advise and consent?" An unwonted silence fell upon the Senate until, finally, Senator Robert Morris, remarking that the President's questions required study, moved that they be referred to a committee of five. According to Senator Maclay of Pennsylvania, who seconded Morris's motion, President Washington "started up in a violent fret. 'This defeats every purpose of my coming here,'" he exclaimed angrily. In order to conciliate the

---

trary view. In a letter written in August, 1788, Washington revealed extensive knowledge of European affairs. Moreover, at this time he laid down a policy from which he never departed. "I hope," he wrote, "that the United States of America will be able to keep disengaged from the labyrinth of European politics and war. . . . It should be the policy of the United States to administer to their wants, without being engaged in their quarrels." Fitzpatrick, *Washington*, XXX, 71–72; Ford, *Jefferson*, IX, 307. Leonard D. White goes so far as to say that Washington was his own Secretary of State. *The Jeffersonians*, p. 183.

[33] Charles, *Origins of the American Party System*, pp. 50–53; Hart, *American Presidency*, pp. 57, 80, 102; White, *Federalists*, pp. 50–66.

outraged Chief Executive, the Senate had to agree to give its answer within three days. Having scored this small victory, Washington left the Senate Chamber with "sullen dignity."[34]

Contrary to Senator Maclay—a waspish-tempered and cross-grained man who, when Washington invited him to dinner, suspected that the President was trying to corrupt him—the last thing the President had in mind was to overawe the Senate by making a display of his authority. Nevertheless, in expecting the Senate to give an immediate answer to the questions he propounded, the President obviously demanded too much of the members. He realized his mistake and when he met the Senate for the second time his demeanor was "placid and serene." After the Senate had expressed its opinion, the President withdrew, well satisfied with the result. And yet he never repeated the experiment of conducting personal consultations with the Senate: during the remainder of his term of office he communicated with that body exclusively by means of written messages. On occasion, most notably in the case of Jay's Treaty, he neglected to ask its advice prior to entering upon negotiations. It is improbable, however, that Washington was so deeply offended by the reception he met with at the hands of the Senate in August, 1789, that he swore "he would be damned if he ever went there again." The formality and precision of written communications were much more to Washington's taste than were the jars and irritations of personal interviews.[35]

Of all the exigencies confronting the Federal government in 1789, revenue was the most critical. The lack of an adequate and dependable source of income was mainly responsible for the collapse of the government established by the Articles of Confederation. In view of the fact that the Federal government had inherited the debts of its predecessor—a heavy burden to impose upon a fledgling government—the American people could no longer hope to evade the responsibility of contributing to its support. The exultation that had accompanied the creation of the more perfect Union in 1788 was tempered by the sobering prospect that a new body of tax collectors, armed with the powers of the Federal government, would soon join local and state officials in separating the American taxpayer from his money.[36]

[34] Maclay, *Journal*, pp. 128–130.
[35] Hart, *American Presidency*, pp. 39, 91–96; Maclay, *Journal*, pp. 131–132.
[36] Boyd, *Jefferson Papers*, 14, p. 645.

It was agreed that the principal source of revenue must be tariff and tonnage duties. In view of the fact that most of the manufactured goods consumed by Americans, as well as important raw products such as molasses, were imported from abroad and that almost half these commodities were transported in foreign ships, tariff and tonnage duties promised to produce sufficient revenue to supply the operational needs of the government and to pay the interest and principal on the foreign and domestic debt.[37]

In the formulation of the fiscal policies of the new government, James Madison asserted over Congress the same high order of leadership that he had exercised over the Constitutional Convention. It required all of Madison's skill as a parliamentarian to carry the revenue bill through Congress. Import and tonnage duties impinged upon vested sectional interests to such a degree that conflict was inevitable. Northern manufacturers wished a high protective tariff; Southern planters believed that their welfare would best be served by a low tariff. New England rum manufacturers demanded a low duty on foreign molasses; many southern representatives wished to impose a high duty upon an article they regarded as a pernicious luxury. Madison attempted to mitigate these sectional conflicts by reminding the representatives of the necessity of subordinating local concerns to the general welfare. As a gesture to those representatives whose constituents considered it "incompatible with the spirit of the constitution, and dangerous to republican principles, to pass such a law unlimited in its duration," Madison was willing to impose a time limit upon the tariff act.[38]

In its final form, the tariff of 1789 represented a compromise between the advocates of high protective duties and those who favored a tariff for revenue only. While an ad valorem charge of 5 per cent was imposed upon most articles subject to duty, specific duties ranging as high as 50 per cent were levied upon steel, ships, cordage, tobacco, salt, indigo, cloth, and so on. Thanks to the timely intervention by the Senate, the duty on molasses was reduced from the six cents per

[37] *Abridgment of Debates*, I, 64; Albert Sidney Bolles, *The Financial History of the United States from 1789 to 1860* (New York, 1894), I, 74.

[38] Hart, *American Presidency*, pp. 62–63, 72; J. B. McMaster, *A History of the People of the United States from the Revolution to the Civil War* (New York, 1883–1913), I, 546–548; Hunt, *Madison*, V, 371–373; *Debates and Proceedings in the Congress of the United States, 1789–1824* (*Annals of Congress*) (Washington, 1834–56), I, 110–111; Henry, *Patrick Henry*, III, 392–393.

gallon requested by the Virginians to two and one-half cents per gallon. This arrangement was typical of the settlement as a whole: as Madison said, the articles subject to a high duty "were pretty generally taxed for the benefit of the manufacturing part of the northern community."[39]

But it was Madison's proposals with regard to tonnage duties which stirred up the most heated controversy in Congress. In effect, Madison called for the enactment of an American navigation system—designed to supersede the navigation systems erected by the individual states during the period of the Articles of Confederation—by which American ships would be favored in American ports over foreign vessels, the goods imported in the United States in American ships would pay less duty than similar goods carried by foreign ships, and the coastwise trade would be reserved to ships flying the American flag. Thus far he had the concurrence of the great majority of the House, but Madison sacrificed his impregnable position by injecting the issue—extraneous to the main question of revenue—of discriminating against the ships and merchandise of foreign countries which had no commercial treaties with the United States.[40]

There was no doubt which country Madison intended to injure and which country he intended to benefit by this measure. Since 1783, Great Britain had refused even to discuss a commercial treaty with the United States and, adding injury to this insult, had refused to surrender the northwest posts or to make compensation for the Negro slaves carried off by the British army when it evacuated New York in 1783. France, on the other hand, had made a commercial treaty with the United States in 1778. Despite the efforts of both countries, however, trade had failed to increase materially after 1783. Instead, American commerce had reverted largely to its prewar channels—which meant that Great Britain continued to serve as the principal entrepôt of American trade with the European continent.

In order to effect a fundamental shift in American commerce from Great Britain and its colonial possessions to France, Madison recommended that British ships should pay a duty of sixty cents per ton

[39] *Abridgment of Debates,* I, 72; Joseph Dorfman, *The Economic Mind in American Civilization* (New York, 1946–49), I, 25; *Pennsylvania Magazine of History and Biography,* XXXVIII (1914), 54; Channing, *History,* IV, 62–63.

[40] Dorfman, *Economic Mind,* I, 14–15; *Abridgment of Debates,* I, 55–56; Harold Hucheson, *Tench Coxe* (Philadelphia, 1938), p. 33.

upon entry into an American port, whereas French ships should pay only thirty cents per ton. That this was equivalent to levying economic war upon Great Britain, Madison admitted; but he promised American merchants and manufacturers a rich harvest, for they and the French would presumably succeed to the markets and the carrying trade from which the British had been dislodged.

In part, Madison's purpose was to endear the people of the United States to the Federal government by demonstrating its capacity to right a great national wrong. He spoke as a nationalist: his objective, he said, was to see "the citizens of one State enabled to assist those of another, and receive mutual benefits and advantages . . . to form a school of seamen, to lay the foundations of a navy, and to be able to support itself against the interference of foreigners." In a commercial war between Great Britain and the United States, he believed, victory would incline to the side that practiced the greatest austerity —and here he thought that virtuous, plain-living American farmers would easily prevail over luxury-loving Britons. "Her interests," he said of Great Britain, "can be wounded almost mortally, while ours are invulnerable."[41]

In some respects, the ideas Madison broached in 1789 anticipated the Reports which Hamilton, as Secretary of the Treasury, later laid before Congress. Madison, it is true, proposed a more violent dislocation of the commerce of the United States than did Hamilton, but both men acted upon the assumption that the government must devote itself to invigorating and protecting commerce and to solidifying the Union by economic means. Like Hamilton, Madison at this time subscribed to the proposition that a commercial North and an agricultural South could coexist in harmony and good will. Both men offered essentially the same prescription for union: "a perfect accordance of interest" between the two sections based upon "mutual concessions" in the interest of the national welfare.[42]

Madison was too honest to deny that most of these concessions would have to come from the South. The tonnage duties, the protective features of the tariff, and the discrimination against British commerce were, he admitted, a bounty paid by the farmers and planters

---

[41] Hunt, *Madison*, VI, 241.

[42] *Abridgment of Debates*, I, 258; W. C. Rives, *History of the Life and Times of James Madison* (New York, 1869–73), III, 16–17; Irving Brant, *James Madison, Father of the Constitution* (Indianapolis, 1950), pp. 245–254.

to the maritime and manufacturing sections of the Union. But he saw
no feasible alternative to his plan of making the "agricultural interest"
—the main wealth-producing part of the community—shoulder a disproportionate share of the financial burden involved in transforming
the United States into a commercial, manufacturing, and maritime
power.[43]

Northern businessmen hardly could have asked for more than Madison offered them in 1789. Had the gift been proffered during the
troubled times of the Articles of Confederation, they no doubt would
have accepted with alacrity and hailed Madison as their benefactor.
But by 1789, rendered cautious by returning prosperity and keenly
aware of their dependence upon British capital, they had lost their
ardor for an economic trial of strength with Great Britain.[44] Moreover,
they displayed a signal lack of enthusiasm for Madison's plan of putting France in Great Britain's place as the principal supplier and
market of the United States. While the merchants agreed with Madison that commerce sorely needed the "fostering care" of government,
they protested that the Virginian was thrusting a heavier burden upon
American shipping than it could bear; without the aid of British ships,
American farm products could not be carried to market. Congressional
spokesmen of New England shipping and manufacturing interests expressed alarm lest southern planters would be ruined by legislation introduced by a Virginia planter![45]

It is significant that Alexander Hamilton, although still a private
citizen practicing law in New York, dissociated himself from Madison's plan of retaliating upon Great Britain. In his opinion, the surest
way of strangling the infant government of the United States in its
cradle was to engage in economic warfare with Great Britain. For
how, he asked, could the debt be paid and the credit of the government restored if import duties—the mainstay of revenue—were dras-
tically curtailed by the stoppage of British imports? It seemed to
Hamilton that in order to gratify their resentment against Great
Britain, Madison and his friends were prepared to wreck the economy
and the government of the United States.[46]

[43] *Pennsylvania Gazette,* May 13, 1789.
[44] A few years later, Alexander Baring observed that a 20 to 30 per cent
return on capital could be made with ease in American commerce.
[45] Maclay, *Journal,* pp. 89, 91, 96–97; *Report on Canadian Archives,* pp.
121–123, 137; Basset, *Federalist System,* pp. 15–16.
[46] *Publications of the Colonial Society of Massachusetts,* XXXVII (Boston,
1954), 668; *Report on Canadian Archives,* p. 25.

Here appeared the first important breach between Hamilton and Madison. "The friends of the Union," the victors in the struggle over the Constitution, had scarcely sat down to the feast before the specter of dissension appeared.[47]

Even though many of the representatives of northern business opposed the plan of discriminating against Great Britain, all of Madison's proposals passed the House of Representatives. But the Senate rejected the section discriminating against Great Britain, the two Virginia senators voting with the majority. The bill was thereupon sent back to the House shorn of this feature; and in that form it was accepted by the House by a vote of thirty-one to nineteen. French and British ships, manufacturers, and raw products were placed upon an equal footing in United States ports. All foreign-owned ships (except those built in the United States) paid a duty of fifty cents per ton, while American-owned ships paid only six cents per ton. With the adoption of this legislation, the United States served notice that, despite its predilection for free trade, it would play the game according to the rules laid down by the mercantilist powers.[48]

The adoption of the tariff and navigation system imposed the first—there were to be many during the Federalist period—sectional strains upon the "more perfect Union" created in 1788. In the South, the tariff and tonnage acts were generally pictured as a victory of northern merchants and shipowners over the "agricultural interest." High tonnage duties meant freight rates injurious to the staple exporting states; and high import duties meant that the South, the principal consumer of imported goods, would be obliged to pay a larger proportionate share than did the North, where manufacturing was much further advanced. Viewed in this light, the government seemed committed in 1789 to nurturing northern commerce and manufacturing at the expense of southern agriculture.[49] Increasingly, during the Federalist era, Southerners tended to regard the Federal government in this light.

[47] Rives, *Madison*, III, 23–24.

[48] *Abridgment of Debates*, I, 56; Bernard Mayo, *Instructions to British Ministers to the United States 1791–1812*, American Historical Association Report (Washington, 1936), p. 12; *Report of the American Historical Association* (1896), I, 608–612; Rives, *Madison*, III, 26; Henry C. Adams, *Taxation in the United States, 1789–1816* (New York, 1884), pp. 38–39.

[49] *Abridgment of Debates*, I, 59, 64, 72, 257; William Hill, *The First Stages of the Tariff Policy of the United States*, Publications of the American Economic Association, VIII (1893), 88–89; Maclay, *Journal*, 380–381; Channing, *History*, IV, 64; Sparks, *Correspondence of the Revolution*, IV, 266.

CHAPTER 2

"The More Perfect Union" in Action

O NE OF the Antifederalists' weightiest objections to the Constitution was that it lacked a Bill of Rights. This omission was deliberate on the part of the framers of the Constitution: because the general government possessed only enumerated powers they saw no necessity of erecting guarantees to civil liberties which were constitutionally outside its jurisdiction. More importantly, they feared that a Bill of Rights would prove to be an entering wedge for amendments to the Constitution that would cripple the Federal government.[1]

Of the 210 amendments submitted by the state ratifying conventions, eighty proposed substantive changes remained after duplications had been deleted. By no means all these amendments were the work of

[1] R. A. Rutland, *The Birth of the Bill of Rights* (Chapel Hill, 1955), pp. 131–133; Herman V. Ames, *The Proposed Amendments to the Constitution,* Annual Report of the American Historical Association for 1896 (Washington, 1897), pp. 80–85; Conyers Read (ed.), *The Constitution Reconsidered* (New York, 1938), p. 127; Arthur Holcombe, *Our More Perfect Union* (Cambridge, Mass., 1950), p. 45; Percy T. Finn, *The Development of the Constitution* (New York, 1940), p. 119; Benjamin F. Wright, *The Growth of American Constitutional Law* (New York, 1946), pp. 26, 126; Hildreth, *History,* IV, 115–117; Joseph Story, *Commentaries on the Constitution of the United States* (abrid., Boston, 1833), pp. 115, 128, 131, 135; Randolph G. Adams, *Selected Political Essays of James Wilson* (New York, 1930), p. 154; Jonathan Elliot (ed.), *Debates in . . . the State Conventions on Adoption of the Federal Constitution* (Washington, 1836–45), II, 454–455; III, 620, 630; Fitzpatrick, *Washington,* XXIX, 465; Sparks, *Gouverneur Morris,* II, 530; H. P. Johnstone (ed.), *Correspondence and Public Papers of John Jay* (New York, 1890–93), III, 305–306, 318; Lodge, *Hamilton,* II, 166; IX, 448, 451; Edward Meade Earle (ed.), *The Federalist* (New York, 1937), pp. 555, 557–558; *Selected Essays on Constitutional Law* (Chicago, 1958), II, 245, 262–263; III, 38.

freedom-loving Americans. The fear of a strong central government and the corresponding devotion to the cause of local rights sometimes served as a mask for bigotry and other forms of illiberality. In New England, for example, one of the objections raised against the Constitution was that by prohibiting religious tests it opened the door for "Jews, Turks and infidels" to infiltrate the government.[2] Nor were the amendments suggested by the state conventions designed primarily to protect civil liberties. The only two amendments which were recommended unanimously were intended to curtail the powers of the Federal government by imposing restrictions upon its power to tax, and to establish the principle that all powers not delegated to the Federal government were reserved to the states. Fully as much importance was attached to amendments prohibiting standing armies in time of peace, restraining the quartering of troops, giving the states control of the militia, providing for an increase in the number of members of Congress, and curtailing the power of the Federal judiciary as to safeguarding civil liberties against infringement by the national government.[3]

While Madison took the position that the omission of a Bill of Rights from the Constitution made little difference one way or the other, he was inclined to give the benefit of the doubt to those who favored it. A Bill of Rights, he observed, "would not be of disservice . . . provided it was so framed as not to imply powers not meant to be included in the enumeration" and, of even greater moment, provided that the amending process did not lead to a weakening of the authority of the Federal government. Amending the Constitution, Madison admitted, was a delicate operation requiring a high degree

[2] Boyd, *Jefferson*, 14, 18; Cecilia M. Kenyon, "Men of Little Faith: The Anti-Federalists on the Nature of Representative Government," *William and Mary Quarterly*, Third Series, XII (1955), 33, 36, 38, 42–43.

[3] None of the amendments recommended by the states touched upon paper money, contracts and tender laws the things that loom so large in the eyes of present-day economic historians. Madison believed that the proposed amendments avoided the true grounds of opposition to the Constitution. "The articles relating to treaties, to paper money, and to contracts," he said, "made more enemies than all the errors of the system, positive and negative, put together." From this circumstance, he inferred that the Antifederalists put forward comparatively innocuous amendments with a view to effecting more fundamental changes later. Edward Dumbauld, *The Bill of Rights* (Norman, Okla., 1957), pp. 30–32; Charles Warren, *The Making of the Constitution* (Boston, 1937), pp. 506–509, 775; Hunt, *Madison*, V, 271; Andrew C. McLaughlin, *A Constitutional History of the United States* (New York, 1935), p. 222; J. C. Ballagh (ed.), *Letters of Richard Henry Lee* (New York, 1911–14), II, 457–458, 463.

of skill and a profound knowledge of its anatomy. He was resolved that the scalpel should not penetrate any vital part of the Federal government; "the passion for amendments," he said, must be confined to the comparatively innocuous subject matter of civil liberties. "If we can make the Constitution better in the opinion of those who are opposed to it without weakening its frame, or abridging its usefulness in the judgment of those who are attached to it," he declared, "we act the part of wise and liberal men to make such alterations as shall produce that effect."[4]

At this particular juncture, expediency alone would have counseled Madison and other Federalist leaders to sanction a Bill of Rights. Some states, notably New York and Virginia, had gone on record in favor of calling a second Constitutional Convention where, the Federalists feared, the Constitution would be rewritten from an extreme states' rights point of view. Moreover, although many of the Antifederalist leaders had pledged themselves to conduct a loyal opposition within the new government, it was imperative, Madison believed, to separate "the well meaning from the designing opponents" of the Constitution. To effectuate such a division within the ranks of the enemy, Madison was prepared to champion a Bill of Rights.[5]

In Congress, Madison made the drafting of a Bill of Rights one of the first orders of business. "Unless Congress shall candidly consider the amendments which have been proposed in confidence by the State conventions," he declared, "federal faith will not be considered very different from the punic fides of Carthage." Despite the protests of members who felt that there were more imperative matters before Congress than conciliating the Antifederalists, the amendments were given precedence over the organization of the Federal judiciary—without which no part of the revenue system could operate, no breach of the laws could be punished, and the authority of the Federal government could not be extended over the states.[6]

[4] Hunt, *Madison*, V, 271–272, 311, 320 (footnote); *Abridgment of Debates*, I, 137, 171; Boyd, *Jefferson Papers*, XIV, 18; Adrienne Koch, *Jefferson and Madison, The Great Collaboration* (New York, 1950), pp. 55–61.

[5] C. F. Adams, *John Adams*, III, 401, 410–411; Ballagh, *Lee Letters*, II, 500–502; Boyd, *Jefferson Papers*, XIV, 340; *Abridgment of Debates*, I, 141, 144; Hunt, *Madison*, V, 309, 320 (footnote); Fitzpatrick, *Washington*, XXX, 185, 195; *Proceedings of the Massachusetts Historical Society*, Second Series, XV (Boston, 1902), 129; Rutland, *Bill of Rights*, p. 171; Benjamin F. Wright, *American Interpretations of Natural Law* (Cambridge, Mass., 1931), p. 138; Sparks, *Correspondence of the Revolution*, IV, 240–241.

[6] Rutland, *Bill of Rights*, p. 171; Brant, *Madison, Father of the Constitu-*

In the interests of simplicity and uniformity, Madison wished to incorporate the amendments in the main text of the Constitution, but Roger Sherman, a representative from Connecticut, declared that Congress had no power to alter the wording or context of a Constitution that had been approved by the people. As a result, it was decided to append separate amendments in the form of a postscript to the Constitution.[7]

Essentially, Madison's task was to resolve the age-old problem of reconciling liberty with authority. In this undertaking he took as his guide the amendments recommended by the Virginia ratifying convention. This convention had enumerated forty changes it deemed desirable in the Constitution, the first twenty being substantially a Bill of Rights almost identical to that incorporated in the Virginia Constitution of 1776. From this source, Madison drew the first eight amendments which constitute the original Federal Bill of Rights. By these proposed changes Madison intended to guarantee the exercise of the "unalienable" rights of man without at the same time impairing the necessary powers of the Federal government.[8]

In order to assuage the Antifederalists' fears of a "paramount Federal authority" and to refute their assertions that the Constitution actually created a "consolidated government" of unlimited powers, Madison proposed the Ninth and Tenth Amendments to the Constitution. These Amendments, which do not properly belong in the Bill of Rights, declared that the "enumeration in the Constitution, of certain rights, shall not be construed to deny or disparage others retained by the people" and that "the powers not delegated to the United States by the Constitution, nor prohibited by it to the states, are reserved to the States respectively, or to the people." The Ninth Amendment was designed to preclude the possibility that powers would be claimed by implication; the Tenth Amendment, lifted almost verbatim from the Articles of Confederation, was intended to confine the Federal government to its allotted sphere.[9]

As sectionalism gained strength in the United States, the Tenth Amendment became the cornerstone of the states' rights interpretation

---

tion, pp. 264–275; Robert Morris to Peters, August 24, 1789, Peters MSS., PHS.

[7] *Abridgment of Debates*, I, 133–135.

[8] Learned Hand, *The Bill of Rights* (Cambridge, Mass., 1958), pp. 1–3.

[9] Several amendments proposed from the floor of the House were defeated,

of the Constitution. In 1789, however, the Federalist leaders of Congress did not suppose that this amendment conferred a grant of new powers to the states or that it interposed obstacles to the exercise of the legitimate authority of the Federal government. The word "expressly," which in the Articles of Confederation had effectively stultified the general government, was deliberately omitted from the Tenth Amendment. Moreover, the Tenth Amendment offered no answer to the all-important question whether or not a particular power had been granted to the Federal government. Notwithstanding, the Ninth and Tenth Amendments represented a retreat, albeit a strategic one, from the "high toned" nationalism that had almost carried the day at the Constitutional Convention.[10]

Late in August, 1789, the House of Representatives approved the submission of seventeen amendments to the states. These amendments were sent to the Senate for its approval. When it appeared that the Senate was not wholly in agreement with the House, a conference between House and Senate committees was held. The report of this conference was accepted by the House on September 24, and by the Senate on September 25, 1789. The latter day is commemorated as the anniversary of the Bill of Rights. But only twelve articles were sent to the states for ratification, and of these twelve only ten were accepted by the states. These amendments went into effect in December, 1791, when Virginia, the eleventh state (the Constitution requires the assent of three-fourths of the states), gave its approval.[11]

Some Antifederalists, particularly those who had made the absence of a Bill of Rights the ostensible rather than the actual basis of their opposition to the Constitution, were chagrined to find that the first eight amendments dealt exclusively with the "unalienable" rights of man. All too clearly, they perceived that they had been outmaneuvered by Madison, for, as Hamilton said, the amendments met "scarcely any of the important objections which were urged, leaving the structure of the government, and the mass and distribution of its powers where they were." Thus, without curtailing the sovereign powers of

---

among them being an amendment to forbid interference by Congress with state regulations of elections and one to prohibit direct taxes unless duties, imposts, and excises were insufficient and a requisition on the states had proved unproductive. *Abridgment of Debates,* I, 138.

[10] Dumbauld, *Bill of Rights,* p. 65; *Selected Essays on Constitutional Law,* III, 14, 107; McLaughlin, *Constitutional History,* p. 202.

[11] Channing, *History,* IV, 158.

the Federal government, Madison had succeeded in depriving the Antifederalists of their most potent weapon against the Constitution. The results were soon manifest: the Bill of Rights helped bring North Carolina into the Union in 1789, and the roster of the original thirteen was completed in June, 1790, when Rhode Island ratified.[12]

The adoption of the Bill of Rights gave no absolute guarantee that civil liberties would remain sacrosanct in the United States. It was now within the power of the judiciary to interpose its authority when fundamental liberties were endangered; but as Judge Learned Hand has observed, "in the end it is they [the voters] and they alone who can and will preserve our liberties, if preserved they are to be." Fortunately for the cause of civil rights, the prediction made by James Madison in 1788 has in general been vindicated by events: "The political truths declared in that solemn manner," Madison said, "acquire by degrees the character of fundamental maxims of free Government, and as they become incorporated with the national sentiment, counteract the impulse of interest and passion." The Bill of Rights has served to keep in the forefront of public consciousness the fact that the power of the government of the United States is limited in scope—the surest guarantee against totalitarianism.[13]

In essence, the task before the First Congress was to breathe life into a newborn frame of government. For the Constitution itself was little more than a set of directions, some of them ambiguous, as to how the Federal government was to be organized. William Penn's aphorism that governments, like clocks, go from the motion given them by men was much in the minds of American leaders in 1789. "The paper will only mark out the mode and the form," remarked a member of the Constitutional Convention. "Men are the substance and must do the business."[14]

The men of the First Congress did the business with rare efficiency. By the end of the session in September, 1789, Congress had filled in

[12] Forrest McDonald, *We the People, The Economic Origins of the Constitution* (Chicago, 1958), pp. 321–340, makes clear that the adoption of the Bill of Rights played little part in Rhode Island's decision to ratify the Constitution. Lodge, *Hamilton*, VIII, 230; Tyler, *Life and Times of the Tylers*, I, 170; Henry, *Patrick Henry*, III, 391, 398, 406; Ballagh, *Letters of R. H. Lee*, II, 499–505, 508.

[13] Boyd, *Jefferson Papers*, XIV, 20, 659–660; Learned Hand, *The Spirit of Liberty* (New York, 1953), pp. 31, 278; Ballagh, *Letters of R. H. Lee*, II, 524.

[14] *Gazette of the United States*, July 14, 1790.

most of the interstices of the government left by the framers of the Constitution. The executive departments of State, War, and the Treasury had been organized, and the judiciary—only the bare outlines of which had been indicated by the Constitution—had been brought into being.

The department that gave Congress the greatest difficulty was the Treasury. During the period of the Articles of Confederation, except for the interregnum during which Robert Morris had occupied the post of Superintendent of Finance, the Continental Congress had maintained direct control of the country's finances. When authority had been delegated, it had been to a board rather than to an individual. And there, in the opinion of many congressmen in 1789, it ought to remain. The fear that a powerful individual at the head of the Treasury would wrest control of the purse from Congress was still very much alive. The course of safety, it was argued, was to reconstitute the Board of Treasury and to make certain that it remained in leading strings to Congress.

The burden of the argument in favor of the creation of an efficient Treasury Department with large powers concentrated in the hands of a single individual was borne by James Madison. "Inconsistent, unproductive, and expensive schemes," he declared, "will be more injurious to our constituents than the undue influence which the well-digested plans of a well-informed officer can have." The impact of Madison's speeches was vastly increased by the fact that the futile efforts of the Continental Congress to solve the country's financial problems were of recent and painful memory. In place of a board, therefore, Congress created a Department of the Treasury headed by a single Secretary.[15]

While the Secretary of the Treasury was made appointive by and responsible to the President, Congress was not prepared to surrender the Treasury Department wholly to the Chief Executive. In the opinion of many of the legislators, the President was already too powerful: "if you give him [the President] complete powers over the man with the strong box," it was said, "he will have the liberties of America under his thumb." It was decided, therefore, that, unlike the heads of the other executive departments, the Secretary of the Treasury must make his reports directly to Congress rather than through the agency of the President, thus making him a sort of liaison officer between

[15] Brant, *Madison, Father of the Constitution*, pp. 258–261.

Congress and the executive. Moreover, Congress reserved the right to examine financial documents and to require information from the Secretary of the Treasury without the interposition of the President.[16]

At the same time, Congress took measures to ensure that the Secretary of the Treasury did not become a power in his own right. It was first suggested that the Secretary be authorized to "digest and report plans for the improvement and management of the revenue, and the support of the public credit." This proposal was opposed by some congressmen on the ground that it was a step toward a financial dictatorship: if the Secretary were permitted to "report" his plans in person to Congress, he might erect himself into a chancellor of the exchequer with a powerful faction at his beck and call. Since the Constitution ordained that revenue bills were to originate in the House of Representatives, it seemed to follow that Congress must confine the powers of the Secretary to giving information only when it was asked for, not when he was disposed to give it. And so, despite Madison's contention that the right to "report" plans was perfectly harmless and would facilitate the exchange of information between Congress and the Secretary of the Treasury, a majority of the representatives voted to authorize the Secretary to prepare and digest but not to report plans.[17]

In establishing the Treasury Department, Congress drew heavily upon the forms and procedures of the Treasury Board. The subordinate officers, such as controller, auditor, registrar, and treasurer, and the system whereby these officials checked and counterchecked each other with a view to preventing unauthorized expenditures were carried over from the old government. Moreover, the experience gained under the Articles of Confederation was exemplified in the prohibition laid by Congress in 1789 upon all officers of the Treasury Department from being concerned in trade or business and in the purchase of public lands and government securities. On the other hand, the duties of the Treasury Department were very different from those of the Treasury Board. The collection of the revenue, for example, could hardly have been said to be a function of the government under the requisition system prevailing under the Articles of Confederation.[18]

[16] Henry Adams (ed.), *Writings of Albert Gallatin* (Philadelphia, 1879), I, 66–67.

[17] Hart, *American Presidency*, 227–228, 230–232.

[18] *Annals of Congress*, X, 980; *Pennsylvania Magazine of History and Bi-*

One of the most palpable defects of the Articles of Confederation was that they failed to provide for a judiciary capable of enforcing the laws of the general government. The Continental Congress had operated upon the states rather than directly upon the people; in consequence, no one was troubled by a Federal tax collector or a Federal judge. The administration of the law, together with control of the purse, rested solely with the states.

The Constitution declared that the judicial power of the United States government should be vested in "one Supreme Court, and in such inferior courts as the Congress may from time to time establish." It was therefore within the powers of Congress in 1789 to have created a system of courts that would have gone far toward realizing Hamilton's vision of the Federal judiciary as "the citadel of the public justice and the public security." But the Federalists in Congress were not agreed upon the extent to which this power should be exercised. Because the Antifederalists had predicted that the Federal judiciary would swallow up the state courts and because the prevailing mood of Congress was to conciliate the "honest opponents" of the Constitution, some congressmen advocated, as a token of good faith, that instead of creating a system of Federal courts the existing state courts be entrusted with the enforcement of Federal laws. In effect, they proposed that Congress create a Supreme Court and then rest upon its labors.

The Judiciary Act of 1789 represented a compromise between this cautious, temporizing policy and the concept of a powerful judiciary providing uniform civil justice and working toward the unification of the country. While a Supreme Court of six members and a system of inferior Federal courts consisting of three circuit and thirteen district courts were created, the principle that the rights of the Federal government could be safely confided to the state tribunals was implicitly followed. The Supreme Court was given limited original jurisdiction and the jurisdiction of the Federal district courts was likewise restricted. The adjudication of cases arising under the Constitution, laws, and treaties of the United States was consigned in the first instance to the

ography, XXXVIII, 138; Lodge, *Hamilton,* VIII, 152–153; Hildreth, *History,* IV, 103; D. R. Dewey, *Financial History of the United States* (New York, 1931), p. 88; J. Franklin Jameson (ed.), *Essays in the Constitutional History of the United States* (Boston, 1889), pp. 148–149, 176–177, 180–181; Leonard D. White, *The Jeffersonians* (New York, 1950), p. 162; Rives, *Madison,* III, 37; *Journal of Economic History,* III (1946), 210–211.

state courts. Instead of making the common law the "law of the United States"—thereby making any common-law question a matter for the cognizance of Federal judges—the Judiciary Act conferred upon the lower national courts only a criminal jurisdiction within the meaning of the common law. Thus, while the Constitution restricted the powers of the state governments, the first Congress actually enhanced the powers of the state courts—and this despite Hamilton's warning in the Constitutional Convention that the administration of justice "has a powerful Influence and must particularly attach Individuals to the state governments."[19]

As a result of the Judiciary Act of 1789, judicial power in the United States was distributed between the Federal government and the states in accord with the guiding principle of the settlement of 1787. No unified system of law pervaded the entire union; each state retained its distinct body of law; and no national tribunal had sufficient authority to lay down uniform rules of procedure and adjudication. In this regard, the United States was still very far from attaining Hamilton's ideal of "ONE WHOLE."[20]

Although Hamilton's suggestion of regional appellate courts under the supervision of the Supreme Court was not adopted, the Judiciary Act did provide that when a state court denied a claim of federal right the case could be appealed to the United States Supreme Court, thereby establishing the principle of judicial review of state legislation despite the absence in the Constitution of any specific mention of

[19] William Crosskey, *Politics and the Constitution* (Chicago, 1952), II, 757, 1040, contends that the intention of the framers of the Constitution was to blend state and national judiciaries into a single unitary system for "establishing justice" and that the Judiciary Act of 1789 was designed "to unite all the laws of the country into a single system" under the supervision of the national judiciary. Crosskey's views have won only limited acceptance. See Henry J. Friendly, "The Historic Basis of Diversity Jurisdiction," *Harvard Law Review* XLIV (1928), 467, 484–490; and Felix Frankfurter, "Distribution of Judicial Power Between United States and State Courts," *Cornell Law Quarterly*, XII (1928), 510, 512–515. Frankfurter points out that in 1787 the principal fear was of the state legislatures, not of the state courts (pp. 520–522). It is probable, however, that some of the framers of the Constitution intended that the Federal courts should have jurisdiction over all cases arising under common law. *Selected Cases in Constitutional Law*, II, 1248; Story, *Commentaries* (abrid. ed.), p. 637; Hand, *Bill of Rights*, pp. 5–7, 69–70; E. H. Scott (ed.), *The Federalist and Other Constitutional Papers* (Chicago, 1894), pp. 573–574.

[20] In *The Federalist*, Hamilton had taken the position that, except where exclusive jurisdiction was vested in the Federal courts, the state tribunals re-

this power. By this means, the Federalist legislators sought to ensure
that the states would not encroach upon the rights of the Federal
government or shake off the restraints laid upon them by the Constitution. Nevertheless, in cases not falling under federal jurisdiction
—which was true of the majority of cases—the decisions of the highest
tribunals in each state were final and without appeal. It was not until
the adoption of the Fourteenth Amendment that all state laws affecting life, liberty, and property were subjected to the review of the
Federal judiciary.[21]

The organization of the executive and judicial departments was not
accomplished without producing some sharp exchanges of opinion.
When, for example, the Department of State was under discussion, an
amendment was proposed whereby the President was authorized to
remove the Secretary from office without the advice and consent of
the Senate. While a large majority of the House of Representatives
was prepared to give the President this power, the members differed
as to whether Congress ought to make the grant or should simply
acknowledge that the power was already conferred by implication by
the Constitution. Madison threw the weight of his prestige and eloquence to the support of the theory that the opening sentence of
Article II (the so-called executive clause) is a general grant of power.
Since the Constitution had vested all executive power in the President,
Madison asserted that Congress had no right to diminish or modify in
any way his executive authority. The bill passed by Congress in June,
1789, not only authorized the President to remove appointees without
the consent of the Senate but implied that this was his right by constitutional grant even though the Constitution nowhere expressly authorized such an interpretation.[22]

The Senate was disposed to go even further toward aggrandizing the
executive power. Early in the session, the Senate affirmed its opinion
that the writs of the Federal government ought to run in the name
of the President. But the House protested that the Senate was up to

tained concurrent jurisdiction. He professed himself solicitous to erect safe-
guards against "an alienation of state power by implication" and he made
clear that the state courts would not be absorbed by the federal judicial bodies.
Here Hamilton spoke not as the nationalist he actually was but as an advocate
for the adoption of the Constitution.
[21] Charles G. Haines, *The American Doctrine of Judicial Supremacy* (New
York, 1914), pp. 154–157; Robert Morris to Peters, September 13, 1789,
Peters MSS., PHS.
[22] In 1867 and again in 1872 Congress attempted to establish the principle
that the President could remove heads of departments only with the advice

its old trick of aping the example of the British government, where writs ran in the name of the King. Since neither side consented to yield, the bill adopted by Congress reflected the impasse between the two houses: while it did not specify that writs should run in the name of the President, it did not, on the other hand, preclude the use of that form. In 1790, the Supreme Court took the matter out of the legislators' hands by directing that all processes of the Supreme Court should be in the name of the President of the United States.[23]

At this particular moment, President Washington himself was less concerned in establishing the President's power of removal than in making judicious appointments to the offices at his disposal. The President was fully aware that in this matter he trod upon slippery ground. "If injudicious or unpopular measures should be taken by the Executive under the New Government with regard to appointments," he said, "the Government itself would be in the utmost danger of being utterly subverted by those measures. So necessary is it, at this crisis, to conciliate the good will of the People; and so impossible is it, in my judgment, to build the edifice of public happiness, but upon their affections." He therefore scrupulously avoided incurring the charge of nepotism: when his nephew, Bushrod Washington, requested an appointment as district attorney Washington refused: "the eyes of Argus are upon me," he said, "and no slip will pass unnoticed that can be improved into a supposed particularity for friends or relatives."[24]

Washington's objective was to draw "the first Characters" of the country into the service of the Federal government. These characters were to be separated from the chaff, the President decided, by the application of three principal criteria: fitness, "former merits and sufferings in the service," and residence. Naturally, the President leaned to "just and candid men who are disposed to measure matters on a Continental Scale." Even so, he appointed some Antifederalists to office in the hope of conciliating the former opponents of the Constitution, thereby closing the gap that had been opened up by the struggle over the Constitution. Finally, in making appointments, President Washington tried to preserve a rough balance between the sections.[25]

---

and consent of the Senate. In effect, this legislation was held unconstitutional, in 1926, by the Supreme Court, Chief Justice Taft presiding.

[23] Hart, *American Presidency*, pp. 41–42, 45–46, 190, 202, 247; Tyler, *Letters and Times of the Tylers*, I, 170; Maclay, *Journal*, pp. 112–116; *The Federalist*, p. 497.

[24] Hart, *American Presidency*, pp. 111–114.

[25] Fitzpatrick, *Washington*, XXX, 413–414; XXXI, 51; Hart, *American Presidency*, pp. 117, 131–132.

As heads of the departments of State, War, and the Treasury, and to the office of Attorney General—the officials of cabinet[26] rank—President Washington appointed respectively Thomas Jefferson, General Henry Knox, Alexander Hamilton, and Edmund Randolph. Since 1784, Jefferson had been United States minister to the Court of France, where he had played an important part in the conduct of American foreign policy. Alexander Hamilton was at this time known as Washington's onetime aide-de-camp, a New York lawyer and politician and —to a few intimates, including Washington—the principal author of *The Federalist*. General Henry Knox, who tipped the scales at three hundred pounds, had been the leading artillerist in the American Army during the War of Independence. Edmund Randolph, no heavyweight in any sense of the word, had been on both sides during the debate over the Constitution, but his timely *volte-face* in favor of ratification had helped carry the day in the Virginia convention.

President Washington—to whom was given the never-to-be-repeated privilege of naming an entire bench—established the precedent of following a geographical rule in filling places on the Supreme Court. Three justices from the South and three from the North were selected by the President. All, however, were stanch Federalists, and none more so than John Jay, the Chief Justice. In many respects, Jay was the quintessence of Federalism: high-minded, public-spirited, devoted to the cause of Union, and a paragon of integrity, he was withal a conservative whose philosophy was succinctly expressed in the aphorism that "those who own the country ought to govern it."

The organization of the Federal government having been effected, the Washington administration was in a position to embark upon a program designed to fulfill the cardinal purposes of the Constitution: the protection of property rights, the extension of the powers of the general government over the economic life of the nation, the furtherance of agriculture, commerce, and manufacturing—in short, in Hamilton's words, to make the new government "majestic, efficient, and operative of great things."[27]

---

[26] After 1792, the Attorney General regularly attended cabinet meetings. White, *Federalists*, p. 164.

[27] White, *Federalists*, p. 507.

CHAPTER 3

Hamilton Takes Command: The Report on Public Credit

IN 1789, the office of Secretary of the Treasury was second in importance only to that of the President. As organized under the act of Congress of September, 1789, the Treasury was the largest of the departments, consisting of an assistant, controller, treasurer, auditor, register, and over thirty clerks. In addition, almost one thousand customhouse officers and internal revenue agents were placed under the Secretary's direction. By comparison, the Department of State seemed almost insignificant: it was staffed by only four clerks, a messenger, and an office keeper; and the War Department could muster only three clerks.[1]

Alexander Hamilton, the first Secretary of the Treasury, was a native of the West Indies. An ardent nationalist, he had proposed in the Constitutional Convention a plan of government for the United States so centralized that the states were reduced to little more than administrative districts of the national government. Throughout his career he acted upon the principle that "American liberty and happiness had much more to fear from the encroachments of the great states, than from those of the general government." Long before he became Secretary of the Treasury, he had sought to convert the national debt into a bond of union. In 1780–81, he had drawn up three separate plans for saving the sinking Continental dollar and in 1784 he played a

[1] *American State Papers* (Washington 1832, 1861), VII, Finance, I, 34; White, *Federalists*, pp. 117–122, 337; *Jeffersonians*, 187.

prominent part in the organization of the Bank of New York. In 1786, he had been the moving spirit at the Annapolis Convention in issuing a call for a Constitutional Convention; he had served in the Constitutional Convention as a delegate from New York and had signed the Constitution without authority from his state. Robert Morris, the former Superintendent of Finance, pronounced him to be a "damned sharp" young man.[2]

When he became Secretary of the Treasury, Hamilton later said, he was "called to the head of the most arduous department in the public administration in a new government, without the guidance of antecedent practice and precedent" and obliged to "trace out his own path, and to adjust for himself the import and bearings of delicate and important provisions in the Constitution and in the laws." But this was a labor that Hamilton entered upon gladly: he had no doubt of his ability to administer his department and to interpret the Constitution without guidance. "Were the people of America with one voice to ask: 'What shall we do to perpetuate our liberties and secure our happiness?' " Hamilton asked rhetorically, "the answer would be: 'Govern well,' and you have nothing to fear from internal disaffection or external hostility." By a vigorous use of the powers granted the general government he hoped to demonstrate to the people that a strong central government was a blessing by "pursuing such measures as will secure to them every advantage they can promise themselves under it."[3]

Having gathered about him men of ability, integrity, and Federalist views, President Washington looked forward hopefully in 1789 to a tranquil administration. The realization of the President's hope depended in large degree upon the continuance of the close co-operation that had hitherto generally prevailed between James Madison, the leader of the House of Representatives, and Alexander Hamilton, the Secretary of the Treasury. From 1782, when Hamilton had been

[2] It was by the intercession of Hamilton's friends, notably James Madison, that Washington was persuaded to appoint Hamilton Secretary of the Treasury. There is no proof that the President offered Robert Morris the post, but there is ample evidence that Morris would have refused had it been offered him. Sparks, *Morris,* III, 18–19; *Journal of Economic History,* III (1946), 210; Sumner, *Finances and Financiers of the American Revolution,* II, 209–210; E. P. Oberholtzer, *Robert Morris* (New York, 1903), pp. 256–258, 315.

[3] Marshall, *Washington,* V, 353–354; *The Federalist,* p. 41; Lodge, *Hamilton,* VIII, 152–153; IX, 460, 465; Rives, *Madison,* III, 37; *William and Mary Quarterly,* Third Series, IV (1947), 220; Holcombe, *Our More Perfect Union,* 286.

elected to the Continental Congress as the representative of New York, these two men had worked together to strengthen the Articles of Confederation and, in 1787, to devise a wholly new form of government for the United States. They had collaborated in writing *The Federalist* and in securing the adoption of the Constitution in New York and Virginia. They shared the conviction that the equilibrium between the states and the Federal government established by the Constitution stood in far greater danger of being upset by the states than by the general government, and that the enemy of freedom in the United States was "democratic majorities" which sacrificed the few to the many. They agreed that an "energetic" central government was necessary to protect property and civil liberties from the state governments, to direct economic activities into the channels most conducive to the national welfare, and to re-establish public credit.[4]

Notwithstanding their close alliance, Madison and Hamilton had worked together mainly as opponents of the system established by the Articles of Confederation. Neither their friendship nor their concurrence of views had as yet been subjected to the ineluctable strains and stresses which accompany the possession of power. While they agreed upon objectives—above all upon the necessity of creating a strong national government—they had reached no meeting of minds as to the means of attaining these objectives. Madison did not share Hamilton's enthusiasm for judicial review as a method of keeping "popular licentiousness" under control; in Madison's opinion, this power ought to be shared equally by the executive, legislative, and judicial branches of the government, and in some instances Congress ought to have the final authority in determining its own powers.[5] Although Patrick Henry opposed Madison's election to Congress on the ground that he was a thoroughgoing nationalist to whom it was unsafe to commit the vital interests of the Old Dominion, it is clear that even in his most nationalistic phase, Madison had never ceased to be a Virginian. He had no intention of reducing the influence of his native state in national affairs: the Virginia plan, which became the basis of

[4] Boyd, *Jefferson Papers*, XIV, 19–21; Brant, *Madison, The Nationalist,* p. 130; Hunt, *Madison,* V, 28–29, 267, 272–275.
[5] E. S. Corwin, *Twilight of the Supreme Court* (New Haven, 1934), p. 5; Charles Beard, *The Supreme Court and the Constitution* (New York, 1922), p. 31; Charles G. Haines, *The American Doctrine of Judicial Supremacy* (New York, 1914), p. 190; Wright, *Growth of American Constitutional Law,* p. 27; *Texas Law Review,* XXXII (1954), 252; Hunt, *Madison,* V, 420.

the deliberations of the Constitutional Convention, was designed to give Virginia and other large states a preponderating influence in the national government. Even while he sought to strengthen the position of northern shipping and manufactures in order to solidify the Union, his devotion to the planting economy of the South remained undiminished. At the time of the Constitutional Convention, he was worried lest the northern states gain a perpetual ascendancy over the southern states, and he advocated property qualifications for the exercise of the suffrage on the ground that, in the not distant future, it would be necessary to protect landed property from the attacks of the property-less proletariat.[6]

Yet in 1789, after Hamilton's appointment as Secretary of the Treasury, there was no reason to believe that the two men stood upon the threshold of a conflict that would irrevocably divide the house of Federalism. Madison had actively promoted Hamilton's appointment to the Treasury; and when the Virginian advocated the granting of extensive powers to the head of that department, he had Hamilton in mind as the man best qualified to exercise them. Aware of his debt to Madison and eager to establish good relations between the Treasury and the House of Representatives, Hamilton asked Madison in November, 1789, to set forth his views as to how the financial exigencies of the government could be most effectively met. From Madison's reply, Hamilton inferred that their earlier agreement still held firm and that he could be certain of the Virginian's continued support.[7]

Next to revenue, the most immediate need of the new government

[6] Tansill, *Documents*, pp. 489–490, 811, 934–935; Ford, *Jefferson*, VI, 310; Elliot, *Debates*, III, 312; Holcombe, *Our More Perfect Union*, p. 149.

[7] Despite Hamilton's conviction that all was well, in actuality Madison's letter made clear that he did not see eye to eye with Hamilton upon all fiscal matters. Certain in his own mind that under the existing system the South was condemned to pay a disproportionate share of the tax burden, Madison favored a land tax, to be imposed by the Federal government. To this advice, Hamilton turned a deaf ear: in the infancy of the government, he had no desire, he said, to impose a tax he felt certain would prove unpopular. Brant, *Madison, Father of the Constitution*, pp. 230–231; Mary L. Hinsdale, *A History of the President's Cabinet* (New York, 1911), pp. 18–20; W. E. Binkley, *The President and Congress* (New York, 1947), pp. 28, 30–31; Frank Monaghan, *John Jay, Defender of Liberty* (Indianapolis, 1935), p. 301; Charles F. Dunbar, *Economic Essays* (New York, 1904), p. 72 (footnote); *Journal of Economic History*, III (1946), 211; Rives, *Madison*, III, 76 (footnote); *Journals of the Continental Congress* (Washington, 1904–37), XXIV, 24, 282; XXV, 872; Lodge, *Hamilton*, IX, 462–463.

was credit. Americans' experience under the Articles of Confederation had demonstrated that no government could endure without the ability to borrow: in its later days, the Continental Congress had presented the spectacle of a government at the end of its financial tether. Manifestly, the Federal government could not live from hand to mouth as had the Continental Congress, spoon-fed at the last by Dutch bankers. In order to induce lenders, both foreign and domestic, to buy the securities of the United States government, it was necessary to convince them that their money would be secure and that it would draw interest.

As a result of the War of Independence, the states as well as the central government had accumulated large debts. Unfortunately for American taxpayers, before the state and Federal governments could regain their ability to borrow, adequate provision must be made for the existing debt. The framers of the Constitution had recognized this necessity and had stipulated in that document that "all debts contracted and engagements entered into before the adoption of the Constitution shall be as valid against the United States under this Constitution as under the Confederation." While this pledge did not compel the new government to redeem the debts of the old government, few members of Congress questioned in 1789 that something must be done for the public creditors. The only real difference of opinion on this score was how much of the existing debt had to be redeemed in order to establish the government's credit.[8]

Most members of Congress were inclined to try to accomplish this objective as cheaply as possible—always, however, with the proviso that the foreign debt, admittedly a "sacred obligation," must be paid in full. The domestic debt, on the other hand, was owed by the people of the United States to their fellow citizens who owned certificates of governmental indebtedness. Inevitably, therefore, "the many were to pay the few."[9] In 1780, the Continental Congress had set a precedent for scaling down this type of debt by setting an official value upon the Continental dollar of forty paper dollars to one specie dollar, thereby reducing the debt from four hundred million to ten million dollars. While in 1789 few congressmen favored such a wholesale repudiation of debt, the idea of paying off the government's creditors at less than

[8] Boyd, *Jefferson Papers,* XIV, 645; *American State Papers,* VII, Finance, I, 78; Lodge, *Hamilton,* VIII, 436; Maclay, *Journal,* p. 330; Noah Webster, *A Collection of Papers on Political, Literary and Moral Subjects* (New York, 1843), pp. 203, 207.

[9] Sparks, *Gouverneur Morris,* III, 17–18; *A Definition of Parties* (Philadelphia, 1794), pp. 7–8.

the face value of their certificates had many advocates. Little injustice or hardship seemed likely to be inflicted by departing from the strict terms of the contract: the debt had been incurred during a period of inflation and many of the original creditors—particularly the soldiers and farmers—had already disposed of their securities to investors and speculators.[10]

Moreover, the magnitude of the debt seemed to compel some abatement. In 1789, the national debt totaled over $50 million, $11,700,000 of which was owing the governments of France and Spain and the private bankers of the Netherlands, while $40 million was in the form of securities held by citizens of the United States. Interest on the French debt had fallen $1,500,000 in arrears and the interest on the debt owing the Dutch bankers had been paid only by further borrowing from the bankers themselves. Without this financial aid, the United States government would not have been able to maintain a diplomatic staff abroad. Even so, the government was unable to pay the ransoms of American sailors held captive by the Barbary corsairs, and the French officers who had served in the United States Army during the War of Independence had not received their annuities since 1785.[11]

If, in order to establish its credit, the government was obliged to pay its debts in whole or in part, most congressmen believed that the sale of western lands provided the most efficacious and painless way of discharging the obligation. With an immense domain beyond the Ohio awaiting settlement, the payment of the debt seemed to be merely a matter of opening up land offices and awaiting the rush of settlers. True, these high expectations had not been borne out by Americans' experience under the government of the Articles of Confederation. Large tracts of land had been sold at giveaway prices to land companies, but the settlers had been kept away by the high cost, the proximity of hostile Indians, and the comparative ease and cheapness of the lands offered by the states. As a result, the land companies soon experienced difficulty in meeting the payments due the government. Potentially, the government of the United States was rich, but at the moment, unfortunately for its creditors, it was land poor.[12]

---

[10] Elliot, *Debates*, II, 80; Rives, *Madison*, III, 78; Channing, *History*, IV, 69; *General Advertiser*, April 24, 1792; *Gazette of the United States*, February 18, 22, 1792.

[11] Boyd, *Jefferson Papers*, XIV, 645; Dewey, *Financial History*, p. 90; Rives, *Madison*, III, 18.

[12] John Page, *An Address* (Philadelphia, 1794), pp. 26–27; *A Review of*

In August, 1789, the creditors of the Federal government residing in Pennsylvania sent a memorial to Congress requesting payment of the interest on the national debt. "A debt originating in the patriotism that achieved the independence may thus," the petitioners observed, "be converted into a cement that shall strengthen and perpetuate the Union of America." This document was referred to a committee of Congress of which James Madison was chairman. On the ground that it was too late in the session for Congress to consider such an important matter, the committee recommended that the petition be referred to the Secretary of the Treasury. With no little relief, Congress accordingly deposited the prickly problem in Hamilton's lap. In October, 1789, Hamilton was instructed to prepare a report upon ways and means of supporting the credit of the Federal government.[13]

With leadership thus thrust upon him, Hamilton proceeded to draw up a Report on Public Credit which reflected his political as well as his financial convictions. Privately, he distinguished sharply between "the generality of considerate men" and "the community at large": in his eyes, the mass of the people were so devoted to their states that they had little affection or loyalty to spare for the national government. Hamilton therefore pinned his hopes of erecting an enduring Union upon the businessmen, the educated, and the professional men who "thought continentally." His financial ideas were equally incisive and firmly held. Rejecting all suggestions that the debt be scaled down in the interests of governmental economy—he recoiled, he said, from "the horrid doctrine of applying the sponge"—Hamilton insisted in his Report that the obligation be paid in full. "A government which does not rest on the laws of justice rests on that of force," he declared. "There is no middle ground."[14] In his view, the only way the new government could establish its credit was to deal honestly with its creditors—for in many instances they were the very people to whom the government must look for future loans. He therefore proposed in his Report to convert the arrears of interest (approximately $13 million) into principal and to fund the entire debt—that is, to pledge a certain part of the government's revenue irrevocably to the payment of interest and

---

the Revenue System (Philadelphia, 1794), p. 45; Abridgment of Debates, I, 115; Ballagh, Letters of R. H. Lee, II, 526.

[13] Annals of Congress, I, 792–795; The Politicks and Views of a Certain Party Displayed (Philadelphia, 1792), pp. 5–6; Dunbar, Economic Essays, 72 (footnote); Louis H. Boutell, Roger Sherman (Chicago, 1896), pp. 225–226.

[14] Lodge, Hamilton, VIII, 447.

principal. When this had been done, he asserted, the national debt would prove to be a national blessing.[15]

In his financial planning for the United States, Hamilton's model was the British financial system and his mentor was William Pitt. Certainly when Hamilton indited his Report on Public Credit, the credit of the British government seemed unshakable: since the creation of the Bank of England it had never defaulted on an obligation and it had never reduced the rate of interest on its securities by an arbitrary act of power. As Hamilton said, the credit of their government had become in Englishmen's minds "an article of faith" and this faith was soundly based upon the government's adherence to the maxim that honesty to creditors was the best policy.[16]

In the heyday of their power under the Articles of Confederation, some states had assumed part of the Federal debt.[17] Now, in 1790, Hamilton proposed that the Federal government turn the tables by assuming the state debts. As he visualized it, such an assumption would serve as a double-edged sword with which to strike at the roots of state sovereignty. In the first place, it promised to bring within the orbit of the Federal government all the state creditors, the most influential part of the community; secondly, it would relieve the states of the necessity of levying taxes, for if the Federal government took upon itself the payment of all the debts, it must perforce have all the revenue—and by

---

[15] *Journal of Business and Economic History,* III (1946), 674; Lodge, *Hamilton,* VIII, 431, 436–437, 441, 472; Seymour Harris, *The National Debt and the New Economics* (New York, 1947), p. 59; Broadus Mitchell, *Alexander Hamilton as Finance Minister,* Proceedings of the American Philosophical Society, Vol. 102, No. 2 (New York, 1958), pp. 117–123.

[16] William Bingham of Philadelphia, one of the wealthiest merchants in the United States, having later returned from England, gave Hamilton valuable information concerning William Pitt's fiscal policies. *Journal of Business and Economic History,* III, 672–676. See E. L. Hargreaves, *The National Debt* (London, 1926), pp. 86, 99–101, 104, 112; Sir James Steuart, *The Works, Political, Metaphysical, and Chronological of the late Sir James Steuart* (London, 1805), III, 144; Earl J. Hamilton, "Origin and Growth of the National Debt in Western Europe," *American Economic Review,* XXXVII (1947), 120–124; Dunbar, *Economic Essays,* pp. 88–89; Francis W. Hirst, *The Credit of Nations* (Washington, 1910), pp. 79–81; David Hume, *Political Discourses* (London, 1752), pp. 209–210; Arthur Hope-Jones, *Income Tax in the Napoleonic Wars* (Cambridge, 1939), pp. 5–6; Charles F. Dunbar, "Some Precedents Followed by Alexander Hamilton," *Quarterly Journal of Economics,* III (1888), 32–59.

[17] E. James Ferguson, "State Assumption of the Federal Debt during the Confederation," *Mississippi Valley Historical Review,* XXXVIIII (1951), 404–406, 411–412, 414–419.

possessing the whole revenue it came into possession of the whole power of the Union. Deprived of the support of their wealthiest citizens and unable to exert their authority by means of taxation, the states, Hamilton fondly imagined, would gradually wither away and their strength would be absorbed by the Federal government.[18]

In the Report on Public Credit which Hamilton submitted to Congress in January, 1790, he supplied his supporters in the legislature with facts and arguments in support of his funding-assumption scheme. To a remarkable degree, the Secretary succeeded in anticipating and answering the objections that were quickly raised against his Report. Nevertheless, while he foresaw the arguments of the opposition, he utterly failed to foresee the source from whence those arguments would emanate. For the organizer and leading spirit of the resistance was James Madison, the very man upon whom Hamilton had counted to guide the funding-assumption measure through Congress.

Madison's opposition to the Report on Public Credit struck Hamilton as "a perfidious desertion of the principles which he [Madison] was solemnly pledged to defend."[19] Nevertheless, as a Virginian, it would have been political suicide for Madison to have taken an unqualified stand in favor of the adoption of Hamilton's Report. Over four-fifths of the national debt was owing citizens living north of Mason and Dixon's line and, except for South Carolina, most of the state debts were likewise concentrated in the North. Inevitably, therefore, Hamilton's plan would have strengthened the position of the North and weakened that of the South. With this circumstance in mind, Henry Lee pointedly asked Madison if he was so ardently devoted to the Constitution that he would adhere to it "even though it should produce ruin to his native country" (Virginia).[20]

18 Lodge, Hamilton, IX, 5, 13, 28–29; Rives, Madison, III, 96; Hunt, Madison, V, 48; Elliot, Debates, II, 132; George Gibbs, Memoirs of the Administrations of Washington and John Adams (New York, 1846), I, 24–25, 45; Annals of Congress, II, 1338, 1608; Maclay, Journal, pp. 232, 236; Marshall, Washington, V, 253.

19 Lodge, Hamilton, IX, 513–515; W. P. and J. P. Cutler, The Life, Journals and Correspondence of the Reverend Manasseh Cutler (Cincinnati, 1888), I, 462.

20 Wilfred E. Binkley, American Political Parties (New York, 1943), p. 44; Lodge, Hamilton, II, 467–468; III, 18; IX, 513–515; Dorfman, Economic Mind, I, 302; Hunt, Madison, VI, 9, 13; Annals of Congress, II, 1518; S. M. Hamilton (ed.), The Writings of James Monroe (New York, 1898–1903), I, 208–210; Henry Lee to Madison, April 3, 1790; George Turberville to Madison, January 23, 1793, Madison MSS., LC.

Even so, Madison was careful to avoid impugning Hamilton's industry and ability, and he made clear that his opposition was directed not against funding and assumption *per se* but against certain aspects of the Secretary's plan. Funding, he conceded, was a "necessary evil." He proposed to mitigate its most pernicious effects by discriminating between the original holders and the purchasers of government securities. Between these two groups—those who had been given securities for services or supplies rendered the government during the War of Independence and those who had purchased these certificates, often at a fraction of their face value—Madison proposed an equitable division of the profit which would otherwise accrue only to purchasers when the debt was funded. The issue between the original holders and their assignees could not be decided, he insisted, by reference to the principles followed in an ordinary case in a court of law: "In great and unusual questions of morality," he said, "the heart is the best judge."[21] To Madison's way of thinking, the Union had been created to achieve more perfect justice and, since injustice had been done the public creditors, the government was obligated to intervene in their behalf.[22]

In his speeches to Congress, Madison dwelt upon the plight of the soldiers—those "hardy veterans" who had been compelled by economic necessity to sell their paper certificates for a pittance of cash. There was, he exclaimed, "something radically immoral and consequently impolitic" to permit the rewards to be transferred from "the gallant Earners of them to that class of people who now take their places."[23]

Since Hamilton's objective was not merely to pay the existing debt but to lay the foundations for contracting future loans on the easiest possible terms, he categorically rejected Madison's plan of discriminating between original holders and purchasers of the debt. *"The established rules of morality and justice,"* he declared, *"are applicable to nations as well as to individuals. . . .* A relaxation of this kind would tend to dissolve all social obligations—to render all rights pre-

[21] Madison to Rush, March 7, 1790, Madison MSS., LC; Ford, *Madison,* VI, 11.

[22] Madison to Carrington, March 4, 1790, Emmet MSS., NYPL; Madison to Rush, March 7, 1790, Madison MSS., LC; Ford, *Madison,* VI, 11; *Annals of Congress,* II, 1407.

[23] Madison to Rush, March 7, 1790, Madison MSS., LC; Fitzpatrick, *Washington,* XXX, 82, 86; *A Review of the Revenue System* (Philadelphia, 1794), p. 6.

carious, and to introduce a general dissoluteness and corruption of morals."[24] To Hamilton's way of thinking, the purchasers of government securities were entitled to every penny of profit resulting from the funding of the national debt: they had supported the government's credit in its darkest hour and they had risked their capital upon a contingency amounting to little less than a revolutionary change in the government.

In this instance Congress was no more inclined than was the Secretary of the Treasury to make equity its guide. Madison's plan lacked the one element that could have commended it to Congress—economy. Accordingly, while many congressmen deplored the sad fate of the soldiers, widows, and orphans who had sold their securities to "unconscionable speculators," they voted down Madison's bill by a large majority. Despite this untoward outcome, Madison's efforts in behalf of the dispossessed appreciably enhanced his reputation as a friend of the common man.[25]

Discrimination between original holders and purchasers was the more necessary, Madison argued, because the debt had become such an object of speculation that if Hamilton's plan were carried out, the speculators would reap a profit comparable to the fortunes amassed by the promoters of the South Sea Bubble.[26] Undeniably, since the adoption of the Constitution, there had been a great deal of speculative buying of government securities by Dutch and American capitalists. The enactment of the revenue law of 1789 had touched off a particularly heavy wave of buying—with the result that by January, 1790, Gouverneur Morris, himself a speculator, estimated that Dutch bankers

[24] Lodge, *Hamilton*, II, 436, 442, 447; III, 17, 20–21; VIII, 466; IX, 15–17; New York *Journal and Weekly Advertiser*, April 5, 1787; Samuel McKee (ed.), *Papers on Public Credit, Commerce and Finance* (New York, 1957), pp. 10–11, 13–15.

[25] Hunt, *Madison*, V, 460; VI, 6 (footnote); *Alexander Biddle Papers*, pp. 36, 82; Hildreth, *History*, IV, 162–166; Marshall, *Washington*, V, 243–244; Dewey, *Financial History*, p. 90; Essex Institute Historical Collections, LXXXIV (1948), 148–149; Dorfman, *Economic Mind*, I, 244–245, 293, 410; McKee, *Papers*, 10–11, 16; Proceedings of the Massachusetts Historical Society, Second Series, XV (1902), 139; Fitzpatrick, *Washington*, XXXI, 28 (footnote); Maclay, *Journal*, pp. 199–201; *Federal Gazette and Philadelphia Evening Post*, February 5, 1790; *Pennsylvania Magazine of History and Biography* (1914), pp. 38, 188; *The Politicks and Views of a Certain Party Displayed* (Philadelphia, 1792), pp. 7–8; Thomas Hartley to Yeates, February 14, 1790, Yeates MSS., PHS.

[26] Hunt, *Madison*, V, 435, 460; Brant, *Madison, Father of the Constitution*, pp. 290–305.

had bought three million pounds of government certificates at an average price of five shillings in the pound.[27] The immediate effect of Hamilton's Report on Public Credit was to raise the price of these certificates as speculators scrambled to get in on a seemingly "sure thing."[28]

The opponents of Hamilton's Report charged that at least part of this "speculative mania" was owing to the fact that certain privileged individuals had prior knowledge of the Secretary's plans. Although suspicion touched even the Secretary himself, there is no evidence that Hamilton divulged the contents of his Report to his friends: on the contrary, resolved to place himself above "eagle-eyed" suspicion, on occasion he flatly refused to discuss the matter. But by appointing William Duer Assistant Secretary of the Treasury, Hamilton virtually ensured that Treasury "secrets" would be leaked to a few wealthy individuals who had the cash necessary to turn such information to profit.[29] And yet, even without Duer's behind-the-scenes manipulations, there would have been widespread speculation in government securities in 1789–90. It required no inside information for capitalists to see that a rapid rise in price was in store. As early as August, 1789, Noah Webster, on the strength of his conversations with various members of Congress, was certain that the debt would be funded. "I wish I had a little property to speculate," lamented Webster. ". . . . There is no part of the world where so many objects of speculation present themselves."[30]

[27] A. C. Morris (ed.), *Gouverneur Morris, Diary and Letters* (New York, 1888), I, 400; *Letters of Benjamin Goodhue,* Essex Institute Historical Collections, LXXXIV (1948), 148; *Columbian Centinel,* August 4, 1790; East, *American Business Enterprise,* pp. 279–280; Craigie to Daniel Parker, October 30, November 14, 1789, Craigie MSS., AAS.

[28] Not all of the speculators in the United States favored the adoption of Hamilton's Report. The land speculators who had committed themselves to purchase land with certificates which, despite their low current price, were accepted by the government at face value in exchange for land were threatened with ruin by Hamilton's plan of raising the price of these securities to par. Nor were all purchasers of government securities properly designated speculators. Many bought for investment purposes. Among the large holders of Massachusetts state securities was Harvard College.

[29] John C. Hamilton (ed.), *Works of Alexander Hamilton* (New York, 1850–51), V, 445–447.

[30] Ford and Skeel, *Notes on the Life of Noah Webster,* pp. 203–204; H. C. Adams, *Taxation in the United States,* p. 61; Craigie to Daniel Parker, October 2, 30, November 5, 1788, Craigie MSS., AAS; B. W. Bond, Jr. (ed.), *The Correspondence of J. C. Symmes* (New York, 1926), pp. 235–236, 250, 254, 256.

As Hamilton's opponents pictured it, much of the buying of state and Federal certificates during the early months of 1790 was by speculators in the know who took advantage of security holders who were ignorant of the contents of Hamilton's Report. Certainly it is true that in January, 1790, several fast-sailing ships, laden with speculators and cash, were sent from Philadelphia and New York to the southern states in the hope of cornering the securities of those states before the holders got wind of Hamilton's recommendations with regard to state debts. But if northern speculators were able to reap a rich harvest in the South, it was not so much owing to the ignorance of Southerners as to their conviction that the funding-assumption measure would be defeated in Congress. In North Carolina, where Hamilton's Report had few supporters, state securities were selling at five shillings on the pound in April, 1790, almost four months after the publication of the Report on Public Credit. Likewise, delay in the adoption by Congress of Hamilton's Report stimulated speculation; as long as the issue was in doubt, buying and selling of government obligation were inevitable.[31] In June, 1790, some issues were selling at a lower price than in the previous January. As Hamilton said, the sellers speculated upon the purchasers and "each made his calculation of chances."[32]

In his Report on Public Credit, Hamilton recommended that the Federal government assume that part of the state debts incurred in the prosecution of the War of Independence.[33] His plan did not em-

[31] Hunt, Madison, V, 435; Ford, Jefferson, I, 160–161; Lodge, Hamilton, II, 470; IX, 507; Horace Johnson to Craigie, January 29, February 29, 1790, Craigie MSS., AAS; Tench Coxe to Irvine, August 24, 1790, William Irvine MSS., PHS; Robert C. Livingston to Alexander Rose, March 20, May 5, 1790; to Richard Wylly, March 19, 1790; to John Green, March 19, 1790, Livingston MSS., NYHS; Ford, Letters of S. B. Webb, III, 157–158; Davis, American Corporations, I, 144, 174–175, 189; Gibbs, Memoirs, I, 24–25; Charles R. King, The Life and Correspondence of Rufus King (New York, 1895), I, January 24, 1790; Jane J. Boudinot, The Life, Public Services, Addresses and Letters of Elias Boudinot (Boston, 1896), II, January 21, 1790.

[32] Lodge, Hamilton, II, 465.

[33] The idea of the assumption of state debts by the Federal government was not new in 1790. It had been proposed by Hamilton and Madison and approved by Jefferson in 1783 and it had been discussed in the Constitutional Convention, where, on August 21, 1787, a committee recommended that there be incorporated in the Constitution a provision authorizing the Federal government to assume the debts "incurred by the several States during the late war, for the common defence and general welfare." This clause was stricken out because "it did not extend to the repayment of that part which the States had

brace the debts as they stood in 1783: Hamilton was concerned only with them as they existed in 1790. In effect, therefore, he penalized the states which had liquidated all or part of their debts since the end of the war. States with low indebtedness would be obliged to help pay the debts of heavily indebted states. Such apparent inequity was necessary, the Secretary contended, to equalize among the states the financial burden inherited from the struggle for independence.[34]

In general, the attitude of the members of Congress toward the assumption of state debts was determined by the size of the debt of the state they represented. Maryland, Georgia, and North Carolina, having small debts, tended to vote against assumption; Pennsylvania, with a debt of about two million dollars, was divided; New York, New Jersey, Massachusetts, and South Carolina, with comparatively large debts, voted in favor. Every New England representative except one wished to see assumption carried, although some privately expressed the opinion that Hamilton was moving too fast.[35] The case of Virginia was exceptional. The Old Dominion had reduced its war debt by half, chiefly by paying it with depreciated paper money and by selling Kentucky lands. (Land warrants sufficient to cover the entire district several times over had been issued.) In 1790, despite these measures, Virginia's debt was not small—it amounted to more than three million dollars —but few Virginians doubted that the Federal government was so deeply in debt to the state that when a settlement was made the entire debt would be extinguished. In actuality, when the final reckoning was made, it was discovered that Virginia, far from being a creditor, owed the Federal government slightly over $100,000.[36]

---

sunk, as well as that which remained unpaid." Hunt, *Madison*, IV, August 18, 21, 1787; *Annals of Congress*, II, 1360; Edmund C. Burnett, *Letters of Members of the Continental Congress* (Washington, 1921), VI, 36, VII, 435; VIII, 703; Brunhouse, *Counterrevolution in Pennsylvania*, p. 199; Gibbs, *Memoirs*, I, 24–25; Tansill, *Documents*, 565; Gorham to Knox, January 20, 1790, Knox MSS., MHS; Craigie to Parker, November 5, 1788, Craigie MSS., AAS; *Pennsylvania Gazette*, November 18, December 2, 30, 1789; Boyd, *Jefferson Papers*, VI, 263–266 (footnote), 270–271.

[34] Lodge, *Hamilton*, VIII, 481–482; IX, 28–32; Marshall, *Washington*, V, 257; Channing, *History*, IV, 71; Henry Cabot Lodge, *Life and Letters of George Cabot* (Boston, 1877), pp. 36–37.

[35] Charles, *Origins*, pp. 24–25; *Annals of Congress*, II, 1364.

[36] Proceedings of the Massachusetts Historical Society, XLVII (1914), 40; *Mississippi Valley Historical Review*, XXXVIII (1951), 21; Charles A. Beard, *Economic Origins of Jeffersonian Democracy* (New York, 1915), pp. 112–113, 193, 195; Ames, *Works*, I, 77; William T. Read, *The Life and Correspondence*

Rather than see Virginia made the victim of such palpable "injustice" as Hamilton's plan envisaged, Madison proposed in Congress that the Federal government assume the debts of the state as they had stood in 1783. Even though this meant doubling the amount of debt Hamilton was prepared to assume, Madison's scheme provided a rallying point for the opponents of the Secretary's Report.[37] Being almost equal in numbers, Hamilton's and Madison's adherents remained deadlocked for almost six months. The debate became increasingly bitter: as John Marshall said, Hamilton's Report "seemed to unchain all those fierce passions which a high respect for the government and for those who administered it, had in a great measure restrained."[38] In March, 1790, the debate was interrupted by a heated exchange between northern and southern members over the subject of Negro slavery. This controversy was precipitated by a Quaker memorial condemning slavery and demanding the abolition of the slave trade. While it did nothing to ease the lot of the slaves, the memorial succeeded in sidetracking the debate and producing more passionate declamations than did the funding-assumption plan itself.[39]

By July, 1790, after four successive defeats, many of the proponents of Hamilton's Report had begun to lose heart. The Madisonians sought to separate funding from assumption, whereas the Hamiltonians, insisting that funding and assumption were indissolubly joined together, refused to vote for one without the other even though such procedure meant defaulting on payments of the foreign debt. Several New England congressmen, disgusted by the obduracy of the Virginians, openly talked of secession; and Senator Richard Henry Lee of Virginia declared that he would prefer the dissolution of the Union to "the rule of a fixed insolent northern majority."[40] Although Hamilton continued

of George Read (Philadelphia, 1870), p. 516; Channing, History, IV, 71–72; McMaster, History, I, 593; J. C. Hamilton, Hamilton, V, 455.

[37] Annals of Congress, II, 1407; Rives, Madison, III, 103–105; Mississippi Valley Historical Review, XXXVIII (1951), 418–421; Edward Carrington to Madison, March 21, 1790, Madison MSS., LC.

[38] Marshall, Washington, V, 234.

[39] It is significant that on this occasion a majority of representatives from Maryland and Virginia displayed little enthusiasm for slavery. The most vehement defenders of the institution came from Georgia and South Carolina. Hunt, Madison, VI, 6 (footnote), 16; Lodge, Hamilton, II, 441; Ames, Works, I, 75–76.

[40] Hunt, Madison, VI, 10–11 (footnote), 13; Rives, Madison, III, 100–101; Cutler, Manasseh Cutler, I, 461; Ford, Letters of S. B. Webb, II, 160–161; Gibbs, Memoirs, I, 46, 48; Hildreth, History, IV, 207–208; Essex Institute

to rally his forces in Congress and to supply his spokesmen with facts and figures with which to refute the arguments of the opposition, it was borne in upon him that even "truly Ciceronian" speeches would not suffice to carry the funding-assumption plan through Congress.[41]

One morning early in July, 1790, Secretary of State Jefferson was preparing to ascend the steps to the President's house when he was accosted by the Secretary of the Treasury. Jefferson observed a certain air of distraction in Hamilton's appearance and speech, but his meaning was clear enough: the Union was endangered by the deadlock in Congress and it was up to Jefferson to use his influence to save the Republic. The next day, with James Madison present, a deal was consummated between Hamilton and the two Virginians: in exchange for locating the capital in Philadelphia for ten years, to be followed by its permanent removal to the Potomac, Jefferson and Madison pledged themselves to change the votes of several southern congressmen in favor of the funding-assumption plan. On his part, Hamilton undertook to win the support of Robert Morris, the most influential member of the Pennsylvania delegation.[42]

Despite these behind-the-scenes maneuvers, to procure a majority in Congress in favor of the assumption of state debts it was found necessary to modify the plan laid down by Hamilton. Thanks largely to the efforts of Congressman Roger Sherman of Connecticut, a compromise was effected between Hamilton's scheme of assuming the existing debts of the states and Madison's proposal to assume the debts as they stood in 1783. By this arrangement, the states with small debts were to be compensated with what amounted to an outright grant by the Federal government. Delaware, with no state debt, received $200,000; North Carolina, with a debt estimated at about $500,000, was awarded $2,400,000; and $3,500,000 was assumed from Virginia, thereby, said Madison, purging assumption "of some of the objections and particularly of its gross injustice to Virginia."[43]

Historical Collections, LXXXIV (1948), 155; Griffith J. McRee, *The Life and Correspondence of James Iredell* (New York, 1857), pp. 281–287; Maclay, *Journal*, pp. 202, 208–209, 237.

[41] Lodge, *Hamilton*, VIII, 469–472; Hildreth, *History*, IV, 207–208.

[42] *Abridgment of Debates*, II, 630; Maclay, *Journal*, p. 263; Essex Institute Historical Collections, LXXXIV (1948), 158; Channing, *History*, IV, 73; Lodge, *Hamilton*, IX, 25; Ford, *Jefferson*, I, 162–164; VI, 172–174; Hildreth, *History*, IV, 212–213; Dumas Malone, *Jefferson and the Rights of Man* (Boston, 1951), p. 507; Noble E. Cunningham, Jr., *The Jeffersonian Republicans* (Chapel Hill, 1957), p. 5.

[43] John H. Morison, *Life of Jeremiah Smith* (Boston, 1845), pp. 52–53;

Accordingly, in August, 1790, by a narrow margin, most of the essential features of Hamilton's Report on Public Credit were enacted by Congress. One of the Virginia congressmen who voted "aye" did so "with a revulsion of stomach almost convulsive," but his sacrifice permitted James Madison to vote to the end against both funding and assumption.[44]

In order to achieve his objective, Hamilton had been compelled to play fast and loose with one of the dearest wishes of his fellow New Yorkers—to keep the national capital in New York City. Fifty thousand dollars had been expended upon the construction of the Federal Hall in New York City—and now the site of government had been bargained away! Jefferson, on his part, had given his approval to a measure which every Virginia congressman except one (and he had died before it came to a vote) had strenuously resisted. Yet both Jefferson and Hamilton were practical men who recognized that politics was largely a matter of give and take.[45]

On second thought, however, Jefferson came to the conclusion that he had done the giving and Hamilton the taking. He feared that the North would repudiate the bargain and that the national capital would remain fast-anchored in Philadelphia.[46] In the meantime, the North would reap the advantages of the funding system and the assumption of state debts and Hamilton would be brought measurably closer to the attainment of his goal of bringing men of wealth within the fold of

Ballagh, *Letters of R. H. Lee*, II, 534; Hunt, *Madison*, VI, July 31, 1790; Marshall, *Washington*, V, 257; Maclay, *Journal*, pp. 230–234; Essex Institute Historical Collections, LXXXIV (1948), 154–155; *Pennsylvania Magazine of History and Biography*, XXXVIII (1914), 199.

[44] Ford, *Jefferson*, I, 162–163; Ballagh, *Letters of R. H. Lee*, II, 534; *Abridgment of Debates*, II, 638.

[45] Stokes, *Iconography*, V, 1267–1268; Saul K. Padover, *Jefferson and the National Capital* (Washington, 1946), p. 14; Essex Institute Historical Collections, LXXXIV (1948), 158–159; *Pennsylvania Magazine of History and Biography* XXXVIII (1914), 204; Lewis Bland Walker (ed.), *The Bland Papers* (n. p., 1859), p. 162.

[46] Had Jefferson been certain that the capital would be removed to the Potomac he would have felt less misgiving over his bargain with Hamilton. From this change of residence he anticipated many benefits to the South: Southern congressmen would be able to attend Congress with less inconvenience; manufactures, commerce, and settlers would be attracted to Virginia and Maryland; and Southerners would be given preference when it came to awarding political offices. The Potomac, Jefferson declared, was "the only point of union which can cement us to our Western friends when they shall be formed into separate states." Boyd, *Jefferson Papers*, VI, 364–365, 371; Dorfman, *Economic Mind*, I, 424.

the national government and of reducing the states to impotence.[47]

It could not be denied that the adoption of Hamilton's Report redounded to the advantage of northern and South Carolina security holders and to the strengthening of the national government. A comparatively small number of individuals were suddenly enriched when, as a result of the funding-assumption law, over $60 million of state and federal certificates of indebtedness, at one time virtually worthless paper, were raised almost to face value. By pledging a large part of its revenue to the payment of interest on this debt, the government regained its ability to borrow: the arrears of interest and principal owing France were paid by means of new loans contracted at a lower rate of interest. As conditions in Europe became increasingly unsettled, foreign capital found in the United States, in Talleyrand's words, "an asylum under the protection of the good faith and wise administration of the United States."[48] Equally important, the new bonds issued by the Federal government—representing a sum ten times larger than the amount of specie in the United States—were converted into a circulating medium which Hamilton acclaimed as "an engine of business, an instrument of industry and commerce."[49]

By no means all Americans rejoiced in these evidences of growing national wealth and power. The defenders of agrarianism saw in Hamilton's fiscal measures an insidious plot to depress agriculture, to make wealthy speculators lords and masters of the United States, to pave the way for the introduction of a monarchical system, and "to sow the seeds of every vice and calamity in our country." The fact that Hamilton had derived many of his ideas from Great Britain did him no honor among American democrats: "When the systems of the vilest and most corrupt government find advocates in the councils of America," it was asked, "shall we dare any longer to say that America is

[47] Hunt, *Madison*, VI, 10–11 (footnote); *National Gazette*, November 10, 1791; Henry, *Patrick Henry*, III, 418–419; Ford, *Jefferson*, I, 162; *An Essay on the Seat of the Federal Government, By a Citizen of Philadelphia* (Philadelphia, 1789), pp. 25–27; Channing, *History*, IV, 29; Cunningham, *Jeffersonian Republicans*, pp. 6–8.

[48] Hans Huth and Wilma J. Pugh, *Talleyrand in America as a Financial Promoter* (Washington, 1942), p. 127; Lodge, *Hamilton*, II, 452, 458; Hildreth, *History*, IV, 275–277.

[49] Tench Coxe, *View*, 364–365; Dewey, *Financial History*, p. 96; McKee, *Papers*, 218–219; Joseph S. Davis, *Essays in the Earlier History of American Corporations* (Cambridge, Mass., 1917), I, 295–299; Proceedings of the Massachusetts Historical Society, XLV (Boston, 1912), 334.

the land of freedom?"[50] Thus was the issue drawn between Hamiltonian finance and American liberty: by treating the people of the United States as a "swinish multitude" fit only to labor for the enrichment of "vultures," "harpies," and "bloodsuckers" (otherwise known as the public creditors) Hamilton, it was said, had, "as with a magic wand, caused princely estates to grow up like mushrooms in a night; and the national debt to increase with the rapidity of a torrent."[51]

In no state was the funding-assumption system more unpopular than in Virginia. During the debate over the ratification of the Constitution, Patrick Henry had predicted that the northern states would attempt to despoil the southern states: "Not satisfied with a majority in the legislative councils," he warned, "they must have all our property. . . . This is a contest for money as well as empire."[52] After 1790, Henry was honored in Virginia as a vindicated prophet whose dire warnings had been taken too lightly. Senator George Mason of Virginia declared Hamilton had "done us more injury than Great Britain & all her fleets & armies." Virginians were convinced that they paid a disproportionate share of the taxes collected by the Federal government; certainly it was true that they received comparatively little in the form of interest on the national debt. In 1795, for example, citizens of Massachusetts received over $300,000 in interest on United States government securities, whereas Virginians received only $62,000 from this source. In the list of holders of public securities Virginia, the largest state in the Union, stood seventh.[53] As a northern congressman observed, the Secretary of the Treasury had driven home to the "Virginia lordlings a mortifying and alarming truth"—namely, that the North was the dominant section of the Union. To this subordination, the Virginia planters, firmly

[50] Henry, *Patrick Henry*, III, 421; *Considerations on the Nature of a Funded Debt* (New York, 1790), pp. 7–8; *Dunlap's American Daily Advertiser*, March 28, 1792; *Pennsylvania Gazette*, February 8, 1790; Fitzpatrick, *Washington*, XXXIII, 94 (footnote); James Sullivan, *The Path to Riches* (Boston, 1792), p. 16; Maclay, *Journal*, p. 329; G. A. Corner (ed.), *Autobiography of Dr. Benjamin Rush* (Princeton, 1951), p. 200.

[51] *John P. Branch Historical Papers*, II (Richmond, 1905), II, 272, 275–276; *Alexander Biddle Papers* (New York, 1943), p. 89; Hunt, *Madison*, VI, 83; John Williams, *Life of Alexander Hamilton* (Boston, 1804), p. 7; *A Definition of Parties* (Philadelphia, 1794), p. 4; Lodge, *Hamilton*, III, 11; VIII, 435; William Manning, *The Key of Liberty* (Boston, 1798), p. 26.

[52] Elliot, *Debates*, III, 319, 322, 474.

[53] Channing, *History*, IV, 93–94; *Report of the American Historical Association for 1896* (Washington, 1897), I, 838.

convinced as they were of the grandeur and self-sufficiency of their state, were never resigned.[54]

Hamilton denied that the South had been sacrificed to the North— the Virginians' contention was, he said, "unsupported by documents, facts, or, it may be added, probabilities." Nor did he admit that the interests of manufacturing and commerce conflicted with those of agriculture: the economy of the United States, he argued, was indivisible and all branches would benefit from a "universal vivification of the energies of industry."[55] Nevertheless, the Virginians were so little persuaded by the Secretary's assurances that in November, 1790, the Virginia legislature sent a Protest and Remonstrance to Congress in which assumption was pronounced to be "repugnant to the Constitution of the United States" and the funding system "dangerous to the rights and subversive of the interests of the people."[56]

This development strengthened Hamilton's conviction that a decisive struggle between Virginia and the national government was inevitable. "This is the first symptom of the spirit which must either be killed, or it will kill the Constitution of the United States," he told John Jay. Instead of sympathizing with Hamilton's eagerness to force a showdown upon Virginia, Jay advised him to wait for the healing effects of time and statesmanship to demonstrate the benefits of the Constitution.[57] While Hamilton reluctantly agreed to hold his hand, he was

[54] So deeply did Virginians resent and distrust Hamilton's financial system that they did not take full advantage of their opportunity to possess themselves of Federal securities. According to the provisions of the Assumption Act, each state was given a quota of Federal securities and the individual holders of state securities were invited to exchange them for new Federal certificates of indebtedness. By March, 1793, the expiration of the period permitted for this exchange, only $18,271,184 had been subscribed. Virginians subscribed for only a small part of the $1,172,350 allowed. *American State Papers,* VII, Finance, I, 150; Studenski and Kroos, *Financial History,* p. 53. See also *Annals of Congress,* II, 1518; Ford, *Jefferson,* I, 215; Hunt, *Madison,* V, 104; Wilfred E. Binkley, *American Political Parties* (New York, 1943), p. 63; *Report of the American Historical Association for 1896* (Washington, 1897), I, 838.

[55] Lodge, *Hamilton,* II, 448, 452, 458; VIII, 462; E. R. Taus, *Central Banking Functions of the United States Treasury* (New York, 1943), pp. 11–12; Dorfman, *Economic Mind,* I, 408; Dewey, *Financial History of the United States,* p. 96; Hildreth, *History,* IV, 275–277.

[56] And yet in 1791, in exchange for a grant of separate statehood, Virginia demanded that Kentucky assume a portion of the Virginia state debt.

[57] Lodge, *Hamilton,* IV, 437; IX, 473–474; Johnston, *Jay,* III, 409–410; Rives, *Madison,* III, 149, 152; Charles Warren, *The Supreme Court in United States History* (Boston, 1937), I, 52–53; George Logan, *Letters Addressed*

never persuaded that there was any permanent solution to the problem short of carving up Virginia and other large states into smaller jurisdictions.

As a result of the funding-assumption legislation, the national debt soared to a total of over $80 million. To service this debt, almost 80 per cent of the annual expenditures of the government were required. During the period 1790–1800, payment of the interest alone of the national debt consumed over 40 per cent of the national revenue. For a nation whose government had been tottering on the brink of bankruptcy a few years before, this might well be regarded as a staggering burden of debt, necessitating an annual revenue of not less than $5 million annually. Nevertheless, Hamilton did not hesitate to increase the load upon American taxpayers in order to further his objective of concentrating economic and political power in the Federal government. In 1790, he had called for an assumption of $25 million in state debts, but Congress, more cautious than the Secretary, reduced the figure to $21,500,000. In 1792, on the ground that the debts of South Carolina and Massachusetts had not been wholly assumed, Hamilton recommended and Congress executed a second assumption of state debts.[58]

Despite Hamilton's denial that assumption had increased the amount of the national debt—it had, he insisted, merely transferred the obligation from agents to principal—in actuality the Federal government had overpaid the states.[59] In 1789, commissioners had been appointed by the central government to determine the amount owing the Federal government by the states; and when their report was finally completed in 1796 it revealed that many states which had imagined themselves to be creditors were actually debtors of the Federal government. Since, however, their debts had already been assumed, the states, with the exception of New York, which discharged $800,000 of the $2 million it owed the Federal government, ignored the findings of the commissioners. As a result, the general government was unable to recapture

to the Yeomanry of the United States. By a Farmer (Philadelphia, 1793), p. 36.

[58] Lodge, Hamilton, II, 439–440; American State Papers, VII, Finance, I, 147; Adams, Gallatin, 169; Paul Studenski and Herman Kroos, Financial History of the United States (New York, 1952), p. 53; Rexford Guy Tugwell and Joseph Dorfman, "Alexander Hamilton, Nation-Maker," Columbia University Quarterly, XXX (1936), 63–64.

[59] Lodge, Hamilton, IX, 32–33; Marshall, Washington, V, 250–251.

these excess payments. But Hamilton did not trouble himself over a few million dollars expended in such a good cause as attaching the state creditors to the national government.[60]

[60] Don C. Sowers, *The Financial History of New York State* (New York, 1914), pp. 256–257; *Annals of Congress,* II, 499, 1364; X, 1039–1040; XIII, 933; Lodge, *Hamilton,* II, 430; 439–440; Henry Adams (ed.), *Writings of Albert Gallatin* (Philadelphia, 1879), III, 133–134; John Watts Kearny, *Sketch of American Finances* (New York, 1885), pp. 22–23, 27–28.

CHAPTER 4

The Bank of the United States and the Report on Manufactures

T HE FUNDING of the national debt and the assumption of state debts had put wealth into the hands of the men who, in Hamilton's opinion, were best qualified to use it for constructive national purposes. This achievement notwithstanding, the United States still lacked two essentials to the proper functioning of the kind of capitalism Hamilton envisaged—an adequate circulating medium and a central bank. In a Report submitted to Congress in January, 1791, Hamilton proposed to remedy both these deficiencies by establishing a corporation to be called the Bank of the United States.

Borrowing heavily from the example of the Bank of England, Hamilton intended that the Bank of the United States should serve as the principal depository of government funds, the fiscal agent of the Treasury in its domestic and foreign operations, and a central control upon the operations of the state banks. The most important function Hamilton assigned to the Bank of the United States was the issuance of bank notes. These notes—payable upon demand in gold and silver and receivable for all payments owing the United States government—were designed to be the principal circulating medium in the Republic.[1]

[1] Bray Hammond, *Banks and Politics in Early America* (Princeton, 1958), p. 133; McKee, *Papers*, pp. 55–59, 66, 93, 218; Lodge, *Hamilton*, II, 449–451; Dunbar, *Economic Essays*, pp. 92–93; James O. Wetterau, "New Light on the First Bank of the United States," *Pennsylvania Magazine of History and Biography*, LXI (1937), 271; *Journal of Economic History*, III (1946), 681; Channing, *History*, IV, 92–93; H. E. Miller, *Banking Theories in the*

The Bank of the United States exemplified Hamilton's theory that a public bank ought to be founded upon the combined credit of the government and private individuals, and that the government ought to exercise supervisory powers while actual management was entrusted to directors most of whom represented the private stockholders. The government of the United States was to own one-fourth of the stock and to appoint five members of the Board of Directors of the Bank, but the ownership of the remaining 80 per cent of the stock and the appointment of twenty directors were left to the investing public. A limit of $10 million, exclusive of deposits, was placed upon the debt of the Bank; and, to ensure that this and other regulations were observed, Hamilton specified that frequent statements were to be supplied by the directors to the Secretary of the Treasury.[2]

Since the United States was sorely deficient in specie, Hamilton's plan of establishing a public bank might appear to be an attempt on the part of the government to lift itself by its own bootstraps. Here was the perennial problem of American banking, but Hamilton got round the difficulty by providing that stock in the Bank of the United States could be purchased with government bonds up to three-fourths of the value of the stock. By this means, Hamilton hoped to set the Bank upon its feet with a minimum of specie, to raise the price of government securities to par by creating a demand, and to give the Bank of the United States a proprietary interest in supporting the credit of the government. In short, the government would support the bank and the bank would support the government; and the rich men of the United States, already the owners of government securities, as stockholders in the Bank of the United States would be bound even more closely to the Federal government.[3]

Hamilton's Report encountered vigorous opposition from the agrarian spokesmen in Congress, one of whom declared that he would no more be seen entering a bank than a house of ill fame. The prospect of an alliance between the government and a bank brought to their minds the image of that dreaded "engine of corruption," the Bank of Eng-

United States Before 1860 (Cambridge, Mass., 1927), pp. 30–31, 79, 92, 95–96, 109–110, 117.

[2] McKee, *Papers*, 83–84; *Journal of Business and Economic History*, III (1946), 681; Hammond, *Banks and Politics*, p. 133.

[3] McKee, *Papers*, 72–73; Channing, *History*, IV, 82–83; *Journal of Business and Economic History*, III (1946), 681; Peletiah Webster, *To the Stockholders of the Bank of North America* (Philadelphia, 1791), p. 4.

land. But fulminations against banks and bankers were of little avail, and James Madison therefore wisely grounded his case against the proposed bank upon its alleged unconstitutionality.

Even in his most nationalistic phase, Madison had doubted that Congress possessed the power to charter a bank. He found no sanction in the Articles of Confederation for the establishment of the Bank of North America. To the act of Congress of 1781 by which this "national" bank was created, Madison gave what he called "an acquiescing, rather than an affirmative vote" in the hope that it would serve as "an antidote against the poisonous tendency of precedents of usurpation."[4] Nor did Madison discover in the Federal Constitution express or implied powers by which Congress was authorized to establish a bank. To remove all doubt on this score he had proposed in the Constitutional Convention that Congress be expressly authorized to charter corporations, but the Founding Fathers had preferred to leave the matter to interpretation.[5]

It was not merely Hamiltonianism to which Madison objected—he now recoiled from the whole concept of a strong, centralized government which he had advocated at the Constitutional Convention. True, Madison did not publicly confess his errors and repent his transgressions against "true republicanism," but after 1790 he made clear that his principal objective was to redress the balance (which he himself had helped to establish) in favor of the states.

The bill incorporating the Bank of the United States passed the House of Representatives by a vote of thirty-seven to twenty, but Madison succeeded in raising grave doubts in the President's mind concerning the constitutionality of the measure.[6] Washington was not

[4] Nor was the Continental Congress sure of its powers in this regard: at the same time that it gave a charter to the Bank of North America, it recommended to the states that they adopt laws of their own incorporating the bank within their respective jurisdictions. Not until 1819, when the United States Supreme Court handed down its decision in the case of McCulloch v. Maryland was the power of Congress to charter corporations established.

[5] James Wilson, *Considerations on the Bank of North America* (Philadelphia, 1789), p. 6; Brant, *Madison, Father of the Constitution*, pp. 126–127; Hunt, *Madison*, I, 179; Davis, *American Corporations*, II, 14–16, 38–39, and *Essays*, pp. 10–11, 50, 55–56; Burnett, *Letters of Members of the Continental Congress*, VI, 289–290; *Pennsylvania Magazine of History and Biography*, LXI (1937), 263, 267; John Taylor, *An Inquiry into the Principles and Policy of the Government of the United States* (Philadelphia, 1794), pp. 7, 14–16, 84; McKee, *Papers*, pp. 72–73; Maclay, *Journal*, p. 353.

[6] The sectional nature of this vote is revealed by the fact that thirty-three

a man of quick, intuitive judgments: when called upon for an immediate opinion, he was often at a loss and, as Jefferson said, gave the appearance of being "unready, short and embarrassed." In consequence, Washington made it an invariable practice to ask advice from the men in whose judgment he placed confidence: it was his boast that during the War of Independence he had never been "presumptuously driven on under the sole guidance of my own judgment and self-will." "For," he explained, "having no other wish than to promote the true and permanent interests of this country, I am anxious, always, to compare the opinions of those in whom I confide with one another; and those again (without being bound by them) with my own, that I may extract all the good I can." But this did not mean that he was easily led by the self-assured, strong-minded men to whom he looked for counsel. Very early in his relations with Washington, Hamilton learned that the Virginian could not be bent to any man's will. As Hamilton said, Washington "consulted much, resolved slowly, resolved surely." Yet he did not always resolve as Hamilton wished.[7]

Accordingly, before signing the bill incorporating the Bank of the United States, Washington requested opinions from Jefferson, Hamilton, and Attorney General Edmund Randolph regarding the power of Congress to create corporations. Jefferson and Randolph took the negative, arguing, as Madison had done, that no such grant had been made to the Federal government and that it could not be implied from any power expressly given. A public bank, they asserted, might be convenient but it was neither necessary nor proper within the meaning of the Constitution.[8]

Although he had not anticipated that the question of the constitutionality of the Bank of the United States would prove decisive, Hamilton was prepared to meet Madison, Randolph, and Jefferson upon their chosen ground. In one of the most notable state papers that ever came from his pen, Hamilton argued the case in favor of the Bank

---

out of the thirty-nine ayes were from states north of the Potomac. Fifteen out of the twenty nays were from Virginia, the Carolinas, and Georgia. South Carolina cast one vote for the bill; one Massachusetts vote was against it. Dewey, *Financial History*, p. 100; Hammond, *Banks and Politics*, p. 117.

[7] Fitzpatrick, *Washington*, XXXIII, 421; XXXV, 103; Ford, *Jefferson*, IX, 307; White, *Jeffersonians*, p. 183; Richard B. Morris, "Washington and Hamilton: A Great Collaboration," *Proceedings of the American Philosophical Society*, Vol. 102, No. 2 (April, 1958), pp. 107–116.

[8] Hunt, *Madison*, VI, 81; Dorfman, *Economic Mind*, I, 438–440, 488; Boutell, *Roger Sherman*, p. 260; *William and Mary College Quarterly*, I, Series III (1944), 100–101.

of the United States by laying down the principle of broad construction of the Constitution. According to his reading of the "necessary and proper" clause, the word "necessary" meant needful, requisite, incidental, useful, or conducive to. Since a bank was necessary to the collecting of taxes, the regulating of trade, and providing for the common defense, it followed that the incorporation of the Bank of the United States was within the powers of Congress. Stated as a general principle, Hamilton's doctrine gave the Federal government, as a sovereign power, the right to employ all the means "necessary and proper" to the attainment of such objectives as were not forbidden by the Constitution or not contrary to the essential ends of society. In the hands of Chief Justice John Marshall, Hamilton's method of interpreting the Constitution later became a force working toward the expansion of the powers of the Federal government over a steadily widening sphere of activities.[9]

Hamilton's opinion, while it did not remove all Washington's doubts, led the President to sign the bill. (To help Washington to make up his mind, the Senate during this interval pointedly held up consideration of a bill the purpose of which was to expedite the government's removal to the Potomac.)[10] On July 4, 1791, the stock of the Bank of the United States was put up for public sale. Within a few hours, crowds of frenzied purchasers had bought all the scrip (warrants entitling the purchaser to buy stock) and hundreds of would-be purchasers had to be turned away. Jefferson declared that the mania for Bank scrip proved that "the delirium of speculation" had gotten wholly out of hand, but Washington chose to regard it as proof of the confidence men of wealth had come to place in the government.[11] It also exhibited the sectional nature of American capitalism, for virtually all

[9] *Selected Essays on Constitutional Law*, III, 42, 256–257; Lodge, *Hamilton*, II, 458–459; VIII, 445; Crosskey, *Politics and the Constitution*, I, 207; Charles Warren, *The Making of the Constitution* (Boston, 1937), pp. 473–476; McKee, *Papers*, pp. 101–102, 110, 130–134; Charles Beard, *The Republic* (New York, 1943), p. 111; Edwin S. Corwin, *The Commerce Power vs. States Rights* (Princeton, 1936), pp. 30–31, 215–216; Marshall, *Washington*, V, 276.

[10] Rives, *Madison*, III, 197–198; *William and Mary Quarterly*, 3rd Series, III (1946), 542–543.

[11] Corner, *Autobiography of Benjamin Rush*, pp. 203–204; *Belknap Papers*, Collections of the Massachusetts Historical Society, Fifth Series, III (Boston, 1877), 265–266; Sullivan, *Path to Riches*, p. 39; Hunt, *Madison*, VI, 43, 55–56; *Jefferson Papers*, Collections of the Massachusetts Historical Society, Seventh Series, I (Boston, 1900), 37; Fitzpatrick, *Washington*, XXXI, 328–329.

the stock was bought by northern and European capitalists.[12]

The Bank of the United States quickly proved its worth to the national economy. By means of bank notes, the country was furnished with a circulating medium and bank credit became one of the most potent devices for stimulating capitalistic enterprise. During the "bancomania" of the 1790's, when state banks were mushrooming on every hand (in 1792, eight banks were established and by 1801 there were thirty-two state banks), the Bank of the United States exercised salutary control over the entire banking system by virtue of its power to require other banks to redeem their notes and checks with hard money. The Bank of the United States loaned the government money—by 1795 the government's debt stood at $6 million—transferred government funds from one section to another, and aided the foreign exchange operations of the Treasury.[13] So vital was it to the growth of national wealth and power that Hamilton declared that even the most uncompromising opponent of the Bank "would, in one month's experience as head of that department of the Treasury, be compelled to acknowledge that it is an absolutely indispensable engine in the management of the finances, and would quickly become a convert to its perfect constitutionality"—an opinion which was endorsed by Albert Gallatin when he became Secretary of the Treasury in 1801.[14]

The importance of the Bank of the United States to the national economy was emphasized by the government's failure to create an adequate system of coinage. In 1791, Hamilton recommended the establishment of a Mint and Congress complied in the spring of 1792. Direction of the Mint was assigned to the State Department because President Washington felt that the Treasury was already overburdened.

[12] J. T. Holdsworth and D. R. Dewey, *The First and Second Banks of the United States* (Washington, 1910), pp. 21–23; *Journal of Economic History,* II (1942), 71; Davis, *American Corporations,* I, 51; *Pennsylvania Magazine of History and Biography,* LXI (1937), 273–274; J. C. Hamilton, *Hamilton,* V, 473–474; Rives, *Madison,* III, 199–200; VI, 55.

[13] Altogether, fourteen successive loans were made by the Bank of the United States to the Federal government. By 1796, almost two-thirds of its capital was tied up in such loans. E. R. Taus, *Central Banking Functions of the United States Treasury, 1789–1941* (New York, 1943), pp. 19–20; Bolles, *Financial History,* II, 145–147.

[14] Bray Hammond, *Banks and Politics,* p. 208; Holdsworth and Dewey, *First and Second Banks,* p. 54; *Pennsylvania Magazine of History and Biography,* LXI (1937), 271; Lodge, *Hamilton,* II, 459; VIII, 462; Hildreth, *History,* IV, 276; Miller, *Banking Theories,* pp. 109–110; Adams, *Gallatin,* I, 80; *Journal of Economic History,* II (1942), 87; McKee, *Papers,* pp. 58, 84–92, 211–213, 239.

But the Mint did not flourish, owing primarily to the fact that there was little bullion in the United States and because Hamilton in his Report on the Mint had overvalued silver. The American "eagles" took flight to England, and unminted silver and gold were drained away to India and China. By 1797, the Mint had issued coins only to the value of about $775,000. So acute was the shortage of hard money that until 1857 the United States used foreign coins as legal tender at specified values.[15]

Although Hamilton was accused of having only the welfare of the speculators at heart, in actuality the Federal government was one of the largest gainers by the establishment of the Bank of the United States. The government made no cash outlay for its stock in the Bank: it was purely a paper transaction in which the government went through the motion of paying the Bank $2 million and receiving the same amount in return in the form of a loan payable in ten annual installments. Hamilton gave individual subscribers to Bank stock eighteen months to pay; the government was permitted ten years.[16]

Knowing Hamilton's ulterior objectives, Madison and Jefferson feared that he would convert the Bank of the United States into an "engine of state" with which to batter down the state banks and with them the state governments. In actuality, however, Hamilton was loath to centralize banking to that degree: although, against Hamilton's advice, branch banks were established by the Bank of the United States in the principal commercial centers of the country, the Secretary of the Treasury did not neglect the interests of the state banks, especially the Bank of New York, of which he was one of the founders. But he left no doubt that the Bank of the United States was intended to serve the needs of businessmen rather than of farmers. When it was suggested that the Bank of the United States should loan money to southern planters on the security of tobacco warehouse receipts, Hamilton refused to consider the idea.[17]

[15] McKee, *Papers*, p. 71; Lodge, *Hamilton*, IV, 4–6, 15–17, 36, 60; VIII, 232; *Annals of Congress*, VII, 750; Dewey, *Financial History*, p. 103.

[16] Lodge, *Hamilton*, II, 449–451; Hammond, *Banks and Politics*, p. 207; Holdsworth and Dewey, *First and Second Banks*, pp. 32, 43; Bolles, *Financial History*, II, 128–130.

[17] Dorfman, *Economic Mind*, I, 438–440; Holdsworth and Dewey, *First and Second Banks*, pp. 14–15; *Journal of Economic History*, II (1942), 73–74; McKee, *Papers*, pp. 81–82; Hutcheson, *Tench Coxe*, p. 27; Davis, *American Corporations*, II, 52–58; Fritz Redlich, *The Molding of American Banking* (New York, 1951), pp. 39, 98–99; *Pennsylvania Magazine of History and Biography*, LXI (1937), 280.

The establishment of branch banks by the Bank of the United States led Hamilton's opponents to erect state banks as a means of defending the sovereign rights of the states and providing banking facilities for farmers. When Jefferson, for example, learned that the Bank of the United States planned to found a branch at Richmond, he suggested to his friends that "a counter-bank be set up to befriend the agricultural man by letting him have money on a deposit of tools, notes, or even wheat, for *a short time.*"[18] And yet, while the agrarian leaders learned the advantages of banks, they did not cease to agitate against the Bank of the United States. John Taylor of Caroline declared that the profits of the bank were a tribute wrung from the people "exceeding any profit extracted from personal slaves." The fact that about thirty members of Congress were stockholders and several members were directors of the Bank of the United States furnished Jefferson and Madison with further proof that Hamilton ruled by corrupting legislators and enriching speculators. It is significant, however, that the spokesmen of the farmers and planters based their case against the Bank of the United States not upon the contention that there was too little control of the Bank by the government but that there was too much governmental supervision. Their slogan was: Let banks be chartered by the states and let them be wholly free of control.[19]

During the administrations of Washington and John Adams, despite Hamilton's protests, Congress failed to appropriate the necessary funds to pay the government's debt to the Bank of the United States. As a result, the government disposed of over half its stock in the Bank and in 1802 President Jefferson sold the last 2,000 shares to the English banking house of Baring. By 1809, foreigners owned 18,000 of the 25,000 shares of the Bank of the United States. From the profits of these sales and the dividends it received over the course of years, the government realized several million dollars. But the Bank, by virtue of its very success, raised up a host of enemies: the state banks resented the control it exercised over their operations and even part of the busi-

[18] Ford, *Jefferson*, VI, July 3, 1792; Dorfman, *Economic Mind*, I, 301; Manning J. Dauer, *The Adams Federalists* (Baltimore, 1953), pp. 67–68; *Journal of Economic History*, II (1942), 76.

[19] Taylor, *An Enquiry*, 19, 22, 74–75; Ford, *Jefferson*, I, 164, 223, 225; *William and Mary Quarterly*, III, 3rd Series (1947), 549; *John P. Branch Historical Papers*, II (Richmond, 1905), 253–254; Dorfman, *Economic Mind*, I, 438; Ballagh, *Letters of R. H. Lee*, II, 541–542.

ness community chafed under the curbs it imposed upon free enter-prise.[20]

The Reports on Public Credit and the Bank of the United States laid the foundations for Hamilton's grand design—the centralization of governmental authority and the industrialization of the United States by means of government aid to business. The Report on Manufactures which he submitted to Congress in December, 1791, was in-tended to provide the capstone to his plans for revolutionizing the American government and economy.

This report was the product of an exhaustive study made by Ham-ilton and Tench Coxe, the Assistant Secretary of the Treasury, of world economic conditions and governmental economic policies. Their in-vestigations revealed that, thanks to private enterprise together with protective duties imposed by the state governments, some branches of manufacturing—notably nails, ships, shoes, and iron and steel—had prospered in the United States. In 1788, a single firm in Beverly, Massachusetts, exported 70,000 pairs of women's shoes to the southern states; a carpet factory at Philadelphia manufactured the carpets used in the chambers of the United States Senate; and there were over fifty paper mills in Pennsylvania alone. When Washington was in-augurated in 1789 he was dressed in a suit of broadcloth manufactured in Connecticut, and he expressed the hope that it would soon "be unfashionable for a gentleman to appear in any other dress." The Pres-ident made it a point to serve only American-made beer and cheese. Clearly, Americans had begun to act upon the principle that the "way to lay a foundation for the future glory, greatness and independence of America" was through manufacturing.[21]

Even so, it was apparent to Hamilton that the United States had done little more than scratch the surface of its potential as a manu-facturing nation. In his Report on Manufactures, he set forth the

[20] *Pennsylvania Magazine of History and Biography*, LXI (1937), 269, 270–271, 284; Dewey, *Financial History*, p. 101; Studenski and Krooss, *Financial History*, p. 71; Redlich, *Molding of American Banking*, pp. 21, 96–99; Miller, *Banking Theories*, pp. 56–57; Hammond, *Banks and Politics*, pp. 198–199, 207–208.

[21] Mathew Carey, *The American Museum*, VI (1789), 236–237; *Pennsyl-vania Gazette*, June 25, 1788; March 19, May 7, 1789; J. C. Fitzpatrick (ed.), *Diaries of George Washington* (Boston, 1925), IV, 38–41; Fitzpatrick, *Wash-ington*, XXX, 186; Adams, *Taxation in the United States*, pp. 30–34; Dorf-man, *Economic Mind*, p. 27; *Report of the American Historical Association for 1896* (Washington, 1897), I, 631–633.

reasons why it was imperative Americans follow the example of Great
Britain, France, and other powers in fostering industrialization. Looking into futurity, he concluded that within a comparatively short span
of time the European market would be closed to American agricultural
products; and that unless the citizens of the United States found some
other outlet, their lumber, wheat, tobacco, rice, and indigo would
perish on their hands. In short, if the United States were to survive
in a world of increasingly restrictive mercantilist systems, Hamilton believed that it had no alternative but to adopt a closed economic system
of its own.[22]

One of the results of Hamilton's survey of American manufacturing
was to underscore the difficulties "infant industries" were obliged to
surmount. Labor and capital were in short supply; most of the immigrants from Europe took up farming and hence were lost as potential
factory workers; and the capital Americans derived from Europe took
the form of credit on consumer goods rather than machinery and tools.
Undaunted by these obstacles, Hamilton argued that the deficiency in
the labor force could be made up by the employment of women and
children in the factories and that labor-saving machinery, operated by
skilled European technicians, would make it possible for Americans to
compete with the most industrialized nations. As for capital, he saw
in the securities of the United States government and the stock of the
Bank of the United States a resource which, if properly employed,
would go far toward overcoming this particular shortage.[23]

Hamilton was not so optimistic—or, as he would have said, so ignorant of human nature—as to imagine that this change could be
effected merely by appealing to the patriotism of American businessmen. In his opinion, the businessmen of the United States were altogether too disposed to remain in the comfortable and profitable rut
of merchandising and shipping; to induce them to venture into manu-

[22] A. H. Cole, *Industrial and Commercial Correspondence of Alexander
Hamilton* (Chicago, 1928), xvii; Davis, *Economic Essays,* pp. 280–283; Mc-
Kee, *Papers,* pp. 249–253; Adams, *Gallatin,* III, 168; Fitzpatrick, *Washington,*
XXX, 491–492; F. S. Oliver, *Alexander Hamilton: An Essay on American
Union* (London, 1915), pp. 235–241.

[23] Samuel K. Mitchell, *The Picture of New York* (New York, 1807), p.
108; Channing, *History,* IV, 62–63; Adams, *Taxation in the United States,* p.
76; *Journal of Economic History,* V (1945), 6; Brown, *Mirror for Americans,*
p. 73; Tench Coxe, *View,* pp. 8–9, 40–42, 54–55; McKee, *Papers,* pp. 193–
198, 206–209, 224–227, 232–233; Dorfman, *Economic Mind,* I, 254–255;
Report on Canadian Archives (1890), p. 104; Paul D. Evans, *The Holland
Land Company* (Buffalo, 1924), p. 8.

facturing, it was therefore necessary to hold out to them the lure of high profits and liberal government aid. The aid Hamilton recommended in his Report on Manufactures was calculated to stir the blood of even the most lethargic and self-satisfied businessman: protective tariffs; bounties for the establishment of new industries; premiums for improvements in quality; awards for the encouragement of inventions, particularly of labor-saving machinery; and exemption from duty of essential raw materials imported from abroad.[24]

Hamilton always believed that his Report on Manufactures was an indispensable supplement to the Federal Constitution: it was a blueprint for a more perfect economic union without which political union could not endure. He envisaged himself as the creator of an indissoluble union of North and South that would ultimately erase sectionalism in the United States. For, if his plans were realized, northern ships would carry southern raw materials to northern factories; and commerce and wealth would flow in a North-South direction instead of pursuing the well-worn transatlantic routes. From this division of labor between the two sections—each doing what nature had intended—Hamilton promised that everyone would benefit: farmers, artisans, shipowners, merchants, and manufacturers all would share in the national wealth. But the greatest boon of all, from Hamilton's point of view, was that the Union would be rendered impervious to sectional jealousies and ambitions.

Southern agriculturalists declined to acclaim Hamilton as their benefactor for having devised a system which consigned them to the status of producers of raw materials for northern merchants, shippers, and manufacturers—it was too much like the system they had experienced as British subjects and against which they were still rebelling. In their opinion, businessmen, whether British or Yankee, were bent upon exploiting the farmer to the hilt, and Hamilton's Report seemed to them to be designed merely to sanction this exploitation under the guise of furthering the national welfare.[25]

As might be expected under such circumstances, they found no difficulty in discovering prohibitions in the Constitution against doing what they did not want done. Hamilton, it was said, was attempting "by arbitrary interpretations and insidious precedents, to pervert the limited government of the Union into a government of unlimited dis-

---

[24] McKee, *Papers*, pp. 273–278.
[25] John Taylor, *An Enquiry*, pp. 41–42.

cretion, contrary to the will and subversive of the authority of the people." It was true that in order to give constitutional sanction to his policy of government aid to business, Hamilton was obliged to interpret the general-welfare clause as a grant of power to Congress to appropriate money for any object which in its opinion was conducive to the general welfare. In the words of the Secretary of the Treasury, the general welfare comprised everything concerning "the general interests of learning, of agriculture, of manufacturing, and of commerce" —a definition which brought every segment of activity within the purview of Congress. Even though Hamilton restricted Congress' authority to appropriating money for these ends—he never claimed that it enjoyed the power of general legislation—his qualification struck Madison and Jefferson as a distinction without a difference. Madison pointed out that if Congress could apply money indiscriminately for the purpose of promoting the general welfare and was at the same time the supreme judge of what constituted the general welfare, it could take religion, education, road building, and so on, under its control. "In short," he declared, "every thing, from the highest object of state legislation, down to the most minute object of police would be thrown under the power of Congress." Since, to Madison's way of thinking, the Constitution had created a limited government tied down to specified powers it could spend money only insofar as it was specifically authorized to do so. "If not only the means, but the objects are unlimited," he remarked, "the parchment had better be thrown into the fire at once."[26]

[26] The dispute revolved round the meaning of the preamble to the Constitution. The preamble declares that the people of the United States have ordained the Constitution in order to "form a more perfect Union, establish Justice, insure domestic Tranquillity, provide for the common defence, promote the general Welfare, and ensure the blessings of Liberty to ourselves and our Posterity." Then follows an enumeration of the powers of Congress. Hamilton read the preamble as though it were intended to give the government latitude to act in situations not covered by the enumerated powers; in Madison's opinion, the government was "tied down to the specified powers which explain and define the general terms. . . . The meaning of the general terms in question must be sought in the subsequent enumerations which limits and details them." But Madison failed to explain satisfactorily why the preamble had been inserted at all. If the government were confined to the enumerated powers, the preamble became an empty rhetorical flourish. The fact that some of the phrases of the preamble had been lifted from the Articles of Confederation did not mean that the framers intended to make the Articles their model. In 1789, Madison had declared in Congress that "it was impossible to confine a government to exercise of express powers; there must necessarily be admitted

Fortunately, it did not prove necessary to consign the Constitution to the flames. When Congress framed the Tariff Act of May, 1792, it incorporated many of the recommendations made by the Secretary of the Treasury; but except in the case of the fisheries, the system of bounties projected by Hamilton was not carried into execution.[27] Disappointed by this outcome, Hamilton turned his attention to the Society for Useful Manufactures in Paterson, New Jersey, by which he hoped to demonstrate to American businessmen the advantages of large-scale industry. But the experiment failed dismally and by 1796 Paterson was hardly more than a ghost town. Samuel Slater, an English mechanic who had arrived in the United States in 1789, was more successful than Hamilton in giving concrete application to the Report on Manufactures. Entirely from memory—British laws prohibited the exportation of machinery or designs—Slater constructed a spinning jenny and in 1793 established at Pawtucket, Rhode Island, the first successful American cotton factory.[28]

As Hamilton was soon made to realize, Americans were much more inclined to invest their capital in land speculation, shipping, and get-rich-quick schemes such as banks, turnpikes, and canal companies than in manufacturing. In 1791, overspeculation in government securities produced a sudden fall in prices; and in 1792 the speculative bubble inflated by William Duer, Alexander Macomb, and other New York financiers who had set out to corner the supply of government securities suddenly blew up in their faces. Although Hamilton came to the rescue by depositing government funds in the New York banks, he was too late to save Duer and his associates. Bankrupt and in danger of an irate mob of citizens who had counted upon him to make them rich, Duer was put in jail, where he remained for most of the re-

---

powers by implication, unless the Constitution descended to recount every minutiae." Hunt, *Madison*, VI, 81; Channing, *History*, IV, 162; Sidney Ratner, *American Taxation, Its History as a Social Force in Democracy* (New York, 1942), pp. 19–20; *Abridgment of Debates*, I, 350–351, 358–359, 362–363; Brant, *Madison, Father of the Constitution*, p. 128; Rives, *Madison*, III, 106, 234–236; Lodge, *Hamilton*, IV, December 5, 1791; Ford, *Jefferson*, I, 177; McKee, *Papers*, pp. 239–240; Madison to Edward Pendleton, January 21, 1792, Madison MSS., LC.

[27] *Abridgment of Debates*, I, 351–353; *Journal of Economic History*, III (1946), 211.

[28] Davis, *American Corporations*, I, 366–368, 400, 417, 499–500; Henry Wansey, *An Excursion to the United States of North America in 1794* (Salisbury, Eng., 1798), pp. 69–70; Hucheson, *Tench Coxe*, p. 158; Cutler, *Manasseh Cutler*, I, 205.

mainder of his life. A few years later, Robert Morris, once the richest man in the United States, landed in the Philadelphia prison as an insolvent debtor. Even Alexander Hamilton himself was much too deeply involved in land speculation for his own financial good.[29]

It was now Hamilton's turn to deplore speculation and to draw "a line of Separation between honest men and knaves, between respectable Stockholders and dealers in the funds, and meer unprincipled Gamblers" and to call for a revival of morality and the old-fashioned virtues. And yet, despite the high mortality rate among the plungers, the economy of the United States burgeoned during the Federalist period. As the *Gazette of the United States* said, dormant wealth "quickened into life and productiveness . . . enterprise has enlarged its sphere and explored new regions of profit."[30] Mining, canal, and turnpike companies were organized; American ships sailed in everincreasing numbers to Europe, India, China, and the northwest coast of America. Prosperity eased the financial problems of the government: a single vessel which arrived in New York during the spring of 1790 paid duties amounting to $30,000 on its cargo. Although President Washington deliberately avoided attributing "to the Government what is due only to the goodness of Providence" and to the unprecedented demand for American agricultural products and shipping created by the European war, he did not overlook the fact that the Federal Constitution and the Federalist administration helped make this prosperity possible by contributing the indispensable element of confidence. The financial stability created by the government, the repute it gained by fulfilling its obligations, the inviolability of property rights, and the credit facilities extended by the Bank of the United States and the state banks encouraged Americans to believe that in the United States possibilities were boundless and that boldness, courage, and enterprise were all that was necessary to unlock the door to great wealth.[31]

By 1792, largely as a result of the leadership assumed by Alexander Hamilton, the heavy war debt dating from the struggle for independ-

---

[29] Charles S. Hall, *Benjamin Tallmadge* (New York, 1943), p. 127.

[30] *Gazette of the United States,* January 23, 1796.

[31] Brown, *Mirror for Americans,* pp. 66 (footnote), 104–106; Wansey, *An Excursion,* p. 236; Adams, *Taxation in the United States,* p. 70; Robert A. East, "The Business Entrepreneur in Colonial Economy," *Journal of Economic History,* III (1946), 26; Davis, *American Corporations,* I, 174–176; Channing, *History,* IV, 102; Lodge, *Hamilton,* II, April 16, 1792; IX, 486, 502, 510.

ence had been put in the course of extinguishment, the price of government securities had been stabilized close to their face value, hoarded wealth had been brought out of hiding, a Federal revenue system had been brought into being, a system of debt management had been created, the power of the Federal government had been decisively asserted over the states, foreign capital had begun to pour into the United States, and the credit of the Federal government had been solidly established. And, finally, in the Report on Manufactures, "the city, the factory, the whole, indeed, of our complex civilization, lay in embryo within the stately body of this document."[32]

[32] *Columbia University Quarterly,* XXX (1938), 62; Lodge, *Hamilton,* II, 446; Maxwell, *Federal Impact of Federalism,* p. 9; Bolles, *Financial History,* II, 17; Davis, *Economic Essays,* pp. 297–299.

CHAPTER 5

Thomas Jefferson and the Philosophy of Agrarianism

IN MARCH, 1790, when Jefferson assumed the post of Secretary of State, his support of the main objectives of the Washington administration seemed assured. During the period of the Articles of Confederation, he had been among the first to urge that the Continental Congress be given powers commensurate with its obligation of paying the national debt and upholding American dignity and rights abroad. He had distinguished himself as a champion of American commercial interests and he had advocated the creation of a navy, "the only weapon," he said, "by which we can act on Europe." He wished to see the Federal judiciary made supreme over the state judiciaries in order that it might prevent the states from encroaching upon the authority of the Federal government. His experience as United States minister to France had deeply impressed upon him the necessity of "firmness and tone" in the central government. Although he had objected to the indefinite re-eligibility of the President and the absence of a Bill of Rights, he had favored the adoption of the Constitution. In 1788, he had pronounced *The Federalist* to be one of the greatest treatises on government ever written.[1]

[1] Boyd, *Jefferson Papers*, XIV, 324, 328, 331, 364–365, 661; Ford, *Jefferson*, I, 149; *American Political Science Review*, XIII (1919), 383; Dorfman, *Economic Mind*, I, 437–438, 445–446; Frank Landon Humphreys, *The Life and Times of David Humphreys* (New York, 1917), II, 18; Edward Channing, "Washington and Parties," *Proceedings of the Massachusetts Historical Society*,

Notwithstanding, Jefferson never admitted to being a Federalist, least of all a Hamiltonian Federalist. Even prior to 1790 he had revealed how little he sympathized with many of the ideals and policies laid down by his colleague at the Treasury: while he was of the opinion that the "tyranny of the legislature" was more to be feared than the ambition and lust for power of the executive, he asserted that "the jealousy of the subordinate governments" toward the exercise of power by the national government was the most "precious reliance" that freedom would endure in the United States. At this time, Jefferson was more inclined than was Madison to trust to "the good sense of the people." Far from sharing the Federalists' panic when Shays rose in rebellion, Jefferson calmly accepted the event as a natural effervescence of popular feeling: when one sailed upon the "boisterous sea of freedom," he said, one expected a little rough going. Shays' Rebellion and other manifestations of what the Federalists called "democratic license" Jefferson attributed to want of information upon the part of the people. There was nothing in the country so radically wrong, he often said, that it could not be cured by good newspapers and sound schoolmasters. For Jefferson had a boundless faith in education: since man was "a rational animal, endowed by nature with rights, and with an innate sense of justice," he had only to be apprised of the truth to act wisely, moderately, and justly.[2]

Because Jefferson made no effort to conceal his opinions, however unpopular they might be in the polite circles of Philadelphia, he was set down by some Federalists in 1790 as "greatly too Democratic for us at present; he left us in that way, but we are infinitely changed, and he must alter his principles." The Federalists who undertook to wean Jefferson from democracy soon discovered that he was a hopeless case.[3]

Jefferson's experience under the "energetic government" administered by Alexander Hamilton revived all of the fears of strong government the Virginian had conceived during the American Revolution.

XLVII (1914), 39; R. R. Palmer, "The Dubious Democrat: Thomas Jefferson in Bourbon France," *Political Science Quarterly*, LXXII (1957), 388–404.

[2] Boyd, *Jefferson Papers*, XI, 45; XIV, 385, 650, 659–661; Ford, *Jefferson*, I, 112, 160; Channing, *History*, IV, 163; Charles M. Wiltse, *The Jeffersonian Tradition in American Democracy* (Chapel Hill, 1935), p. 140; Mott, *Jefferson and the Press*, p. 3.

[3] *Report on Canadian Archives* (1890), pp. 138–140, 246; Wiltse, *Jeffersonian Tradition*, pp. 81–84, 94; Richard Hofstadter, *The American Political Tradition and the Men Who Made It* (New York, 1948), p. 37; Humphreys, *David Humphreys*, II, 20.

What was occurring in the United States seemed to confirm his earlier conviction that "the natural progress of things is for liberty to yield and government to gain ground." While he never lost confidence in the people's devotion to republicanism, he feared that Hamilton and the "Monocrats," solidly entrenched in office, disposing of great wealth, and in a position to mold public opinion through the newspapers, would prove too powerful for the "republican interest."[4] And so Jefferson became the champion of minimal government—"a few plain duties to be performed by a few servants." He considered Adam Smith's *Wealth of Nations* to be the best book ever written on economics and, eagerly embracing the philosophy of laissez faire, he contended that government could best contribute to the public prosperity by letting individuals, businessmen included, manage for themselves.[5]

So distrustful of the Federal government did Jefferson become that in 1791 he even denied it the power to aid agriculture by incorporating an Agricultural Society. If the power to erect corporations were conceded to the government, he predicted, "it would soon be used for no other purpose than to buy with sinecures useful partisans." To the proposal that the Federal government construct roads, Jefferson objected that it would open up "the richest provision for jobs to favorites that has ever yet been proposed. . . . The mines of Peru would not supply the monies which would be wasted on this object." Manifestly, during the Federalist era, Jefferson was so intent upon circumscribing the powers of the Federal government that he ignored its potentialities as a constructive force for the public welfare.[6]

In part, Jefferson's abiding fear of strong government stemmed from his determination to preserve the American farm from the heavy hand of organized business, which, to his way of thinking, always attempted to convert government into an instrument for extracting

[4] Wiltse, *Jeffersonian Tradition*, p. 94.

[5] *American Political Science Review*, XIII (1919), 383; Ford, *Jefferson*, VII, January 26, 1799; August 13, 1800; Wiltse, *Jeffersonian Tradition*, pp. 214–216, 220–222; Jefferson to Volney, December 9, 1795, Jefferson MSS., LC; Charles, *Origins of the American Party System*, pp. 74–77.

[6] Wiltse, *Jeffersonian Tradition*, pp. 137–138; Ford, *Jefferson*, VII, August 13, December, 19, 1800; *Proceedings of the American Philosophical Society*, Vol. 87, No. 3 (1943), pp. 203–205, 207; Merle Fainsod and Lincoln Gordon, *Government and the American Economy* (New York, 1941), p. 84; *American Political Science Review*, XIII (1919), 383; Hofstadter, *American Political Tradition*, pp. 176–177; Sobei Magi, *The Problem of Federalism* (New York, 1931), pp. 76, 82.

money from the mass of the people, especially farmers.[7] Jefferson loved farming with an ardor which, to city-bred Federalists, passed understanding. Of course, as the owner of thousands of acres of land and of a considerable number of slaves, he was happily spared the more onerous side of an agriculturalist's life. In his eyes, farming was not simply a matter of grubbing a living from intractable soil; it was a way of life ordained by God for his "Chosen People," the school of "substantial and genuine virtue . . . the focus in which he [the Creator] keeps alive that sacred fire, which otherwise might escape from the face of the earth." For Jefferson, the pursuit of happiness ended on a farm; the true Republican was the man with the hoe and a hundred acres besides. He could conceive of no more ennobling or enduring joy than for a man to look upon his land and say: "This is mine and it will be my children's."[8]

The worst that could happen, in Jefferson's opinion, was for Americans to rush into the Industrial Revolution, exchanging their farms for factories and the open countryside for the slums of large cities. Jefferson never doubted that Americans had created as nearly perfect a society as mankind had yet achieved; to him, the industrialization of the United States was comparable to the exodus from Paradise. Nevertheless, much as he wished to see factories and "the mobs of great cities" confined to their natural habitat in Europe, he recognized that he could not indulge his partialities and prejudices when they ran counter to the aspirations and interests of the majority of the American people. He was prepared to acquiesce in the will of that majority even when it was at variance with his better judgment: if the American people wished to sail the seas, congregate in cities, and labor in factories, he believed that it was the duty of a statesman to yield to their wishes. In consequence, Jefferson altered his policy, but not his pre-

[7] Jefferson distinguished between American merchants "trading on British capitals" and those who did business on their own or locally borrowed capital. He assumed that American businessmen who were beholden to British creditors would support Great Britain even against their own country. Yet, as Fisher Ames observed, "in Virginia, which owes fifty times as much as Connecticut, the British influence has never been great enough to obtain payment. . . . So far have British debts been from creating British influence, that they have given rise to the most rancorous hatred." Seth Ames, Fisher Ames, II, 161–162.

[8] A. Whitney Griswold, "The Agrarian Democracy of Thomas Jefferson," American Political Science Review, XL (1946), 667; Ford, Jefferson, VI, 145; IX, 292; Roscoe Pound, Federalism as a Democratic Process (New Brunswick, 1942), p. 88; Francis W. Croker, Democracy, Liberty and Property (New York, 1942), p. 115.

dilections, in accord with changing circumstances and the popular will. After the War of 1812, for example, he called for "an equilibrium of agriculture, manufactures and commerce"—the very objective that Hamilton had held in view.[9] And yet, to the end, Jefferson hoped that household manufactures would triumph over the factory system. At Monticello he established a small nail factory operated by slave children.[10]

Always his main point of reference was the quality rather than the number of the inhabitants of the United States. What did it profit a nation, Jefferson asked, if, even though it were rich and powerful, the mass of its citizens was an illiterate, poverty-stricken, mutinous proletariat? He attached paramount importance to farming because he believed that it produced the kind of citizens best qualified to meet the exacting demands of republican government. The choice between shipping and manufactures resolved itself in his mind into a question of the relative desirability of the type of citizen begotten by these occupations. His own preference was for shipping rather than for manufactures because, he said, "comparing the characters of the two classes I find the former [mariners] the most valuable citizens." Seamen, he admitted, were anything but models of propriety, but they seemed respectable and even virtuous in comparison with the factory workers of large cities. Here, Jefferson exclaimed, were found the real enemies of republicanism, "the panders of vice and the instruments by which the liberties of a country are generally overturned."[11]

Where agriculture was concerned, it is apparent that Jefferson was as much concerned with the social as with the economic conditions it created. Nor did he exclude political considerations: he never strayed far from his main point—that agriculture, "the great American interest," constituted the most solid bond of union of the diverse sections of which the American Union was constructed. He recognized that if the farmers could be organized politically, nothing—not even the

[9] Jefferson was keenly interested in the development of agricultural machinery, such as the threshing machine, and he aided Eli Whitney in securing a patent for the cotton gin. *Collections of the Massachusetts Historical Society,* Seventh Series, I (1900), 47–49, 58.

[10] Boyd, *Jefferson Papers,* VIII, 426; Ford, *Jefferson,* I, 214; VI, 145; IX, 333, 351; *American Political Science Review,* XL (1946), 667–670; W. S. Carpenter, *The Development of American Political Thought* (Princeton, 1930), p. 106; Wiltse, *Jeffersonian Tradition,* p. 80.

[11] Dorfman, *Economic Mind,* I, 434; Hofstadter, *American Political Tradition,* p. 30; Dauer, *Adams Federalists,* pp. 16–17.

Hamiltonian "phalanx" of bankers, speculators, and businessmen—could stand against them. Furthermore, as a political leader, Jefferson displayed a flexibility hardly to be expected in one who cleaved so self-righteously to principles. "He who would do his country the most good he can," he said, "must go quietly with the prejudices of the majority until he can lead them into reason."[12] When victory depended upon the support of the "degraded," "vicious," "debauched," and "mobbish" workingmen of the eastern cities, Jefferson welcomed them as allies. He even permitted bankers to squeeze through the needle's eye and to wear the raiment of "true republicans."

Conscious that the mass of the people were on his side, Jefferson enjoyed a serenity of mind and a cheerful confidence in the future which were denied Hamilton. In the Virginian's humanistic optimism all things were possible for an enlightened people; the beneficent Intelligence that had created and governed the world on a rational plan had merely begun to open the doors to man's enquiring mind. He regarded the people, particularly the educated and landowning part thereof, as "the most honest and safe, though not the most wise depository of the public interest"; but, while the people could be fooled some of the time, their folly was less pernicious than the wisdom of oligarchs. If the people were rightly informed, Jefferson was confident that they would do right, even to the extent of electing the best men to political office.[13]

As regards the national debt, Jefferson demanded that it be liquidated forthwith, not only because he had a horror of debt—he held it to be a mortgage unjustly imposed by one generation upon posterity —but because he believed that Hamilton wished "it never to be paid, but always to be a thing with which to corrupt and manage the legislature." Like Madison, Jefferson detected "a sympathy between the speeches and the pockets of all those members of Congress who held certificates."[14] Despite Hamilton's roseate view of the country's financial position, Jefferson insisted that the debt was increasing steadily

[12] Jefferson to Caesar Rodney, October 23, 1805, Gratz MSS., PHS; Charles, *Origins of the American Party System*, p. 86.

[13] Charles Beard, *The Enduring Federalist* (New York, 1948), pp. 16–17; Boyd, *Jefferson Papers*, XI, 526; Wiltse, *Jeffersonian Tradition*, pp. 63–64, 68–69, 81, 210–211; Hofstadter, *American Political Tradition*, pp. 25–26; Ford, *Jefferson*, VII, January 26, February 23, 1799; Charles, *Origins of Party System*, pp. 77–78; *Proceedings of the American Philosophical Society*, Vol. 87, No. 3 (1948), pp. 203–205.

[14] Corner, *Benjamin Rush*, p. 217.

and that it had already reached a point "beyond the possibility of payment." Moreover, the Virginian was certain in his own mind that the Secretary of the Treasury deliberately made his financial reports intricate and confusing in order to mislead the public, and that he had involved himself in such complexities that he himself could not find a way out of this self-created labyrinth. The only way of putting the country on the right track, said Jefferson, was to adhere religiously to the maxim that "the accounts of the United States ought to be, and may be made as simple as those of a common farmer, and capable of being understood by common farmers."[15]

While Jefferson took it for granted that "absolute acquiescence in the decisions of the majority" was "the vital principle of republics," he excepted majorities created by corruption. He did not doubt that Hamilton owed his influence in Congress less to the rectitude of his policies than to the finesse with which he played upon the acquisitive instinct of his followers. As Jefferson visualized it, Hamilton presided over a Great Barbecue, otherwise known as the funding system, and by dint of cutting choice slices for his friends he assured himself of a majority in Congress. But the evil did not end here: as a result of this unholy alliance between businessmen and government, said Jefferson, "natural aristocrats"—the men of virtue and talent to whom power rightfully belonged—were excluded from public office while "tinsel aristocrats" swarmed into high places. Jefferson estimated that fourteen out of fifteen of these artificial aristocrats were rogues and predators. In Europe, he had seen society divided into "two classes, wolves and sheep." He was resolved that it should not happen here.[16]

To save republicanism from these evildoers, Jefferson urged that all holders of government securities and bank stock be excluded from holding seats in Congress. Not until the legislature had been thoroughly purged of this "corrupt element" was he prepared to accept its acts as a bona fide expression of the majority voice. It is significant, however, that much as Jefferson reprobated the acquisitive instinct as it manifested itself in businessmen, stock speculators, and bankers, he withheld

[15] Ford, *Jefferson*, I, 200, 204, 215; VII, March 2, 6, 1796; Lodge, *Hamilton*, VII, 304; IX, 516; *Letters Addressed to the Yeomanry of the United States. By a Farmer* (Philadelphia, 1793), p. 36; John Taylor, *An Enquiry*, p. 247; *Columbia University Quarterly*, XXX (1938), 60.

[16] Ford, *Jefferson*, I, 160, 215; VII, August 30, 1795, September 1, 1797; Wiltse, *Jeffersonian Tradition*, pp. 74–75, 81, 94; Carpenter, *Development of American Political Thought*, p. 106; Maclay, *Journal*, p. 310.

his strictures when that instinct took the form of land speculation. Nor did he ever propose that the owners of slaves, together with the owners of stocks and bonds, be denied admittance to Congress.[17]

Jefferson did not rest his case against Hamilton with the charge of aiding and abetting the rise of a plutocracy in the United States; in the eyes of the Secretary of State, his adversary was guilty of the even more heinous crime of seeking to subvert republicanism and to erect a monarchy in its stead. Every Report which emanated from the office of the Secretary of the Treasury struck Jefferson as part and parcel of an insidious monarchical "plot." As he saw it, Hamilton lived for the day when he could place a diadem upon the brow of George Washington and acclaim him "Highness." In that event, Jefferson felt certain that although the voice which issued from the American throne would be that of George Washington, the script would be the work of Alexander Hamilton.[18]

His suspicions nurtured by John Beckley, the clerk of the House of Representatives and an indefatigable scandalmonger, Jefferson concluded that Hamilton was "a man whose history from the moment at which history can stoop to notice him, is a tissue of machinations against the liberty of the country which . . . has heaped it's honors on his head." Where his rival was concerned, Jefferson's credulity was unbounded: he even gave credit to a report that Hamilton was the author of *Plain Truth,* a pamphlet written in 1776 to oppose American independence.[19]

Particularly in Hamilton's efforts to aggrandize the power and prestige of the Presidency did Jefferson see the monarchical leaven at work. Since the Constitutional Convention, where Hamilton had delivered a speech in praise of monarchy, he seemed to have become more subtle, not more republican: if he could not make Washington a king in name, he would make him a king in fact, leaving only the

---

[17] *A Definition of Parties* (Philadelphia, 1794), pp. 15–16; Ford, *Jefferson,* I, 160, 215; Morison, *Jeremiah Smith,* p. 59; Corner, *Benjamin Rush,* p. 227.

[18] Ford, *Jefferson,* VI, 78; VII, April 24, 1796; *Answer to Alexander Hamilton's Letter* (New York, 1800), pp. 4–5; *Letters to Alexander Hamilton, King of the Feds, by Tom Callender* (New York, 1802), p. 23; John Page, *An Address to the Citizens of the District of York* (Richmond, 1794), p. 20; Hamilton, *Monroe,* I, 268–269; Lewis Leary, *That Rascal Freneau* (New Brunswick, 1941), p. 206.

[19] Ford, *Jefferson,* IX, 269; Noble E. Cunningham, Jr., "John Beckley: An Early American Party Manager," *William and Mary Quarterly,* Third Series, XIII (1956), 40–52.

semblance of republican government to beguile the people into believing that they were still free. But, as Jefferson well knew, a monarchy required the prop of a privileged aristocracy. It was painfully obvious to him from whence this aristocracy was to come: the stockjobbers, merchants, and bankers were being groomed by Hamilton to play the part of members of an American House of Lords. From that eminence they would presumably occupy themselves in keeping the "swinish multitude" in order.[20]

Thus Jefferson recognized no differences between "stock-jobbers and king makers": those who worshiped Mammon were prepared to bend the knee before a king. While he did not suppose that the "monarchical conspiracy" had sunk its roots deep into the body politic—"the bulk below," he remarked, "is sound and pure"—it was not until he attained the Presidency that he proclaimed the doctrine that Federalists and Republicans were brothers under their party labels. During the period of Federalist ascendancy, he declared repeatedly that Hamilton and his followers were dedicated to the overthrow of the Constitution and the creation of a monarchy in the United States. Between monarchism and republicanism, he saw no middle ground. "I hold it as honorable to take a firm and decided part," he said in 1796, "and as immoral to pursue a middle line, as between the parties of Honest men, & Rogues."[21]

No doubt Jefferson and his partisans sincerely believed in the existence of a "monarchical conspiracy." But no politicians, however pure —and the Jeffersonians arrogated to themselves the full measure of "republican purity"—could have overlooked the enormous possibilities of attaching the name "monarchists" to their political opponents. As a Federalist wryly observed, the word was an epithet—"a substitute for argument, and its overmatch."[22]

Applied to the Federalists, it did violence to the facts. If any real danger of monarchy existed in the United States, it was during the period of the Articles of Confederation, when conservatives were

[20] John Taylor, *A Definition of Parties,* pp. 15–16; Stan V. Henkels (ed.), *Washington-Madison Papers* (Philadelphia, 1892), p. 76.

[21] Ford, *Jefferson,* I, 233, 257, 284; VI, 78; VII, February 9, 1797; Taylor, *A Definition of Parties,* pp. 15–16; Lodge, *Hamilton,* II, 554.

[22] Moncure D. Conway, *Omitted Chapters of History . . . Edmund Randolph* (New York, 1888), pp. 11, 38; Ames, *Fisher Ames,* II, 159; William Smith, *The Pretensions of Thomas Jefferson to the Presidency Examined* (Philadelphia, 1796), p. 19; Ford, *Jefferson,* IX, 263 (footnote); Lodge, *Hamilton,* VII, 300.

alarmed by the precarious position of property rights. But these troubles were now past and the new government afforded ample protection to property. In the funding-assumption measures adopted in 1790, men of wealth had received a financial windfall calculated to endear them to the general government; even Jefferson was compelled to admit that the beneficiaries of Hamilton's fiscal policies were not likely to bite the hand that fed them. Nor did their personal predilections impel them toward monarchy. In the Constitutional Convention, Franklin had observed that there was "a natural inclination" in the mass of mankind toward kingly government because, he said, "it gives more the appearance of equality among citizens; and that they like." But that the Federalist grandees emphatically did not like: high-spirited, independent-minded, and domineering men, they could not easily bring themselves to acknowledge a master. As Gouverneur Morris pointed out, it was absurd to suppose "that the upper ranks of society will, by setting up a king, put down themselves." Their taste ran much more strongly toward an oligarchic republic than toward a monarchy.[23]

What Jefferson stigmatized as incipient monarchy was in actuality "energetic" government and burgeoning capitalistic enterprise. When he reported in 1790 that he often stood alone at Philadelphia dinner parties as "the only advocate on the republican side of the question," it was his brand of republicanism that he was defending. His opponents in these debates were not monarchists but men who wished to render the republican form of government "competent to its purposes" to strengthen the position of commerce and manufacturing in the American economy, and to wield political power in the interests of the businessmen in the United States.[24]

As for Hamilton himself—the moving spirit, by Jefferson's reckoning, of the monarchical plot—he complained that by accusing him of trying to subvert the established government, his enemies not only impugned his republicanism but cruelly insulted his intelligence. For, he

[23] Henry, *Patrick Henry*, III, 394; Johnston, *Jay*, III, 205, 213, 227; Ames, *Fisher Ames*, II, 348–349, 389, 391–392; Thomas C. Amory, *The Life of James Sullivan* (Boston, 1859), II, 392–394; Morris, *Gouverneur Morris*, II, 525; S. E. Baldwin, *Life and Letters of Simeon Baldwin* (New York, 1919), pp. 388–389; H. R. Warfel, *Noah Webster, Schoolmaster to America* (New York, 1936), p. 148; George Bancroft, *History of the Formation of the Constitution of the United States* (New York, 1882), II, 417, 423; *Proceedings of the Massachusetts Historical Society*, LXIII (1930), 497.

[24] Ford, *Jefferson*, I, 159–160, 257; IX, 263 (footnote), 269; Tyler, *Life and Times of the Tylers*, I, 169.

said, only a man far gone in folly could suppose that monarchism was possible in a country where the people were so democratic in their ideas and so egalitarian in their tastes as to raise grave doubts whether they would long remain and submit to the restraints imposed upon them by the Federal Constitution. He regretted that he was compelled to deal with this singularly cross-grained breed of men who balked at deferring to rank, birth, or merit. But Hamilton always took a realistic rather than a romantic view of human nature—his romanticism was reserved for the nation, not for its citizens—and he resigned himself early in his career to making the best of the strange republican world in which his destiny was cast. Robert Troup, one of his most intimate friends, declared that Hamilton "never had the least idea that we had materials, in the country, at all suitable for the construction of a monarchy; and consequently he never harboured any intention whatever of attempting that form of government."[25]

However he might appear to his enemies, Hamilton always visualized himself as the one man who could make republicanism a success. In his opinion this entailed, among other things, protecting popular government from its friends and well-wishers. For republicans seemed to Hamilton to have a peculiar weakness for killing the thing they loved. If monarchy were ever established in the United States, for example, Hamilton felt sure that it would eventuate "from convulsions and disorders, in consequence of the arts of popular demagogues." Here Hamilton believed that he had touched upon the weakest spot of republicanism—its tendency to produce demagogues and the proclivity of the people to follow these Pied Pipers of democracy. The road to political office in the United States, Hamilton decided, was by "flattering the prejudices of the people, and exciting their jealousies and apprehensions, to throw affairs into confusion." While he absolved Jefferson and Madison of any intention of bringing such disaster upon the country, he believed that it would be the inevitable result of their actions.[26]

Considered solely as a theory, republicanism had a strong appeal for Hamilton. "I desire above all things," he said, "to see the equality

[25] *William and Mary Quarterly,* IV (1947), 221; Noah Webster, *Papers,* p. 330; Morris, *Gouverneur Morris,* II, 526; Lodge, *Hamilton,* II, 459–461; Ford, *Jefferson,* VI, 103; Correspondence of General Hamilton and Judge Purdy, February 25, 1804, Nathaniel Pendleton MSS., NYHS; Tyler, *Letters and Times of the Tylers,* II, 169; Ames, *Fisher Ames,* II, 104.
[26] Lodge, *Hamilton,* IX, 527–535.

of political rights, exclusive of all hereditary distinction, firmly established by a practical demonstration of its being consistent with the order and happiness of society." But when it came to reducing this prepossessing theory to practice, Hamilton felt grave doubts and misgivings. The question uppermost in his mind—and it was never answered fully to his satisfaction during his lifetime—was whether republican government was compatible with order, stability, and the maintenance of the Union. Nevertheless, he was resolved to give popular government a fair trial. Everything he did during his tenure of the Secretaryship of the Treasury was intended to contribute to the success of the "republican experiment."[27]

At certain times during his career, Hamilton gave evidence of possessing the ability—rare in a man so deeply committed in the issues of the day—of viewing himself and his adversaries objectively. On one such occasion, Hamilton's insight led him to discern the real nature of his difference with Jefferson. "One side appears to believe that there is a serious plot to overturn the State governments, and substitute a monarchy to the present republican system," he wrote in 1792. "The other side firmly believes that there is a serious plot to overturn the general government and elevate the separate powers of the States upon its ruins. Both sides may be equally wrong. . . ."

In at least one particular, Jefferson was right: Hamilton was resolved to make the executive department the nerve center of the government, the "cement of the union," the chief stabilizing influence and the checkrein upon demagoguery. By thus exalting the Chief Executive, Hamilton did not believe that liberty would be endangered, for he had learned from history that republics were destroyed not by executive encroachments but by "the licentiousness of the people." Unless the "executive impulse" were made the mainspring of the Federal government, he saw no prospect of success for the "republican experiment": good government, he said, "must always naturally depend on the energy of the executive department." Under this conviction, he construed the President's powers as broadly as the Constitution permitted and assigned to the Chief Executive the duty of leading and informing the people.[28]

[27] *Ibid.,* IX, 532–534; Thomas P. Govan, "The Rich, the Well Born and Alexander Hamilton," *Mississippi Valley Historical Review,* XXXVI (1950), 676–680.
[28] Victor H. Paltsits, *Washington's Farewell Address* (New York, 1935), p. 206; Edward S. Corwin, *The President, Office and Powers* (New York, 1940),

Hamilton branded as "malignant and false" Jefferson's charge that ownership by congressmen of government securities or stock in the Bank of the United States constituted prima facie evidence of corruption. "It is a strange perversion of ideas," he observed, ". . . that men should be deemed corrupt and criminal for becoming proprietors in the funds of their country. . . . As to improper speculations on measures depending before Congress, I believe never were any body of men freer from them."[29] But he had long since ceased to be surprised by anything Jefferson and his friends said or did—they seemed to consider themselves to be the only honest men in the country, and every man who differed from them in opinion "an ambitious despot or a corrupt knave."[30]

At no time in his career did Hamilton attempt to violate the Constitution, nor has his interpretation of the powers granted the Federal government under that document been nullified by subsequent decisions of the Supreme Court of the United States. The truth is, at the very time that Jefferson was accusing him of planning the overthrow of the Constitution, Hamilton was holding it up to veneration as a sacred ark. But when Jefferson took over the Presidency, Hamilton was prepared to give up the Constitution for lost: in such hands, "the frail and worthless fabric," he said, would never carry the American people to national power and greatness.[31]

Hamilton's achievement was not merely that he had set the finances of the country in order. The Constitution had created a government of three distinct branches, each of which was protected from the encroachments of the others by a system of checks and balances. In 1790, the question was: Could a government so constrained by its internal organization function effectively or was it condemned to inaction produced by deadlock between the departments? Certainly it is true that if the doctrine of the separation of powers were applied in its full rigidity, there was little hope that the new government would prove more effective in meeting emergencies than had the Articles of Con-

pp. 2–4, 18, 252–253; Lodge, *Hamilton,* VII, 285; Binkley, *President and Congress,* p. 24.

[29] Evidence tending to confirm Jefferson's accusations has been cited in Charles Beard, "Some Economic Origins of Jeffersonian Democracy," *American Historical Review,* XIX (1914), 282–298, and Clark, *Origins of the American Party System,* pp. 32–33, 44–45.

[30] Lodge, *Hamilton,* II, 454–455; Ames, *Fisher Ames,* I, 142.

[31] J. C. Miller, *Alexander Hamilton, Portrait in Paradox* (New York, 1959), pp. 533–534.

federation. Hamilton demonstrated that the Federal government was capable of fulfilling one of the cardinal objectives of the "more perfect union" created in 1787—the direction of the financial and economic concerns of the country.[32]

---

[32] Hart, *American Presidency,* p. 57; *Harvard Law Review,* XLIV (1928), 130–131; R. V. Harlow, *History of Legislative Methods before 1825* (New York, 1917), p. 140; Dunbar, *Economic Essays,* p. 71.

CHAPTER 6

The Quarrel Between Hamilton and Jefferson

THE RIVALRY between Jefferson and Hamilton was not confined to taking opposing views of domestic policies and arguing finely drawn constitutional points. From the time Jefferson took office as Secretary of State, he and Hamilton were engaged in a spirited contest to determine the foreign policy of the United States. The cry of "executive influence" was first raised not against President Washington but against the Secretary of the Treasury. And, in truth, Hamilton conducted himself more like a prime minister than as a mere head of a department; generally speaking, he acted upon the principle that "most of the important measures of every government are connected with the treasury."[1] He was no respecter of departmental boundaries: so completely did he dominate Henry Knox, the Secretary of War, that he became hardly more than a minion of the Treasury. After experiencing the imperious ways of the Secretary of the Treasury, Jefferson concluded that his colleague was bent upon usurping all executive power and converting President Washington into a *roi fainéant*.[2]

No doubt President Washington's practice of consulting the cabinet members upon general questions of governmental policy—except those relating to finance, where he relied almost wholly upon Ham-

[1] Lodge, *Hamilton*, IX, 531.

[2] Harlow, *History of Legislative Methods*, pp. 140, 149–150; Ford, *Jefferson*, I, 215; VI, 103–104; Rives, *Madison*, III, 230; Dunbar, *Economic Essays*, p. 71; White, *Jeffersonians*, p. 134; Dumas Malone, "Alexander Hamilton on Balance," *Proceedings of the American Philosophical Society*, Vol. 102, No. 2 (1958), pp. 129–135.

ilton—encouraged the Secretary of the Treasury to give rein to his ambition. But even if the President had not invited Hamilton's opinion upon the conduct of the government's affairs, it is improbable that he would have remained within the sphere delimited by his office. For Hamilton was a man who grasped power because he believed that he, and he alone, could make effective use of it. This was true of foreign policy quite as much as of finance.[3]

Early in 1790, when war seemed imminent between Great Britain and Spain, Lord Dorchester, the governor general of Canada, sent his aide-de-camp, Major Beckwith, to New York to ascertain the attitude of the Washington administration toward a possible British request to move troops across United States territory in order to attack the Spaniards in Louisiana. Beckwith quickly discovered that of all the members of the cabinet Hamilton was by far the most strongly inclined to accommodate Great Britain in this matter. Fearing that if the United States refused permission the British would march anyway, thereby involving the two countries in war, the Secretary of the Treasury recommended that the government permit the British to march across United States territory. Moreover, by extending to Great Britain the amenities of a benevolent neutrality, Hamilton believed that the grateful Britons would allow the United States to carve itself a piece of territory at the peace table. If and when that repast was spread before the United States, Hamilton was of the opinion that the Republic ought to insist first of all upon the free navigation of the Mississippi to the sea. "We must have it," he told Major Beckwith.[4]

In his conversations with the Secretary of the Treasury, Major Beckwith found it difficult to believe that he was dealing with a former enemy of Great Britain. "Originally one people," he told Beckwith, "we have a similarity of tastes, of language, and general manners. . . . I have always preferred a connexion with you to that of any other

[3] Adams, Gallatin, I, 66–67; Harlow, History of Legislative Methods, pp. 148–149; Lodge, Hamilton, X, October 3, 1795; Ford, Jefferson, VI, 103–104; Proceedings of the Massachusetts Historical Society XXXV (1914), 43; H. M. Bishop and Samuel Hendel, Basic Issues of American Democracy (New York, 1948), p. 110; Humphreys, David Humphreys, II, 22, 26; John A. Carroll and Mary W. Ashworth, George Washington, First in Peace (New York, 1957), VII, 44–47.

[4] W. C. Ford, The United States and Spain in 1790 (Brooklyn, 1890), pp. 104–105; Report on Canadian Archives (1890), pp. 125–126, 139, 162–163, 175; Fitzpatrick, Washington, XXXI, 88, 102; S. F. Bemis, Jay's Treaty, A Study in Commerce and Diplomacy (New York, 1923), pp. 43–62, 68–79.

country, *we think in English.*" Blood might be thicker than water; but Hamilton was well aware that when Englishmen and Americans got together, blood was likely to grow hot. Still, providing that these quick-tempered cousins kept their prejudices and resentments under control, Hamilton saw no "solid grounds of national difference" between the two countries. On the contrary, he believed that they complemented each other economically as well as linguistically: "You have a great commercial capital and an immense trade," he observed, "we have comparatively no commercial capital, and are an agricultural people."[5]

Far from sharing Hamilton's eagerness to roll out the carpet for the redcoats, Jefferson insisted upon bringing up with Colonel Beckwith such awkward topics as British intrigues with the western Indians, plots to break up the Union, and the presence of British troops in the western posts seven years after the British government had promised to evacuate them "with all convenient speed." President Washington favored the firm line adopted by Jefferson, but this circumstance did not prevent Hamilton from warning Colonel Beckwith against dealing with the Secretary of State. While he was careful not to impugn Jefferson's patriotism, Hamilton indicated that his colleague had picked up abroad an unfortunate prejudice against Great Britain and a no less distressing predilection for France. It was to be expected, therefore, that Jefferson would raise objections to an Anglo-American accord. "I should wish to know them," Hamilton told Beckwith, "in order that I may be sure they are clearly understood and candidly examined." In effect, Hamilton offered to supply the British government with arguments with which to combat the American Secretary of State.[6]

Nor did Hamilton hesitate to interfere in the exploratory talks being carried on in London by Gouverneur Morris. In 1790, Morris had been instructed by the President to sound out the British ministry on the subjects of a commercial treaty and the evacuation of the Northwest posts. Morris, who at this time was deeply resentful of British treatment of his country, threatened Pitt's government with commercial

[5] *Report on Canadian Archives* (1890), 125–126, 162, 165; Lodge, *Hamilton*, VI, July 8, 22, 1790; S. F. Bemis (ed.), *American Secretaries of State* (New York, 1927–29), II, 111.

[6] Channing, *History*, IV, 160; *Report on Canadian Archives* (1890), pp. 135–136, 148–149; Ford, *Jefferson*, I, 181, 186, and *United States and Spain*, pp. 24, 28, 30, 46, 52, 54.

reprisals and the formation of a league of armed neutrals. To Beckwith, Hamilton confided his dissatisfaction with Morris's conduct at the Court of St. James's: in those purlieus, he said, deference, candor, and politeness were expected of every American diplomat. Unwilling to trust delicate matters of state to such a bungler as Morris, Hamilton suggested that if a treaty were seriously contemplated, the negotiations ought to be transferred to the United States, where he could keep an eye on them. True, he did not presume to say that these matters ought to be taken out of the hands of the Secretary of State, but he left no doubt that at the first sign of Anglophobism on the part of Jefferson the Secretary of the Treasury would move in with all his forces.[7]

Having felt the full force of the sweep of Hamilton's ambition, Jefferson was not likely to fall into the error of underestimating his adversary. He set down the Secretary of the Treasury as a man of exceptional ability, energy, and strength of character and he credited him with possessing an "acute understanding, disinterested, honest and honorable in all private transactions, amiable in society and duly valuing virtue in private example." Indeed, he was willing to concede Hamilton every merit except that of being right. In his eyes, the West Indian figured as a natural aristocrat gone wrong—a bright young man who had drifted into the evil ways of monarchism, high finance, and corrupt politics. Nevertheless, he was not unsusceptible to Hamilton's charm, nor did he suppose that the younger man disliked him personally: "Each of us, perhaps," he said later, "thought well of the other as a man." But neither man could bring himself to think well of the other's ideas.[8]

In 1791, fearful that the "French party" would triumph in the United States and that the commerce of the Republic would be diverted to France, the British government sent a minister plenipotentiary to the United States. The first official representative of the British government in the United States—it was eight years since Great Britain had recognized the independence of its revolted colonies—was George

[7] Ford, *Jefferson*, I, 166; *Report on Canadian Archives* (1890), pp. 161–163; Morris. *Gouverneur Morris*, II, 388, 499; Lodge, *Hamilton*, IV, September 15, 1790; Robert Troup to Hamilton, June 15, 1791, Hamilton MSS., LC.

[8] Bernard Fay. "Early Party Machinery in the United States," *Pennsylvania Magazine of History and Biography*, LX (1936), 377; Ford, *Jefferson*, I, 166, 186, 231; IX, 269.

Hammond. With him, Hamilton maintained a relationship that could hardly have been closer had the United States and Great Britain been allies. There were few state secrets that were not known to George Hammond. On the other hand, if American diplomacy—thanks to Alexander Hamilton—was an open book to the British minister, he did not always take pleasure in what he read therein.

While Jefferson was seeking to preserve republicanism and his own position in the administration against Hamilton's "machinations," the Secretary of the Treasury was complaining that he was being made the victim of Jefferson's rancor and "lust of power." It was soon after Jefferson came to New York to assume the duties of Secretary of State that Hamilton detected an undercurrent of hostility in the Virginian's bearing. The closer Hamilton observed this shifty-eyed Southerner— Jefferson seldom looked directly at people when he addressed them— the deeper grew his conviction that Jefferson was trying to destroy him politically. In 1791, Jefferson and Madison set out on a "botanizing tour" of New York in the course of which they paid a social call upon Governor Clinton and Aaron Burr. Hamilton gave ready credence to the report spread by his friends that the Republican leaders, under the pretext of studying the flora of New York, had met in secret conclave for the purpose of encompassing his downfall. Later that same year, Jefferson attempted to persuade the President to remove the Post Office from Hamilton's jurisdiction and transfer it to the State Department. Although the Post Office eluded him, Jefferson succeeded in having the Mint placed under his control despite Hamilton's protests that it was "a most material link in the money system of the Treasury." Every measure emanating from the Treasury, including the funding system, seemed to have incurred Jefferson's displeasure: his opinion on the constitutionality of the Bank of the United States was delivered, Hamilton complained, "in a manner which I felt as partaking of asperity and ill humor towards me"; and he made no concealment of the satisfaction he took in every discomfiture suffered by the Secretary of the Treasury. On the strength of this evidence, Hamilton concluded that his rival nursed an overweening ambition to dominate the government and that he would not rest content until he had installed himself in the Treasury—from which vantage point Hamilton expected him to subvert "the Union, peace, and happiness of the country." Not for a moment did Hamilton admit that he had given the Virginian any provocation for waging a vendetta against him; his only offense, he said, was that he had proved himself to be "the steady, invariable, and decided friend of broad national principles of government."[9]

Both men, being absolutely certain that they were right, were prone to regard criticism as evidence of malice as well as of wrong thinking. As a result, they went into battle exposed to the shafts of their adversaries and they rent the air with cries of anguish when the iron went home. "I find the pain of a little censure, even when it is unfounded," said Jefferson, "is more acute than the pleasure of much praise."

The greatest pleasure of all, for both Jefferson and Hamilton, consisted in censuring the other. They found no want of provocation for such castigations, but it was not until 1792 that they carried their quarrel before the public, exhibiting and asking commiseration for the wounds they had received in the arena battling for the right. Nor did they omit to proclaim their own unimpeachable virtue and to warn the public against the evil designs of the other.[10]

Of the twelve newspapers published in Philadelphia in 1791, the most important was the *Gazette of the United States,* edited by John Fenno. Established in 1789 in order "to endear the General Government to the people," this sheet enjoyed the largest national circulation of any newspaper of the day. The *Gazette of the United States* was not wholly dependent upon its circulation or advertising revenues: Fenno received printing contracts from the Treasury Department, and on several occasions Hamilton loaned him money. The Secretary of the Treasury derived full value from this outlay: "No printer was ever so *correct* in his politics," said Fisher Ames. Certainly no printer ever praised the talents and virtues of Alexander Hamilton more fulsomely. If Washington were the Father of His Country, Hamilton seemed to readers of the *Gazette of the United States* to be the First-Born Son.[11]

[9] Lodge, *Hamilton,* VII, 264–265, 271, 304; IX, 516, 529–531; *Gazette of the United States,* September 22, 1792; Cunningham, *Jeffersonian Republicans,* pp. 11–12; Edward Dumbauld, *Thomas Jefferson, American Tourist* (Norman, Okla., 1946), pp. 237–238; Philip M. Marsh, "The Jefferson-Madison Vacation," *Pennsylvania Magazine of History and Biography,* LXXI (1947), 70–72.
[10] J. C. Hamilton, *Hamilton,* V, 518–519, 522; Leary, *That Rascal Freneau,* pp. 208–209.
[11] Leary, *That Rascal Freneau,* 191, 196; Mott, *Jefferson and the Press,* p. 15; Ames, *Fisher Ames,* I, 240; *National Gazette,* October 24, 1792; Nathan

In Jefferson's opinion, Fenno's "hymns and chaunts" to the glory of the Secretary of the Treasury seemed to presage the West Indian's elevation to the Presidency; and, as for the *Gazette of the United States* itself, it was, he said, "a paper of pure Toryism, disseminating the doctrines of monarchy, aristocracy, and the exclusion of the influence of the people." Under the conviction that the Republic was in danger, Jefferson and Madison resolved to establish in Philadelphia a newspaper dedicated to counteracting the "poison" disseminated by the *Gazette of the United States* and to exposing Hamilton as the archenemy of republican government, a practitioner of corruption and an adventurer who had wormed his way into the good graces of the President. As editor of this projected anti-Hamiltonian newspaper they picked Philip Freneau, the "Poet of the Revolution," who had forsaken poetry for journalism. Employing all the circumlocution with which he habitually worked his ends, Jefferson offered Freneau a clerkship in the State Department which, while it paid only $250 a year, required so little work that—so Freneau was assured—the happy incumbent could pursue "any other calling" he might choose. Thus, without mentioning the subject of a newspaper, Jefferson, with Madison's help, made clear to Freneau what he was expected to do with his leisure. It was not until a friendly printer agreed to put up the money that Freneau consented to come to Philadelphia, where, in 1791, he established the *National Gazette*.[12]

As an antidote to the *Gazette of the United States,* the *National Gazette* fully lived up to Jefferson's expectations. All of Freneau's formidable literary talent was devoted to the cause of destroying Hamilton's good name. Seldom has a public man in the United States been put to the rack by a journalist more expert in tightening screws where it hurt the most. If at the end of this ordeal by journalism Hamilton

---

Schachner, *Alexander Hamilton* (New York, 1946), p. 299; Dumas Malone, *Jefferson and the Rights of Man* (Boston, 1951), p. 424; Samuel E. Forman, *The Political Activities of Philip Freneau,* Johns Hopkins Studies in Historical and Political Science, XX (1902), 35–79.

[12] Mott, *Jefferson and the Press,* pp. 16–17, 181–188, 196; Leary, *That Rascal Freneau,* pp. 243–246; Hunt, *Madison,* VI, 55, 117–118; Rives, *Madison,* III, 196 (footnote); *American Historical Review,* LI (1946), 69–73; John Beckley to Madison, September 2, 1792, Madison MSS., NYPL; Cunningham, *Jeffersonian Republicans,* pp. 13–19; Philip Marsh, "Vindication of Mr. Jefferson," *South Atlantic Quarterly,* XLV (1946), 61–67; Philip Marsh, "Monroe's Draft of the Defense of Freneau," *Pennsylvania Magazine of History and Biography,* LXXI (1947), 74–76.

had a shred of reputation left, it was not owing to lack of effort on the part of Philip Freneau. And while this unpleasantness was going on, Jefferson blandly went his way: Freneau was holding down a job in the State Department at the same time that he was engaged in cutting Hamilton to pieces, but Jefferson affected to be no more than an innocent bystander.

Freneau's barbs stung Hamilton the more cruelly because they were always accompanied by the most honeyed praise of Thomas Jefferson. If the *National Gazette* ran short of adjectives in describing Hamilton's crimes against republicanism, it experienced similar difficulty in finding words to convey a proper sense of the transcendent virtues of the Secretary of State. Jefferson was hailed as "that illustrious Patriot, Statesman and Philosopher," "the Colossus of Liberty" who single-handed prevented monarchy and aristocracy from overwhelming the land. These effusions afforded the Secretary of the Treasury food for thought; and when he discovered that Freneau was employed in Jefferson's department as a translator, the Secretary of the Treasury drew the conclusion that he was being made the victim of a hired character assassin.[13]

Lacking proof that Jefferson had deliberately hired Freneau for this purpose, Hamilton could do no more than insinuate in July, 1792, in the *Gazette of the United States* under the pseudonym "T.L.," that the State Department paid Freneau a salary for abusing public men in order "to oppose the measures of government, and, by false insinuations, to disturb the public peace." If this were true, it explained a good deal about Freneau's activities: "In common life," Hamilton observed, "it is thought ungrateful for a man to bite the hand that puts bread into his mouth; but if the man is hired to do it, the case is altered."[14]

A few weeks later, his suspicions that Jefferson and Madison had been instrumental in setting up the *National Gazette* verified by trustworthy evidence, Hamilton returned to the charge—still, however, retaining his pseudonym—and this time he did not mince words. Thereupon, Jefferson's supporters rushed into print in his defense: Attorney General Randolph wrote a series of articles vindicating the

[13] Lodge, *Hamilton*, VII, 271; IX, 519–520; *National Gazette*, September 8, October 24, 1792; January 12, 1793; *Gazette of the United States*, September 15, 1792.

[14] Lodge, *Hamilton*, VII, 230–231, 236–242, 251; Leary, *That Rascal Freneau*, p. 208; *The Nation*, LX (1895), 198.

Secretary of State, and Hamilton answered him under the signature "Scourge." Thus the administration was divided into warring camps and for the first time the American people became aware of the fact that the cleavage in Congress had penetrated the executive branch of the government.[15]

While the *National Gazette* pilloried Hamilton as a monarchical serpent in the republican paradise, Hamilton inveighed against Jefferson as a disunionist. For proof, the Secretary of the Treasury went back to the days when the Federal Constitution was awaiting action by the state ratifying conventions—at which time Jefferson had recommended that nine states ought to ratify and that three states ought to withhold their approval pending the adoption of certain amendments. From this incident Hamilton drew the moral that the Virginian was prepared to hazard "an eventual schism in the *Union*" in order to forward his scheme of emasculating the Constitution. Defeated in that objective, Jefferson, said Hamilton, had devoted himself to cultivating the spirit of faction "which, unless soon checked, may involve the country in all the horrors of anarchy."[16]

As might be expected from a man who bore so little love for the Union, Jefferson—so Hamilton alleged—thought nothing of playing fast and loose with the national honor. In the Treasury records, Hamilton dug up a letter written by Jefferson in 1787 urging that the French debt be sold to a group of Dutch bankers. Since the United States was not at this time in a position to pay its debts, Hamilton told his readers that Jefferson intended to cheat the Dutch bankers in order to curry favor with France. "What a blemish on our national character," the Secretary of the Treasury declared in the newspapers, "that a debt of so sacred a nature should have been transferred at so considerable a loss to so meritorious a creditor!" Hamilton was careful to omit the all-important point that this plan was supported by some of his capitalist friends who were at this time speculating in the national debt.[17]

[15] Philip Marsh, "Freneau and Jefferson: The Poet-Editor Speaks for Himself about the National Gazette Episode," *American Literature*, VIII (1936), 183–187, and "The Griswold Story of Freneau and Jefferson," *American Historical Review*, LXI (1946), 69, 72; J. C. Hamilton, *Hamilton*, V, 518–519, 522; Leary, *That Rascal Freneau*, p. 212; Lodge, *Hamilton*, VII, 233; *Gazette of the United States*, September 15, 1792.

[16] Lodge, *Hamilton*, VII, 254, 276; IX, 531–532; *Gazette of the United States*, September 22, 1796; Cunningham, *Jeffersonian Republicans*, pp. 23–27.

[17] Lodge, *Hamilton*, VII, 259–261, 281, 297; John Beckley to Madison,

Jefferson, as Hamilton portrayed him in the newspapers, was a gullible visionary who had fallen victim to the "French disease" in its most virulent form—French philosophy. He pictured Jefferson in "a certain snug sanctuary, where, seated on his pivot-chair, and involved in all the obscurity of political mystery and deception . . . he compounds his poison thro' the medium of the National Gazette." To Hamilton's mind, it was debatable whether Jefferson had done more harm to the United States or to France. Naturally "prone to projects which are incompatible with the principles of stable and systemic government," Jefferson had found kindred spirits among the French *enragés,* and together they had brought ruin upon France. At a time when, according to Hamilton, the need was for "a well poised government properly checked," Jefferson had promulgated "wild schemes of government" which, unfortunately for the French people, had been adopted. Having thus made the Virginian responsible for the excesses of the French Revolution, Hamilton had no difficulty in explaining why Jefferson exhibited such singular anxiety for its success—"a parent loves his offspring though he sees her deformities." Commendable as was parental love, Hamilton could not forgive Jefferson for trying to marry this misshapen brat to the pure and virtuous American Republic.[18]

To portray Jefferson to the American people in his true colors was, Hamilton admitted, a difficult task if for no other reason than that the Virginian habitually operated behind a smoke screen of "a monstrous affectation of pure republicanism, primitive simplicity, and extraordinary zeal for the public good." How, therefore, to expose this man, "cautious and sly, wrapped up in impenetrable silence and mystery," as a demagogue driven by the inordinate ambition and lust of power that had destroyed past empires? If the truth were known, Hamilton flatly declared, this shy, retiring philosopher would be revealed as "the most intriguing man in the United States," fit for stratagems and spoils and the dirtier forms of politics. As Hamilton said, he ought to know: he had been marked down as the chief victim of the Virginian's malice.[19]

September 2, 1792, Madison MSS., NYPL; Bolles, *Financial History,* pp. 252–255; William Smith, *The Pretensions of Thomas Jefferson to the Presidency Examined* (Philadelphia, 1796), pp. 3–4.

[18] Lodge, *Hamilton,* VII, 275; *Gazette of the United States,* September 22, 1792.

[19] Lodge, *Hamilton,* VII, 233, 271, 275; IX, 535; *Gazette of the United States,* September 22, 1792.

While Hamilton gave vent in the newspapers to his anger, Jefferson remained silent and aloof, leaving Freneau and other friends to answer the Secretary of the Treasury. Such treatment merely exasperated Hamilton the more: as the dispute went on his tone became progressively more shrill and his allegations more far-fetched. Chief Justice John Jay, a cooler head than Hamilton, advised him to vindicate his reputation by writing his memoirs, preferably to be published posthumously. But Hamilton replied that he could not wait for posterity to do him justice—the national government was in danger of being destroyed, in which event it would matter very little what posterity thought of him.[20]

Patently, the conflict between Hamilton and Jefferson was not wholly based upon principle, nor was it always kept upon the lofty plane of ideological differences. The two secretaries were engaged in a struggle for power; and the question who would be the heir apparent of President Washington was never far removed from the forefront of their consciousness. The objective of each man, therefore, was to ingratiate himself and to blacken the other in the eyes of the President. Jefferson was the first to prefer charges against his rival. In February, 1792, he told Washington that Hamilton was responsible for the alarming growth of a get-rich-quick mania "which had introduced its poison into the government itself." Later he asserted that the Treasury "already possessed such an influence as to swallow up the whole Executive power, and that the future President (not supported by the weight of character which he [Washington] possessed) would not be able to make head against this department." In July, 1792, he informed the President that Hamilton had pronounced the Constitution to be "a shilly shally thing of mere milk & water, which could not last, & was only good as a step to something better." And in September, 1792, he complained to Washington that the Secretary of the Treasury was vilifying him (Jefferson) in the newspapers.[21]

Notwithstanding that he was slower than was Jefferson in laying his grievances before the President, Hamilton did not permit himself to be outdone in this regard by his rival. In August, 1792, he notified Washington that he could no longer remain silent under the aspersions

[20] J. C. Hamilton, *Hamilton,* V, 518–519, 522; *Gazette of the United States,* September 22, 1792.
[21] Ford, *Jefferson,* I, 174, 177, 204, 256; Hunt, *Madison,* VI, 318–319; Lodge, *Hamilton,* IX, 531; *The Pretensions of Thomas Jefferson to the Presidency Examined,* p. 2.

cast upon him by the *National Gazette.* "I feel that I merit them in no degree," he exclaimed; "and expressions of indignation sometimes escape me, in spite of every effort to suppress them." "It is a curious phenomenon in political history (not easy to be paralleled)," he later observed, "that a measure which has elevated the credit of the country from a state of absolute prostration to a state of exalted pre-eminence should bring upon the authors of it obloquy and reproach."[22]

President Washington, who had hoped that his "declining years" would be spent in peace and repose—in 1788, he had supposed that the American people would be "delighted with a government instituted by themselves and for their own good"—was dismayed by this turn of events. While he had long known there were serious differences of opinion between Jefferson and Hamilton, he had no idea, he told the two cabinet officers, that the quarrel had been carried to such a pitch as to endanger the existence of the Federal government. Therefore, while protesting his affection for both men and admitting that their views were "pure and well meant," he urged them to make "mutual yieldings." "Mankind cannot think alike," he said, "but would adopt different means to attain the same end." Being certain in his own mind that Jefferson and Hamilton had the same end in view, he tried to mark out a line by which both could walk in peace and understanding.[23]

The President made clear, however, that it was not to be a line laid down by Jefferson. He refused to give credence to the assertions of the Secretary of State that there was a monarchical plot afoot and that Hamilton was one of the prime conspirators: "He did not believe," he roundly declared, "that there were ten men in the United States whose opinions were worth attention who entertained such a thought" as subverting the republican form of government established by the Constitution. Nor would the President agree that Hamilton's financial schemes had been injurious to the country. It was not true, he said, that the assumption of state debts had increased the debt, "for . . . all of it was honest debt." What history would say of the work of the Secretary of the Treasury, Washington did not pretend to know, but for his part he was inclined to give Hamilton the benefit of the doubt: Washington had seen "our affairs desperate & our credit lost, and that

[22] Lodge, *Hamilton,* II, 427, III, 9.
[23] Ford, *Jefferson,* I, 215; Fitzpatrick, *Washington,* XXX, 496; XXXII, 130, 137, 185–186; XXXV, 119; Cunningham, *Jeffersonian Republicans,* pp. 26–28; Cunliffe, *George Washington, Man and Monument,* pp. 166–169.

this was in a sudden & extraordinary degree raised to the highest pitch." And, the President told Jefferson, he regarded attacks upon the administration as attacks upon himself: "He must be a fool indeed to swallow a little sugar plumb here & there thrown out to him."[24]

Much to his chagrin, Washington discovered that the two cabinet officers did not subscribe to his view that, since they were working toward the same objectives, compromise was simply a matter of reconciling unimportant differences between them.[25] Even though Hamilton offered to embrace any plan devised by the President that promised to bring peace to the administration—a singularly generous offer in view of his conviction that he was "the most deeply injured party"—his advice to Washington was to choose between the two heads of departments and to support with all his powers the man of his choice. A continuance of the division in the executive department, he told Washington, "must destroy the energy of government, which will be little enough with the strictest union." If Jefferson wished to attack the policies and officers of the government through a "hireling," Hamilton recommended that he resign forthwith: in private life he would be free to indulge to his heart's content his favorite sport of vilifying those with whom he disagreed. On his part, Jefferson denied any complicity in the establishment of the *National Gazette* or in determining its editorial policies. He, too, offered to resign, but only on condition that his retirement did not appear to be forced by the Secretary of the Treasury.[26]

The readiness on the part of Jefferson and Hamilton to offer their resignations visibly distressed the President. After all, Washington had accepted the Presidency with the understanding that he would remain only until "he saw matters fairly set going." In the spring of 1792, persuaded that the hour of deliverance was at last at hand, he had started to compose a Farewell Address. But Hamilton, Jefferson, Madison, and many others beseeched him to accept another term; and the President had reluctantly consented to put away the draft of his valedictory and to endure another four-year term of exile from his beloved Mount Vernon. Now his advisers were threatening to leave him to

[24] Ford, *Jefferson*, I, 165, 199–201, 204–205, 215, 231, 257.

[25] Henry Adams, *The Life of Henry Adams* (Philadelphia, 1879), p. 159; Lodge, *Hamilton*, VII, 284–288.

[26] Lodge, *Hamilton*, VII, 304–306; Ford, *Jefferson*, I, 204; Fitzpatrick, *Washington*, XXXII, 185–186.

wrestle alone with the thorny problems created by their quarrels.[27]

In the end, the President succeeded in persuading Hamilton and Jefferson to maintain at least a semblance of harmony in the administration. Despite this patched-up truce, Jefferson did not cease his efforts to drive Hamilton from public life loaded with obloquy. In January, 1793, the Virginian drafted a ten-point indictment of Hamilton's conduct of the Treasury by means of which he hoped to force Hamilton's resignation. As was his settled habit, Jefferson did not allow his hand to appear in these proceedings: the bill of complaints against Hamilton was presented to Congress by William Branch Giles, a member of the House of Representatives from Virginia. Despite the fact that Madison voted "guilty" on all counts, the Secretary of the Treasury was vindicated by a considerable majority. Jefferson took this defeat hard, but he consoled himself with the reflection that the most that could be said in Hamilton's favor was that a "corrupt" legislature had exonerated a "corrupt" Secretary of the Treasury. It was a case, he thought, of the pot and the kettle calling each other white.[28]

Moreover, even though decorum was preserved in the cabinet, the newspaper war went on unabated. The *National Gazette* continued to hold up Hamilton to execration and the *Gazette of the United States* lost none of its zeal for flaying Jefferson. But the *National Gazette* lost money and Freneau's job in the State Department (he found that he had to hire translators to do much of the work for him) cost him almost as much as his salary brought in. Although Jefferson went out of his way to procure subscriptions for the *National Gazette*, he was not prepared to invest his own money in it. As a result, in October, 1793, during the yellow fever epidemic in Philadelphia, the *National Gazette* suspended publication and Freneau retired to New Jersey.

[27] Ford, *Jefferson*, I, 175.

[28] *The Nation*, LXI (1895), 163–165; Hildreth, *History*, IV, 395–396, 400–401; Lodge, *Hamilton*, III, 63–64, 107, 109–110, 125, 152–153, 164, 169, 191; Ford, *Jefferson*, I, 222, 229; Charles F. Jenkins (ed.), *Jefferson's Germantown Letters* (Philadelphia, 1906), p. 123; Marshall, *Washington*, V, 385–388; Hunt, *Madison*, VI, 210–211; Fitzpatrick, *Washington*, XXXIII, 95; J. C. Hamilton, *Hamilton*, V, 596–598; D. R. Anderson, *William Branch Giles* (Menasha, Wis., 1914), pp. 21–22; *Collections of the Massachusetts Historical Society*, Fifth Series, III (1877), 323; *Proceedings of the Massachusetts Historical Society*, XV, Second Series (1902), 141; George Hammond to Lord Grenville, March 7, 1793, Hammond MSS., Henry Adams Transcripts, Library of Congress.

That a similar fate did not befall the *Gazette of the United States* was owing in part to the alacrity with which Hamilton and other prominent Federalists reached into their pockets whenever Fenno found himself in financial difficulties.[29]

Nevertheless, the final victory rested with Jefferson. Instead of enhancing his own reputation by attacking Jefferson in the newspapers, Hamilton succeeded in focusing attention upon the Virginian as the leader of the anti-Treasury forces. The shy, retiring man in the State Department, already famous as one of the leaders in the struggle for liberty against George III, now stood forth as the people's champion against the combined forces of finance, corruption, and monarchism.[30]

[29] Allan Nevins, *The New York Evening Post* (New York, 1922), p. 13; John Fenno to Hamilton, November 9, 1793, Hamilton MSS., LC; F. L. Mott, *American Journalism* (New York, 1950), pp. 126–127; Warfel, *Noah Webster,* p. 223.

[30] *Dunlap's American Daily Advertiser,* September 22, October 10, 1792; *General Advertiser,* January 5, 1793; Leary, *That Rascal Freneau,* pp. 208–209; J. C. Hamilton, *Hamilton,* V, 518–519, 522.

CHAPTER 7

The Emergence of Political Parties

IN 1792, the conflict between the ideas and economic interests personified by Hamilton and Jefferson began to crystallize in the form of political parties. To the framers of the Constitution, this was a sinister turn of events: far from supposing that political parties were essential to the proper functioning of republican government, they regarded them as a source of weakness and division. "If we mean to support the Liberty and Independence which it has cost us so much blood and treasure to establish," Washington said in 1790, "we must drive far away the daemon of party spirit and local reproach."[1] The objective of the men who assembled in Philadelphia in 1787 was to create a Union so perfect that the people would be united in furthering the national welfare. Had the ideal of the Founding Fathers been realized, the United States would have been a one-party state in which the distinctions of Whig and Tory, Federalist and Antifederalist were absorbed by an all-embracing American patriotism.[2]

In 1788–89, Federalism was more a state of mind than an organized

[1] Fitzpatrick, *Washington,* XXXI, 48.

[2] Such political parties as existed in the United States during the period of the Articles of Confederation were on the state rather than on the national level. A good example of such parties is afforded by the so-called Constitutionalists and Anti-Constitutionalists in Pennsylvania. These two groups contested for control of the state from 1776 to 1790. Harry Marlin Tinkcom, *The Republicans and Federalists in Pennsylvania, 1790–1801* (Harrisburg, 1950), pp. 4–6. See also Sparks, *Gouverneur Morris,* I, 200; George Hammond to Lord Grenville, March 7, 1793, Hammond MSS., LC; Dauer, *Adams Federalists,* p. 3.

political party. Federalists were found in all the states, but there was little concerted political activity on a national scale. Even the adoption of the Federal Constitution was accomplished by its proponents working independently in the various states. True, some correspondence passed between the leading Federalists in the key states—notably between Alexander Hamilton in New York and James Madison in Virginia—but such organization as the Federalists enjoyed was along state rather than national lines. With the ratification of the Constitution, however, the Federalists were compelled to depend increasingly upon unified political action. A national government could be properly administered only by national-minded men. As the "friends of the Constitution," the Federalists campaigned vigorously for office in 1788–89 and succeeded in electing a large majority in both houses of Congress. Plainly, the idea was gaining ground that only a certain denomination of men ought to be trusted with the management of national affairs.[3]

In general, the Federalist spokesmen were the national-minded, conservative, well-to-do members of the community who believed that the cure for the "excess of democracy" was a strong national government. If the aphorism "those who own the country ought to run it" had been realized, the Federalists were the kind of people who would have been installed in the seats of power. As befitted a body of men who thought continentally, the Federalists were not divided along sectional lines: both northern merchants and southern planters were found within the fold. In general, Federalism was weakest in the West, strongest in the cities (where the laborers, lawyers, and artisans were almost as ardent in its support as were the businessmen), and firmly established among the prosperous farmers and planters of the eastern seaboard.[4]

The gravest weakness of the Federalists was that their power was based upon a coalition of northern businessmen and southern planters. In all probability, this uneasy alliance would have succumbed sooner or later to the strains and stresses generated by the divergent economic interests and social and political attitudes of Northerners and Southerners. As might be expected, victory—in this case, the adoption of the Constitution—hastened the dissolution of the coalition, but the event was not ensured until 1790, when Hamilton launched his fiscal and

[3] Charles, *Origins of the American Party System*, pp. 5–6.
[4] Dauer, *Adams Federalists*, pp. 25, 285.

economic programs. In March, 1790, Washington was informed that "many who were warm Supporters of the government, were changing their sentiments from a conviction of the impracticability of Union with States, whose interests are so dissimilar to those of Virginia."[5] Of the committee appointed in 1790 by the Virginia legislature to draft a protest against the funding-assumption acts, seven were originally supporters of the Constitution. Hamilton himself admitted that his differences of opinion with Madison over discrimination between original holders and purchasers of government securities had "laid the foundation of the great schism which has since prevailed."[6] Madison traced the quarrel to the same source: by encouraging the spirit of speculation, he said, Hamilton had "wantonly multiplied" enemies to the Federal government and "disgusted the best friends of the Union," compelling them to choose "between the loss of the union, and the loss of what the union was meant to secure."[7]

Thus, despite the fact that Hamilton's objective was to promote the unity and national power of the United States, his policies led to the creation of two political parties representing the two dominant economic groups in the country: the planting-slaveholding-farmer interest and the mercantile-shipping-financial interest. By 1792, the opponents of the Secretary of the Treasury had adopted the name "Republicans," leaving to the Hamiltonian residue the denomination of "Federalists." These parties were divided by economic and ideological differences greater than those which have generally existed between major American political parties.[8]

While the Federalists and Republicans lacked the appurtenances of present-day political parties, they were true parties in the sense that they acted upon clearly formulated ideas, they had leaders of marked intellectual and political ability, and they aspired to administer the government for the benefit of sections and economic groups. It is

[5] Fitzpatrick, *Washington*, XXXI, 28.

[6] Lodge, *Hamilton*, VIII, 466; Rives, *Madison*, III, 149.

[7] Ford, *John Quincy Adams*, I, April 5, 1790; Adams, *Gallatin*, III, 131, 149; Stuart Gerry Brown, *The First Republicans* (Syracuse, 1954), pp. 51–55; Cunningham, *Jeffersonian Republicans*, pp. 8–9, 23; Harry Ammon, "The Formation of the Republican Party in Virginia, 1789–1796," *Journal of Southern History*, XIX (1953), 309–310.

[8] Noah Webster, *Papers*, p. 332; J. S. Basset, *The Federalist System* (New York, 1906), p. 42; *Gazette of the United States*, January 15, 1795; Charles, *Origins of the American Party System*, pp. 20–23; Dauer, *Adams Federalists*, pp. 7, 23–24, 263–264.

significant that these political parties first manifested themselves in Congress, from whence they percolated down to the electorate. The division of the American people into Federalists and Republicans—one of the most striking features of the political scene during the Federalist era—was the work of leaders who were most immediately in touch with the conduct of national affairs.[9]

When Hamilton saw an organized opposition to his policies developing in Congress, he concluded that Antifederalism was again menacing the Union. When he did not apply to his opponents the harsher epithets of "disorganizers" and "Jacobins," he made it a point to call the Republicans "Antifederalists." The use of this name was justified only in the sense that some Republicans were former Antifederalists: in New York and Pennsylvania, for example, the personnel of the Republican party came largely from those who had opposed the ratification of the Constitution. But not all the centers of Antifederalism became Republican strongholds: Rhode Island, the state most adamantly opposed to the Federal Constitution, became for a time a Federalist state; and Massachusetts, although almost evenly divided in 1788 between Federalists and Antifederalists, won distinction during the decade of the 1790's by its rock-ribbed Federalism. And not a few of the leaders of Antifederalism—notably Richard Henry Lee and Patrick Henry—switched their allegiance to the party of Alexander Hamilton.[10]

Whatever their former political convictions may have been, Republicans vigorously denied that their party was Antifederalism Revived. Unlike the Antifederalists, Republicans professed ardent devotion to the Constitution and the "beautiful equilibrium" it established between the central and state governments. If the Republicans were to be believed, their principal purpose was to preserve that sacred document from the profane hands of Federalists who wished to pervert it into "a consolidation of the union in a Republic *one and indivisible*.[11]

Leadership of the Republicans fell to James Madison, who as its

[9] White, *Jeffersonians*, p. 46; Cunningham, *Jeffersonian Republicans*, pp., 115, 257; Orin G. Libby, "Political Factions in Washington's Administrations," *Quarterly Journal of the University of North Dakota*, III (1912).

[10] Charles Beard, *Economic Origins of Jeffersonian Democracy* (New York, 1915), p. 256; Charles, *Origins of the American Party System*, pp. 9, 96–97.

[11] Ford, *Jefferson*, I, 165; IX, 313; Rives, *Madison*, III, 145–146 (footnote); *American Historical Review*, II (1896), 101; *National Gazette*, December 8, 1792.

THE EMERGENCE OF POLITICAL PARTIES

organizer and policy maker gave the Federalists good cause to lament his defection from their ranks. During the early period of its existence, the Republican party was sometimes called the "Madisonians." Upon every score except that of service to the cause of American Independence, Madison's stature was equal to that of Jefferson, and in one particular—the work of organizing the Republican party and equipping it with a political philosophy—his contribution was even greater than that of his fellow Virginian. Part of the reputation Jefferson enjoyed as a leader of the Republican party was owing to the assiduity with which Madison acclaimed him as a paragon of virtue and wisdom. And while Jefferson was tasting the sweets of retirement at Monticello, Madison was in Philadelphia marshaling votes and directing the party's strategy in Congress.[12] If the reward had gone to the man who had done most for the Republican party, James Madison would have been its first candidate for the Presidency.[13]

Jefferson's contribution to the Republican party was made mostly behind the scenes—his favorite sphere of operations. As a political leader, the Secretary of State preferred to work through others rather than to permit his hand to appear, to write a letter rather than to make a speech, and to remain outwardly every man's friend rather than to engage openly in quarrels. Above all, it was by means of unremitting attention to his correspondence that Jefferson did his part toward organizing a militant opposition to Hamilton: a constant stream of letters poured from his pen, "every letter beginning with protestations of his disgust at politics and total forgetfulness of public affairs, but as constantly ending in hints, suggestions and recommendations as to the best method of carrying on the campaign."[14] In part, at least, Jefferson was a political leader by grace of the United States mails.[15]

[12] Joseph Charles maintains that Jefferson did not assume leadership of the Republican party until 1797, after his election as Vice-President. *Origins of the American Party System*, p. 85.

[13] Hunt, *Madison*, VI, 129; Adrienne Koch, *Madison and Jefferson, The Great Collaboration* (New York, 1950), pp. 291–294; *Gazette of the United States*, December 13, 1794; Charles, *Origins of the American Party System*, pp. 80–83; Cunningham, *Jeffersonian Republicans*, p. 69.

[14] Joseph Charles contends that "Jefferson did not create a party: a widespread popular movement recognized and claimed him as its leader." This is an extreme position; it is clear that Jefferson played a far more active role than Charles credited him with. *Origins of the American Party System*, pp. 82–83, 90.

[15] Cunningham, *The Jeffersonian Republicans*, p. 258; Bernard Fay, "Early Party Machinery in the United States," *Pennsylvania Magazine of History and Biography*, LX (1936), 337–338, 382; Hildreth, *History*, IV.

Republicanism was a "grass roots" philosophy; by comparison, Federalism was born and bred on the city streets. Republicanism reflected the prevailing ideals and antipathies of the majority of the American people: the fear of a strong, overbearing central government, of the rule of "stock jobbers, stockholders, bank directors, and brokers"— a mere "kennel of sharpers"—and of a large national debt. When Republicans declaimed against expensive government, they touched a deep chord in the American people; and when they defended local rights and privileges against the Federal government, they were hailed as "heroes of liberty." At the same time, with no sense of incongruity, Republicans spoke in the name of the slaveholders and as champions of the South's "peculiar institution."[16]

Behind Southerners' distrust of a strong national government lay the fear that such a government would interfere with the institution of slavery. In 1790, the presentation of a memorial from the Pennsylvania Society for Promoting the Abolition of Slavery touched off an alarm among southern members of Congress palpably out of all proportion to its real importance. The committee to which this memorial was referred tried to calm the agitated Southerners by pointing out that Congress was restrained from interfering with the emancipation of slaves, that it could not prohibit the importation of slaves until 1808, and that it had no authority to take any action respecting the care, welfare, or education of slaves "in the principles of morality and religion." Moreover, in 1793, by a large majority, Congress enacted a Fugitive Slave Law (entitled "An Act respecting fugitives from justice and persons escaping from the service of their masters") which permitted an owner to seize a fugitive and to carry him back to servitude simply by presenting an affidavit of ownership. State as well as Federal officials were required to enforce the law, and a fine of $500 was ordered imposed upon anyone who obstructed the activities of the law-enforcement officers.[17]

Even so, the South was not disposed to relax its vigilance.[18] As a

[16] *Virginia Magazine of History and Biography,* XLVI (1938), 289; Hunt, *Madison,* VI, 58–59; Frederick B. Tolles, *George Logan of Philadelphia* (New York, 1953), pp. 111–114, 128.

[17] *Abridgment of Debates,* I, 72, 75, 239, 417; Basset, *Federalist System,* pp. 178–189.

[18] In those northern states where slavery had not already been abolished by interdiction, statute law, or judicial decree, emancipation societies were at work. John Jay was one of the prime organizers of the Society for Promoting the Manumission of Slaves. Partly as a result of the activities of this organiza-

southern congressman said, slavery was so inextricably bound up with the social and economic life of the region "that it could not be eradicated without tearing up by the roots their happiness, tranquillity and prosperity; that if it were an evil, it was one for which there was no remedy, and therefore, like wise men, they acquiesced in it." "We took each other," he told the northern members, "with our mutual bad habits and respective evils, for better, for worse: the Northern States adopted us with our slaves, and we adopted them with their Quakers."[19]

One of the most striking anomalies of American political history was the emergence of the great slaveholding planters of the South as the leaders of the party which prided itself upon its liberalism, its devotion to republican institutions, and its concern for the welfare of the masses. For the wealthy planters and the small self-sufficient farmers of the South were not natural allies; on the contrary, they were divided by social, political, and economic differences that seemingly precluded the possibility of united action. But Hamiltonianism —and later, abolitionism—exposed Southerners to a common danger and gave them a common cause. In a conflict with northern finance capital, the farmers, large and small, of the South rallied round the aristocratic leaders who spoke in the name of American agriculture.[20]

It is not surprising that most of the leaders of the agrarians' crusade against "the avaricious, monopolizing Spirit of Commerce and Commercial Men" came from Virginia.[21] The society of the Old Dominion was uncontaminated by businessmen; even of the professions only law was deemed suitable for a gentleman. Family, landed property, and the ownership of slaves were the criteria of gentility; wealth derived

---

tion, New York adopted a program of gradual emancipation. In return, the New York Federalists won the "Negro vote"—that part of the free colored population that was qualified to vote. Dixon Ryan Fox, "The Negro Vote in Old New York," *Political Science Quarterly*, XXXII (1938), 252–255; E. Wilder Spaulding, *New York in the Critical Period* (New York, 1932), pp. 31, 49.

[19] *Abridgment of Debates*, I, 232.

[20] John Davis, *Travels of Four Years and a Half in the United States of America* (Bristol, Eng., 1803), ed. A. J. Morrison (New York, 1802), pp. 388–389; Beard, *Economic Origins of Jeffersonian Democracy*, 398–399; John Taylor, *An Argument Respecting the Constitutionality of the Carriage Tax* (Richmond, 1795), pp. 9–10; *Four Letters Addressed to the Yeomanry of the United States. By a Farmer* (Philadelphia, 1792), p. 11; *American Political Science Review*, XXII (1928), 873–874.

[21] Ballagh, *Letters of Richard Henry Lee*, II, 35; John Taylor, *An Enquiry*, pp. 78–79.

from trade or commerce, unless seasoned by a generation or two of gentlemanly pursuits and landed wealth, did not admit one to the charmed circle of the First Families of Virginia. No state of the Union could compare with Virginia in point of size, population, and the wealth and pride of its patricians.[22]

The political philosophy of agrarianism was most fully developed by John Taylor of Caroline, a Virginia planter, economist, and politician.[23] Taylor served in the United States Senate from 1791 to 1793, but most of his life was spent upon his plantation writing books on agriculture and political economy. In the opinion of this "philosopher of Jeffersonian Republicanism," the "moneyed aristocracy"— the most hateful kind of a ruling class—had firmly planted its foot upon the neck of the American farmer. Stocks and bonds, cunning and greed, had triumphed, he lamented, over wheat and tobacco, innocence and simplicity. Under Hamilton's aegis, Taylor believed, the interests of five million people were being sacrificed to the avarice of five thousand: the most productive class in the community was compelled to labor for the enrichment of a parasitic group which exemplified what Taylor called "the modern, sordid, money-loving meanness of mind." A devout believer in hard money, he condemned paper money and bank credits as devices of cheats and sharpers for fleecing the public.[24]

Taylor's idea of Paradise was a government of farmers, by farmers and for farmers. He considered it highly significant that "the divine intelligence . . . selected an agricultural state as a paradise for its first favorites" and had "prescribed the agricultural virtues as the means for the admission of their posterity into heaven."[25] Since agriculture was clearly the dominant interest of the United States—at this time it might truly have been said that the business of the American people was sowing and reaping—Taylor argued that if the government

[22] In 1790, the population of Virginia was 747,000—almost as many people as lived in all the New England states. The second most populous state, Pennsylvania, had 434,000 inhabitants. Today Virginia is much smaller in size than it was in 1790. In 1792, Kentucky became a separate state and in 1863 West Virginia was lopped off from the Old Dominion.

[23] *American Political Science Review*, XXII (1928), 870; Hunt, *Madison*, VI, 123; *Virginia Magazine of History and Biography*, XLVI (1938), 290.

[24] John Taylor, *An Enquiry*, pp. 40, 45; Coker, *Democracy, Liberty and Property,*, p. 413; William Manning, *The Key of Liberty*, p. 55; Tolles, *George Logan*, pp. 115–116; Leary, *That Rascal Freneau*, p. 266; *Virginia Magazine of History and Biography*, XLVI (1938), 291–292.

[25] *Virginia Magazine of History and Biography*, XLVI (1938), 288–289.

acted at all, it ought to make the welfare of the farmers its paramount concern. But the sturdy, independent yeomen in whose name Taylor spoke were not expected to clamor for government aid whenever the going got rough; instead, they were supposed to ask only that they be left alone and permitted to work out their own salvation. Taylor's ideal was a simple, frugal, do-little government that knew it best served the interests of the American people by keeping its hands out of their affairs and out of their pockets. From unhappy experience, Taylor had learned that when government intervened in the economy it was usually to foster special privilege.

Coming from John Taylor, the owner of thousands of acres and scores of slaves, denunciations of a "privileged aristocracy" seemed paradoxical. During the American Revolution, Dr. Samuel Johnson had caustically inquired how it happened that the "loudest yelps" for liberty came from the drivers of Negroes; now these same drivers of Negroes were extolling equality.[26] This anomaly afforded the Federalists material for declamations against the Republicans' claim to be the spokesmen of the common people of the United States. "Men who can count in their train a hundred slaves, whose large domains, like feudal barons, are people with the humblest vassals," said James Bayard, the Federalist congressman from Delaware, "are styled democrats. . . . These high priests of liberty are zealously proclaiming freedom on one hand while on the other they are rivetting the chains of slavery." Even Washington was startled by this discrepancy; in 1788 he had supposed that "the habitual distinctions which have always existed among the people" of the South would predispose them toward aristocracy and royalty.[27]

Of course, the southern grandees were careful not to apply their democratic ideas to conditions at home: democracy was strictly for export to the northern states. When William Branch Giles, a Virginia planter and congressman, declared that "he should view the banishment of the privileged orders from the world as the surest harbinger of the approach of the millennium," he was not preaching social revolu-

[26] In 1791, James Madison declared that he was "greatly interested in that species of property" (slaves) and that he would "not lessen the value by weakening the tenure of it." Hunt, *Madison*, VI, 60.

[27] Fitzpatrick, *Washington*, XXIX, 190; *Massachusetts Historical Society Proceedings*, LXIII (1930), 497; Manning J. Dauer and Hans Hammond, "John Taylor, Democrat or Aristocrat?" *Journal of Politics*, VI (1944), 381–403.

tion in the South.[28] Nor did John Taylor admit any inconsistency between economic and social realities and his political philosophy. As he
saw it, in the freemasonry of agriculture, all white free landowners
were equal: the mystic bond created by the ownership of land and the
agricultural way of life erased distinctions and leveled inequalities. And,
as a final saving grace, the landed interest, by virtue of the fact that
it constituted the majority, could never form an aristocracy or oppress
the minority because, said Taylor, "the many have no motive to oppress the few."[29]

While John Taylor's writings helped to mobilize the farmers against
the growing power of northern businessmen, it remained for a Yankee
to reinvigorate southern agriculture beyond the fondest hopes of the
planters themselves. Eli Whitney's invention of the cotton gin made
possible the spread of cotton cultivation—and with it, Negro slavery—
over a large part of the southern United States. In actuality, the period
of Federalist rule was memorable less for the advances scored by commerce and manufacturing than for the tremendous expansion of southern agriculture which began in 1793.

The leaders of the Federalist party were lawyers, merchants, and
large landowners. But the leadership did not faithfully reflect the composition of the party as a whole. Manifestly, there were not enough
landed magnates, businessmen, and professional men in the United
States to form a political party; had not Federalism attracted the votes
of the farmers and the town artisans, it never would have attained
power in the United States. The party appealed especially to the more
prosperous farmers living near the cities and engaged in growing cash
crops. In Lancaster County, Pennsylvania, for example, there were a
number of farmers of the Federalist persuasion worth from fifty to
several hundred thousand dollars. Even in New England, the merchants, lawyers, and shipowners who constituted the nucleus of the
party leaned heavily upon the well-to-do farmers and the Congrega-
tional clergy.[30]

Being men of wealth and high social position, the Federalist leaders
fell easily into the assumption that there was a close connection be-

[28] *Annals of Congress*, III, 547.

[29] Channing, *History*, IV, 214; Taylor, *An Enquiry*, p. 52.

[30] S. E. Morison, *The Maritime History of Massachusetts* (Boston, 1922),
p. 174; *Collections of the Colonial Society of Massachusetts*, XXXVI (1954),
662; Dauer, *Adams Federalists*, pp. 18–19.

tween the ownership of property and the possession of the talents necessary to the efficient administration of government. The men who had made good in trade, speculation, and the professions were the proper custodians of the national welfare; they alone possessed the ability, wisdom, sobriety, public spirit, and love of good order upon which the success of all government, and especially republican government, depended. It was plain at least to the Federalists that the people of the United States could ensure their happiness and prosperity only by accepting the principle that "those who have more strength and *excellence,* shall bear rule over those who have less."[31] Surely the frankest politicians who ever graced the American scene, the Federalists made no pretence of being other than what they were: upper-class Americans who had a natural-born right to rule their inferiors in the social and economic scale. Even within the party itself, the rank and file were never permitted to indulge the pleasing illusion that they were the social equals of the leaders. Particularly in the northern cities, good society was coeval with the Federalist party: a gentleman was a Federalist but, unhappily, it did not follow that every Federalist was a gentleman.

Despite the fact that Federalism sought to carry over the aristocratic bias of colonial society into the Republic, it did not represent the last stand of an old order. Rather it marked the first concerted effort on the part of the business and professional class, together with prosperous landowners, to arrogate to themselves direction of the nation's affairs. Having already solidified their economic position, the Federalist merchants, lawyers, speculators, bankers, and landowners undertook to put in practice the maxim that those who owned the country ought to run it.

In part, it was upon the necessity of making the United States a first-rate power that the Federalists based their claim of a right to rule. Under the Articles of Confederation, they argued, national security had been jeopardized by a weak and inefficient central government—an experience which ought to have taught Americans that their peace, happiness, and safety depended upon establishing a powerful national government and giving the full measure of confidence to those best qualified to administer it. Accordingly, the Federalists tried to inculcate

[31] R. G. Adams (ed.), *Selected Political Essays of James Wilson* (New York, 1930), pp. 230–231; John Ward Fenno, *Desultory Reflections on the Political Aspects of Public Affairs,* II (New York, 1800), 32–33.

in the American people a love of the Union which subordinated local interests to the good of the whole nation and put the welfare of the United States over loyalty to any foreign country whatever. "I would wish my countrymen to feel like Romans, to be as proud as Englishmen," said Gouverneur Morris; "we are neither Frenchmen nor Englishmen, we are Americans." The Federalists were the champions of an ideal without which the Republic could not have endured.[32]

During the period of their ascendancy, the Federalists constantly inveighed against the "pernicious," the "baleful," the "abominable" doctrine of states' rights. Here, they exclaimed, was the eternal enemy of national prosperity and greatness, the opening wedge for demagoguery, foreign intrigue, and civil war. At this time, of course, the Federalists were not aware that the time would come when they embraced this hateful thing and acclaimed it a refuge against Jeffersonian Democracy.[33]

The Federalists were wedded to a philosophy of human nature which proved more enduring than their nationalism: in the end, these patricians were left with little except their contempt of the people. To a considerable degree, this attitude was derived from the struggle between creditors' rights, and majority rule which had been waged in the states during the period of the Articles of Confederation and which had seriously undermined the optimistic faith in human possibilities that had illuminated the Declaration of Independence. Viewing human nature through a glass darkly, the Federalists recoiled from what they saw: instead of being temperate, wise, and virtuous, mankind in the mass seemed to be actuated by cupidity, envy, and malice. "The most ferocious of all animals, when his passions are roused to fury and uncontrolled, is man," said Fisher Ames. "Men are often false to their country and their honor, false to duty and even to interest, but multitudes of men are never long false or deaf to their passions."[34] "The many," said George Cabot, "do not think at all"—they were purely creatures of feeling. Ames and Cabot believed that this assessment was the product of a candid and dispassionate examination of human nature. The leaders of the Federalist party were not merely politicians—they were students of psychology who had mastered, to their own satisfaction, what in the eighteenth century was called "the science of human nature."[35]

[32] *Gazette of the United States,* August 8, 1790; *Annals of Congress,* XI, 84.
[33] *Gazette of the United States,* May 1, 1800.
[34] Ames, *Fisher Ames,* II, 79–80; 394–395.
[35] Lodge, *George Cabot,* pp. 119–120; Johnston, *Jay,* IV, 215–216.

Men being what they were, the Federalists concluded that government must be rendered capable of resisting the passions of the people. "The delusions of democracy, like other delusions of the human mind," it was pointed out, "cannot be resisted by reason and truth alone. . . . Reason will not answer—reason will not protect your houses, ships and stables from thieves. You must have for protection the controlling *fear of God and fear of Government.*"[36]

In the democratic state, as the Federalists viewed it, no one feared either God or government; instead, popular majorities ruled without let or hindrance and the sovereign people gave free rein to every whim and desire, however transitory and injurious to the public welfare. Federalists prided themselves upon being Fighters against Democracy: in their eyes, none were more worthy of honor than those who did battle against egalitarians and demagogues. In 1801, Noah Webster boasted that he had spent "the largest part of eighteen years in opposing Democracy." He thought that if the American people understood their true interests, they would gratefully commemorate his efforts to save them from that slough of despond.

In combating democracy and all its works, the Federalists supposed that they were upholding the cause of freedom. Their purpose, as they conceived it, was to save the country from the despotism produced by "popular delusion, injustice and tyranny." They proclaimed themselves to be the friends of "temperate liberty"—not the kind which came like a whirlwind effacing established institutions and leveling distinctions, but the mild, benignant variety which cast the mantle of the law over the rights and property of every individual. "American liberty," said Fisher Ames, "calms and restrains the licentious passions, like an angel, that says to the winds and troubled seas, be still." True freedom, they pointed out, could not be enjoyed unless some rights were curtailed: "Honest men must submit to the force that is necessary to govern rogues. . . . To make a nation free, the crafty must be kept in awe, and the violent in restraint."[37] In their own eyes, the Federalists

[36] *Impartial Herald* (Suffolk, Conn.), May 21, 1799; C. F. Volney, *A View of Climate and Soil of the United States* (Philadelphia, 1804), pp. xii–xiii; S. E. Morison, *Life and Letters of Harrison Gray Otis, Federalist, 1765–1848* (Boston, 1913), I, 280; Morison, *Jeremiah Smith*, p. 96.

[37] John Jay, who represented the more liberal wing of Federalism, said: "Civil liberty consists not in a right to every man to do just what he pleases, but it consists in an equal right to all the citizens to have, enjoy and to do, in peace, security and without molestation, whatever the equal and constitutional laws of the country admit to be consistent with the public good." Johnston, *Jay*, III, 395.

were the true heirs of the American Revolution: the patriots of 1776, they said, had never defined liberty as the privilege of a mob to do as it pleased. Tyranny, they knew, bore many faces, and they were resolved to fight it whether it came in the guise of King George and his ministers or the American populace.[38]

In keeping with their view of human nature, the Federalists did not credit the mass of the people with sufficient intelligence to make themselves a threat to the established order. In themselves, the people were nothing; it was only when they were set in motion by demagogues that they became dangerous. In short, the people needed leadership—and they found it, the Federalists lamented, in the most unscrupulous, self-seeking, and unprincipled members of society. "The republicanism of a great mass of people," said Fisher Ames, "is often nothing more than a blind trust in certain favorites, and a less blind and still more furious hatred of their enemies." The trouble was that the people were unable to distinguish between their true friends and enemies; as a result, democracy became the rule by the worst passions of the worst men in the community.[39]

The mark of a demagogue, in the Federalists' opinion, was not only that he gave the people an inflated sense of their own importance but that he set the poor against the rich. To the Federalists, the central theme of history was the struggle between the opulent members of the community and "the discontented and factious at the head of the poor. . . . The jealousy of the rich is a passion in the poor which can always be appealed to with success on every question, and . . . the engine by which a giddy populace can be most easily wrought on to do mischief." Chancellor Kent summoned history to prove his contention that "there is a constant tendency in the poor to covet and to share the plunder of the rich; in the debtor to relax or avoid the obligations of interest; in the indolent and profligate to cast the whole burden of society upon the industrious and virtuous; and there is a tendency in ambitious and wicked men to inflame those combustible materials." Federalists agreed that "the poor we have always with us,"

[38] Ames, *Fisher Ames, II,* 212, 360, 392–394; Henry Adams (ed.), *Documents Relating to New England Federalism, 1800–1815* (Boston, 1887), p. 341; Volney, *A View,* pp. xii–xv; Lord Acton, *Essays on Freedom and Power* (Boston, 1948), pp. 209–210; Ford and Skeel, *Noah Webster,* I, 482; Gibbs, *Memoirs,* II, 319.

[39] Lodge, *George Cabot,* p. 322; Johnston, *Jay,* IV, 204; Warfel, *Noah Webster,* pp. 264, 267.

1. The State House in Philadelphia
(Courtesy, Print Room, New York Public Library)

2. Philadelphia in the 1790's
Engraving by William Birch
(Courtesy, Historical Society of Pennsylvania)

3. JOHN JAY

Painting by John Trumbull

(Courtesy of State of New York and
Frick Art Reference Library)

4. ALEXANDER HAMILTON

Replica after full-length painting
by John Trumbull

(Courtesy, Yale University
Art Gallery)

5. EDMUND RANDOLPH

F. J. Fisher copy of Gilbert Stuart painting

(Courtesy of State of Virginia and Dementi
Studio, Richmond, Virginia)

6. JOHN ADAMS

Painting by Charles Willson Peale

(Independence National Historical
Park Collection)

HIGH FEDERALISTS

7. FISHER AMES

Miniature by John Trumbull

(Courtesy, Yale University Art Gallery)

8. ROBERT GOODLOE HARPER

Ivory miniature by
Robert Field
(Courtesy, Maryland Historical
Society)

9. TIMOTHY PICKERING
By anonymous American artist
(Courtesy, Frick Art Reference
Library)

10. OLIVER WOLCOTT, JR.

By G. L. Nelson after
Trumbull
(Courtesy of First National
City Bank of New York and
New-York Historical Society)

11. Inauguration of Washington

Engraved for Washington Irving's *Life of Washington*

12. Mount Vernon

Engraving of drawing by William Birch

(Courtesy, Print Room, New York Public Library, Phelps Stokes Collection)

13. GEORGE WASHINGTON

Crayon drawing by C. B. J. F. de Saint-Mémin, said to be the last portrait done from life, as reproduced in Elizabeth B. Johnston's *Original Portraits of Washington* (1882)

(New York Public Library)

AMERICANS
ABROAD

14. JOHN QUINCY ADAMS

Painting by
John Singleton Copley

(Courtesy, Museum of
Fine Arts, Boston)

15. GOUVERNEUR MORRIS

Painting by James Sharples

(Courtesy of John S. Turnbull
and Frick Art Reference Library)

16. JAMES MADISON

Painting by Charles Willson Peale

(Courtesy of Gilcrease Foundation,
Tulsa, Oklahoma, and Hirshl and
Adler Galleries, Inc., New York City)

17. THOMAS JEFFERSON

Painting by
Charles Willson Peale

(Independence National
Historical Park Collection)

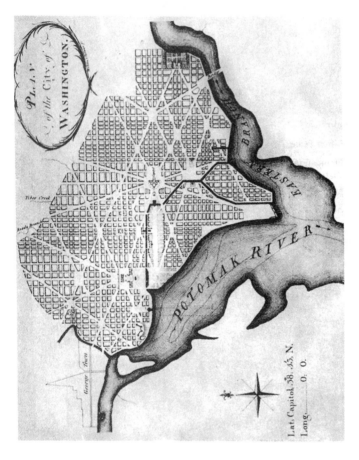

18. Plan of City of Washington

From *Universal Asylum and Columbian Magazine*, March, 1792

(Courtesy, Rare Book Room, New York Library)

19. Georgetown and Federal City
Engraving of Beck painting
(Courtesy of Print Room, New York Library, Phelps Stokes Collection)

PRINCIPALS
OF THE
X, Y, Z
AFFAIR

20. CHARLES COTESWORTH PINCKNEY

Miniature by Charles Fraser

(Courtesy, Carolina Art Association,
Gibbes Art Gallery, Charleston, S.C.)

21. TALLEYRAND

Miniature by anonymous
French painter
(Courtesy, C. Townsend Ludington and
Frick Art Reference Library)

22. JOHN MARSHALL

Etching by Allen Rosenthal after
painting by Chester Harding

(Courtesy, Print Room, New York
Public Library)

23. ELBRIDGE GERRY

By unknown artist, after
John Vanderlyn

(Courtesy, The Fogg Art
Museum)

24. JAMES MONROE

Ivory miniature by Jean François Sené

(Courtesy, The James Monroe Law Office
Museum, Fredericksburg, Virginia, and
the Frick Art Reference Library)

25. ALBERT GALLATIN

Painting by Gilbert Stuart

(Courtesy, The Metropolitan Museum of Art,
Gift of Frederic W. Stevens)

JEFFERSONIAN REPUBLICANS

26. THOMAS PAINE

Painting by John Wesley Jarvis

(Courtesy, National Gallery of Art)

27. "Mad Tom in a Rage," a Federalist cartoon attacking Jefferson, who is pictured as a brandy-soaked anarchist tearing down the pillars of government.

(Courtesy, Library of Congress)

28. "Griswold-Lyon Fight"

(Courtesy, Print Room, New York Public Library)

but they could not say as much for the rich: exposed to assaults of ignorance and poverty, the rich seemed to have but a slim chance of survival in a democratic state.[40]

As for warning the people to beware of the wiles of demagogues, the Federalists feared it was wasted effort. For one thing, the people seemed incapable of resisting the blandishments of these seducers of unquiet souls: a few honeyed words and they were ready to yield all. In the second place, the Federalists were inclined to regard demagogues as an inevitable concomitant of freedom: "The more free the citizens," they said, "the bolder and more profligate will be their demagogues." Since poverty was also regarded as an inescapable by-product of freedom, it seemed to the Federalists that in the United States demagogues would never want materials upon which to work. Already, mourned Noah Webster, the "preposterous doctrine of equality" had "stripped old men of dignity and wise men of their influence."[41]

In a democracy, the Federalists believed that the normal course of events was from disaster to catastrophe. Bad as was majority rule, they did not suppose that it was the last word in abominations. Men could not long endure the chaos produced by popular majorities which did the bidding of demagogues: the only good that Federalists could say of democracy was that it was soon over. In itself, democracy was merely a way station on the way to the Inferno: in Fisher Ames's words, "like death, it is only the dismal passport to a more dismal hereafter." That hereafter was the despotism of one man whose mission it was to put an end to freedom, including the freedom of the majority to do as it pleased. And for this service, the dictator was hailed by the people as their savior—as indeed he was, for he had saved them from their worst enemy, themselves.[42]

There was no danger that a Federalist would be mistaken for a demagogue. Federalists prided themselves upon their disdain of "the vile love of popularity": even if political office depended upon it, they swore that they would not truckle to the people. They repeatedly declared that they would rather be right than be popular, and it is in-

[40] Gibbs, *Memoirs,* I, 331; Lodge, *George Cabot,* 180, 231; Morris, *Gouverneur Morris,* II, 429; Sparks, *Gouverneur Morris,* III, October 10, 1802; Harold R. Pennman (ed.), *Sait's American Parties and Elections* (New York, 1948), p. 22; Ford and Skeel, *Noah Webster,* p. 267.

[41] Ford and Skeel, *Noah Webster,* I, 479.

[42] Ames, *Fisher Ames,* I, 324; II, 353, 382; Sparks, *Gouverneur Morris,* II, April 23, 1803; April 11, 1804; Adams, *New England Federalism,* p. 341.

dicative of their state of mind that they believed it was rarely possible
to be both. "I have frequently been the servant of the people, always
their friend," said Gouverneur Morris; "but not one moment of my
life their flatterer, and God forbid that I ever should be." In 1797,
Rufus King accounted it a paradox that the people were "less wrong
than their government, which, everywhere seems to be destitute of both
wisdom and courage."[43]

The Federalists were careful to distinguish between democracy and
republicanism. At the same time that they expressed their detestation
of democracy, they professed veneration for republicanism. They regarded democracy as the uncontrolled will of the people operating
through the government, whereas republicanism imposed restraints
upon the power of the people, taught respect for law and order, and
discriminated between liberty and licentiousness.[44]

Despite their abhorrence of democracy, Federalists admitted that it
was an integral part of every well-ordered government. But—and upon
this point Federalists were especially emphatic—it was not the whole
of government. Their ideal was a "mixed government" composed of
democracy, aristocracy, and monarchy poised in such delicate equilibrium that no single element could make itself dominant over the government. The branch allotted to the people was the House of
Representatives—and this, said the Federalists, was all any people
who wished to be truly free had a right to ask. For if the democratic
part of the government succeeded in making itself supreme—and the
Federalists believed that it was the nature of democracy to grasp at
all power—despotism resulted.[45]

Thus the Federalists were willing to acclaim the people sovereign
but not to invest them with the plenitude of authority usually attached
to that title. Government of the people they could accept, but not
government by the people. Instead of the people ruling the government, the Federalists wished to see the government rule according to
the Constitution. The people, in short, were to reign but not to rule,
that important function being reserved for "the choice sort of people,"
sober and discreet men, seasoned by wealth and education and dedicated to keeping the passions of the populace within bounds. To whom

[43] *Annals of Congress,* XI, 41; Rufus King to Hamilton, August 5, 1797,
Rufus King MSS., NYHS.
[44] Ames, *Fisher Ames,* II, 79, 81, 212–214.
[45] Adams, *New England Federalism,* p. 363; *Gazette of the United States,*
August 18, 1793.

else could this description apply but to the leaders of the Federalist party? And, in fact, as organizers and managers of businesses and banks, the Federalists brought skills to the government which it sorely needed; even their enemies admitted that they were men of rare constructive administrative ability. During their tenure of power, no Federalist officeholder was found guilty of malfeasance.[46]

In essence, the Federalists' doctrine was that men cannot live by liberty alone; order and stability were often in conflict with the popular will, and in such instances order and stability must prevail. The real danger to liberty, from their point of view, came from the people themselves: where the people were all-powerful, liberty perished. Nor did they deny the converse of this maxim: where the government was all-powerful, liberty was extinguished. They were not advocates of an omnipotent government; their ideal was a government capable of moderating "the unruly passions of men" but at the same time limited in its powers. For while the Federalists looked to the general government for protection against the "rapacious democrats" in the states, they did not ignore the possibility—and, after 1796, a very real possibility it was—that the democrats would gain control of the general government itself. Unlike Edmund Burke, the great English conservative, they did not consecrate the state—there was too much danger that it would fall into the wrong hands.

Beset by democrats, demagogues, and disorganizers, the Federalists looked upon the President as their rock of salvation. To him they gladly assigned the responsibilities of leadership in both foreign and domestic affairs. "It is upon the Executive we depend for the execution of the laws and for general protection," declared a Federalist congressman. He is "the cement of our Union, the representative of the whole people." A Federalist was expected to construe the powers of the President broadly and to defend his prerogatives against legislative encroachment. In this regard, Fisher Ames set a model for his party: it was said that Ames seldom spoke without casting aspersions upon the House of Representatives and bestowing praise upon the President.[47]

Nevertheless, when it came to strengthening executive powers, many Federalist congressmen experienced a sharp conflict of loyalties. On the

[46] Ames, *Fisher Ames*, II, 140, 348; Lodge, *George Cabot*, pp. 318–319, 340; Adams, *New England Federalism*, p. 341.
[47] White, *Jeffersonians*, p. 29; Ames, *Fisher Ames*, I, 212–213, 216; Acton, *Essays on Freedom and Power*, pp. 211–212.

one hand, they were eager to erect the Presidency into a tower of strength against "popular licentiousness"; on the other hand, *esprit de corps* attached them to their own particular branch of the government. For the most part, however, the fear that the rule of Congress would mean the triumph of democracy—"it will play the mob at last," Fisher Ames predicted—kept Federalist members of Congress loyal to the executive. Not only did they look with equanamity upon the aggrandizement of the executive—they cheerfully abnegated powers of Congress in order to ensure that he did not want authority.[48]

Experience had taught the Federalists that the principal work of government must be in neutralizing "the follies and vices of men." Nevertheless, they did not take a wholly negative view of the functions of government; besides holding down the lid on the democratic caldron, they expected government to act in behalf of the business interests of the country by means of tariffs, bounties, and other aids. As British subjects, Americans had learned the advantages as well as the disadvantages of mercantilism; and now, emancipated from British control, they wished to perpetuate the advantages of that system. "Government," they said, "is formed to promote the general good, and that government is best which tends most directly to that end."[49]

When Federalists saw the Great Beast—a democratic majority led around by demagogues—stalking the land, they trembled for property rights, particularly the kind of property rights they represented. As a creditor class and the owners of stocks, bonds, ships, factories, and the like, they were vulnerable to the attacks of small landowners bent upon expropriating unpopular forms of wealth without affecting, of course, their own real estate holdings. Against this doctrine that certain forms of wealth were reprehensible and therefore subject to whatever interference the majority deemed desirable, the Federalists asserted that wealth of every kind whatsoever was equally meritorious and entitled to the protection of the laws. They admitted no real difference between fluid wealth and real estate; and money acquired by trade, banking, or speculation was quite as honorific in their eyes as wealth derived from the tillage of the soil. Upon the sanctity of property rights they based all the rights of man; if property could be invaded by a government

[48] Lodge, *Hamilton*, VI, 201–202; Ames, *Fisher Ames*, I, 212–213.
[49] *Annals of Congress*, XI, 38; John Jay, *An Address to the People of the State of New York* (New York, 1797), p. 5.

acting at the behest of a majority, no other rights were safe. In the necessity of protecting property and ensuring the tranquillity of society, Federalists found the ultimate sanction of all government.[50]

In portraying themselves as the champions of property rights against democratic majorities, the Federalists drew upon their experience under the Articles of Confederation. At that time, some states had enacted laws which, besides invalidating the vested rights of creditors, had struck against freedom of speech and the civil rights of unpopular religious minorities. Thus the Federalists were presented with an opportunity to stand forth as the defenders of minority rights in general —of asserting the principle that the majority was not everything, that the minority had indefeasible rights that could not be rightfully invaded by "the sudden impulse of mere majorities." Instead of rising to this challenge, the Federalists confined themselves to championing the cause of the "opulent minority" of manufacturers, speculators, professional men, and well-to-do farmers. They upheld only one of the rights of man—the right of property. Toward the other inalienable rights, they showed scant respect. Indeed, before it had run its course, Federalism demonstrated that freedom stood in quite as much danger from a minority composed of the wise, the rich, and the good as from a democratic majority.[51]

While the rights of property occupied a central place in Federalists' thinking, it was far from being the sum total of their philosophy. Their range of vision was more spacious: it embraced the Good Society in all its aspects, political, social, and economic. The Federalists' objective was to mold the United States in accord with their vision of an established order securely protected against demagogues and democratic majorities. This vision took the form of a highly aristocratic, class-conscious society in which gentlemen knew their privileges and the lower orders knew their place—the price, the Federalists insisted, of order, stability, and progress.[52]

Federalism was not a wholly static political philosophy: it changed with the times, but its progress was not in the direction of liberalism. Under the impact of the shattering events of the 1790's, conservatives tended to become archconservatives. The innovators of 1788 had by

---

[50] Ames, *Fisher Ames,* II, 166.

[51] Ames, *Fisher Ames,* II, 166; Acton, *Essays on Freedom and Power,* p. 209.

[52] Change, said John Jay, should be brought about "soberly, by sober and discreet men, and in due manner, measure and proportion." Johnston, *Jay,* IV, 216.

1800 become the dedicated champions of things as they were. "We have sailed round the world of novelty," said John Ward Fenno, a Federalist newspaper editor, "without making any discovery worth retaining, except that our discoveries are worthless." The one discovery that Fenno wished his countrymen to retain was that "Providence hath wisely ordained a chain of grades and subordinances, from the peasant to the peer." The authoritarian element became progressively stronger in the party; distrust of the people became more pronounced. Increasingly, Federalists revealed themselves to be more intolerant, more disposed to castigate "popular delusions," and more inclined to throw up their hands in despair at the iniquities of the times. Had the Federalists been in a position in 1800 to draw up a Constitution for the United States, it would have borne little resemblance to the frame of government which emanated from the Philadelphia Convention in 1787.[53]

In proclaiming these ideas, the Federalist leaders were a minority within a minority. Sensible as they were that they did not have the support of the mass of the American people, they were denied the comfort of knowing that their views were shared by a majority of their own partisans. Fisher Ames lamented that there were not one hundred people in Massachusetts who subscribed wholeheartedly to his views, but he did not for that reason think any the less highly of his ideas or adhere to them less pertinaciously. If their opinions condemned them to isolation, it was in their eyes a splendid isolation comparable to Olympus or Sinai.[54]

The Federalists never experienced the exhilarating sensation of riding the wave of the future; instead, they feared that they were about to be engulfed by that wave and to perish "miserably on the shoals of democracy"—the graveyard of republics. Seldom, as a result, was a Federalist politician a happy or optimistic man. Even in moments of victory, the leaders of the party were oppressed by forebodings of future disasters: they might win battles but they seemed certain to lose the war. Their work appeared to be built upon sand; in the United States, everything changed and, the Federalists feared, for the worst. Keeping down the democrats in a country teeming with "faction and revolution" was to be an endless task much beyond the strength of a little band of gentlemen, however devoted to the cause of upholding reason and good order. George Cabot expressed a mood common

[53] Fenno, *Desultory Reflections,* II, 32.
[54] Adams, *Gallatin,* p. 199.

among Federalists when he wrote in 1797: "Our friends have hope & even expect that things will all go well, but . . . I always expect the contrary." Given Cabot's philosophy, gloom and despondency were to be expected: "In the present state of society," he observed, "folly and the vices which are its natural offspring, have a power which cannot be overcome." Gouverneur Morris came to the conclusion that it was as futile to attempt to instill wisdom in the people as to preach religion to unbelievers: "They are to be converted only by suffering," he observed. "They must be schooled with adversity, where their false friends are their teachers. After some smart correction, they may be more manageable."[55]

Dismal as was the present, the Federalists feared that the future had even worse in store. For them, there was no millennium: always the few wise and virtuous would be obliged to struggle against brutishness and greed of the many. The mold of human nature had been cast for all time—and so, said John Jay, "there will be wars, and commotions, and tyrants and factions, and demagogues and . . . they will do mischief as they have opportunity." What was even more disheartening, irrationality and vice would always prove an overmatch in this world for rectitude and goodness. Nothing endured except human folly and the envy of the poor for the well-to-do.[56]

If demagoguery flourished in the United States under the conditions that existed in the 1790's, what would it be like, the Federalists asked themselves, when, as a result of capitalistic development, the United States would be the home of "many poor, and a few rich, many grossly ignorant, an inconsiderable number learned, and a few eminently learned"? The Federalists regarded themselves as the destined victims of an economic and political process that would leave the proletariat triumphant. In their eyes, this was the end, not the beginning, of the Good Society.[57]

While the Federalists rejoiced that the United States was not yet a democracy, they trembled at the symptoms of the dread malady they beheld on every hand. Zealously as they labored to arrest its progress, they were more than half convinced that the case was hopeless. Cer-

[55] Ames, *Fisher Ames,* I, 237, 348; II, 204, 368; Gibbs, *Memoirs,* II, 319; Lodge, *George Cabot,* 322; Sparks, *Gouverneur Morris,* III, April 11, 1809; Morison, *Otis,* I, 280.

[56] Johnston, *Jay,* IV, 204, 215–216; Gibbs, *Memoirs,* I, 264; Lodge, *George Cabot,* pp. 119–120; Ames, *Fisher Ames,* I, 263; J. C. Hamilton, *Hamilton,* V, 200.

[57] Ames, *Fisher Ames,* II, 142; Lodge, *George Cabot,* p. 180.

tainly they never claimed that they had hit upon the cure; at the end of his life, Fisher Ames was still saying that "our disease is democracy. It is not the skin that festers—our very bones are carious, and their marrow blackens with gangrene." But it was small consolation to Ames that he had detected the malignancy at the outset and that his prognosis had been verified: the diagnosis was correct but the patient died.

This sense of insecurity was aggravated by the Federalists' realization that the United States was a republic in form only: at heart the people were "democrats playing at republicanism" and it was only a matter of time before they would seek to change the form as well as the substance of the government. As Republicans of an earlier vintage, the Federalists suspected that they were trying to sell an out-of-date political philosophy to a people who hankered for absolute liberty. Already, they lamented, the people were unwilling to suffer any superiority in rank, to pay deference to those high in the economic and social scale, and to yield obedience to government when the laws ran contrary to their wishes. And so the Federalists steeled themselves for the coming triumph of democracy in the same frame of mind with which they might have awaited the Deluge.[58]

As the conservative mood grew upon them, Federalists began to fear the proletariat of the cities no less than did Jefferson. "The rabble of great cities is the standing army of ambition," they said. ". . . . Cities are seats of vanity, ignorance and vice" where the basest passions held sway. In Massachusetts, said Stephen Higginson, Boston contained "all the seditious, and degenerate"—a happy hunting ground for demagogues in search of a democratic majority.[59]

To save them from the mobbish workingmen of the cities, the Federalists looked to the farmers—as well they might—for the American electorate consisted at this time of about half a million citizens, the overwhelming majority of whom were farmers. They rejoiced that at least one state—Connecticut—was "not troubled with ungovernable chief towns, nor with any other convenient harbours for villains or parricides." Like Jefferson, they regarded farmers as "cautious and reflecting men" whose passions were moderated by the fact that they had a substantial stake in the country. To keep these estimable citizens out of the hands of "the tempters in the seaports, and their mobs" became

[58] Gibbs, *Memoirs*, II, 319; J. C. Hamilton, *Hamilton*, V, 201–202; Ames, *Fisher Ames*, I, 237, 398.

[59] J. C. Hamilton, *Hamilton*, V, 571; Gibbs, *Memoirs*, I, 127–130; Lodge, *George Cabot*, pp. 318–319; Ames, *Fisher Ames*, I, 182, 441.

a constant concern to the Federalists. Thus the Federalists loved the
farmers no less than did Jefferson, but they loved and lost—for in the
end the farmers embraced Republicanism. Yet it is noteworthy that in
their protestations of affection the Federalists never gave priority to
the welfare of the farmers; instead, they contented themselves with
pointing out that the interests of business and agriculture were indissolubly united and that what benefited the one must benefit the other.[60]

Although Jefferson did not make universal suffrage an immediate
objective of the Republican party—he thought that universal suffrage
ought to wait upon universal education—the Federalists strenuously
opposed it with or without education on the ground that government
ought to be by "the choice sort of people." Indeed, as the 1790's pro-
gressed, the Federalists became increasingly insistent upon property
qualifications for voting. Their only regret was that so many Americans
were permitted to vote since so many voted the wrong way. Even with
limited suffrage, the Federalists believed, "the rights of property and
the principles of liberty" were in jeopardy from the electorate. Gouverneur Morris predicted that if the suffrage were expanded, the people
would sell their votes to the highest bidder. Noah Webster declared
that "a republican government can be rendered durable in no other
way than by excluding from elections men who have so little property,
education, or principle, that they were liable to yield their own opinions
to the guidance of unprincipled leaders." The future dictionary maker
urged that the age limit for voting be raised to forty-five years and
that no man be eligible for public office until he had reached the age
of fifty.[61]

Much as the Federalists affected to hold public opinion in contempt,
they did not act upon the maxim: "The public be damned." They admitted—although it cost them many a pang—that in a government
constituted as was that of the United States, public opinion ultimately
prevailed. They therefore sponsored petitions and addresses, took an
active part in local government, and established newspapers. The *Gazette of the United States,* the New York *Minerva,* the Hartford

[60] Thomas C. Amory, *Life of James Sullivan* (Boston, 1859), II, 138;
Gazette of the United States, August 1, 1795; Gibbs, *Memoirs,* I, 127–128,
331; Ames, *Fisher Ames,* I, 182; II, 441–442.
[61] Ford and Skeel, *Noah Webster,* I, 479; Warfel, *Noah Webster,* pp. 264,
267; Dauer, *Adams Federalists,* p. 211.

Courant, and *Porcupine's Gazette* were among the most influential
of the Federalist newspapers; and these newspapers enlisted the talents
of such redoubtable writers as Alexander Hamilton, John Jay, Rufus
King, and Noah Webster.[62]

Instead of currying favor with the people, the Federalists attempted
to instruct them in "salutary truths." As preceptors of the American
people, the Federalists were so busy laying down "truisms" and hand-
ing out advice that they had no time to consider their pupils' opinions
in matters of state. Not, however, that they thought that the people
had anything to say worth listening to: the labor of imparting wisdom
was, in their estimation, strictly a one-way process—from the top to
the bottom.[63]

It is significant that the Federalists' efforts were mainly directed
toward the "rectification" of popular errors. Whenever they conceived
public opinion to be wrong—and it was rare that they considered it
to be otherwise—they undertook to set it right. It became almost an
article of the Federalists' creed that anything popular was contrary
to the best interests of the community. It was not an attitude calculated
to produce mutual esteem and confidence between the people and
their government.

It was a peculiarity of the "truths" with which they sought to edify
the American people that they were not easy to swallow. Against the
glittering fallacies retailed by Jefferson and his partisans, the Federalists
acknowledged that their own unvarnished wares could not compete. In
the political market, they complained, the base and meretricious drove
out the unblemished and genuine article.

In the struggle between the Federalist and Republican parties for
control of the national government that began in 1792, the Federalists'
principal sources of strength were that they had saved the country
from "chaos" in 1787–88; that they represented the forces of law and
order against democratic "levelism"; that they were the guardians of
the rights of property and the upholders of the dignity and honor of
the United States abroad. But the most precious asset of the Federalists
was President Washington; under the shelter of his renown, Hamilton
was able to bring to fruition his plans for transforming the American

[62] *Annals of Congress,* XI, 91–92.

[63] Ford and Skeel, *Noah Webster,* I, 479; McLaughlin, *American Democracy,* pp. 81–83; James Cheetham, *Reply to Aristides* (New York, 1804), p. 87.

economy.[64] True, Washington, as befitted the Father of His Country, was above party, yet he favored the domestic policies of the Secretary of the Treasury and kept him in office despite the clamor of his political enemies. To the end, he believed that Hamilton was sincerely seeking to promote the welfare of the country. Like a good Hamiltonian, Washington made it his practice "to contemplate the United States, as one great whole . . . and to consult only the substantial and permanent interests of our country." But Washington was a Federalist of a very special kind: his nationalism did not prevent him from trusting the people. In words reminiscent of Thomas Jefferson he declared that "the *mass* of our Citizens require no more than to understand a question to decide it properly."[65]

In the early stages of the party contest, the Federalists enjoyed the advantage of better organization, more administrative experience, and control of Federal offices. Even so, as early as the presidential election of 1792, the Republicans were able to register a significant measure of support for George Clinton, their candidate for the Vice-Presidency. A unanimous vote for Clinton was cast by the electors of New York, North Carolina, and Georgia. New York's adherence in this election to the "southern interest" was a portent of the later alliance between New York and Virginia—an alliance which exerted decisive influence upon the political history of the United States.

By 1793, observers of the congressional scene were comparing the discipline and regimentation of the two parties to Prussian and French military units: they wheeled, maneuvered, and voted, it was remarked, like soldiers obeying the orders of their officers. Each party considered the other to be superior in this respect: Jefferson lamented that the Hamiltonians exhibited in Congress all the precision of a "squadron"; and Fisher Ames warned his fellow Federalists that if victory were to go to the party that displayed the most activity and resourcefulness, the Republicans were certain to prevail. Thus rivalry and emulation tended to stimulate party activity.[66]

During most of the period of Federalist ascendancy, the House of Representatives was almost evenly divided between the two parties. In

[64] Hart, *American Presidency*, p. 67.

[65] Fitzpatrick, *Washington*, XXXIV, 252; XXXVI, December 4, 1797.

[66] George Hammond to Lord Grenville, March 7, 1793, Hammond MSS., LC; *Pennsylvania Magazine of History and Biography*, LXVI, 458; Charles, *Origins of the American Party System*, pp. 92–93; John Taylor, *A Definition of Parties*, p. 2; Ames, *Fisher Ames, Works*, I, 127.

1796, for example, there were fifty-six Republicans and forty-nine Federalists in the House. Two years later, the Federalists had a majority of five. In the Senate, on the other hand, the Federalists consistently chalked up a majority. Nevertheless, especially in the House of Representatives, many members refused to wear the livery of either party; instead, they made a point of voting as the interests of their state and section, rather than the party leaders, dictated. Even as late as the Third Congress (1795–96) almost half the members of the House prided themselves upon being free of party ties and obligations.[67]

The greatest danger to the Union forged at Philadelphia in 1787 was sectionalism; and no form of sectionalism was more dreaded by the framers of the Constitution than the division of the country into political parties. President Washington attempted to avert this evil by apportioning the highest offices at his disposal equally between the North and South: in 1789–90 he appointed Northerners to the posts of Secretary of the Treasury and Secretary of War, whereas the Secretary of State and the Attorney General were Southerners. This balance of power was preserved until 1795, when President Washington reluctantly admitted that the genii of sectionalism, inadvertently uncorked by Hamilton, could not be laid simply by giving the rival sections equal representation in the cabinet. Henceforth, instead of striving to maintain a sectional balance among the heads of departments, Washington insisted upon political orthodoxy among his advisers—orthodoxy being, of course, Federalism. "I shall not, whilst I have the honor to administer the government," he said in September, 1795, "bring any man into any office of consequence knowingly whose political tenets are adverse to the measures which the general government are pursuing; for this, in my opinion, would be a sort of political suicide."[68]

The sectional composition of the cabinet after 1795 reflected the political state of the country. By 1793, from the Federalist point of view, Virginia had become the enemy's country. While vestiges remained in the Northern Neck and in the area around Alexandria and Richmond, elsewhere the ruin of the party was almost complete.

---

[67] Channing, *History*, IV, 150–151; *Quarterly Journal of the University of North Dakota*, Vol. 3, Nos. II, III, IV; *Proceedings of the Massachusetts Historical Society*, XLVII (1914), 40–41; *American Historical Review*, XIV (1909), 787; *Gazette of the United States*, March 4, 1794.

[68] Beard, *Economic Origins of Jeffersonian Democracy*, p. 66.

Among the lawyers of the Old Dominion—a sure indicator of the shift that had occurred since 1790—only Bushrod Washington and Charles Lee remained loyal to Federalism.[69] In the South, South Carolina stood as a lonely outpost in what Federalists regarded as a democratic wasteland. But this outpost was not only under attack from without; the enemy was already in the Federalists' midst. The western part of the state was strongly Republican; only in Charleston and the lowland planting areas did Federalism hold its ground. Unhappily for the Federalists, the continuance of their rule depended upon maintaining a system of representation which discriminated against the western counties. Since the retention of the vote of South Carolina was essential to a Federalist victory in presidential elections after 1792, the northern leaders of the party habitually kept their eyes glued to the political barometer in this key state.[70]

The great majority of the American people were hardly more than spectators of the struggle being waged in Congress and at the polls between Republicans and Federalists. In the early 1790's, in some elections which exercised vital bearing upon national concerns, only about 3 per cent of the population voted. Not that 97 per cent of the potential electorate was disfranchised by property requirements from voting; the small turnout was owing, rather, to the failure of qualified voters to take the trouble to register their opinion. Outside New England, where the majority of citizens took part in elections at least on the town-meeting level, the custom of going to the polls was not widely practiced. It is significant that it was not until the appearance of political parties, with their arresting slogans, leaders who dramatically personified the political issues of the day, and techniques for getting out the vote, that any large number of Americans took advantage of their right to vote. The impressive increase in the popular vote of 1800 over that of 1788—far greater than was warranted by the increase in population—resulted primarily from the interest generated in politics by the rival political parties.[71]

[69] Elizabeth Cometti, "John Rutledge, Jr., Federalist," *Journal of Southern History*, XIII (1947), 196–202; Hamilton, *Monroe*, I, 252; Gibbs, *Memoirs*, I, 300, 303, 373; Hunt, *Madison*, VI, 123; Fitzpatrick, *Washington*, XXX, 9, 37, 509.

[70] Ulrich B. Phillips, "The South Carolina Federalists," *American Historical Review*, XIV (1909), 292–312.

[71] Beard, *Economic Origins of Jeffersonian Democracy*, p. 99; DeConde, *Entangling Alliance*, p. 87; Cunningham, *Jeffersonian Republicans*, p. 259.

CHAPTER 8

Genêt and the French Alliance

AS A divisive force in American politics, the French Revolution cut a deeper swath than did even Hamiltonian finance. At first, most Americans rejoiced in the French Revolution: they were too close to their own revolution not to feel strongly sympathetic toward a people struggling against despotism. The key to the Bastille was sent to Washington by Lafayette, thereby symbolizing the consanguinity of the two revolutions. But as early as 1789, some American conservatives began to view the course of events in France with misgivings; and in August, 1790, Washington, while insisting that the French people must be left free to work out their own destiny, protested against the dangers "resulting from too great eagerness in swallowing something so delightful as liberty." By 1793, it had become one of the canons of the Federalist party that the French Revolution was an outpouring from the depths of society of irreligion, anarchy, and massacre. In Federalist eyes, there was no more affinity between the American and French revolutions than between virtue and vice.[1]

The Republicans preserved their enthusiasm for the French Revolution despite the riots, the massacres, the execution of the King and Queen, and the Jacobin Terror. Although Jefferson preferred to see a limited monarchy—better suited, he thought, than a republic for the "uninformed mass"—he believed that regardless of the excesses to

---

[1] Stuart Gerry Brown (ed.), *The Autobiography of James Monroe* (Syracuse, 1959), pp. 54–55; Lodge, *Hamilton*, IV, April, 1793; VII, 266, 361; Hunt, *Madison*, VI, 321; Charles D. Hazen, *Contemporary American Opinion of the French Revolution* (Baltimore, 1897), p. 11; Ford, *Jefferson*, I, 268.

which the Revolution gave rise, it would end happily in the triumph of order and liberty. He deplored the fate of the victims of the Terror, but their deaths seemed to him necessary and, in some cases, salutary: "The liberty of the whole earth was depending on the issue of the contest," he said, "and . . . rather than it should have failed, I would have seen half the earth devastated."[2]

In championing the cause of the French Revolution, Jefferson was certain that he had the great majority of Americans on his side. In January, 1793, he asserted that ninety-nine out of a hundred of his countrymen wished well to the French Revolution. Jefferson himself was of the opinion that France was Americans' "true mother country, since she has assured to them their liberty and independence." A few years later, the French minister observed that in the United States "men still exist who can say, here a ferocious Englishman slaughtered my father; there my wife tore her bleeding daughter from the hands of an unbridled Englishman." Conversely, these same men could say: "Here a brave Frenchman died fighting for American liberty; here French naval and military power humbled the might of Britain." It was said that during the celebrations staged by Americans in 1795 to commemorate the French conquest of Amsterdam, more cannon were fired "than the French fired in achieving it." And not only powder was consumed: "They huzzaed like so many wild Indians, or rather devils," remarked an onlooker, "and swilled down the brandy till they were scarcely able to crawl home on all fours." Proper posture, sneered the Federalists, for democrats![3]

Even though the horrors of the French Revolution were three thousand miles away, the Federalists felt the hot breath of the "canaille" upon their necks. Those Americans who praised the French for "exterminating the monster aristocracy" presumably would not suffer aristocracy to exist in the United States. And when the guillotine was set up in Market Street, Broadway, and State Street, some finely powdered Federalist heads would roll in the sand! It was a consolation to the Federalists—albeit a slim one—that when they went, the Vir-

[2] Gilbert Chinard, *Thomas Jefferson, The Apostle of Americanism* (Boston, 1929), pp. 278–297; Ford, *Jefferson*, VI, January, 1793, 293.

[3] *Correspondence between John Adams and William Cunningham* (Boston, 1823), pp. 35–36; *National Gazette*, June 27, 1793; *General Advertiser*, January 21, 1797; *Historical Magazine*, VIII (1864), 19; William Cobbett, *Works* (London, 1835), I, 46–47.

ginia aristocrats, the bluest-blooded patricians of them all, would go with them.

Thus Americans looked upon each other with heightened suspicion and distrust. "Behold France," exclaimed Fisher Ames, "an open hell, still ringing with agonies and blasphemies, still smoking with sufferings and crimes, in which we see . . . perhaps our future state." Behold England, exclaimed the Republicans, a den of iniquity ruled by a privileged aristocracy, a corrupt monarchy, a "perpetual" government debt, an army and navy—"in which we see . . . perhaps our future state." Americans took their choice and picked their political party accordingly.[4]

The French Revolution became the paramount issue in American politics when, early in 1793, France proclaimed itself a republic, declared war upon Great Britain, and appointed Citizen Edmond Genêt minister to the United States. By abolishing the monarchy, France joined the ideological camp of the United States; by going to war with Great Britain, it raised the question of American aid under the Treaty of Alliance of 1778; and by sending Genêt to the United States, it precipitated a crisis in Franco-American relations.

Both Hamilton and Jefferson wished to preserve the neutrality of the United States, but they differed markedly as to how this objective could be best achieved. Hamilton argued that the treaties of commerce and alliance, which dated from 1778 and by the terms of which the United States guaranteed France in possession of its West Indian islands and opened its ports to French privateers, should be declared "temporarily and provisionally suspended." While the Secretary of the Treasury admitted that treaties between nations remained in force regardless of changes in the form of government of either signatory, he insisted that this rule applied "only in reference to a *change*, which has been finally *established* and secured." It did not apply, he asserted, when, as in the present case, such a change was "pending and in contest and which may never be consummated." He also contended that the United States was under no obligation to defend the French West Indies, because such action would expose the nation "to

[4] *National Gazette,* May 22, 29, 1793; Charles D. Hazen, *Contemporary American Opinion of the French Revolution,* Johns Hopkins Studies in Historical and Political Science, XVI (Baltimore, 1897), 164–188; Noah Webster, *Papers,* p. 40; Ames, *Fisher Ames,* II, 112; R. R. Palmer, *The Age of Democratic Revolution* (Princeton, 1959), pp. 16–17.

a *great extremity* of danger." The treaty with France specified American aid only in case of a defensive war; and Hamilton took full advantage of the fact that France had declared war upon Great Britain in January, 1793. As for Citizen Genêt, Hamilton strenuously opposed his reception by the United States government—to receive Genêt, he said, was to recognize the French republic and the binding force of the Franco-American treaties.[5]

Jefferson was horrified by the cavalier attitude assumed by Hamilton toward the treaty obligations of the United States. In the cabinet meetings held early in April, 1793, the Secretary of State took the position that the Franco-American treaties were compacts between peoples, not merely between governments. The question of the defense of the West Indies and the danger it entailed of war with Great Britain might be safely left, he said, to the future; nor was it the present duty of the United States to decide whether France was engaged in defensive or offensive war. And, finally, Jefferson insisted that Genêt be received as the representative of the duly constituted government of France.[6]

Nor were the two cabinet officers agreed upon the question how the United States ought to acquaint the world with its intention of remaining neutral in the European war. Hamilton's reading of the Constitution left no doubt in his mind that the President possessed the power in the absence of Congress to proclaim and enforce "the neutrality of the nation." From that document, however, Jefferson drew the opposite conclusion: since the warmaking power was vested in Congress, he inclined to the view that only Congress could properly commit the country to neutrality. Moreover, whereas Hamilton favored an immediate declaration of neutrality, Jefferson wished to delay action in the hope that the belligerents would make concessions to the commerce of the United States and other nonbelligerents in order to ensure their neutrality. In short, he proposed to put a price tag upon the neutrality of the United States.[7]

[5] Hamilton was seemingly unaware of the fact that he was trying to reverse a decision already reached by the administration. On March 12, 1793, the Secretary of State had instructed Gouverneur Morris, the American minister in Paris, to recognize the National Assembly as the legal government of France. DeConde, *Entangling Alliance*, p. 191. See also Ford, *Jefferson*, I, 208.

[6] DeConde, *Entangling Alliance*, pp. 194–197; Charles M. Thomas, *American Neutrality in 1793: A Study in Cabinet Government* (New York, 1931), pp. 75–76; Ford, *Jefferson*, I, 224.

[7] DeConde, *Entangling Alliance*, pp. 187–188.

In the cabinet discussions, Hamilton lost on two of the points in controversy: President Washington decided not to declare the treaties suspended and he decided to receive Citizen Genêt, thereby making the United States the first nation to accept an emissary from the French Republic. In the matter of the competence of the Chief Executive to issue a proclamation of neutrality, however, the President adopted Hamilton's views. Disclaiming any suggestion that he could bind Congress and asserting that "his main view was to keep our people in peace," Washington nonetheless resolved to meet the crisis by an epoch-making exercise of presidential authority, calculated to make the President a greater power than even George III in the formulation and conduct of foreign policy. The elimination of the word "neutrality" from the proclamation removed Jefferson's objection, although not his doubts and misgivings, and on April 19, 1793, the cabinet unanimously recommended that the President save the peace by issuing in the name of the government of the United States a proclamation of "neutrality."[8]

The President's proclamation gave assurance to foreign nations that the United States intended to pursue "a conduct friendly and impartial towards the belligerent powers." To that end, it prohibited American citizens from "aiding or abetting hostilities" or otherwise engaging in unneutral acts within the jurisdiction of the United States.

While Republicans were content that the United States should remain neutral, they hotly resented the use of the word "impartial" and the constraints placed upon their freedom of action by the President. Had Washington forgotten, they asked, that France was "under God, the saviour of America," and that upon the continued friendship of France "the future glory, honor, welfare, commerce, agriculture and manufactures of *America* essentially depend"? Hugh Henry Brackenridge, a Republican leader of western Pennsylvania, summed up the attitude of his party when he declared that "the cause of France is the cause of man, and neutrality is desertion." What these citizens wanted was to enjoy all the immunities of neutrality and still exercise the privilege of aiding France against the "Despots of Europe." They thought solely in terms of American rights; when President Washing-

[8] Edwin S. Corwin, *The President, Offices and Powers* (New York, 1940), p. 213; George Hammond to Lord Grenville, April 2, 1793, Hammond MSS., LC.

ton reminded them of their duties, they raised the cry that he was acting unconstitutionally.[9]

Wary of attacking the President directly, Republicans attributed his
dereliction to his "evil counsellors," the chief of whom, of course, being Alexander Hamilton. The Secretary of the Treasury gave credence
to this suspicion that he was responsible for the neutrality proclamation
by the ardor with which he defended it in the newspapers. Under the
pseudonym of "Pacificus" Hamilton published a series of articles purporting to show that the President was within his constitutional rights;
that the proclamation was binding upon the nation; that war upon
the side of France would be an unmitigated disaster for the United
States; and that France was and always had been—even when aiding
the United States during the War of Independence—actuated by self-
interest.[10]

Fearful that these doctrines would warp the government into monarchism, Jefferson appealed to his friend James Madison: "For God's
sake, my dear Sir, take up your pen, select the most striking heresies,
and cut him to pieces in the face of the public." Taking the name
"Helvidius," Madison set forth the true "republican" canons: Congress
controls foreign policy; the powers of the President in the diplomatic
field are instrumental only; the executive department is more prone
to war than is the legislature—"war is, in fact, the true source of executive aggrandizement"—and the proclamation of neutrality was a
unilateral interpretation of the Franco-American treaties and enjoined
an impartiality that was irreconcilable with Americans' moral obligations. Madison advocated neutrality, but he insisted that it be
proclaimed by Congress. The former exponent of executive powers was
now bent upon whittling the Chief Magistrate down to a stature considerably smaller than that of Congress.[11]

The proclamation of neutrality sought to guard against contingen-

[9] C. M. Newlin, *The Life and Writings of Hugh Henry Brackenridge*
(Princeton, 1932), pp. 130–131.

[10] Hamilton's doctrine that the "executive power" clause of the Constitution "embraces a prerogative in the diplomatic field which is plenary except
as it is curtailed by more specific clauses of the Constitution has consistently
prospered." Corwin, *The President*, pp. 252–253; John C. Miller, *Alexander
Hamilton, Portrait in Paradox* (New York, 1959), pp. 370–372.

[11] Hunt, *Madison*, I, 633, 640, 650–651; VI, 135, 138, 174; Rives, *Madison*,
III, 335, 354.

cies likely to involve the United States in war. But there was one contingency it had not taken into account—the ebullient personality of Edmond Genêt, the newly appointed French minister to the United States. An ardent young revolutionist who regarded caution and discretion as hardly better than treason to the republic, Genêt undertook to convert the United States into a base of operations from which to conquer Louisiana, the Floridas, and Canada and to equip privateers to prey upon British shipping. Genêt assumed that as an ally of his country, the United States government would decently avert its eyes while he proceeded to make it a belligerent in all but name. After all, during the War of American Independence, France had done no less for the United States, and Genêt asked only that he be accorded the same privileges that had been granted Benjamin Franklin by France. The French minister purchased the services of George Rogers Clark to lead an expedition against Louisiana and the Floridas, and he lavishly distributed commissions in the *Armée du Mississippi* and the *Armée des Floridas*. But Clark was an alcoholic and his prestige had been badly tarnished since he had conquered the West for Virginia. Moreover, Genêt's grandiose schemes required much more money than the French government had placed at his disposal. The Frenchman had the bright idea of asking Secretary of the Treasury Hamilton for an advance upon the money owing France by the United States government, but Hamilton declined to finance Genêt's schemes. The French minister received an equally unceremonious rebuff from Secretary of War Knox: when he asked for cannon ostensibly for use in the West Indies, he was informed that the United States government would not loan him a pistol.[12]

Despite these rebuffs, the warmth of the welcome Genêt received everywhere in the United States—his journey from Charleston to Philadelphia was like a triumphal progress—convinced the excitable young diplomat that the people were wholly committed to the cause of France. In Philadelphia, no pretense of neutrality was observed: "The bosoms of many hundreds of freemen beat high with affectionate

[12] DeConde, *Entangling Alliance,* pp. 199, 212, 237–239; King, *Rufus King,* I, 466; A. C. Primrose (ed.), *The Windham Papers: Life and Correspondence of the Right Honorable William Windham, 1750–1810* (London, 1913), I, 128; Walters, *Dallas,* 46–48; *A Message of the President, December 5, 1793* (Philadelphia, 1794), pp. 45–46, 93; *American Historical Review,* II (1896), 476.

transport, their souls caught in the celestial fire of struggling liberty." At a dinner given in honor of Genêt, over a hundred prominent Philadelphians gathered to sing the "Marseillaise," "with two additional odes composed by Citizen Genêt," who came attired in a liberty cap. A few days later, a French frigate brought into Philadelphia a British vessel as a prize. When the British colors were seen reversed and the French flag flying above, the large crowds lining the waterfront "burst into peals of exultation."[13]

Similarly, Genêt's conferences with Secretary of State Jefferson left no doubt in the Frenchman's mind that he had a warm friend at court. Genêt had been instructed to make a commercial treaty with the United States—he described it as a "true family compact"—and Jefferson, always eager to strengthen the economic ties between the two countries, welcomed this opportunity of diverting American trade from Great Britain to the new French Republic. And, indeed, there was some reason for optimism on Jefferson's part: in February, 1793, the National Convention decreed that all ports of the French colonies were opened to the vessels of the United States. These vessels were to pay no higher duties on cargoes than were paid by ships of French origin.[14]

Upon the strength of this evidence of the good will of France and his own liking for Genêt—"it is impossible," said Jefferson, "for any thing to be more affectionate, more magnanimous, than the purport of his mission"—the Secretary of State took the French minister into his confidence as unreservedly as did the Secretary of the Treasury in the case of the British minister. As Genêt later said, Jefferson "initiated me into mysteries which have inflamed my hatred against all those who aspire to an absolute power"—meaning, of course, Hamilton and his partisans. Like a good Jeffersonian, Genêt declared that he preferred "the modest and pure society of good farmers, plain citizens, honest citizens" to that of "distinguished personages, who speculate so patriotically on the public funds, on the lands and paper of the State." Genêt soon arrived at the conclusion that of all the principal officers of the United States government, only Thomas Jefferson was wholeheartedly devoted to Liberty, Equality, and Fraternity. When he was asked whether the members of the cabinet were fools, Genêt answered: "Jefferson is no fool."[15]

[13] Ford, *Jefferson*, VI, April 25, 1793; *General Advertiser*, May 26, 1793; *National Gazette*, May 22, 1793.

[14] *Message of the President*, p. 94.

[15] Monaghan, *Jay*, 352; Noah Webster, *Papers*, 325; *Report of the American*

At this time, so ardent was Jefferson's love of France that he abetted Genêt's plans for making the United States a base from which to launch an attack upon Spanish and British territory. Among the undercover agents sent by the French minister to the American West in order to organize the frontiersmen for a foray into Louisiana and Canada was André Michaux, a well-known French botanist. Even though Jefferson knew that Michaux had in mind more important business than collecting specimens, he made no effort to stop the Frenchman. Jefferson's justification for this unneutral conduct was his hope that as a reward for its compliance the United States would be given the Floridas, and that France, after conquering Louisiana, would permit American citizens the free navigation of the Mississippi.[16]

In his own estimation, Jefferson was upholding the cause of "a fair neutrality." The only member of the cabinet guilty of harboring unneutral opinions was, he said, Alexander Hamilton. The Secretary of the Treasury seemed to be "panic-struck if we refuse our breech to every kick which Great Britain may chuse to give it. . . . Some propositions have come from him which would astonish Mr. Pitt himself with their boldness. If we preserve even a sneaking neutrality, we shall be indebted for it to the President, & not to his counsellors."[17]

Genêt peremptorily demanded that the United States enforce against the British the principle, written into the Franco-American treaty of 1778, that free ships make free goods. As matters stood, he pointed out to the Washington administration, the British confiscated French goods aboard American ships but French cruisers were forbidden to molest British property being conveyed in American ships. In consequence, he said, the French were "punished for having believed that the American nation had a flag, that they had some respect for their laws, some conviction of their strength, and entertained some sentiment of their dignity." In July, 1793, he insisted that the government take steps to

Historical Association for 1898 (Washington, 1899), pp. 543–544; George Hammond to Lord Grenville, July 7, 1793, Hammond MSS., LC; *American State Papers*, I, September 18, 1793; Joseph Fauchet, *A Sketch of the Present State of Our Political Relations* (Philadelphia, 1797), pp. 24–25; Ford, *Jefferson*, VI, April 25, 1793; Rives, *Madison*, III, 336–337.

16 DeConde, *Entangling Alliance*, pp. 248–250; Channing, *History*, IV, 130–131; *American Historical Review*, I (1895), 932–933; II (1896), 475–476; III (1897), 669–670; Lodge, *George Cabot*, p. 75; *American State Papers, Foreign Affairs*, I, 455.

17 Ford, *Jefferson*, VI, April 25, 1793; George Hammond to Lord Grenville, March 7, 1793, Hammond MSS., LC.

restore to French citizens the property of which they had been deprived by British seizures of American ships. At the same time he told Jefferson that he would respect "the political opinions of the President only until the representatives of the people met to confirm or reject them." "A true neutrality," he pointedly declared, "does not consist in the cowardly abandonment of their friends in the moment when danger menaces them."[18]

Genêt brought with him to the United States enough blank commissions for privateers to have swept British shipping from the seas. He himself actively participated in the arming and equipping of these sea rovers. Many Americans fell in enthusiastically with Genêt's plans, for privateering offered them an opportunity of making a handsome profit and at the same time gratifying their animosity against Great Britain. Accordingly, American ships were converted into French privateers and Americans went down to the sea in ships flying the tricolor.[19]

That the President's proclamation had not altered the prevailing pro-French sympathies of the people was revealed in July, 1793, when two American citizens, Henfield and Singletary, were arrested for engaging to serve aboard a French privateer in Charleston. The two men were brought to Philadelphia for trial in the Federal court. Since there was no Federal law prohibiting foreign recruiting in the United States, the Attorney General based the case on the common law offense of disturbing the peace. The jury, strongly predisposed in favor of France, acquitted the prisoners, whereupon Henfield further endeared himself to his admirers by re-enlisting on a French privateer. Accounting this a victory over the government, Genêt advertised in the newspapers for all "Friends of France" to enlist in the French service regardless of the proclamation of neutrality.[20]

Altogether, Genêt commissioned twelve privateers in the United States, and these ships captured over eighty British merchantmen, some of the captures taking place within the territorial waters of the United States. These prizes were brought into American ports, where they were tried, condemned, and sold by French consuls for whom Genêt claimed extraterritorial privileges.[21]

[18] *Message of the President*, pp. 27, 64, 68; *American State Papers*, I, September 27, 1793.
[19] G. W. Allen, *Our Naval War with France* (New York, 1909), pp. 11–12.
[20] DeConde, *Entangling Alliance*, pp. 216–217.
[21] George Hammond to Lord Grenville, July 7, 1793, Hammond MSS., LC.

All this, Genêt blandly informed the United States government, was permitted by the Franco-American treaties of 1778. Since these treaties were not explicit upon many points (the treaty of commerce, for example, simply stated that enemy privateers were not to be fitted out or permitted to sell prizes in the ports of either signatory), President Washington decided in July, 1793, to call upon the judges of the Supreme Court for an opinion upon the questions raised by Genêt's activities. But the judges declined to take these matters under consideration unless they were brought before them through the regular legal channels—a procedure too time-consuming to be of any avail in the existing emergency. In consequence, the government was obliged to act without benefit of the judges' advice.[22]

In the "Rules Governing Belligerents," drawn up early in August, 1793, the administration undertook to prevent Westerners from organizing filibustering expeditions against Spanish territory and the equipping of French privateers in American ports. These rules prohibited foreign nations from outfitting ships and recruiting volunteers within the territory of the United States and created machinery for the enforcement of the neutrality proclamation. In one particular, however, the French were given preferred treatment over Great Britain: by Washington's order, the French were permitted to sell prizes in United States ports—"not," as Hamilton later pointed out, "because the treaty gave her a right, but because he did not see clearly any law of the country, or of nations, that forbids it." However, in 1794, the Supreme Court ruled that French consular tribunals established by Genêt in the United States for the purpose of condemning prizes were illegal.[23] At the same time, the Court declared the competence of the courts of admiralty of the United States to take cognizance of such captures.[24]

Although in August, 1793, the administration ordered the ships already commissioned by Genêt to stay out of American ports, it would have taken a sizable army and navy to keep the irrepressible Frenchman within bounds. Unfortunately for the Federal government, it had no

[22] DeConde, *Entangling Alliance*, pp. 91, 99, 210; Ford, *Jefferson*, Writings, I, 229–230, 255; George Hammond to Lord Grenville, June 10, August 10, 1793, Hammond MSS., LC; Fauchet, *A Sketch*, p. 12.

[23] DeConde, *Entangling Alliance*, pp. 91, 99, 223; Ford, *Jefferson*, VI, May, 1793.

[24] In 1793, Jefferson protested against these courts on the ground that their actions constituted an invasion of United States sovereignty.

navy and the small peacetime army was engaged in holding down the Indians on the frontier. Its only recourse, therefore, was to rely upon Treasury agents and, where they proved unable to curb Genêt, to request the governors of the states to call out the militia. Even though the governors were for the most part willing to co-operate, the Federal government itself was bemused by indecision and vacillation. As a result of Jefferson's unwillingness to resort to force—he feared that France would take offense—Genêt was able to arm and send to sea the captured British merchantman *Little Sarah*, renamed the *Petite Démocrate*. This fast-sailing privateer made a rich haul of British shipping off the Delaware Capes. It was left to Hamilton to square matters with the British minister, but the Secretary of the Treasury found it increasingly difficult to talk his way out of the corner into which Genêt was pushing the United States government. After the *Petite Démocrate* incident, the British minister informed his government that the administration was unable "to enforce any measures in opposition to the views of the French faction." Unless Genêt was stopped short in his career it seemed entirely possible that he would raise the tricolor and proclaim himself proconsul.[25]

In August, 1793, he took a long stride in that direction by threatening to appeal to the people over the head of President Washington. Conscious of the mounting displeasure of the government and certain that he could count upon the support of the mass of the people, he demanded that the President call Congress into special session in order that the representatives of the people could judge between the President of the United States and the minister of the French Republic; if Washington refused to summon Congress, Genêt declared, he would take his case directly to the public. It is indicative of how far Genêt was gone in folly that he confidently expected the people to repudiate Washington and to throw in their lot with France.[26]

By this time, Jefferson was throughly cured of his earlier enthusiasm

[25] Thomas, *American Neutrality*, pp. 142–143, 197–198, 227; *Report of the American Historical Association for 1898* (Washington, 1899), p. 531; George Hammond to Lord Grenville, February 22, 1794, Hammond MSS., LC; Fitzpatrick, *Washington*, XXXIII, 4–5 (footnote); Ford, *Jefferson*, I, 240–241, 259; Lodge, *Hamilton*, V, July 8, 1793; Walters, *Dallas*, pp. 47–48; Carroll and Ashworth, *Washington*, VII, 100–107.

[26] Monaghan, *Jay*, 355–358; *Independent Chronicle*, November 8, December 23, 1793; January 6, 9, 1794; *Message of the President*, pp. 29–30; A. J. Dallas to Gallatin, November 8, 1793, Gallatin MSS., NYHS; Walters, *Dallas*, p. 50.

for the French minister. He now described Genêt as "hot-headed, all imagination, no judgment, passionate, disrespectful & even indecent towards the President." If this wild-eyed young revolutionary were permitted to run loose, Jefferson feared that the "republican interest" would be ruined and that the United States and France would go to war—utterly improbable as that event had seemed before Genêt arrived in this country. Nevertheless, Jefferson continued to distinguish between the French government and its representative: it was the minister, he insisted, not the government, who was at fault. When, therefore, Hamilton recommended that a peremptory demand for Genêt's recall be sent to the French government, that his diplomatic functions be suspended, and that his correspondence with the United States government be published, the Secretary of State insisted upon observing the diplomatic niceties. But even he finally agreed that the presence of the French minister in the United States could no longer be tolerated. Genêt's recall was requested. (At the same time, the United States recalled Gouverneur Morris, the American minister, whose relations with the French government had become almost as strained as Genêt's relations with the Washington administration.) In December, 1793, President Washington laid before Congress Genêt's correspondence, but the sins of the minister were not visited upon his government; instead, Washington informed Congress that Genêt's conduct contained "nothing of the friendly spirit of the nation which sent him." And, over Hamilton's objections, the President included in his message an account of the depredations committed by the British as well as by the French upon American commerce.[27]

Jefferson need have given himself no concern about offending the French government by taking action against Genêt. During Genêt's absence from France, a new upheaval had swept out the Girondists and installed the Jacobins in power. As a Girondist, Genêt was declared a public enemy, his acts were disavowed by the new French government as "criminal maneuvers," and he was ordered to return to France, where, no doubt, he would have expiated his "crimes" on the guillotine. The now terrified French minister looked to the administration he had tried to turn out of office to save him from

[27] DeConde, *Entangling Alliance*, pp. 297–302; Ford, *Jefferson*, I, 247, 252–253, 259–260; VI, August 3, 25, 1793; Jenkins, *Jefferson's Germantown Letters*, pp. 96–97, 148, 168; *Message of the President*, p. 45; Peter Porcupine, *A Little Plain English* (Philadelphia, 1795), p. 96; Fitzpatrick, *Washington*, XXXIII, 138, 171–172.

Fauchet, the new French minister, who had been ordered to send Genêt back to France for trial. Given sanctuary in the United States, he married the daughter of Governor Clinton of New York and settled down quietly as a country gentleman, lost wholly to public view until his death in 1836 recalled briefly the memory of this stormy petrel of diplomacy.[28]

[28] *Independent Chronicle,* January 6, 1794; *American State Papers,* I, October 19, 1793; Henry Wansey, *An Excursion,* p. 92.

CHAPTER 9

The Crisis of 1794

ALTHOUGH the European war brought prosperity to Americans, they were unable to follow John Adams's advice that they line their pockets while philosophically watching Europeans cut each others' throats. For, regardless of Americans' desire to enjoy the sweets of neutrality, they found themselves exposed to the aggressions of the belligerents. From the beginning of the War of the French Revolution, American commerce was under the threat of being ground between the French and British millstones. Of the two, the British pressed the more heavily, for Great Britain was the dominant sea power. France, weak at sea, desperately needed American shipping; the very survival of the French West Indies depended upon the free transit of American merchant ships. For this reason, early in the war, the French government proclaimed its adherence to the doctrine of the freedom of the seas. Nevertheless, the French government did not hesitate to violate this principle whenever it appeared that American neutrality was redounding to the advantage of Great Britain. Early in 1793, France began to seize American ships and confiscate their cargoes without compensation; and eighty American ships were embargoed at Bordeaux for almost a year.[1]

Whenever France violated American rights and seemed on the point

[1] DeConde, *Entangling Alliance*, pp. 76–77, 80, 148–149, 162, 354; Ford, *Jefferson*, VII, January 26, 1799; George Hammond to Lord Grenville, July 7, September 13, 1793, Hammond MSS., LC; Thomas, *American Neutrality*, pp. 253–254, 256–257; Mayo, *Instructions to British Ministers*, p. 47 (footnote).

of bringing down upon itself the wrath of the United States government, the British could be depended upon to commit some even more heinous offense and to make themselves the target of Americans' anger. The British planted dragon's teeth in the United States, but they never ceased to be surprised that a crop of Anglophobes sprang up. In June, 1793 Great Britain proclaimed a blockade of France with a view to starving that country into subjection, and orders were issued directing the seizure of all neutral ships carrying supplies to France. But worse was to come: in the autumn of 1793 a British fleet and army were sent to the Caribbean to conquer the French West Indies. In support of this operation, on November 6, 1793, an Order in Council authorized the commanders of British ships of war to seize and bring into British ports all neutral vessels carrying provisions or other supplies to the enemy's islands or transporting the produce of those islands. This measure was patently aimed at the American merchant marine, the principal carrier of provisions to the French West Indies and of the produce of those islands to the outside world.[2]

To ensure that the bag of American ships would be as large as possible, this Order in Council was kept secret until late in December, 1793. Thanks to this ruse, British cruisers and privateers were able to capture about 250 unsuspecting and unarmed American ships, almost half of which were condemned in British West Indian admiralty courts. The officers of His Majesty's Navy, who by long-standing custom shared in the profits of these seizures, had seldom found war more profitable. The fact that the victims were Yankees merely added savor to the business.[3]

In December, 1793, before the news of the British depredations reached the United States, Jefferson retired from public life. His departure came as no surprise: in 1792 he had fixed upon "the termination of our first federal period of four years as the proper epoch for retirement"—an event which, he declared, he awaited "with the fondness of a sailor who has land in view." During the summer of 1793 he had informed the President that he would resign at the end of the year

[2] Carl J. Karlsrud, *Maritime Neutrality to 1780* (Boston, 1936), pp. 79–82, 130–137, 142–143, 150, 154–155, 336–337; Noah Webster, *Papers*, 109–110; Ford, *John Quincy Adams*, I, October 3, 1796; *Parliamentary History*, XXX, 1273–1275; King, *Rufus King*, III, 549; *American Historical Review*, XXIV (1919), 27; Mayo, *Instructions to British Ministers*, 42 (footnote); Channing, *History*, IV, 135; Adams, *John Quincy Adams*, I, 138.

[3] Mayo, *Instructions to British Ministers*, pp. 48–49; Bemis, *Jay's Treaty*, pp. 154–160.

even though his withdrawal meant that Hamilton would be left in possession of the field.

The interminable controversy with Hamilton had left Jefferson weary of public office. The Virginian was not a man who delighted in altercations; on the contrary, he wanted to be everybody's friend and he was surprised and hurt when he was not accepted on his own terms. He was convinced, moreover—although the record does not bear him out—that when he and Hamilton were "daily pitted like two cocks" in the cabinet, it was the fine-feathered Secretary of the Treasury who usually strutted off victorious.[4] On his part, Hamilton was far from certain that he had triumphed over his rival or that he would immure himself at Monticello, where, preoccupied with his experiments, his books, and his violin, he would remain a mere spectator of the political scene. Indeed, in the autumn of 1793, it seemed probable that Hamilton would precede his adversary into a retirement from which there was no returning: the Secretary of the Treasury fell ill of yellow fever and for a time his life was despaired of. But Hamilton recovered and by November, 1793, he was back at his desk.[5]

Late in 1793, as his valedictory upon retiring as Secretary of State, Jefferson sent to Congress a Report on the Privileges and Restrictions on the Commerce of the United States in Foreign Countries. He had been engaged since 1791 in collecting the information that went into this report. For Jefferson, it was a labor of love, inasmuch as it was designed to prove by statistical evidence that France's commercial policy was far more friendly toward the United States than was that of Great Britain. The contrast was particularly striking, he observed, in the West Indies, where Great Britain barred United States ships from its colonies while France admitted them freely. And, he continued, France was prepared to make a new commercial treaty which would further relax restrictions on Franco-American trade, whereas the British refused even to enter into discussions with the United States.[6]

Despite the friendly disposition of France, the great bulk of American trade was with Great Britain or its colonies—a situation that Jef-

[4] Ford, *Jefferson*, VII, January 22, 1797; Lodge, *Hamilton*, IX, 530; Bemis, *American Secretaries of State*, II, 102.

[5] John Powell, *Bring Out Your Dead* (Philadelphia, 1952), pp. 42–50.

[6] Ford, *Jefferson*, VI, 357, December 16, 1793; George Hammond to Lord Grenville, February 22, 1794, Hammond MSS., LC; Bemis, *Jay's Treaty*, pp. 186–188.

ferson called upon Americans to correct forthwith by diverting their commerce to France. While he admitted that free trade was the ideal toward which the United States ought to strive, Jefferson was not inclined to practice this ideal toward Great Britain; to break that country's "unnatural" monopoly of American exports and imports, he advocated a system of restrictions and regulations comparable to those of Great Britain. By this means, said Jefferson, the United States would build up an impregnable barrier of defense in its merchant marine and would foster "the precious efforts and progress of *household* manufactures." But it is plain that Jefferson did not have economic considerations solely in mind: he believed that American foreign policy ought to be based upon the fact that France and the United States shared a common republican ideology.[7]

Thus, said Hamilton, Jefferson "threw this FIREBRAND of discord into the midst of the representatives of the states . . . and instantly *decamped* to Monticello." But James Madison blew the firebrand into even hotter flame by introducing into Congress in January, 1794, a series of "Commercial Propositions" calling for retaliatory duties upon British ships and merchandise. The purpose of these regulations was to foster the growth of the American merchant marine, to encourage American manufacturers, and to end the "dangerous" dependence of the United States upon British markets and credits. In essentials, Madison was proposing an American mercantilist system oriented in favor of France.[8]

To answer Madison on the floor of Congress, Hamilton primed William L. Smith of South Carolina with facts and figures purporting to show that in general Great Britain showed greater favoritism to American shipping and agricultural exports than did France, and that in any event France could not take the place of Great Britain as a market for American products and as a supplier of manufacturers. But even more decisive was the argument that Madison's plan would lead to war with Great Britain. Moreover, in the eyes of the Federalists, Madison's proposals had "Made in France" indelibly stamped upon them: France, not the merchants and shipowners of the North, seemed likely to profit by the violent dislocation of trade the Virginian advocated.[9]

[7] Koch, *Jefferson and Madison*, pp. 22–23.
[8] *Annals of Congress*, III, 212, 382–383; William Smith, *The Pretensions of Thomas Jefferson to the Presidency Examined*, pp. 25–26, 28–29; Bemis, *Jay's Treaty*, pp. 189–193.
[9] This debate brought to light significant facts regarding American com-

Virginians' eagerness to engage in economic war with Great Britain was not shared by northern merchants. Having been taught by adversity to hold the British navy in respect, they were not inclined to impale themselves upon the triton shrieking slogans about neutral rights. Nor could they overlook the fact that if Madison's proposals passed, the merchants would probably never recover a farthing of their property seized by British privateers and brought into the West Indian admiralty courts for adjudication. As a result, it was observed that Madison's commercial propositions "had not a single commercial man to advocate them in Congress." When Virginia invited New England "not only to partake, but to monopolize all the riches of her commerce," New Englanders spurned the proffered gift on the ground that as much capital was invested in ships and factories "as was consistent with the general welfare," and that it was unjust to benefit shipowners and manufacturers at the expense of "that most useful and respectable description of men, the farmer and planter." It was left to the spokesmen of the planters and farmers of the United States to wax eloquent upon the rights of American ships and sailors, and to bewail the sad lot of American manufacturers exposed to the cutthroat competition of unconscionable Englishmen.[10]

The decision whether the United States should show partiality toward France or toward Great Britain was not settled by statistics or oratory upon the floor of Congress. In this dispute, the conduct pursued by the two warring powers toward the United States was almost certain to prove decisive—and it was here that the British seemingly

merce. Three-fourths of American imports—chiefly hardware, cloth, tropical produce—came from Great Britain and its colonies. Great Britain was the entrepôt of American export trade: most of the tobacco imported into Great Britain from the United States was re-exported to the Continent. Even so, the balance of trade between the United States and Great Britain was tipped in Britain's favor. *Annals of Congress,* III, 219, 324, 329, 331–333, 342, 415, 521; Ames, *Fisher Ames,* II, 161.

[10] In reality, Madison did not intend to benefit the North quite as much as Northerners seem to have supposed: when he spoke of stimulating manufactures, he meant household manufactures, in which the South was not far behind the North. *Annals of Congress,* III, 221. See also *Gazette of the United States,* April 23, May 20, 1794; Gibbs, *Memoirs,* I, 107; Rives, *Madison,* III, 408; Ames, *Fisher Ames,* I, 135, 144; Morison, *Jeremiah Smith,* pp. 61–62; *An Address from William Smith to His Constituents* (Philadelphia, 1794), pp. 5–7, 11; *James Sprout Historical Monographs,* No. 3 (Chapel Hill, 1902), p. 99; Ballagh, *Letters of R. H. Lee,* II, 581–582; *Gazette of the United States,* February 12, 1794.

went out of their way to affront and alienate even their warmest friends in the United States. Besides directly violating American neutral rights, the British were accused of a particularly heinous form of indirect aggression—attacking American shipping through the Barbary corsairs. As a result of the good offices of the British government, a treaty was concluded in 1793 between Portugal and Algiers. Until this time, the Portuguese navy had blocked the Straits of Gibraltar to the pirates and, on occasion, had convoyed American ships through dangerous waters. With the cessation of hostilities between Portugal and Algiers, however, the corsairs irrupted into the Atlantic and the protection of the Portuguese navy was withdrawn from American ships. To many Americans, this untoward development signified only one thing: Great Britain intended to use the Barbary pirates to drive American shipping from the Mediterranean.[11] Thus, exclaimed James Monroe, the United States was being "kicked, cuffed and plundered all over the Ocean" by ships flying the Union Jack and the Crescent of the Prophet.[12]

This did not exhaust the "crimes" of which the British stood accused before the bar of American political opinion. All the disasters suffered by American armies in the West were attributed to British intrigue with the Indians. George III was pictured unleashing a brace of bulldogs, one representing the Indians, the other depicting the Barbary pirates, against the United States. The guns, powder, and even the tomahawks with which the redskins carried terror to the American frontier were believed to have been supplied by Englishmen for the purpose of killing innocent Americans. Apart from the bloodshed, Madison estimated that Great Britain was costing the United States three and a half million dollars a year as a result of the Indian war, loss of the fur trade, Algerine depredations, the additional cost of insurance, and dependence upon British shipping to carry American products safely to market.[13]

This much was undisputed: in 1794, the British had six thousand troops in North America, one thousand of whom were stationed on

[11] In actuality, Great Britain's objective in bringing about peace between the Portuguese and the Algerines was to free the Portuguese navy for use against France. Mayo, *Instructions to British Ministers*, p. 50.

[12] Fitzpatrick, *Washington*, XXXIII, 331; *Independent Chronicle*, January 9, February 20, 1794.

[13] *Annals of Congress*, III, 378, 439; *American Historical Association Report for 1898* (Washington, 1899), p. 467; Fitzpatrick, *Washington*, XXXI, 267–268; Bemis, *Jay's Treaty*, pp. 109–133.

American soil. The military posts within the borders of the United States, which the British had promised in 1783 to surrender "with all convenient speed," were still in their possession and they had given no sign that they contemplated moving out. The possession of these posts gave the British control of the fur trade and with it the allegiance of the Indians. Moreover, it made the United States appear in the eyes of the Indians as a second-rate power that might be pushed around by a few determined and well-armed tribesmen.[14]

Despite the British government's disavowal of any improper relations with the Indians, President Washington, who prided himself upon keeping a cool head, no matter how flagrant the provocation, held the London government accountable for the troubles on the frontier. Of what avail was it, he asked, for His Britannic Majesty to proclaim his innocence when he did not punish his agents in Canada and the United States who instigated the Indians to take the warpath and furnished them with arms?[15]

To make trouble for the United States, the British had only to give the Indians weapons; the animus against the United States was supplied by the Indians themselves. With mounting anger they saw their tribal lands being confiscated by white settlers and their lives put at the mercy of a "lawless banditti" of frontiersmen. An American officer reported that "the people of Kentucky will carry on private expeditions against the Indians and kill them whenever they meet them, and I do not believe that there is a jury in all Kentucky will punish a man for it." Washington saw no prospect of tranquillity on the frontiers until Congress had defined and regulated the methods by which Indians could alienate land; until the Indian trade had been brought under control; and until it had been made as much a crime to kill an Indian as a white man. In short, said the President, Americans had to learn to treat the Indians justly.[16]

Certainly the policy being pursued toward the Indians seemed to be bringing only disaster upon the United States. Early in 1790, the Northern Indians, having resolved to hold the Ohio River line against the advance of the white settlers, took the warpath and routed General Harmar's army at the Maumee River. ("I expected little," said Washington, "from the moment I heard he [Harmar] was a drunkard.")

[14] Ford, *Jefferson*, I, 196–198; Mayo, *Instructions to British Ministers,* pp. 7, 14; *Report on Canadian Archives* (1890), pp. 167, 173.

[15] Mayo, *Instructions to British Ministers,* pp. 74, 75 (footnote); Fitzpatrick, *Washington,* XXXIII, 310, 479, 484.

[16] Fitzpatrick, *Washington,* XXXI, 320; XXXIV, 99.

General St. Clair, the governor of the Northwest Territory, met with an even more costly reverse. With an army composed of "men collected from the streets . . . from the stews and brothels of the cities" and militiamen, many of whom had been hired as substitutes and commanded by officers who had little or no experience in Indian fighting, General St. Clair marched against the tribesmen in the autumn of 1791. At sunrise on November 4, 1791, the Indians attacked the American camp, advancing from tree to tree until they were within range of the troops. The American artillery and musket fire was largely wasted on the Indians, but the smoke became so thick that the troops were unable to see the enemy. Officers were singled out by the braves with such deadly effect that the militia turned tail and bolted for home, plundering the officers' tents on their way. The battle turned into a melee in which over nine hundred Americans were killed or wounded. Although General St. Clair, who, being incapacitated with gout, had watched the battle propped up with pillows in a wagon, was hauled to safety, few other officers survived the slaughter. "I saw a Captain Smith," reported a soldier, "just after he was scalped, sitting on his backside, his head smoking like a chimney." As far away as Pittsburgh, the frontier was thrown into panic, but providentially the Indians did not follow up their advantage.[17]

Instead of blaming the troops for this disaster, Congress sought a scapegoat in the military leaders of the expedition and the cabinet officers responsible for supplying the army. A congressional investigating committee—the first of its kind—requested permission from the Secretary of War to see the papers relevant to the campaign. The President and cabinet agreed that when such requests were addressed to the President rather than to the heads of the departments concerned, they ought to be complied with "so far as the public good would permit." In this instance, it was decided that all the papers might safely be entrusted to the committee. As a result of its investigations, the committee exonerated General St. Clair, Hamilton, and Knox and placed the blame for the defeat upon the contractors who had failed to supply the army with proper equipment. The Secretary of the Treasury was given larger powers over the supply of the armed forces. Not until 1798 was this function transferred to the War and Navy departments.[18]

[17] Fitzpatrick, *Washington*, XXXI, 156; Lt. McDonough to his brother, November 10, 1791, Clements Library MSS.
[18] Marshall, *Washington*, V, 531; Anderson, *Giles*, p. 26; Hunt, *Madison*, V, 337; Taylor, *Definition of Parties*, p. 12.

Madison introduced his "commercial propositions" into Congress before reports of British confiscations of American shipping under the Order in Council of November 6, 1793, reached the United States. These resolutions were on the point of passage by Congress when the country was stunned by the news from the West Indies. As a result of this turn of events, Madison's proposals lost much of their cogency: there was no point in talking about enlarging the American merchant marine when it was being swallowed up by the British navy. Moreover, economic retaliation against Great Britain no longer wholly suited the public temper. A second War of Independence was necessary, it began to be said, to teach Englishmen that the United States was truly a sovereign nation: "We must adopt such a mode of retaliation as will stake their kingdom to the centre," a Republican newspaper asserted. Some patriots exclaimed that they were prepared to take on "the whole mob of European kings, with all their murdering legions and cut-throats." In Philadelphia, a bas-relief of George III that had survived the Revolution was removed in 1794 lest it provoke mob violence. The British minister and consul were subjected to insults and threats from "knots of street politicians," but with typical British composure they stood their ground "with a very cool indifference." They needed all the equanimity they could muster: "Our blood is in a flame," exclaimed an American. ". . . . The avenging arm of America once uplifted, should chastize and pursue a corrupt and base tyrant till his worthless life is terminated upon a scaffold."[19]

It was a peculiarity of the Republicans' conduct of affairs that, eager as they were to force an economic showdown with Great Britain, they vehemently opposed every effort to strengthen the defenses of the United States. It was enough for them that the United States was upholding its rights and that its enemy was Great Britain; against that foe, hundreds of thousands of Americans would spring to arms or, if guns were wanting, to pitchforks. But they had little fear that Great Britain would commence hostilities against the United States: already heavily engaged in war with France, it was supposed that the British could not afford to take on another adversary, especially when that

[19] Bemis, *Jay's Treaty*, pp. 192–195; *Independent Chronicle*, January 17, December 23, 1793; May 29, 1794; Madison to Jefferson, March 2, 1799, Madison MSS., LC; *Report of the American Historical Association for 1897* (Washington, 1898), pp. 546–550; Charles Francis Adams, *The Life of John Adams* (Boston, 1874), II, 173; George Hammond to Grenville, May 10, 1794. Hammond MSS., LC.

adversary was Great Britain's best customer. Republican newspapers told the people of the United States that Great Britain was "reduced to her last gasp, and were America to seize her by the throat, she would expire in agonies at her feet."[20]

Republicans expected to strangle the former mother country neatly and effectively without resorting to the more sanguine forms of mayhem. In their thinking, Great Britain figured as a nation whose policies were always determined by its material interests—and those interests seemingly compelled the islanders to yield to their former subjects overseas. It became an article of faith among Republicans that "commercial weapons" would suffice to bring Great Britain to any terms the United States chose to dictate. As Jefferson said, "war is not the best engine for us to resort to, nature has given us *in our commerce*, which, if properly managed, will be a better instrument in obliging the interested nations of Europe to treat us with respect."[21]

Hamilton shared neither Jefferson's optimism nor his theory that economics inexorably determined British foreign policy. The Secretary of the Treasury and his congressional followers felt certain that "the pride of Great Britain will yield to her interest" and that in the "war of regulations," instead of playing according to the rules laid down by the Republicans, the British would "change the game from manifests and shipping papers to powder and ball." Hamilton knew Englishmen too well to imagine that they would wait passively while an economic noose was fixed around their necks by Americans. After all, the United States was an ally of France—and the first hostile move by Americans was almost certain to be interpreted by the British government as proof that the United States had decided to commit itself to the cause of France.[22]

From war with Great Britain, the Federalists anticipated a host of evils: the drying up of the import duties from which the government drew most of its revenues; the overthrow of the Hamiltonian fiscal

[20] *National Gazette,* June 5, August 14, 1793; *General Advertiser,* February 12, March 18, 1794; *Independent Chronicle,* November 20, 1793, January 5, October 20, 1794; Madison to Jefferson, March 14, 1794, Madison MSS., LC; Hunt, *Madison,* VI, 209, 220; Rives, *Madison,* III, 408; Eugene Perry Link, *Democratic-Republican Societies, 1790–1800* (New York, 1942), p. 55 (footnote).

[21] Rives, *Madison,* III, 394; Bradford Perkins, *The First Rapprochement* (Philadelphia, 1955), p. 27.

[22] *General Advertiser,* January 23, 1795; Lodge, *Hamilton,* V, April 14, 1794.

system; the involvement of the United States in "the tragedy of Europe"; and the re-enactment in the United States of all the horrors of the French Revolution, including the guillotining of "aristocrats." As for victory over Great Britain, that seemed to the Federalists as improbable as it was undesirable. Certainly, Great Britain was not likely to be seriously inconvenienced by Americans' military might. The United States Army was fully occupied in fighting Indians; the militia was poorly trained and equipped; the arsenals were half empty; and the fortifications of the principal seaports had fallen into decay. The United States, in short, presented the spectacle of a nation armored in righteousness and rectitude but in little else.[23]

Even though they had no heart for war with Great Britain, the Federalists attempted to prepare the country for a clash of arms. "My primary objects," said Washington, ". . . have been to preserve the country in peace if I can, and to be prepared for war if I cannot." To remedy the more palpable weaknesses in American defenses, the Federalists leaders in Congress proposed that an army of 15,000 men be raised, that the President be authorized to request the states to hold 80,000 militia in readiness, that new taxes be imposed, and that a navy be created.

Admittedly, the United States was most vulnerable to attack on blue water, for the Navy was nonexistent, the last ship of the old Continental Navy having been sold in 1784. Even so, James Madison urged that the United States hire the Portuguese Navy rather than construct a fleet of its own; and William B. Giles declared that he "considered navies altogether as very foolish things," the prime cause of the ruinously high taxes to which Englishmen were subjected. As a Federalist speaker pointed out, there was a marked contrast between the kind of language Republicans used against Great Britain and their attitude toward the Barbary corsairs: "The same men whose proud spirits could not brook a pacific interview with one of the most powerful nations in the world, can now humbly crouch to supplicate a peace with the barbarians of *Algiers* on their own terms."[24]

[23] *Annals of Congress,* III, 424, 584, 592; Gibbs, *Memoirs,* I, 107; Ames, *Fisher Ames,* I, 143, II, 160; Duc de la Rochefoucauld-Liancourt, *Travels,* II, 510; *Report of the American Historical Association for 1896* (Washington, 1897), I, 630.
[24] *Annals of Congress,* III, 583; Ames, *Fisher Ames,* II, 158–160; *Independent Chronicle,* June 5, 1794; Hamilton, *Monroe,* I, 286; *General Advertiser,* February 12, March 18, April 3, 1794.

Nevertheless, in February, 1794, Congress authorized the construction of six frigates. All the representatives from Virginia save one voted with the minority.[25] These frigates were expected to be used against the Barbary corsairs, but by an unexpected turn of fate they received their baptism of fire in action against the French. As for the Algerines, instead of receiving shot and shell from American naval vessels, they received a tribute in the form of hard cash. In 1794, the United States government agreed to pay the Dey of Algiers $760,000 and an annual stipend of about $24,000. If this settlement was humiliating for the United States, it was the kind of humiliation to which the European naval powers had long submitted.

In no mood to temporize with that "Leviathan, which aims at swallowing all that floats on the ocean," Congress dropped Madison's Commercial Propositions in the spring of 1794 only to take up a more drastic plan of retaliation. Even stanch Federalists were infected with Anglomania: on March 27, Jonathan Dayton of New Jersey proposed that the United States government sequester the debts owing by American citizens to British merchants and hold them as a security for American property captured by British cruisers. These debts totaled about £4 million, at least half of which was owed by Virginia planters, much of it dating from before the Revolution. Here, therefore, was a plan of action that promised to confer financial advantages upon the planters at the same time that it inflicted injury upon "perfidious Britons." True, the people singled out for punishment were guilty of no greater crime than that of advancing credit to their transatlantic customers, but many Virginians had reached the point where they blamed their creditors for having loaned them money.[26]

From the viewpoint of the Hamiltonian Federalists, the sequestration of debts was worse than Madison's Commercial Propositions; Hamilton declared that he preferred "the manly energies of fair and open war" to "the tricks of a swindler." He did not doubt that sequestration would lead to war, but it would be war in the worst of causes—

[25] *Annals of Congress*, III, 438, 447, 459; Madison to Gates, February 23, 1794, Gates MSS., NYHS; George Hammond to Lord Grenville, February 22, 1794, Hammond MSS., LC; Anderson, *Giles*, pp. 29–30.

[26] Rives, *Madison*, III, 411; Lodge, *Hamilton*, VII, 358; Hunt, *Madison*, VI, 209; *Annals of Congress*, III, 250, 536, 544–549; Fitzpatrick, *Washington*, XXXIII, 414; Ames, *Fisher Ames*, II, 158; Ford, *John Quincy Adams*, I, April 22, 1794; Carroll and Ashworth, *Washington*, VII, 162–165.

to enable debtors to escape from paying their creditors their just dues. As for the credit of the United States government, Hamilton was prepared to deliver a funeral oration over its bier if the sequestration bill passed; no foreigners would ever invest their capital in the public securities or loan money to the private citizens of a country that descended to such barefaced fraud. Jefferson and Madison regarded British credit as a bane; to Hamilton, it was the very life blood of the American economy.[27]

The attempt to inflict economic penalties upon Great Britain in 1794 opened a chasm between the North and South. John Singleton Copley reported that talk of separation was common in Philadelphia and that even the possibility of civil war was not discounted; and John Adams declared that "nearly one half the continent is in constant opposition to the other." In May, 1794, Senator Rufus King of New York informed John Taylor of Virginia that North and South had come to the parting of the ways: since New England would never submit to southern domination and North and South "never had and never would think alike," a "dissolution of the union by mutual consent" seemed the only way out of the impasse. Thus the attempt to coerce Great Britain seemed more likely to weaken and divide the United States than to injure the former mother country.[28]

Even though in January, 1794, the British government repealed the Order in Council of November, 1793, and instructed the admiralty courts in the West Indies to cease their indiscriminate condemnation of American vessels, tension mounted steadily during the spring of 1794. In February of that year, Lord Dorchester, the governor general of Canada, told an assemblage of Indian chiefs that war between Great Britain and the United States was almost certain and that "a line must then be drawn by the warriors." Colonel John Simcoe, the officer in command of the British-occupied American forts, acting un-

[27] Adams, *John Adams*, II, 172–173; Lodge, *Hamilton*, V, April 14, 1794; *Report of the American Historical Association for 1897* (Washington, 1898), pp. 548–549; Stan V. Henkels (ed.), *Washington-Madison Papers* (Philadelphia, 1892), pp. 73–74; *An Address from Robert Goodloe Harper to His Constituents* (Boston, 1796), pp. 13–14.

[28] George Hammond to Lord Grenville, May 10, June 27, 1794, Hammond MSS., LC; *Report of the American Historical Association for 1912* (Washington, 1913), p. 707; C. F. Adams, *John Adams*, II, 160; *Pennsylvania Magazine of History and Biography*, IX (1885), 483; Gaillard Hunt (ed.), *Division Sentiment in Congress in 1794* (Washington, 1905), pp. 21–23; Gibbs, *Memoirs*, I, 136.

der orders from Lord Dorchester, began the construction of a fort on the Miami rapids, well within United States territory. Simcoe declared that the object closest to his heart was "with adequate force and on a just occasion to meet . . . [Washington] face to face." The British government indicated that these were not empty menaces by sending ships of the line to North Atlantic stations with instructions to be prepared for any eventuality.[29]

To the President and his advisers, war seemed almost inevitable in the spring of 1794; the only question in their minds was whether it would be precipitated by the British government or the Republican party.[30] And yet, although the Republicans insisted that it was only a mote in Hamilton's eye, the Secretary of the Treasury discerned a faint ray of hope that peace could be preserved. He believed that the British government was composed of reasonable men who, could they be persuaded that the United States was not bent upon aiding France under the cover of neutrality, would be more than willing to make a liberal settlement with the United States. One of the Secretary's strongest arguments against the punitive measures advocated by the Republicans was that they would defeat all hope of effecting a negotiated settlement with Great Britain.[31]

In March, 1794, resolved to stop the drift toward war, a group of Federalist senators, backed by Hamilton, urged the President to send a minister plenipotentiary to Great Britain. Although Hamilton himself was the choice of most of the party leaders, Washington decided that the Secretary of the Treasury was too controversial a figure for a mission of such extreme delicacy. Instead, he designated Chief Justice John Jay as minister plenipotentiary to Great Britain. But it was Hamilton rather than Secretary of State Edmund Randolph who was responsible for drafting Jay's instructions. Rigorously deleting everything calculated to give umbrage to Great Britain—"energy, without asperity," he said, "seems best to comport with the dignity of national

[29] Report on Canadian Archives (1890), p. 282; D. B. Read, The Life and Times of John Graves Simcoe (Toronto, 1890), pp. 207–211, 231–232; George Hammond to Lord Grenville, August 3, 1794, Hammond MSS., LC; Fitzpatrick, Washington, XXXIII, 310; Rives, Madison, III, 418–419 (footnote); Perkins, First Rapprochement, p. 105; Bemis, Jay's Treaty, pp. 161–177.

[30] Noah Webster, Papers, 218–220; Gazette of the United States, May 20, 1794; American Historical Review, XIV (1909), 780.

[31] George Hammond to Lord Grenville, March 7, 1793, Hammond MSS., LC; Fitzpatrick, Washington, XXXIV, 293–295, 398; Gibbs, Memoirs, I, 133–134.

language . . . We are still in the path of negotiation: let us not plant
it with thorns"—he directed Jay to secure the cession of the western
posts, reparation for losses sustained by the actions of British cruisers
and admiralty courts, compensation for the slaves carried away by the
British army in 1783, and, despite Randolph's opposition, a commercial
treaty with Great Britain.[32]

Jay's appointment came just in time to avert a final Republican
effort to take reprisals upon Great Britain—a measure certain to have
rendered negotiations nugatory. In April, 1794, a bill providing for
nonintercourse with Great Britain passed the House of Representatives
and was defeated in the Senate by the casting vote of Vice-President
Adams. The Republicans had to be content with an embargo imposed
upon American ships. Intended to prevent the capture of American
ships by British cruisers, the embargo was lifted when it was found
that it gravely injured the trade of the South. Thus, by the narrowest
of margins, the government was committed to a policy of attempting
to resolve its differences with Great Britain by negotiation rather than
by economic coercion. Hamilton had won a victory over Jefferson and
Madison, but it remained to be seen whether the Secretary of the
Treasury's trust in the pacific methods of diplomacy would be vindicated by the results of Jay's mission.[33]

Rep. Despite several attempts/efforts
    to take reprisals on G.B. —
        Hamilton negotiated
        this treaty toward
            G.B.

---

[32] Bemis, *American Secretaries of State*, II, 116; Conway, *Randolph*, p.
220; Lodge, *Hamilton*, X, March 28, 1796; Monaghan, *Jay*, 371; James Monroe, *A View of the Executive* (Philadelphia, 1797), vi; Hamilton, *Monroe*,
I, 290; Bemis, *Jay's Treaty*, pp. 196–199; Carroll and Ashworth, *Washington*,
VII, 169–170; Ralston Hayden, *The Senate and Treaties, 1789–1817* (New
York, 1920), p. 92.
[33] *Annals of Congress*, III, 313, 677, 680, 682; Hamilton, *Monroe*, II, 6;
Hunt, *Madison*, VI, 211; Marshall, *Washington*, V, 544; Rives, *Madison*, III,
394; Adams, *John Quincy Adams*, I, 39.

CHAPTER 10

The Whisky Rebellion and Jay's Treaty

WITH John Jay on his way to England, the Federalists began to hope that the worst was over. But their respite from the threat of war proved to be of brief duration. In 1794, the storm center shifted from the foreign to the domestic scene. The Washington administration was compelled to deal with an insurrection in western Pennsylvania at the very time that the issue of peace or war with England hung in the balance.

In response to appeals by Hamilton, Congress had in 1791 authorized an excise tax upon distilled whisky. Republicans as well as Federalists had voted for the measure; despite the unpopularity of the tax, it was generally agreed that the assumption of state debts had saddled the country with financial obligations that could be discharged in no other way.[1] To augment the tariff rates seemed likely to encourage smuggling and discourage consumption. Hamilton himself was unwilling that merchants—the stanchest supporters of his policies—should bear further financial burdens, and he was eager to forestall the states by preempting the excise as a source of revenue for the Federal government.

The Secretary of the Treasury knew that he was committing the government to a trial of strength with Westerners, but he deliberately courted the contest. Even though some of the more oppressive features

[1] All the senators from North Carolina, South Carolina, and Virginia voted for the excise. Three New England senators, including both senators from Massachusetts, voted against it. In the House of Representatives, most of Jefferson's friends voted aye. See Dewey, *Financial History*, pp. 105–106; Gibbs, *Memoirs*, I, 62–63, 157; Maclay, *Journal*, p. 387; *A Short History of Excise Laws* (Philadelphia, 1795), pp. 97–98, 100–101.

of the excise were eliminated from the act of 1791, the fact remained
that excises had provoked resistance whenever they had been levied
by the state governments during the period of the Articles of Confederation. Apart from the invasions of privacy necessitated by the collection of the tax, there were special reasons why an excise on whisky
was certain to arouse the wrath of Westerners. In their minds, the
tax was associated with the assumption of state debts, an unpopular
measure in the West. The duties were oppressively high—about 25 per
cent of the net price of a gallon of whisky. In the interior parts of the
country, where neither bank notes nor hard money circulated, whisky
was a medium of exchange: in hundreds of scattered country stores,
wet goods were bartered for dry goods. Moreover, as long as the Mississippi remained closed to Americans, the distillation of whisky was the
only feasible way of moving grain to market. For these reasons, many
western farmers had a still "out back" and reckoned their fluid wealth
in Monongahela rye.[2]

Westerners were not reconciled to the excise by Hamilton's arguments that it was the most equitable tax that could be devised, that
if they did not like it they could stop drinking whisky, and that Americans consumed altogether too much spirits for their own good. The
College of Physicians of Philadelphia drew up a memorial supporting
the contentions of the Secretary of the Treasury, but General James
Jackson stoutly asserted in Congress the right of his constituents to get
drunk—"that they have been long in the habit of getting drunk and
that they will get drunk in defiance of a dozen colleges or all the
excise duties which Congress might be weak or wicked enough to impose."[3]

The whisky distillers were not the only sufferers by the excise. Hamilton laid down the principle that whenever a domestic industry attained sufficient maturity to bear taxation, it ought to be subject to
internal revenue duties. In 1794, accordingly, snuff and loaf sugar,
two flourishing American industries, were singled out by Congress, at
the Secretary of the Treasury's recommendation, for this unwelcome

[2] Beard, *Economic Origins of Jeffersonian Democracy*, p. 256; Dewey,
Financial History, p. 106; *American State Papers*, VII, Finance, I, 156, 158;
Pennsylvania Archives, Second Series (Harrisburg), IV, 50–51, 141; Brant,
Madison, Father of the Constitution, p. 209; Leland D. Baldwin, *Whisky
Rebels: The Story of a Frontier Uprising* (Pittsburgh, 1939), pp. 94–95, 108.
[3] *General Advertiser*, January 18, 1791; April 28, 1792; Tench Coxe, *View*,
p. 15; *Gazette of the United States*, February 12, 1791; May 19, 1792;
American State Papers, VII, Finance, I, 156; Lodge, *Hamilton*, II, 435.

treatment. The result was an outcry from the manufacturers that they were being made the victims of discriminatory, confiscatory, and unconstitutional taxes. The snuff manufacturers of Pennsylvania drew up a memorial urging the businessmen of America to unite against "the first approaches of tyranny." They received unexpected support from the Virginia Republicans, not hitherto celebrated for devotion to the welfare of American businessmen. But the Treasury stood firm and the manufacturers ceased to protest when they discovered that the excise duties could be safely imposed upon the consumer.

There were rumblings of discontent in the West as early as 1792, but the storm did not break until the summer of 1794.[4] In the four western counties of Pennsylvania, excise officers were terrorized; the Pittsburgh mail was robbed; Federal judicial proceedings were stopped; and a small body of regular troops guarding the house of General John Neville, excise inspector for western Pennsylvania, was forced to surrender. On August 12, at a meeting at Braddock's Field— a location presumably chosen "in terrorem and by way of hint to the effeminate federalists, what a set of bloody-minded fellows they had to deal with"—the insurgents threatened to attack Pittsburgh. Bloodshed was averted only by the townspeople's decision to join the malcontents.[5]

After a presidential proclamation calling upon the insurgents to disperse and the appointment of a commission authorized to offer amnesty in exchange for pledges of obedience to the laws had failed to produce satisfactory evidence of a peaceful disposition on the part of the "Whisky Rebels," President Washington called upon the states to furnish 12,900 men to take the field.[6] This overwhelming force was

[4] One of Westerners' grievances—that those accused of infractions of the excise laws were obliged to stand trial in Philadelphia—had been removed by an act of Congress passed in May, 1794. But the indictments that furnished the ostensible cause of the outbreak in the West were served under the old law.

[5] H. M. Brackenridge, *History of the Western Insurrection* (Pittsburgh, 1859), pp. 144–145; Beard, *Economic Origins of Jeffersonian Democracy*, p. 256; William Findley, *History of the Insurrection in Western Pennsylvania* (Philadelphia, 1796), pp. 74–75; Bennett Milton Rich, *The Presidents and Civil Disorder* (Washington, 1941), p. 6; Alexander Graydon, *Memoirs of a Life Chiefly Passed in Pennsylvania Within the Last Sixty Years* (Harrisburg, 1811), p. 372; Adams, *Gallatin*, p. 94; J. C. Hamilton, *Hamilton*, IV, 281; Lodge, *Hamilton*, II, 435; Carroll and Ashworth, *Washington*, VII, 184–186; Raymond Walters, Jr., "Spokesman of Frontier Democracy: Albert Gallatin in the Pennsylvania Assembly," *Pennsylvania History*, XIII (1946), 166.

[6] By the terms of an act of Congress of 1792, the militia could not be called

necessary, the President declared, because "we had given no testimony to the world of being able or willing to support our government and laws." The President agreed wholeheartedly with Hamilton that "the crisis was arrived when it must be determined whether the Government can maintain itself."[7] Disaffection was spreading in Maryland, Georgia, and the Carolinas; unless the government acted promptly and decisively, the entire West might take up arms. The result of the President's call to arms left the issue in no doubt: there were so many volunteers that the army threatened to become unmanageable because of sheer size. The insurgents, who had flattered themselves that they would march to Philadelphia, "accumulating in their course, and swelling over the banks of the Susquehanna like a torrent—irresistible and devouring in its progress," found themselves confronted by an army larger than Washington had commanded during the War of Independence.[8]

If anything ought to have made Westerners carry out their threat of fighting to the last ditch, it was the presence of the Secretary of the Treasury in the army. Leaving Oliver Wolcott in charge of the Treasury, Hamilton journeyed with Washington to Harrisburg, where the troops were assembled. The President remained with the army only a few weeks, but Hamilton was with the troops almost to the end of the campaign.[9]

Not a little to Hamilton's disappointment, for he yearned to smite the rebels with the full force of the army, the "Whisky Boys" did not have the courage of their potations. The troops encountered nothing more menacing than liberty poles bearing placards reading "Liberty and No Excise. O, Whisky." As for the rebels in arms, not one showed

out until a Federal judge had certified that the courts were unable to cope with the opposition to the laws. On August 4, 1794, Associate Justice James Wilson of the United States Supreme Court certified that the situation in western Pennsylvania was beyond the control of United States marshals or ordinary judicial proceedings.

[7] *Pennsylvania Archives,* Second Series, IV, 105–107, 144–145; Adams, *Gallatin,* p. 138; Fitzpatrick, *Washington,* XXXIV, 28–30; Walters, *Dallas,* p. 56; Boudinot, *Elias Boudinot,* II, 87–88.

[8] Albert Gallatin to Hannah N. Gallatin, December 3, 1794, Gallatin MSS., NYHS; Baldwin, *Whisky Rebels,* p. 222; Findley, *History of the Insurrection,* p. 180; Brackenridge, *Western Insurrection,* pp. 144, 145; *Pennsylvania Archives,* Second Series, IV, 432–433; Adams, *Gallatin,* p. 143; Walters, *Dallas,* pp. 58–59; Carroll and Ashworth, *Washington,* VII, 212–213.

[9] Boudinot, *Elias Boudinot,* II, August 7, 1794; *Gazette of the United States,* August 20, 1794; *Independent Chronicle,* November 24, 1790.

himself even though the army marched across the Alleghenies in search of these elusive malcontents. In truth, however, the advocates of violent resistance to the laws were few in number and the influence of the moderate leaders, including the Presbyterian clergy, soon asserted itself. The moving spirits of overt resistance, David Bradford and James Marshel, fled across the Ohio. It was a forlorn hope that a few frontiersmen, menaced by the Indians at their rear, could withstand the military force of the United States.[10]

As a result, the bag of prisoners taken by the army was meager in the extreme. Nonetheless, the administration made the most of its catch: twenty prisoners were paraded down Market Street in Philadelphia and kept in prison for months. But there was not a single person of prominence or influence among them; in this respect, the result hardly seemed worthy of the magnitude of the government's effort. Only two prisoners were found guilty of high treason—levying war against the United States—but Washington pardoned both. One, he said, was a "simpleton," the other "insane."[11]

Even though, as Jefferson said, "an insurrection was announced and proclaimed and armed against, but could never be found," Hamilton declared that the government had gained "reputation and strength" by demonstrating that it was capable of compelling obedience to the laws. The quick collapse of resistance in the West was made to appear as a vindication of Hamiltonian "energy." Nevertheless, the firmness and vigor shown by the administration in dealing with this crisis were not reflected in any upsurge of its popularity among the voters. Fisher Ames, a philosopher in politics, observed that "a regular government, by overcoming an unsuccessful insurrection, becomes stronger; but elective rulers can scarcely ever employ the physical force of a democracy without turning the moral force, or the power of public opinion, against the government."[12]

[10] Adams, *Gallatin*, I, 5, 10–11; Charles Biddle, *Autobiography* (Philadelphia, 1883), p. 262; Lodge, *Hamilton*, VI, August 28, 1794; Gibbs, *Memoirs*, I, 155; Adams, *Gallatin*, p. 148; Gallatin to Hannah N. Gallatin, December 3, 1794, Gallatin MSS., NYHS.

[11] Rich, *Presidents and Civil Disorder*, pp. 15–18; Boudinot, *Elias Boudinot*, II, 87; Findley, *History of the Insurrection*, pp. 261, 279; Adams, *Gallatin*, p. 149.

[12] Ford, *Jefferson*, VII, May 26, 1795; A. McLane Hamilton, *The Intimate Life of Alexander Hamilton* (New York, 1911), p. 231; Ford, *John Quincy Adams*, I, November 7, 1794; Ames, *Fisher Ames*, II, 362; Graydon, *Memoirs*, p. 372; Hunt, *Madison*, VI, 220.

The authority of the Federal government had been amply vindicated in 1794, but President Washington was not willing to let the matter rest there. He believed that the government's victory would not be complete until the real fomenters of the insurrection had been pointed out to the American people. From the first manifestation of trouble in the West, President Washington was sure in his own mind that he was witnessing "the first formidable fruit of the Democratic Societies." "I early gave it as my opinion to the confidential characters around me," he said, "that, if these Societies were not counteracted (not by prosecutions, the ready way to make them grow stronger) or did not fall into detestation from the knowledge of their origin . . . that they would shake the government to its foundation." Under this conviction, he inserted in his message to Congress of November, 1794, a denunciation of the "self-created societies" as the prime movers of the Whisky Rebellion.[13]

The Democratic Societies were products of the enthusiasm for the French Revolution that had swept the United States in 1793. Genêt was the founder of the Philadelphia Society, the "mother society" of a brood that numbered over forty. These societies corresponded with each other as had the Corresponding Societies during the American Revolution; they were dedicated to the extirpation of "aristocracy" and "monarchism" (in which they included Hamiltonian finance) in the United States; they actively campaigned in behalf of candidates who met their approval; they undertook to tell the American people who were their friends and who were their enemies; they instructed representatives and senators in their duty; they organized and brought out the voters, particularly in the urban centers; and they fervently upheld the cause of France.[14]

All this might seem innocent enough: the Democratic Clubs were simply the Americans for Democratic Action of their generation. But the year was 1794 and the shadow of the French Revolution fell menacingly upon the United States. In the eyes of skittish Federalists, these clubs were the precursor of all the horrors of "Jacobinism." "Beheading Federalists is the present reigning fashion in France," remarked a Federalist newspaper, "and . . . it is too delightful a recreation, not to be universally enjoyed." It was not doubted that in

[13] Lodge, *Hamilton*, X, November 27, 1794; Fitzpatrick, *Washington*, XXXIII, 475–476, 506–507, 524; XXXIV, 3; Gibbs, *Memoirs*, I, 179; Carroll and Ashworth, *Washington*, VII, 215–225.

[14] *National Gazette*, June 8, 1793; Link, *Democratic-Republican Societies*, pp. 11–13, 20, 43, 103, 124, 155.

their secret conclaves the members of the Democratic Clubs plotted the overthrow of the government by force. For these reasons, Washington regarded the societies as "the most diabolical attempt to destroy the best fabric of human government and happiness, that has ever been presented for the acceptance of mankind."[15]

It was easier for the President to indict than to convict the Democratic Societies of responsibility for the Whisky Rebellion. Resistance to the excise had appeared long before Genêt "brought the eggs of these venomous reptiles to our shores." Westerners' resentment was not only directed against the excise: the failure of the government to secure the navigation of the Mississippi and the cession of the Northwest posts; the land policies that permitted a few individuals to engross large amounts of land; the necessity of standing trial in Philadelphia —these grievances likewise long antedated the appearance of the Democratic Societies. Although some of the leaders of the Democratic Society in western Pennsylvania played a prominent part in the riots, elsewhere so many members of the clubs volunteered for service against the rebels that it was said that "the Democratic Society of Pennsylvania could have made a quorum in the field."[16]

Nor, indeed, could any of the numerous societies in the United States escape the reproach of being "self-created." The Society of the Cincinnati (of which Washington was president), St. Andrew's Society, and St. George's Society owed their origin to the initiative of a few individuals. The Society of the Sons of Saint Tammany, sometimes called the Columbian Order, came into being as a sort of poor man's Cincinnati. The members celebrated Saint Tammany's Day (the first of May) and patriotic holidays by dressing like Indians, smoking the peace pipe, and drinking toasts until the Wigwam rang with their war whoops. The Tammany braves indignantly denied their "self-created society" had anything to do with the Whisky Rebellion, but they did not claim to be ignorant of whisky.[17]

Thus the question laid before the House of Representatives in

[15] Ford, *Jefferson*, VII, May 7, 1794; Edmund Randolph to Washington, October 21, 1794, Washington MSS., LC.

[16] The leaders of the two Philadelphia Democratic Societies were physicians, lawyers, and businessmen. There were three clubs in western Pennsylvania: the Mingo Creek Society, the Republican Society of the Yough, and the Democratic Society in Washington County. Of these clubs, the Mingo Creek Society was the most radical. Fitzpatrick, *Washington*, XXXIII, 475–476, 507; XXXIV, 3; Walters, *Dallas*, p. 63; Morison, *Jeremiah Smith*, 67–68; *Gazette of the United States*, February 21, March 2, 7, April 12, 1794.

[17] Rives, *Madison*, III, 470; Hunt, *Madison*, VI, 221–223; *Pennsylvania*

November, 1794—to sustain or to repudiate President Washington's condemnation of "self-created societies"—was fraught with implications not foreseen by the President. On the one hand, it was pointed out that, by refusing to concur with the President and Senate, the House would in effect be "rekindling the fire-brands of sedition . . . unchaining the demon of anarchy." On the other hand, Madison declared that it was unconstitutional for Congress to censure the clubs: opinions were not the object of legislation; the right of discussing, writing, and publishing could not legally be invaded by the Federal government; and "the censorial power is in the people over the Government, and not in the Government over the people." So adamant were Madison and his supporters that the Federalists could do no more than effect a compromise which barely saved the President's dignity: "combinations of men" was substituted for "societies."[18]

President Washington would have been well advised to have let the Democratic Societies die a natural death instead of attempting to hasten their end by singling them out for his official disapproval. By so doing, he tended to impair the real strength of his position in American politics—his Olympian aloofness from the partisan struggles that raged about him. The condemnation of the Democratic Societies planted the idea in Republicans' minds that President Washington was at heart a Federalist or—even worse—a Hamiltonian. As it transpired, there was no real necessity for the President to risk his popularity upon this issue: within a year, the Democratic Societies had ceased to exist, not so much because of Washington's censures as because of the decline and final extinction of the societies in France itself and of the increasingly critical attitude adopted by Americans toward the French Revolution.[19]

The suppression of the Whisky Rebellion was the last important event in Hamilton's career as a member of the cabinet. He had announced his intention of retiring from the Treasury if the congressional

Magazine of History and Biography, XXVI (1902), 216–218, 433; Stokes, Iconography, V, 1267, 1291–1292, 1437; Findley, History of the Insurrection, 166–167.

[18] Letters of Germanicus to the Citizens of the United States (Philadelphia, 1794), pp. 8–9; Gazette of the United States, April 24, June 21, 1794; Rives, Madison, III, 470; Hunt, Madison, VI, 221–223.

[19] Adams, Gallatin, III, 104–105; Hunt, Madison, VI, 222–223; Pennsylvania Magazine of History and Biography, LXII (1938), 348; Baldwin, Whisky Rebels, p. 270.

elections proved favorable for the Federalists. As it turned out, the elections went against the Federalists. In January, 1795, Albert Gallatin—regarded by Federalists as one of the principal fomenters of the Whisky Rebellion and the man whom Hamilton hoped to bring back to Philadelphia in chains—was elected to Congress. A year previous to this election, the Federalists had succeeded in expelling Gallatin from the United States Senate (where he had quickly made himself a thorn in Hamilton's side) on the ground that he had not been a citizen for seven years, as required by the Constitution, but in the House of Representatives Gallatin was in an even better position to make trouble for the Federalists. Besides being a first-rate political leader (after Madison's retirement, he directed the Republican forces in the House of Representatives), Gallatin was a financial expert: alone among the Republicans he was capable of challenging Hamilton upon the Secretary of the Treasury's own ground.[20]

This untoward turn of events strengthened Hamilton's decision to retire. He was thoroughly disillusioned about public service: the low pay, the abuse and vilification, "the jealousy of power and the spirit of faction," inflicted unbearable hardships, he said, upon those who tried to serve the people. Nevertheless, when he left Philadelphia in January, 1795, he thought of himself as retiring from office, not from power; and even as a New York attorney he continued to exert vast influence upon the cabinet and the President.[21]

By stepping down from the "fiscal throne," Hamilton was spared the frustration and humiliation at the hands of the Republicans in Congress that fell to the lot of his successor in the Treasury, Oliver Wolcott. The House of Representatives asserted its control of finance through the instrumentality of the Committee of Ways and Means, and in 1797 Gallatin succeeded in further tying the hands of the Secretary of the Treasury by instituting a system of specific in place of general appropriations. With Hamilton gone and the Republicans bent upon asserting the prerogatives of Congress, the Treasury ceased to be an important policy-making department of the government.[22]

[20] Adams, *Gallatin*, pp. 121, 142, 154, 167, 214; Rives, *Madison*, III, 274–275; Studenski and Krooss, *Financial History*, pp. 71–72; Lodge, *Hamilton*, IX, 521; Findley, *History of the Insurrection*, p. 259.
[21] A. M. Hamilton, *Intimate Life*, pp. 231–232; Lodge, *Hamilton*, X, May 2, 1797.
[22] Studenski and Krooss, *Financial History*, pp. 71–72; Binkley, *President and Congress*, pp. 52–54.

In the autumn of 1794, when the United States seemed on the verge of civil war, John Jay was trying to avert war with Great Britain. But Jay arrived in London at an unpropitious moment for extracting concessions from the British government. In June, 1794, the British were flushed with victory over the French, and, during most of the summer and autumn, the American plenipotentiary conducted negotiations with Lord Grenville, the Foreign Secretary, against a background of British military and naval triumphs in the West Indies.[23]

Nevertheless, Jay discovered a surprising amount of cordiality in the British government. William Pitt and Lord Grenville were eager to settle the dispute with the United States and even the King spoke kindly to Jay. Not to be outdone in civility, Jay praised George III's "justice and benevolence"—singular words coming from a signer of the Declaration of Independence. But Jay prided himself upon having discarded all the awkward "ancient Prejudices" that stood in the way of a settlement with Great Britain; and to see him at a weekend party frolicking with lords and ladies, it was difficult to believe that he had once been proscribed as an enemy of Great Britain.[24]

Throughout his negotiations with Lord Grenville, Jay acted upon the principle that "the quarrel between Britain and America was a family quarrel, and that it is time it should be made up." He did not threaten the British with economic or military reprisals; nor did he bring up the possibility that the United States would join the Armed Neutrality recently formed by the Scandinavian powers to uphold neutral rights against the British navy. Without the authorization of President Washington, Alexander Hamilton had already told the British minister that the United States had no intention of associating itself with the Armed Neutrality. Both Jay and Hamilton assumed that menaces would defeat the whole purpose of Jay's mission and that

[23] The tide of battle began to turn against the British in the autumn of 1794. Defeat in the Low Countries and the defection of Prussia led Lord Auckland to term 1794 "the most calamitous year of the century." See J. C. Hamilton, *Hamilton*, V, 54; Jay to Hamilton, July 18, 1794, Hamilton MSS., LC; Sir A. W. Ward and G. P. Gooch, *The Cambridge History of British Foreign Policy, 1783–1919* (Cambridge, Eng., 1922–23), I, 245, 252–254; J. W. Fortescue, *British Statesmen of the Great War*, p. 191; *Parliamentary History*, XXI, 683, 1036–1037, 1052–1053, 1133; Paul Frischauer, *England's Years of Danger*, xiv; John Adolphus, *The History of England* (London, 1843), VI, 25–26, 29–30, 32–33.

[24] Jay to Washington, November 19, 1794, Washington MSS., LC; Perkins, *First Rapprochement*, pp. 22–23.

a conciliatory attitude alone offered hope of success. And, in truth, the British government would have sent Jay packing had it believed that the Washington administration was hostile. The British did not want war with the United States—as a British minister said, the Americans "are so much in debt to this country that we scarcely dare to quarrel with them"—but the issue of war or peace depended to a large degree upon the conduct pursued by the United States toward the belligerents. It was precisely because the Federalists seemed to stand as a barrier to "the Torrent of Jacobin Principles" in the United States that Lord Grenville was disposed to make concessions.[25]

It was not Alexander Hamilton but James Monroe who weakened Jay's position in London.[26] Monroe had been appointed American minister to France at almost the same time Jay was sent to England. Monroe was a Republican and ardently pro-French in his sympathies —to which he gave expression by embracing the President and delivering a rousing speech to the National Assembly. Upon this conduct, Lord Grenville looked coldly: he told Jay that if Monroe represented the attitude of his government, it would be difficult for His Majesty's ministers to regard it as truly neutral. And unless the British government was persuaded that the United States intended to remain neutral, it was not likely to surrender the Northwest posts or to make a commercial treaty with the republic.[27]

To secure these objectives, Jay was obliged in effect to renounce the freedom of the seas. The maritime principles which the United States had bound itself to uphold in its previous treaties with foreign powers—free ships make free goods, neutrals are entitled to trade freely with belligerents in noncontraband goods, and the contraband list must be confined to a few warmaking articles—were jettisoned by Jay as the price of Anglo-American harmony. In their place, the British concept of belligerents' rights was written into the treaty: naval

[25] *American Historical Review*, XXIV (1919), 29–33, 36–38, 42–43; Adams, *John Adams*, IX, 86–87; Conway, *Randolph*, p. 221; Mayo, *Instructions to British Ministers*, pp. 55, 61, 67–68; Lodge, *Hamilton*, VII, 359; Hammond to Lord Grenville, August 3, 1794, Hammond Correspondence, LC.

[26] S. F. Bemis contends that in effect Hamilton sacrificed the position of the United States by renouncing the threat of joining the Armed Neutrality. *Jay's Treaty*, pp. 218–231, 269.

[27] Jay to Hamilton, September 11, 1794, Hamilton MSS., LC; James Greig (ed.), *The Farrington Diary* (London, 1923), I, 56; Johnston, *Jay*, IV, 27, 33–34, 114–115; Mayo, *Instructions to British Ministers*, p. 66; J. C. Hamilton, *Hamilton*, V, 27.

stores were held to be contraband; provisions, under some ill-defined circumstances, could not be carried in neutral ships to enemy ports; and the United States acquiesced in the so-called "Rule of 1756" by which trade with enemy colonies prohibited in time of peace could not be legalized in time of war. To preclude the possibility of discriminatory legislation against British ships and merchandise, Great Britain was granted most-favored-nation treatment; and it was agreed that private debts were not amenable to sequestration. Finally, the United States gave assurances that it would not permit its ports to be made a base of operations for the ships and privateers of His Britannic Majesty's enemies and that the sale of prizes in American ports would no longer be permitted.[28]

In exchange for these concessions, the British government promised to surrender the Northwest posts by June, 1796. The other outstanding disputes between the two countries—the amount of compensation for spoliations, the claims of British creditors who had been deprived of their money by legal obstructions in the United States, the disputed Northwest Boundary between the United States and Canada—were referred to the arbitrament of joint commissions. The British agreed to pay for the spoliations upon American commerce, but the United States government had to promise to pay the claims of British creditors against American citizens. Conspicuously absent from the treaty was any mention of compensation for slaves belonging to American citizens emancipated by the British army in 1783; nor were there any guarantees against the impressment of American sailors by the British navy.[29]

As he had been directed by Hamilton, Jay made a commercial treaty with Great Britain, the terms of which were contained in the twelfth article. Here it was stipulated that American ships were to enjoy, under certain restrictions, the privilege of trading with India. The British West Indies, hitherto closed to American ships, were opened to vessels of seventy tons or less. Thus, while Jay succeeded in breaching the mercantilist walls Great Britain had erected round its empire, the crack was so small that hardly more than a fishing smack could get through. To secure even this limited trade to the British West Indies, Jay was compelled to promise that molasses, sugar, coffee,

[28] S. F. Bemis, *John Quincy Adams and the Foundations of American Foreign Policy* (New York, 1949), pp. 42–45; James Callender, *The American Annual Register* (Philadelphia, 1797), p. 287; Fitzpatrick, *Washington* XXXVI, 234.
[29] Bemis, *Jay's Treaty*, pp. 232–251, 258–261.

cocoa, or cotton would not be carried in American ships to any part of the world except the United States.[30]

In agreeing to this self-denying ordinance, Jay was not guilty of indifference to the future importance of cotton in the American economy.[31] In actuality, Jay was a good Hamiltonian who believed that the United States ought to manufacture for itself all the cotton it grew. As for the treaty as a whole, the only concession that Jay might have secured by a more resolute demeanor was a stipulation requiring payment for the Negro slaves the British had carried away from the United States during the War of Independence. But Jay pressed this point halfheartedly: he had already admitted that on this score the United States was in the wrong and as a prominent abolitionist he could not but rejoice that the slaves had gained their freedom.[32]

From the viewpoint of the British government it had displayed remarkable magnanimity toward the United States. Lord Grenville felt that he had gone as far as he could without forfeiting the support of Parliament; even so, the ministry was obliged to defend itself in the House of Commons against charges of pro-Americanism and indifference to the Acts of Trade and Navigation. By way of answer to these allegations, Pitt declared that the treaty had been "dictated on both sides by a spirit of fairness and mutual accommodation."[33]

The terms of Jay's Treaty were kept secret until the Senate had been given an opportunity to act. It seemed probable that the Senate would reject incontinently Jay's handiwork; only after the obnoxious twelfth article had been stricken out were the proponents of the treaty able to secure the necessary two-thirds majority. Again the voting was on sectional lines: only two New England senators voted against it; both senators from Virginia cast their votes with the minority.[34]

Despite the injunction of secrecy, the text of the treaty was leaked

[30] Bemis, *American Secretaries of State*, II, 116; Conway, *Randolph*, p. 220; Perkins, *First Rapprochement*, pp. 70–71.

[31] By gaining the privilege of limited trade with the British West Indies, Jay probably hoped that "we should completely possess all of the West India trade and form inflexible habits of dependence upon our supplies, which at the end of the term ought to lead to better conditions. In the meantime our consumers here would obtain West India articles on more moderate terms." Gibbs, *Memoirs*, I, 213.

[32] Gibbs, *Memoirs*, I, 180; *An Address from Robert Goodloe Harper to His Constituents* (Boston, 1796), pp. 7, 17; Bemis, *Jay's Treaty*, pp. 212–217, 267–268.

[33] Johnston, *Jay*, IV, 163–164; Perkins, *First Rapprochement*, p. 5.

[34] Charles, *American Party System*, p. 105 (footnote); Perkins, *First Rapprochement*, pp. 30–32.

168 THE FEDERALIST ERA

to Benjamin Bache, publisher of the Philadelphia *General Advertiser,* or *Aurora.* To those Americans who believed that the British Lion was "perishing in his den of iniquity," Jay's Treaty came as a nasty shock. "To what state of degradation are we reduced," they exclaimed, "that we *court* a nation more perfidious than Savages—more sanguinary than Tigers—barbarous as Cannibals—and prostituted even to a proverb," especially when, without firing a shot, the United States might have hastened the doom of this monster. No doubt the Republicans would have opposed any treaty with Great Britain—in their eyes, the eternal enemy of liberty and the moving spirit of "the great confederacy against human happiness." But Jay's Treaty went beyond anything they had expected; to them it seemed that the American negotiator had linked the United States with the "Caligula of Great Britain" in his scheme of "starving a whole people out of their liberties."[35]

At first, the cry against the treaty was, said Washington, "like that against a mad dog." John Jay wryly observed that he could have found his way across the country by the light of his burning effigies in which he was represented selling his country for British gold. The Boston town meeting condemned Jay's Treaty without even reading it, and in a meeting in New York City Hamilton was pelted with stones when he attempted to speak in its favor. A Philadelphia orator urged his audience to "kick this damned treaty to Hell," and even well-to-do merchants, the pillars of the Federalist party, seemed disposed to give it the boot. For having kissed the hand of the Queen of England, it was said that Jay deserved to have his lips "blistered to the bone." In July, 1795, Charles Pinckney of South Carolina moved to request the President to take steps to have Jay impeached. Jay had put himself beyond the Republicans' wrath by resigning the office of Chief Justice to accept the governorship of New York. It is significant that he was elected before the terms of his treaty had been made public.[36]

In defense of Jay's Treaty, Alexander Hamilton and Rufus King wrote a series of newspaper articles under the signature "Camillus." But the principal reliance of the Federalists to carry the treaty with the country was the popularity of President Washington.

[35] Ford, *Jefferson,* VII, November 30, 1795; *Remarks Occasioned by the Late Conduct of Mr. Washington* (Philadelphia, 1797), p. 1; *Features of Mr. Jay's Treaty* (Philadelphia, 1795), p. 36; John Page, *An Address* (Richmond, 1796), p. 14; Perkins, *First Rapprochement,* pp. 32–33.
[36] *Independent Chronicle,* December 25, 1794; Perkins, *First Rapprochement,* pp. 32–35.

Even the President, however, was far from certain in his own mind that Jay's Treaty warranted his approval. And yet, since he saw no alternative except war with Great Britain, he suppressed his own doubts and reservations and was on the point of signing the treaty when reports arrived that the British had begun to seize American ships carrying foodstuffs to France.[37] Deeply angered by what he regarded as British perfidy, Washington went to Mount Vernon resolved not to sign. In August, 1795, he was summoned to Philadelphia by the astounding news that Secretary of State Edmund Randolph, who had strongly advised the President to withhold his signature, had been detected in an intrigue with Fauchet, the French minister.[38]

Randolph's dereliction might have gone undetected had it not been for British disregard of the three-mile limit established by the United States. Captain Home of H.M.S. *Africa* stopped and searched the American sloop *Peggy* in American coastal waters in the hope of taking prisoner Citizen Fauchet, the French minister to the United States. Fauchet had left the ship in Connecticut, but his papers were aboard and these Captain Home removed from the *Peggy*. The British government deliberately kept Fauchet's papers in reserve until they would do the most good. In July, 1795, with Jay's Treaty hanging in the balance, the British minister presented these documents to the United States government. From them it appeared that Randolph, who had opposed the use of force against the Whisky Rebels, had divulged state secrets to Fauchet and had appealed to him to bribe several prominent Pennsylvania Republicans (presumably Governor Thomas Mifflin and Secretary of the Commonwealth A. J. Dallas) to restore peace in western Pennsylvania.[39] "Thus," observed Fauchet to his superiors in

[37] The United States admitted that provisions were contraband only when being conveyed to some port absolutely blockaded or under siege. According to international law, a blockade to be binding must be effective; and to be effective it was generally agreed that there must be a sufficient naval or military force to make running the blockade hazardous.

[38] Conway, *Randolph*, p. 269; Fitzpatrick, *Washington*, XXXIV, 293–295, 399; Irving Brant, "Edmund Randolph, Not Guilty!" *William and Mary Quarterly*, Third Series, VII (1950), 180–189; Charles, *American Party System*, pp. 104–106; Josiah T. Newcomb, "New Light on Jay's Treaty," *American Journal of International Law*, XXVIII (1934), 687; W. C. Ford (ed.), "Edmund Randolph on the British Treaty," *American Historical Review*, XII (1907), 587–599.

[39] Randolph subsequently explained that he referred only to some American flour merchants who, possessed of information damning to the British, feared to divulge it lest they be ruined by their creditors. Fauchet was asked to loan

Paris, "with some thousands of dollars the Republic would have decided on civil war or on peace! Thus the consciences of the pretended patriots of America have already their scale of prices!" It was all Hamilton's fault, said Fauchet, that American politicians had their price: "He has made of a whole nation a stock-jobbing, speculating, selfish people." But the French minister declined to lay out any of his government's money upon such dubious characters.[40]

Reading Fauchet's dispatches, Washington drew the inference that Randolph's purpose had been to raise ready cash for himself and his political friends, most of whom were Republicans. Whatever the Secretary of State may have had in mind, it was clear that he had compromised himself so deeply with the French minister that his usefulness to the government was at an end. In a full cabinet meeting, Randolph was asked to read Fauchet's dispatch. As he read, the President and the heads of departments watched him intently for telltale signs of guilt. When Randolph was asked for an explanation of his conduct, his answer failed to carry conviction either with the President or the members of the cabinet. Knowing that he already stood condemned by his colleagues, Randolph resigned as Secretary of State. He subsequently retired to Virginia, where he wrote his *Vindication,* which, however, was more notable for its intemperate attack upon Washington than for a convincing justification of Randolph's conduct. He de-

money to these individuals, not to corrupt American politicians. In 1796, Randolph published *Political Truth, or . . . an Inquiry into the Truth of the Charges Preferred against Mr. Randolph.* The subject has been exhaustively examined by Irving Brant in "Edmund Randolph, Not Guilty!" *William and Mary Quarterly,* Third Series, VII (1950), 180–198. It is clear that the British government was determined to ruin Randolph, whom it regarded as one of its most inveterate enemies in the United States. Nor was Hamilton displeased to see Randolph dismissed from the government. Jefferson had frequently complained that Randolph was a trimmer—"the most indecisive person I ever had to do business with . . . half for it, and half against it, according to custom." Yet he was far more of a Jeffersonian than a Hamiltonian. In the majority of cases he sided with Jefferson on important cabinet divisions. Bemis, *American Secretaries of State,* II, 99–100; Conway, *Randolph,* pp. 198–201, 207–208; Mary L. Hinsdale, *A History of the President's Cabinet* (New York, 1911), p. 25; Ford, *Jefferson,* I, 263; Rives, *Madison,* III, 380–381 (footnote); Mayo, *Instructions to British Ministers,* pp. 73–75, 126; Gibbs, *Memoirs,* I, 230; *Windham Papers,* I, 126.

[40] Gibbs, *Memoirs,* I, 266–267, 271; Walters, *Dallas,* p. 71; *A Translation of Citizen Fauchet's Intercepted Letter* (Philadelphia, 1795), pp. 10, 16; *Report of the American Historical Association,* II (1903), 413–414, 444–445, 450; Charles, *American Party System,* pp. 107–108; DeConde, *Entangling Alliance,* p. 417.

clared that he had suffered at Washington's hands the injustice of an "assassin" and he asserted that his only crime consisted of attempting to save republicanism in the United States from the so-called Father of His Country.[41] Randolph had reason to complain, not of his dismissal, for he had wholly forfeited his position in the government, but of the treatment meted out to him after his forced retirement from office. He was charged with a deficit of more than $50,000 in his department, and, since the head of a department was held accountable for shortages, he and his family were obliged to make good the entire amount.[42]

At the risk of making it appear that American policy was based upon considerations other than the merits of the treaty itself, Washington signed Jay's Treaty even though Randolph's alleged conniving with the French minister had occurred over a year before. The British had not repealed the Order in Council to which Washington objected and they did not do so until after he had signed the treaty. The truth is, Randolph's actions convinced the President that French influence was rife even in the highest councils of the government and that unless a settlement was made with Great Britain the United States stood in grave danger of being converted into a French satellite.

Unhappily for the Federalists, by affixing his signature to Jay's Treaty, President Washington did not put an end to the controversy that had bedeviled the country since June, 1795. Public opinion was still highly critical of the treaty; and the Republican leaders, emboldened by the knowledge that they had a large amount of public backing, were resolved to kill the treaty in the House of Representatives.

[41] After the Randolph affair, Washington abandoned all hope of achieving union by giving representation in the cabinet to different political points of view. In 1795, he declared that he would not appoint to any office of consequence a man "whose political tenets are adverse to the measures which the general government are pursuing; for this, in my opinion, would be a sort of political Suicide." Hinsdale, *History of the President's Cabinet*, pp. 24–25; Fitzpatrick, *Washington*, XXXIV, 315. See also Henkels, *Washington-Madison Papers*, pp. 161–162; Octavius Pickering and Charles Upham, *Life of Timothy Pickering* (Boston, 1867–73), III, 216; Conway, *Randolph*, 328; J. C. Hamilton, *Hamilton*, VI, 39; Lodge, *Hamilton*, X, 115–116, 123; Channing, *History*, IV, 144; Gibbs, *Memoirs*, I, 265–266; Carroll and Ashworth, *Washington*, VII, 265–268.

[42] Stephen G. Kurtz, *The Presidency of John Adams* (Philadelphia, 1957), p. 264.

This state of affairs produced the first party caucus held in Congress. In order to commit the Republican party as a whole to a predetermined course of action in the House of Representatives, the party leaders called a meeting of members of Congress known to be hostile to Jay's Treaty. Even though this meeting failed to produce agreement, it was a significant step toward the creation of a unified, disciplined party responsive to policies laid down by its leaders.[43]

In March, 1796, by a vote of sixty-two to thirty-seven, the House of Representatives adopted a motion introduced by Edward Livingston of New York, calling upon the President to submit to its scrutiny all the papers relating to Jay's Treaty excepting "such papers as any existing negotiation may render improper to be disclosed." By this action, the House attempted to give concrete application to the theory that the concurrence of the lower house of Congress was necessary to give validity to treaties and that by virtue of its control of appropriations it possessed a discretionary power of carrying a treaty into effect.[44]

After taking counsel with his cabinet and with Alexander Hamilton, who, at the age of forty, served the Federalist party somewhat in the capacity of an elder statesman, Washington decided to deny the House's request. In his message to Congress, the President went farther than his advisers deemed prudent: not only did he declare that treaties duly ratified by the Senate and signed by the President were the supreme law of the land, but he cited as proof of the correctness of his interpretation of the Constitution his personal knowledge of the proceedings of the Constitutional Convention. During the meetings of that body, he pointed out, a proposal to give the House a voice in the treaty-making power had been rejected.[45]

The grounds upon which the President based his refusal to gratify the wishes of the House brought James Madison into the thick of the dispute. Up to this point, Madison had tried to cool the party hot-

[43] On a lower level of party organization, machinery for nominating candidates was beginning to be set up in the states, notably in New York and Pennsylvania, where the parties were nearly equally divided and where, consequently, rivalry was kept at a high pitch. Committees representing articulate groups and interests were established to nominate candidates and to promote their election by the distribution on a state-wide basis of letters, newspaper articles, and handbills.

[44] Henkels, *Washington-Madison Letters*, p. 76; David Redick to Gallatin, April 20, 1796, Gallatin MSS., NYHS; *Features of Mr. Jay's Treaty* (Philadelphia, 1795), p. 36.

[45] Kurtz, *Presidency of John Adams*, pp. 35, 40; Hamilton to Wolcott, April, 1796, Wolcott MSS., CHS; Lodge, *Hamilton*, X, March 28, 1796.

heads. The peremptory tone of Livingston's original motion had offended Madison, and he had succeeded in attaching an amendment acknowledging the President's right to withhold documents prejudicial to existing negotiations. But as the leading authority on the Constitution in the House of Representatives, Madison could not permit Washington's interpretation of that document to pass unchallenged. Above all, he rejected the President's dictum that the proceedings of the Constitutional Convention must govern the interpretation put upon the Constitution. That piece of parchment, he declared, was "nothing but a dead letter, and life and validity were breathed into it by the voice of the people." And that voice was to be heard not in the debates of the Constitutional Convention but in the proceedings of the state ratifying conventions.[46]

In actuality, what Madison did in 1796 was not to refer the question to the people but to set up his own interpretation of the Constitution against Washington's. Madison's views were contained in resolutions introduced by William Blount to the effect that while the House did not claim any agency in making treaties "when a Treaty must depend for its execution . . . on a law or laws to be passed by Congress . . . it is the Constitutional right and duty of the House of Representatives to deliberate on the expediency or inexpediency of carrying such treaty into effect." It was not necessary, the Madison-Blount resolutions held, for the House to state the purpose for which such information was wanted; it was sufficient that the House had expressed a desire for the information. If a majority of representatives were dissatisfied with the provisions of a treaty which called for the expenditure of money to carry it into effect, that majority, Madison contended, enjoyed the right of withholding the necessary appropriation and thereby in effect nullifying the treaty.[47]

These resolutions appealed not only to the opponents of Jay's Treaty but to the even larger number of representatives who were eager to uphold the constitutional rights of the legislature against the executive. Nor were the representatives in the mood to thank the President for having, out of his wisdom, set them straight concerning

[46] Morison, *Jeremiah Smith*, p. 98; Oliver Ellsworth to Trumbull, March 13, 1796; Oliver Wolcott to Washington, March 26, 1796, Washington MSS., LC; Draft of a Speech for Washington, March 29, 1796, Hamilton MSS., LC; Fitzpatrick, *Washington*, XXXV, 29.

[47] Perkins, *First Rapprochement*, p. 40; Brown, *First Republicans*, pp. 113–116; Cunningham, *Jeffersonian Republicans*, pp. 80–83.

the Constitution. In consequence, the Blount-Madison proposals were carried by a majority of fifty-seven to thirty-five, indicating that not a few Federalists voted with the Republicans. Thus the President, his own party badly split, was confronted by a large majority of the House of Representatives led by James Madison.

Hamilton met this crisis by mobilizing the businessmen behind Jay's Treaty and the President's constitutional theory.[48] Public meetings were called to protest the action of the House, and a veritable flood of petitions in favor of Jay's Treaty, some of them from western farmers, poured in upon the representatives, and, at the same time, the predominantly Federalist Senate threatened to postpone the ratification of the Spanish and Algerian treaties until the House agreed to carry Jay's Treaty into execution. The Republican strategy seemed, therefore, to have succeeded in dividing the people and in creating a situation fraught with danger to the Union. The dilemma of the Republicans was aggravated by the fact that they desperately wanted the advantages of Jay's Treaty—above all, the cession of the western posts —which would be forfeited if the House refused to implement the treaty.[49]

Beset by these doubts and misgivings and unnerved by the petitions that poured in upon them, the Republicans' majority in the House began to wither away.[50] By the end of April, 1796, the two parties were almost evenly divided. At this juncture, Fisher Ames of Massachusetts delivered one of the most moving speeches ever heard in the House of Representatives. Probably it decided no votes, but it made Ames's reputation as one of the great orators of American history. The Federalist representative from Massachusetts, ill, cadaverous, his voice so

[48] In *The Economic Origins of Jeffersonian Democracy*, pp. 268, 282–283, Charles Beard declared that Jay's Treaty alienated a considerable part of the business community and that this element went over to Jefferson. This defection from Federalism, clearly apparent in 1800, did not originate in disgust with Jay's Treaty but with the narrow and exclusive policies pursued by Federalist banks and the Federalist-dominated state legislatures. It represented an effort on the part of enterprising and ambitious men who saw no future for themselves either within the Federalist party or the Federalist business community.

[49] Ford, *Jefferson*, VII, June 1, 1797; *Annals of Congress*, V, 1224, 1247.

[50] In 1796, Alexander Baring remarked, apropos of Washington's calling out 12,000 men to suppress the Whisky Rebellion and refusing an application on the part of the House of Representatives for papers, "both these were actions a King of England would not dare to have done, yet here it was considered the mere execution of a constitutional duty."

weak that at first he could scarcely be heard, begged the House's attention for a few moments—if his health would permit him to speak that long. Thereupon he launched into an oration that lasted for over an hour, during which time the congressmen were riveted to their seats both by his eloquence and by the momentary prospect of seeing him collapse and be carried from the House.[51]

Although Ames played freely upon the heartstrings—the state of his health provided numerous opportunities for pathos—his arguments were in general closely reasoned. By asserting its "unconstitutional" claims to sit in judgment upon treaties duly ratified by the Senate and signed by the President, the House, Ames pointed out, was forfeiting all the advantages gained from Jay's Treaty—millions of dollars in spoliation claims, the western posts, the confirmation of our neutrality, and the ending of the dispute with Great Britain. In renouncing these certainties, the United States was embarking upon a sea of troubles—national dishonor, division at home, the reopening of the dispute with Great Britain, the sacrifice of neutrality, and the resumption of Indian war—in which the frail bark of Union might well be dashed to pieces. "By rejecting the posts," he warned the House, "we light the savage fires, we bind the victims. . . . The darkness of midnight will glitter with the blaze of your dwellings. You are a father—the blood of your sons shall fatten your corn-field: you are a mother—the war whoop shall wake the sleep of the cradle."

When Ames finally sat down, there was hardly a dry eye in the House "except," remarked John Adams, "some of the jackasses who had occasioned the necessity of the oratory. These attempted to laugh, but their visages grinned horrible ghastly smiles."[52]

On April 29, 1796, the day after Ames's monumental forensic effort, the question of carrying the treaty into execution came before the House as a committee of the whole. The vote revealed that the representatives were evenly divided for and against implementing the treaty; whereupon Frederick Muhlenberg, the chairman of the House and a Republican, cast his vote in favor. This proved decisive: the next day, when a roll call vote was called for, the bill was passed by a vote of fifty-one to forty-eight.[53] For this "base desertion" of his party, Muhl-

---

[51] Morison, *Jeremiah Smith*, p. 97.

[52] *Annals of Congress*, V, April 28, 1796; Adams, *Gallatin*, pp. 164–165; Charles, *American Party System*, pp. 115–116; Perkins, *First Rapprochement*, pp. 41–42; Carroll and Ashworth, *Washington*, VII, 345–385.

[53] The New England states voted twenty-four to four in favor of the treaty;

enberg failed of re-election to the House in the next election. But a swifter and more dramatic retribution overtook him: a few days after he broke the deadlock in the House he was stabbed by his brother-in-law, a rabid Republican.[54]

In May, 1796, less than a month after the House of Representatives had yielded in the struggle against Jay's Treaty, the British announced that they were ready to surrender the posts as required by it. It is a commentary upon the bellicose speeches delivered by Republican congressmen that the United States army lacked sufficient troops at this time to garrison all the posts. In order to prevent depredations by the Indians when the British left the posts, the United States government requested His Britannic Majesty to permit the redcoats to remain temporarily in the forts until sufficient American troops could be brought up.[55]

Even though Jay's Treaty continued to be condemned by Republicans as a sacrifice of American rights and honor, simply by confirming neutrality of the United States it made possible a large increase in American shipping and trade. As Fisher Ames said in 1796: "The vast crop of our neutrality is all seed wheat, and is sown again, to swell, almost beyond calculation, the future harvest of prosperity." From 1795 to 1800, the value of American exports to the British Empire increased 300 per cent. During this period, thanks to Jay's Treaty, the United States became Great Britain's best customer.[56]

A considerable part of this trade was with India. Jay's Treaty legalized the existing trade between the United States and India and thereby put American shipmasters in a more favorable position than private British shippers, who were forbidden to trade with the ports under the control of the East India Company. Yet, while the monopoly of the Company was broken, Americans were not permitted complete freedom of action in India: by the terms of the treaty they were pro-

the vote of Virginia was eighteen to one against; only four votes from the region south of the Potomac were ayes. It is significant that the sum involved in this controversy was only $90,000.

[54] Kurtz, *Presidency of John Adams*, pp. 72–73; *Collections of the Colonial Society of Massachusetts*, XXXVI (1941), 664; Perkins, *First Rapprochement*, p. 42.

[55] Perkins, *First Rapprochement*, pp. 42–43, 47, 73–75, 78–79; Adams, *Gallatin*, 165–166; Gibbs, *Memoirs*, I, 335; Hunt, *Madison*, VI, 413; G. J. McRee, *Life and Correspondence of James Iredell* (New York, 1857), II, 475; Morison, *Jeremiah Smith*, 95–96.

[56] Perkins, *First Rapprochement*, pp. 13–14.

hibited from engaging in the Indian coastwise trade and from carrying exports to any place or port except the United States. This latter restriction was successfully evaded as early as 1797 with the consent of the British government; and by 1801, American ships were carrying the produce of India to Europe as freely as did the ships of the East India Company itself.[57]

Much the same thing happened in the British West Indies, where, as a result of the expunging of Article XII of the treaty, the prohibition upon the entry of American ships still stood. But the British West Indies were dependent upon the United States for flour, meal, salted meat, dried fish, and lumber. In order to procure sufficient quantities of these supplies, the governors of the British islands opened their ports by proclamation to American ships, and their actions were almost invariably upheld by the home government. As a result, American ships enjoyed virtually unlimited access to the British West Indies and American exports of sugar to Europe more than doubled from 1795 to 1800.

From an economic point of view, it proved to be highly fortunate for the United States that Article XII of Jay's Treaty, which prohibited the export of cotton from the United States, had been struck out by the Senate. When Jay agreed to this self-denying ordinance, cotton was not an important article of export; but the invention of the cotton gin by Eli Whitney in 1793 led to a spectacular burgeoning of cotton cultivation. In 1796, six million pounds of cotton were exported from the United States; in 1801, twenty million pounds were sent overseas. The bulk of American cotton was exported to England, thereby forming another economic ligament between the United States and Great Britain. Of even more decisive importance upon the course of American history, the rise of the cotton industry gave Negro slavery in the South, hitherto weakened by economic adversity and revolutionary idealism, a new lease on life.

Jay's Treaty had consigned some of the thorniest problems inherited from the treaty of peace of 1783 and the War of the French Revolution to arbitration by mixed commissions. The St. Croix River boundary was determined in 1798 with comparative ease, but the commissions appointed to deal with the problems of prewar debts and spoliations of American shipping ran into serious trouble. The British made such excessive demands upon the United States for debts the

[57] *Ibid.*, pp. 70–71.

collection of which had been allegedly impeded by the state governments that the American members of the commission walked out in
1799. The commission was thereupon suspended and the issue was not
settled until a Claims Convention was signed by both governments in
1802 by the terms of which, instead of the £3 million claimed by British merchants, the United States government agreed to pay £600,000.
The Seizures Commission appointed to settle the amount owing by
Great Britain for spoliations of American commerce was likewise suspended in 1799. When it resumed its meetings in 1802, it awarded the
United States $6 million compensation for losses sustained through the
illegal activities of British cruisers and admiralty courts.[58] The treaty
also directed that the boundary between the United States and Canada should be adjusted to give Great Britain access to the Mississippi
River. British subjects were permitted to trade with the Indians south
of the boundary and American citizens were allowed to trade with
the Indians north of the line, with the exception of the territories
administered by the Hudson's Bay Company. President Washington objected that this arrangement would benefit the British far more than
the Americans, but Hamilton, with greater prescience, predicted that
American enterprise and capital would soon penetrate the northern
part of the continent, binding it economically to the United States
rather than to Great Britain.

When Jay's Treaty is compared with the Treaty of Ghent, by which
the War of 1812 was brought to a close, the victories of peace appear
far more renowned than those of war. At Ghent, a war undertaken in
the name of free trade and sailors' rights was terminated by a treaty
which made no mention of either. Jay's Treaty, on the other hand,
gave the United States privileges in the trade of the British Empire
upon which the Republic capitalized to the full. Nevertheless, from
a political standpoint the treaty proved costly to the Federalists; seldom
have peacemakers been less blessed. It gave the Republican party a
platform; it strengthened Jefferson's position in the presidential election of 1796, and it exposed the Federalists to the charge of having
abandoned American neutral rights. Finally, it brought President
Washington into the center of the maelstrom of American politics.
After 1795, the Father of His Country markedly shrank to the stature
of the leader of a political party. Washington never met Jefferson
after the ratification of Jay's Treaty, with the result, said James Mad-

[58] *Ibid.,* pp. 116–122, 138–149.

ison, that not a "ray of republican truth could penetrate to the President."[59]

Within the national government itself, the principal struggle for power lay between the executive and legislative departments. The judiciary was hardly more than a spectator of this conflict. For the first fourteen years of its existence, the Supreme Court failed to play the commanding role Hamilton had assigned it in *The Federalist*. There were no epoch-making decisions handed down from that tribunal; not a few Justices resigned in order to accept appointments in the state judiciaries; and on several occasions the office of Chief Justice went begging. In 1800, when John Jay declined reappointment as Chief Justice, he gave as his reason his conviction that "under a system so defective it would not obtain the energy, weight and dignity which was essential to its affording due support to the national government; nor acquire the public confidence and respect which, as the last resort, of the justice of the nation, it should possess." During the period 1790–1800, only six cases involving important points of constitutional law were decided by the Supreme Court.[60]

For this state of affairs, the Judiciary Act of 1789 was in some measure responsible. This act established the District, Circuit, and Supreme Courts of the United States and provided for appellate jurisdiction from the state courts—thereby conferring upon the Supreme Court power to pass upon the constitutionality of state laws. As though to ensure that the taxpayers got full value from the services of the Federal judges, Congress directed that the Justices of the Supreme Court preside over the Circuit Courts. This meant that the Justices were kept almost constantly on the road: to serve upon the Supreme Court, it was humorously said, required the agility of a jockey as well as the erudition of a judge.[61]

[59] Ford, *Jefferson*, I, 168; VI, 293; IX, 450; Fitzpatrick, *Washington,* XXXV, 119; Rives, *Madison,* III, 538; Hinsdale, *History of the President's Cabinet*, pp. 10–13; Marshall, *Washington*, V, 210; Jasper Dwight, *A Letter to George Washington* (Philadelphia, 1796), pp. 10–11; *Proceedings of the Massachusetts Historical Society*, LVII (1924), 129; Charles, *American Party System*, pp. 116–119; Perkins, *First Rapprochement*, pp. 5–6.

[60] Charles G. Haines, *The American Doctrine of Judicial Supremacy* (Washington, 1914), pp. 156–157; Edmund Randolph to Washington, August 5, 1792, Washington MSS., LC.

[61] Morris, *Gouverneur Morris, Diary*, II, 567; *Selected Essays on Constitutional Law*, III, 16; J. E. Oster, *The Political and Economic Doctrines of*

During the rare intervals when the judges were not in the saddle
they found time to invalidate state laws which impeded the collection of debts, including accrued interest, by British creditors and
which impaired the obligations of private contracts.[62] But when the
Supreme Court put itself in direct conflict with a sovereign state, the
Justices came off the field with their robes trailing in the dust. In
1793, in the case of *Chisholm* v. *Georgia,* the Court upheld the right
of a citizen to institute an original suit for breach of contract in the
Supreme Court against a state of which he was not a resident. The
Georgia legislature took steps to prevent the execution of the Court's
decision and the issue was not resolved until 1798, when the Eleventh
Amendment to the Constitution was adopted by the requisite number
of states. The Eleventh Amendment represented a victory for the states
over the Court. It provides that "the Judicial power of the United
States shall not be construed to extend to any suit in law or equity,
commenced or prosecuted against one of the United States by a
citizen of another State, or by Citizens or Subjects of any foreign
State."[63]

Because of the prohibition imposed by the Federal Constitution upon
ex post facto laws, it was expected that the Federal courts would put
a stop to the practice of the state legislatures of interfering with the
decisions of the state courts affecting the rights of property, particularly those based upon contract. But here the Supreme Court declined
to act: in 1798, in the case of *Calder* v. *Bell,* the Court held that the
ex post facto clause related only to criminal statutes, not to private

John Marshall (New York, 1914), p. 282; McLaughlin, *Foundations of
American Constitutionalism,* p. 302; Story, *Commentaries on the Constitution,*
p. 624; E. S. Corwin, *Twilight of the Supreme Court* (New Haven, 1934),
p. 4; Warren, *Supreme Court,* I, 91, 94, 100; Holcombe, *Our More Perfect
Union,* p. 363; *The Federalist,* p. 529; Ames, *Proposed Amendments to the
Constitution,* p. 156.

[62] So expensive and time-consuming were appeals from the state courts to
the United States Supreme Court that during the twelve years in which the
Federalists were in power only three cases were appealed.

[63] Here the judges acted contrary to Hamilton's dictum in *The Federalist*
that a state could not be called at the bar of a Federal court. "It is inherent
in the nature of sovereignty," Hamilton said, "not to be answerable to the
suit of an individual *without its consent.*" Hamilton also asserted that a
sovereign state could not be compelled to pay its debts except by its free will.
In 1918, however, the Supreme Court asserted the right of the Federal government to compel a state to pay its debts. *The Federalist,* p. 529; Scott, *The
Federalist and Other Essays,* p. 539; Ames, *Proposed Amendments to the
Constitution,* p. 156.

property or contractual rights. As though to confound further their
more national-minded supporters, the Justices added a dictum to the
effect that acts having a retrospective effect might be necessary and
proper and that therefore the hands of government ought not be tied
by judicial restraints: private rights must yield to public exigencies.[64]

In 1792, in the first Hayburn case, a District Court declared an act
of Congress unconstitutional. This decision was warmly applauded by
the Republicans, who urged the Federal courts to continue the good
work by declaring the act of Congress incorporating the Bank of the
United States to be in violation of the Constitution.

Three years later, the Supreme Court itself was called upon to decide the constitutionality of an act of Congress. In 1794, at the instigation of the Secretary of the Treasury, Congress imposed a tax
upon carriages. This tax was deeply resented by the southern planters,
to whom carriages, decorated with coats of arms, were one of the
emblems of gentility. John Taylor of Caroline was prepared to contemplate disunion: "A union emphatically and solemnly contracted,
is dissolved," he declared categorically; "states which impose unequal
taxes, are masters, those which pay them, slaves." Before resorting to
this extremity, Taylor decided to plead before the Federal courts that
the carriage tax was a direct tax and therefore unconstitutional.[65]

The Constitution declares that no direct tax shall be laid unless
apportioned among the states "in proportion to the census or enumeration, of the inhabitants of the United States." This stipulation had
not been observed by Congress in the case of the carriage tax, for it
had been assumed that the tax was an excise, not a direct tax. When
suit was brought against David Hylton, a Virginian, in the Circuit
Court of the United States for the evasion of the tax, John Taylor,
acting as Hylton's counsel, challenged the interpretation put by Congress upon its handiwork. Although Hylton lost the suit, the judges
of the Circuit Court were divided in their opinion. Acclaiming this

[64] In this decision, Hamilton found, not for the last time, *The Federalist*
cited against his real convictions. Justice Chase, stating his opinion against
the application of the ex post facto clause to civil causes, quoted "Publius."
B. R. Curtis, *Reports of Decisions in the Supreme Court of the United States*
(Boston, 1855), I, 273–274.
[65] John Taylor, *An Argument Respecting the Constitutionality of the Carriage Tax* (Richmond, 1795). pp. 4. 7–8. 10–12; Bolles, *Financial History*, II,
112; Adams, *Gallatin*, III, 95; *Proceedings of the Massachusetts Historical
Society*, Second Series, XV (1902), 140–141; Maxwell, *Fiscal Impact of
Federalism*, p. 6; Dewey, *Financial History*, I, 107.

lack of unanimity in the Circuit Court as proof of the rightness of his position, Taylor urged Virginians to refuse to pay the tax when it fell due the following year. To vindicate its authority, the government was obliged to bring the case before the Supreme Court. Alexander Hamilton, now a private citizen practicing law in New York City, was called in as co-counsel by the Attorney General of the United States. In a speech lasting three hours, Hamilton argued the case in favor of the government's position on the ground that the powers of the Federal government ought to be broadly interpreted. In doubtful cases, he told the Court, "no construction ought to prevail calculated to defeat the express and necessary authority of the Government. . . . It would be contrary to reason and to every rule of sound construction to adopt a principle for regulating the exercise of a clear constitutional power which would defeat the exercise of the power."[66]

In its decision, the Supreme Court upheld Hamilton's contention that the carriage tax was an excise and gave its sanction to his method of interpreting the Constitution. From this reverse, the Virginia Republicans learned the futility of appealing to the Supreme Court to uphold their constitutional theories. This lesson bore fruit three years later in the Virginia and Kentucky Resolutions, wherein was set forth the doctrine that the final interpretation of the Constitution rested with the states rather than with the Supreme Court.[67]

[66] Lodge, *Hamilton*, VIII, 381–382; J. C. Hamilton, *Hamilton*, VI, 83–84; *Gazette of the United States*, February 26, 1796; Sidney Ratner, *American Taxation, Its History as a Social Force in Democracy* (New York, 1942), p. 28; A. J. Dallas, *Reports of Cases in the Courts of the United States and Pennsylvania* (Philadelphia, 1799), III, 172; William Bradford to Hamilton, July 2, 1795, Hamilton MSS., LC.

[67] Dallas, *Reports*, III, 173–175, 179–184.

CHAPTER 11

Western Conspiracy and Washington's Farewell Address

IT TOOK money and hard fighting, as well as diplomacy, to dispose of the Indians who since 1790 had been ravaging the frontier and hurling back the armies sent to subdue them. From 1790 to 1796, almost five-sixths of the general expenses of the government were swallowed up by the war in the West; and before the country was pacified, a total of $5 million had been expended. But in August, 1794, the Indians were finally crushed by Anthony Wayne at the Battle of Fallen Timbers. Decimated and discouraged, the Indians buried the hatchet and signed the Treaty of Greenville in 1795. In this treaty, at a cost of $10,000, the United States purchased from the Indians the southeastern quarter of the Northwest Territory and the site of Vincennes, Detroit, and Chicago. Equally important, peace was restored to the northwestern frontier and the way was now open for the settlers to flock in.[1]

Large-scale emigration to the western territory was not altogether to the liking of many Federalists. They feared that such a movement of population would depopulate the eastern states; deplete the labor force of the older communities, where manufacturing was on the rise; and diminish the political influence of the East and of the Federalist party. John Jay seriously considered the possibility that hordes of "white savages" would one day overrun the East, much as the bar-

[1] Lodge, *Hamilton*, III, 36; Ames, *Fisher Ames*, I, 118; Bemis, *Jay's Treaty*, pp. 177–183, 263–264.

barians had overrun Rome. Federalists of Jay's stamp therefore tended to favor gradual settlement by compact bodies of settlers, the survey of lands prior to occupancy, high prices for public lands in the interests of revenue, and the sale of large parcels of land to corporations rather than small amounts to individual settlers.[2]

In general, the Federalists succeeded in writing these provisions into the Land Act of 1796, under which the government administered the territory acquired by the Treaty of Greenville. This act required survey before purchase and settlement; land could not be sold at less than $2 an acre (four times the price charged for comparable state lands); and the terms set upon credit were too exacting to permit many settlers to buy directly from the government. In 1800, this act was amended to permit the purchase of minimum tracts of 320 acres, and four years' credit was granted to purchasers.

As a seller of land, the Federal government was obliged to compete with the states, several of which had extensive landed domains. Not only were these state lands cheaper than those put on the market by the Federal government; occasionally corruption was practiced by land speculators in the state legislatures upon a scale that dwarfed the activities of William Duer and his associates. In 1795, for example, the Georgia legislature granted the speculators who had organized four "Yazoo" land companies almost thirty million acres of land in Indian territory for about one and a half cents per acre.[3] Every member of the Georgia legislature that signed away this imperial domain had been purchased by the Yazoo companies with grants of land. Popular indignation was so strong, however, that in 1796 a newly elected legislature rescinded the sale. But much of the land had already been sold to bona fide purchasers, who raised the cry of fraud against the Georgia legislators who had undone the work of their corrupt predecessors. The Constitution forbids the states from violating contracts, and in the case of *Fletcher* v. *Peck* (1810) Chief Justice John Marshall invoked this clause to prevent Georgia from rescinding the sale of the Yazoo lands.

[2] *Collections of the Colonial Society of Massachusetts,* XXXVI (1941), 647, 666; Gibbs, *Memoirs,* I, 75, 323; White, *Jeffersonians,* pp. 513–514; B. W. Bond, Jr. (ed.), *The Correspondence of John Cleves Symmes* (New York, 1926), p. 274; Robert Liston to Lord Grenville, July 6, 1796, Liston Correspondence, Henry Adams Transcripts, LC; Johnston, *Jay,* III, 172.

[3] The Yazoo territory comprised a large rectangle extending from the Mississippi to the middle of Georgia.

NORTHWEST BOUNDARY GAP

St. Lawrence R.

Pointe au Fer
Dutchman's Point
Oswegatchie
Oswego

Michilmackinac

Niagara

Detroit

Pittsburgh

Marietta

Cincinnati

Louisville

Lexington

Ohio R.

Knoxville

Nashville

San Fernando

Tennessee R.

Hiwassee R.

Tombecbee R.

Ft. Confederacion

Flint R.

Los Nogales

Natchez

WEST FLORIDA

EAST FLORIDA

ATLANTIC OCEAN

GULF OF MEXICO

Mississippi R.

THE NORTHWEST AND SOUTHWEST
1783–1798

Indian barrier state proposed by British and Indians

Extreme Spanish territorial claims

U.S. settlements

U.S., Treaty of 1783

+ + + Greenville Treaty Line, 1795

◉ British posts until 1796

◇ Spanish posts until 1798

● U.S. frontier towns

Scale of Miles
0   100   200   300

Even though the Federalists' land policies conflicted with Western-ers' desire to act upon the time-honored principle of "first come, first served," and take up lands without tarrying for the surveyor, the West underwent a rapid expansion during the latter part of the Federalist era. Two new western states were admitted to the Union—Kentucky in 1792 and Tennessee in 1796. Even state capitals began to move west: Pennsylvania changed its seat of government from Philadelphia to Lancaster; Richmond replaced Williamsburg as the capital of Vir-ginia; Albany succeeded New York City as the capital of New York; and Springfield divided honors with Boston. While the East tended to lose political influence, particularly in the Senate, commercially and industrially many of the seaboard cities profited from the west-ward movement. New York City, Philadelphia, and Baltimore—all with outlets to the west—grew rapidly in wealth and population, whereas Boston and Newport, geographically cut off from the richest western markets, developed at a less rapid pace.

Although the power of the Indians had been broken in the North-west, formidable tribes still blocked the expansion of the American frontier in the South. Here the Creeks, the Choctaws, and the Chero-kees, incensed by the land grabbing of American frontiersmen and speculators, found the Spanish authorities in Louisiana and the Floridas eager to aid them in their quarrel with the United States. Spain claimed sovereignty over these tribes and encouraged them with arms and the promise of an independent Indian buffer state which would drive the American settlers in Tennessee and Kentucky east of the Appalachians. Moreover, whereas the United States contended that the boundary line between the Republic and Spanish territory was the thirty-first parallel, Spain insisted that the boundary lay just south of the Ohio River. Thus the problem confronting the United States in the Northwest and the South was essentially the same: in both areas, the Indians were armed and otherwise abetted by a European power unfriendly to the United States.[4]

The United States had repeatedly attempted to make a settlement with Spain, but to no avail; the Madrid government continued to hope that the troublesome Republic in North America would fall apart and thereby relieve His Catholic Majesty of the necessity of

[4] Fitzpatrick, *Washington*, XXXII, 126–128, 130, 189; Ford, *Jefferson*, I, 206–207; Randolph to Washington, July 15, 17, 1794, Washington MSS., LC.

coming to terms. As a result, the Mississippi, where it flowed through Spanish territory, remained closed to Americans; and the port of New Orleans was open only to Spanish shipping. But by 1794, Spanish policy toward the United States seemed to have reached a dead end: the Union still held firm, efforts to detach the West from the rest of the country had failed, and pressure was mounting among Westerners for an attack upon Spanish Louisiana and the Floridas. In the summer of 1794, therefore, the Spanish government indicated its willingness to open negotiations with the United States. In view of the importance of the occasion, the Madrid government requested that a minister of higher rank and dignity than William Short and William Carmichael, the American commissioners in Spain, be appointed to conduct the negotiations. The Washington administration responded to this overture by appointing Thomas Pinckney, the American minister to Great Britain, as envoy extraordinary and sole plenipotentiary to the court of Spain.[5]

Pinckney delayed his departure for Spain until May, 1795. Seldom has procrastination worked more decisively in favor of the United States. While Pinckney tarried in England, William Short, who, after Carmichael's retirement early in 1795 carried on as sole United States minister to Spain, prepared the way for the arrival of the envoy extraordinary. Of even more importance, however, was the rapid deterioration in 1794–95 in Spain's position as a belligerent in the war against France.[6]

Like all of Spain's wars in the eighteenth century, its involvement in the War of the French Revolution as a British ally was a costly failure. In 1795, therefore, Godoy, the so-called "Prince of the Peace," who, thanks to his position as the paramour of the Queen, was in effective control of the Spanish government, determined to pull out of the war by making a separate peace with France. Godoy acted in full realization of the risks involved—a British declaration of war and an attack upon the vulnerable Spanish empire. Moreover, the fact that the United States had recently made a treaty with Great Britain filled the Spanish minister with forebodings of an Anglo-American alliance directed against Spain. Since he was as yet unaware of the

---

[5] Fitzpatrick, *Washington*, XXXII, 117–118, 126–127; Basset, *Federalist System*, pp. 69–83; Hunt, *Madison*, V, 337.

[6] S. F. Bemis, *Pinckney's Treaty* (New York, 1926), pp. 219, 354.

terms of Jay's Treaty, Godoy's apprehensions were nourished by his ignorance and his suspicions.[7]

Spanish policy was notorious for its temporizing and equivocation, but Pinckney found in Madrid an unwonted air of urgency and decision. Indeed, the American diplomat was startled to hear Godoy propose an alliance between the United States and Spain—ultimately to be expanded into a triple alliance of France, Spain, and the United States—with mutual guarantees of territory in the New World. Pinckney politely but firmly declined to discuss this grandiose scheme: as he told Godoy, the United States had no desire to entangle itself further in the affairs of Europe, nor was it prepared to offer any guarantees of Spanish territory. Instead of wasting time upon such fruitless matters, Pinckney suggested that they get down to business: the settlement of the boundary dispute, an acknowledgment by Spain of Americans' right to navigate the Mississippi, and the establishment of a port or landing place near the mouth of the Mississippi for the transshipment of goods from river boats to ocean-going vessels.[8]

It was soon made painfully clear to Godoy that while the Americans demanded much, they were disposed to concede very little. When Pinckney indicated the price the United States set upon its good will, Godoy was horrified. He swore that Spain would never yield the right of deposit upon which Pinckney insisted. Yet despite the bold front he assumed toward Pinckney, the Prince of Peace was in reality a hollow man, hagridden by his fears. Pinckney saw Godoy's weakness and played upon it skillfully. When the discussions broke down over the right of deposit, the American plenipotentiary asked for his passports. As he had foreseen, Godoy capitulated. But upon one point he stood firm to the end: under no circumstances would Spain open its colonial empire to American ships and merchandise.

In virtually every other respect, Pinckney succeeded in writing into the treaty signed at San Lorenzo in September, 1795, the text of his instructions. The United States secured the grant (not, however, the right) of the navigation of the Mississippi through Spanish territory and the privilege of deposit at New Orleans for three years. At the expiration of that period, the deposit was to be renewed at New Orleans

[7] *Ibid.*, pp. 305–306, 314–315, 354.
[8] W. P. Cresson, *James Monroe* (Chapel Hill, 1946), p. 114; Bemis, *Pinckney's Treaty*, pp. 275, 286, 316–322.

or at some other place on the river. As for the boundary, Spain went all the way to satisfy the Americans: the thirty-first parallel was fixed as the boundary between the United States and Spanish Florida. Both countries pledged themselves to restrain by force all hostilities against the other on the part of the Indians under their jurisdiction.

On the subject of neutral rights, the Spaniards were equally accommodating. Pinckney was able to incorporate in the treaty a full statement of the American doctrine of the freedom of the seas: free ships make free goods; naval stores and provisions to be treated as noncontraband; and the right of neutrals to trade freely with belligerents except in cases of actual blockade or siege.[9]

These provisions of the Treaty of San Lorenzo contrasted so markedly with Jay's Treaty that many Americans concluded that Pinckney was a better diplomat than Jay. But the two men were dealing with countries so wholly different in their circumstances, power, and attitude toward neutral rights that comparison was impossible. Pinckney did not persuade a reluctant Godoy to insert these articles in the Treaty of San Lorenzo; fearful that his country would soon be at war with Great Britain, Godoy was eager to secure for Spain whatever advantages might accrue from the neutral shipping of the United States.

Having made a treaty in a state of mind bordering upon panic, Godoy soon repented of his precipitancy. Great Britain did not declare war upon Spain, nor did Jay's Treaty bear out his apprehension that Great Britain and the United States had made an alliance directed against Spain. Godoy therefore reverted to his earlier policy of intriguing with the Indians and the western settlers, and refusing to open the deposit at New Orleans guaranteed by the treaty.

Any thoughts Godoy might have entertained in 1796 that the United States could be bilked out of its rights were abruptly dispelled by the exposure of a plot involving a United States senator to attack Louisiana and the Floridas. Abortive as this plot was, it served notice upon the Spaniards that time was running out and that the probable alternative to executing the treaty was war.[10]

Senator William Blount was a Federalist who had become rich by using political office to further his business interests. As governor of

[9] Bemis, *Pinckney's Treaty*, pp. 332–333, 338–339; Arthur P. Whitaker, *The Mississippi Question, 1795–1803* (New York, 1934), pp. 52–54.

[10] Bemis, *Pinckney's Treaty*, p. 351.

the Tennessee territory, he had built up vast real estate holdings. Land speculation became his dominant passion and he surrendered himself to it utterly. In one North Carolina county alone he owned over a million acres. He became an ardent advocate of Tennessee statehood largely for the reason that he expected it would lead to aggressive action by the United States government against the Creek Indians, whose continued forays against the white settlements held down the price of his lands. But the government refused to go to war against the Creeks—with the result that when Tennessee became a state and Blount was elected to the United States Senate, he broke with the administration and declared himself to be a Republican.[11]

Deeply in debt—he would have landed in a debtors' prison had he not enjoyed senatorial immunity—Blount's only hope was to sell his lands at a profit. Unfortunately for him and other land speculators, the supply of immigrants from Europe upon which the prosperity of the West depended had been cut off by the European war. In 1796 that war took an unexpected turn when Spain and Great Britain, former allies, went to war. Immediately the West began to buzz with rumors that the French were about to take over Louisiana and the Floridas—an event certain to depress further the sinking land values in the southwestern territories of the United States.

With his real estate empire collapsing about his head, Blount looked in desperation to his friend John Chisholm, a former British soldier turned Indian agent. Chisholm produced a plan: with the aid of the British government, a filibustering attack upon the Spanish possessions would be launched from the United States. Blount eagerly fell in with this scheme and early in 1796 Chisholm got in touch with Robert Liston, the British minister to the United States. Even though Liston was cool toward the project, he held several meetings with Chisholm and in March, 1796, he paid Chisholm's expenses to England and gave him a letter of introduction to Lord Grenville, the British Foreign Secretary.[12] Early the next year, Blount went West to take charge of the conspiracy upon the actual scene of operations.[13]

---

[11] William H. Masterson, *William Blount* (Baton Rouge, 1954), pp. 249, 266, 270, 278, 294, 296–297, 300–301, 349–350.

[12] Robert Liston to Grenville, March 16, 1797, Liston MSS., LC; Masterson, *Blount,* pp. 302–304; *Albany Centinel,* January 2, 1798; Perkins, *First Rapprochement,* pp. 99–100.

[13] To Liston, Chisholm indicated that he had in mind the conquest of the Floridas, Louisiana, New Mexico, "and a Diversion that might ultimately

In London, Chisholm was bluntly informed by the British government that it would have no part of a plan that violated the sovereignty of the United States. In all probability, therefore, the Blount-Chisholm conspiracy would have been buried in the records of the Foreign Office had not one of Blount's letters fallen into the hands of the United States government. Liston entreated the administration not to make public the letter lest it appear that the British government was involved in the affair, but President John Adams refused to swerve from what he regarded as a dictate of duty. When the Attorney General expressed the opinion that Blount had rendered himself subject to impeachment, President Adams directed that the letter and other relevant papers be laid before Congress. While Adams seemed disposed to act upon the principle, let justice be done regardless of Anglo-American relations, Secretary of State Pickering was careful to point out that the British government had been innocent of any wrongdoing.[14]

In 1797, by a vote of twenty-five to one, Blount was expelled from the United States Senate. Soon afterward he went back to Tennessee, where he was acclaimed as a hero; Governor Sevier delighted to call him friend; and in 1798 he was elected Speaker of the Tennessee House of Representatives. Owing to Blount's absence in Tennessee, his impeachment trial was postponed until December, 1798. Counsel for the defendant argued that the Senate lacked jurisdiction since Blount was no longer a member of the Senate and that, in any event, no criminal act was charged. The case was never brought before the House of Representatives; in January, 1799, the Senate decided that senators were not impeachable civil officers and dismissed the impeachment for want of jurisdiction. With this victory, Blount's political comeback in Tennessee seemed assured, but in 1800 his career was abruptly terminated by death.[15]

Long before Blount was removed from the scene, the fears and forebodings that determined Godoy's foreign policy had been reactivated by the activities of the Senator from Tennessee. Fearful that war would break out between France and the United States, that the United States would ally itself with Great Britain, and that the Span-

contribute to the Independence of South America if this were considered as a measure essential to the Interests of Great Britain."

[14] Liston to Lord Grenville, June 24, 1797, Liston MSS., LC; John Dawson to Madison, August 13, 1797; Madison to Jefferson, December 24, 1797, Madison MSS., LC.

[15] Masterson, *Blount,* pp. 339, 341.

ish empire would be divided between the two English-speaking countries, Godoy ordered that the Treaty of San Lorenzo should be carried out to the letter. Accordingly, in 1798, the deposit was opened at New Orleans and American frontiersmen rode the Father of the Waters unvexed to the sea.[16]

The Blount conspiracy brought into sharp relief the danger of foreign influence in the domestic affairs of the United States—one of the gravest weaknesses, in Hamilton's opinion, of the republican form of government. Americans were soon treated to other and more sinister examples of foreign meddling in their internal concerns. In all these instances, the offending nation was France.[17]

No Republican congressman worked harder to defeat Jay's Treaty than did Citizen Adet, the French minister to the United States. In March, 1796, he undertook to direct Republican strategy in Congress by conferring with the party leaders, and when they seemed unwilling to act upon his ideas he took matters into his own hands. It was Adet, for example, who, after the Senate had ratified Jay's Treaty, procured a copy of the still-secret treaty from Senator Stevens Thomas of Virginia and arranged for its publication in Benjamin Bache's *Aurora* in the hope that the American people would repudiate the work of the Senate. Again, in the fight in the House of Representatives against appropriating money to execute Jay's Treaty, it was Adet who exhorted the Republicans to resist to the bitter end.[18]

Besides making himself a force to be reckoned with in American politics, the French minister was occupied in planning the French conquest of Louisiana. In his schemes, the United States figured as a staging base for the army of invasion. Adet also revived the project of the secession from the United States of the region west of the Appalachians. In March, 1796, he dispatched General Victor Collet to prepare the ground for this coup, but Collet held the government of the United States in such contempt that he made no secret of the purpose of his mission. The administration, thoroughly alarmed by these disclosures, set aside $500 to hire secret agents to shadow Collet and report on his activities.[19]

[16] Paltsits, *Washington's Farewell Address*, p. 205; Bemis, *Pinckney's Treaty*, pp. 351–352.
[17] Fitzpatrick, *Washington*, XXXV, 189–190.
[18] DeConde, *Entangling Alliance*, pp. 427, 455–456, 458.
[19] DeConde, *Entangling Alliance*, pp. 446–447, 451.

John Jay had been instructed to make no arrangements with Great Britain incompatible with the terms of the Franco-American treaties of 1778. In the opinion of the Republican leaders in Congress, Jay had utterly ignored this stipulation: Robert R. Livingston predicted that France would regard the treaty as not "much short of a direct declaration of hostilities." As though to ensure this result, the Republican spokesmen charged that France had been betrayed by Jay and Hamilton; that the treaty put the United States in the camp of France's enemies; and that the Franco-American treaties had been reduced to the status of scraps of paper. "The treaty," it was said, "was designed to operate against France; a nation in the act of imitating the example of America, and checked in the attempt by England, the only enemy of the liberty of America."[20]

The French Directory needed no prodding by American Republicans to prejudice it against Jay's Treaty. A glance at Jay's handiwork sufficed to convince the Directors that they had indeed been sold down the river by the Washington administration. They discovered that while the United States flag no longer afforded protection of supplies consigned to France, it protected goods destined for British ports. And—the cruelest cut of all—the United States had seemingly consented to become Britain's accessory in starving France into subjection. It was of little avail for Hamilton to point out that the only complaint France could legitimately make was that the United States had refused to plunge into war with Great Britain. In Paris, the United States began to be classed among the enemies of France.[21]

The responsibility for reconciling France to Jay's Treaty devolved upon James Monroe. At the time of Monroe's appointment President Washington still believed in preserving a balance in the administration between the two parties: a Federalist having been sent to England, it followed that a Republican ought to go to France. But Monroe's conduct in Paris quickly demonstrated the impracticability of conducting foreign policy upon this premise.

Had it been the objective of the Washington administration to align the United States with France, Monroe would have been one

[20] Fauchet, *A Sketch,* pp. 13, 16–17, 26; *American State Papers,* I, 578; Sparks, *Correspondence of the Revolution,* IV, 474; Fitzpatrick, *Washington,* XXXIV, 263, 266; Adams, *Gallatin,* 158; Hunt, *Madison,* VI, 242–244; Rives, *Madison,* III, 511; Lodge, *Hamilton,* X, November 11, 1796.

[21] Mayo, *Instructions to British Ministers,* pp. 133 (footnote), 134; Ford, *John Quincy Adams,* I, April 4, 1796; *Proceedings of the Massachusetts Historical Society,* XLIV, 44 (1911), 407; DeConde, *Entangling Alliance,* p. 437.

of the most successful diplomats in American history. Unfortunately for his reputation and the peace of mind of his superiors in Philadelphia, he devoted his energies wholly to counterworking the administration; as Washington said, Monroe seemed to wish to scrap Jay's Treaty and then to ask France's pardon "for having made it, and enquire of France what more she required." Monroe even went to the length of accusing Jay of having accepted a bribe for signing the treaty. He corresponded more frequently with his Republican friends than with the State Department; he wrote propaganda for Republican newspapers; and he gave shelter in Paris to Tom Paine, who repaid the hospitality by writing a venomous diatribe against President Washington, whom he addressed in this vein: "As to you, Sir, treacherous in private friendship (for so you have been to me, and that in the day of danger) and a hypocrite in public life, the world will be puzzled to decide, whether you are an apostate or an impostor, whether you have abandoned good principles, or whether you ever had any."[22]

There was never any doubt of Monroe's principles. In 1794, he had favored the seizure of the western posts and the invasion of Canada —a course of action far more appropriate, in his opinion, than stooping to negotiate with "the enemy of mankind." As minister to France, his cardinal objective was to weld France and the United States into an intimate and indissoluble union. From this connection he anticipated many blessings: by attaching itself to the "great republic," the United States would secure a protector of its neutral rights and might even be invited to sit in at the peace table when the British empire was being carved up.[23]

President Washington suffered qualms whenever he considered what the British would make of Monroe's unneutral conduct, but despite the adjurations of Secretary of State Pickering the Virginian con-

[22] Kurtz, *Presidency of John Adams*, p. 121; Cresson, *Monroe*, p. 144; De-Conde, *Entangling Alliance*, p. 366; *Proceedings of the Massachusetts Historical Society*, LXI (1928), 367; Hamilton, *Monroe*, II, 122, 150, 154, 156, 161; III, 6–7, 13, 20, 53–54, 64; Fitzpatrick, *Washington*, XXXIV, 249; XXXVI, 197–198, 215, 218, 224–225, 229, 239; Gibbs, *Memoirs*, I, 367; Lodge, *George Cabot*, 110; Philip Foner (ed.), *The Complete Writings of Thomas Paine* (New York, 1945), II, 922–923; G. S. Hillard (ed.), *Life, Letters and Journals of George Ticknor* (Boston, 1878), II, 113.
[23] DeConde, *Entangling Alliance*, pp. 369, 375–377; Hamilton, *Monroe*, II, 64, 257, 303.

tinued to play the part of a worshiper at the shrine of the French Revolution. Finally, in 1796, its patience at an end, the administration recalled Monroe. The Virginian took this action as a personal affront and demanded that the government state its reasons for withdrawing him from Paris—a demand which the Secretary of State rejected on the ground that it would expose the executive "to perpetual altercations and controversies with the officers removed." As was the settled practice among the politicians of this period, Monroe appealed from the President to the public by publishing a pamphlet entitled *A View of the Conduct of the Executive.* Here he accused the administration of all the crimes in the political calendar, not excluding that of trying to deliver the country bound and gagged to the mercies of King George III.[24]

Everything Monroe did in France tended to fortify the Directory's view that the people and the government of the United States were at odds and that the Washington administration could easily be toppled from power. This conviction, together with Adet's failure to prevent the execution of Jay's Treaty in 1796, served to persuade the Directors of the necessity of using stronger methods against the refractory republicans overseas: in 1796, Monroe was informed by the Minister of Foreign Affairs that Jay's Treaty had abrogated the military alliance and commercial treaty of 1778, that Adet was to be recalled from the United States, and that "the customary relations between the two nations shall cease." And all this, Monroe was given to understand, was merely preparatory to revolutionizing the United States and bending it to France's will. Before leaving Paris, Monroe appealed to the Directory to withhold its hand until the outcome of the impending presidential election was known. As a personal favor to the outgoing minister, the Directors generously consented to postpone the overthrow of the United States government—but only on condition that "Washington must go."[25]

[24] Fitzpatrick, *Washington,* XXXIV, 249; XXXV, 101–103; Hamilton, *Monroe,* II, 160; Oliver Wolcott to Washington, January 30, 1798, Washington MSS., LC; Brown, *First Republicans,* pp. 116–121; Stuart Gerry Brown (ed.), *The Autobiography of James Monroe* (Syracuse, 1959), pp. 131–134, 141–147.

[25] *Proceedings of the Massachusetts Historical Society,* LXVII (1945), 374–375; Hamilton, *Monroe,* II, 455–459, 467; DeConde, *Entangling Alliance,* pp. 378–379; Adams, *Gallatin,* p. 186; *American Historical Review,* XXXIX (1934), 254–255; Ford, *John Quincy Adams,* II, February 1, 1797; King,

Unknown to the French, Washington had already made up his mind not to stand for a third term. Sick of politics, wounded by the envenomed shafts of Republican journalists, and eager to sit down to dinner with Martha alone—a pleasure, he said, he had not enjoyed for twenty years—the President was determined to retire from the splendid misery of the Presidency to the peace and quiet of Mount Vernon. But before taking leave of the people whom he had served in war and peace for more than twenty years, Washington wished to hand down his political testament in the form of a Farewell Address. In the summer of 1796, with the aid of Hamilton and John Jay, he drew up his valedictory, which in September, 1796, appeared in the newspapers throughout the country.[26]

While the Farewell Address was the product of the collaboration of Washington, Hamilton, and, to a lesser extent, Jay, and the President worked from a draft prepared four years before by James Madison, the ideas therein expressed were the common property of the Federalist party. Every point made in this valedictory had been enunciated by Washington, Hamilton, and other leading Federalists at one time or another. It contained, in short, the essence of the political philosophy of Federalism.[27]

Almost two-thirds of the Farewell Address was devoted to the domestic situation of the United States and to the problems created by the rise of political parties. Here Washington offered his countrymen a guide to the pursuit of happiness: only through a close and enduring union, he declared, could they obtain the felicity they sought. He pleaded for the most perfect kind of union of all—a union of hearts and minds that transcended state, party, and sectional considerations, an "American character" wholly free of foreign attachments. Only by making American interests the touchstone of all their actions, Washington declared, could the people of the United States attain national power and greatness. He warned his countrymen against the baleful effects of sectionalism—"geographical distinctions"—and of the excessive party spirit which tended to divide Americans and to

Rufus King, II, April 3, 1797; *What Is Our Situation? By an American* [Joseph Hopkinson] (Philadelphia, 1798), p. 14.

[26] Fitzpatrick, *Washington,* XXXIV, 401; XXXV, 49, 103–104 (footnote), 254; Paltsits, *Washington's Farewell Address,* p. 39; H. E. Scudder (ed.), *Recollections of Samuel Breck* (Philadelphia, 1877), pp. 252–253; *Pennsylvania Magazine of History and Biography,* LX (1936), 384.

[27] Fitzpatrick, *Washington,* XXX, 71; Johnston, *Jay,* IV, 232.

make them the tools of European powers. In 1796, the threat to the Union and the Federal Constitution was uppermost in Washington's mind—hence his emphasis upon the importance of fostering common ideals and promoting "institutions for the general diffusion of knowledge."[28]

As regards foreign policy, the President recommended friendship and commerce with all nations but involvement in the wars and domestic affairs of none. Against Europe, Washington erected the doctrine of the two spheres: the United States had a set of primary interests in which Europe did not share—and Europe, in turn, had interests which were peculiarly its own. And yet Washington did not say that the United States ought to retire into an isolationist shell: while he warned against long-term alliances, he did not deny that circumstances might make short-term alliances essential to the security of the Republic. He insisted that the French alliance—a perpetual alliance—must be strictly observed, but throughout the Farewell Address it is implied that Americans ought to have learned from their connection with France the disadvantages of such ties and the necessity of demonstrating to European governments that "we act for *ourselves* and not for *others*."[29]

It was Republican spokesmen such as Albert Gallatin of Pennsylvania and John Nicholas and William Branch Giles of Virginia, rather than President Washington, who proclaimed the doctrine of isolationism. These men denied that the United States had any concern in the balance of power in Europe. "We may lament the fate of Poland and Venice," said Gallatin, "and I never can myself see, without regret, independent nations blotted from the map of the world. But their destiny does not affect us in the least. We have no interest whatever

---

[28] Joseph Charles and Alexander DeConde contend that much of Washington's Farewell Address was written by Hamilton and that it was merely "political propaganda" intended to influence the outcome of the impending elections. The view that it was largely written by Washington and was designed by him to serve as a political testament to the American people is more accurate. Charles, *American Party System*, p. 48; DeConde, "Washington's Farewell, the French Alliance, and the Election of 1796," *Mississippi Valley Historical Review*, XLIII (1957), 648–650. See also Beard, *The Republic*, p. 48; A. M. Hamilton, *Intimate Life*, p. 286; Paltsits, *Washington's Farewell Address*, p. 176.

[29] Fitzpatrick, *Washington*, XXXV, 452–453, 457, 481; S. F. Bemis, "Washington's Farewell Address," *American Historical Review*, XXXIX (1934), 256–259; Bemis, *John Quincy Adams and the Foundations of American Diplomacy*, pp. 62–64.

in that balance, and by us it should be altogether forgotten and neglected." Nicholas declared that the United States stood in relation to Europe "as mere buyers and venders of their manufactures." He deemed it desirable to do away with all foreign intercourse of the United States and to reduce the diplomatic staff to a mere skeleton. Jefferson expressed the wish that "there was an ocean of fire between that island [Great Britain] and us." Another Republican declared that the United States might concern itself as properly with "the wandering excursions of the Arabs or unite in some rash crusade against infidels at Mecca or at Palestine" as with the affairs of Europe. Only by strictly minding its own affairs, they argued, could the United States remain at peace, for, as William Duane put it, Great Britain was determined to involve the United States in war "as an old Bawd drags her daughter to prostitution as the only source of support under the weight of turpitude and old age."[30]

The reception accorded the Farewell Address revealed that President Washington had good reason to deplore the baneful effects of party feeling in the United States. His decision to retire was almost the only act of his second administration that was approved by the Republican press. In 1797, Benjamin Bache—the grandson of Benjamin Franklin and nicknamed "Lightning Rod, Junior" because of his penchant for administering high-voltage shocks to prominent Federalists in the Philadelphia *Aurora*—pronounced Washington to be "the source of all the misfortunes of our country. . . . If ever there was a period for rejoicing," he continued, "this is the moment. Every heart in unison with the freedom and happiness of the people ought to beat high with exultation that the name of Washington from this day ceases to give a currency to political iniquity and to legalized corruption." The President was even accused of having been a secret traitor during the War of American Independence. Political rancor could hardly be carried farther.[31]

Washington having removed himself from the race, the Federalists put forward John Adams as their candidate for the Presidency, while

[30] Mathew L. Davis, *An Oration* (New York, 1800), p. 17; Dwight, *Letter to George Washington*, pp. 39–40; Lester J. Cappon (ed.), *The Adams-Jefferson Letters* (Chapel Hill, 1959), I, 260.

[31] Pickering and Upham, *Timothy Pickering*, II, 96–97; *General Advertiser*, January 21, 1797; *Pennsylvania Magazine of History and Biography*, LX (1936), 79; Cunningham, *Jeffersonian Republicans*, pp. 93–94.

the Republicans pinned their hopes upon Thomas Jefferson. From the Directory's point of view, John Adams was no more acceptable than "old man Washington"; this crusty, intractable New Englander had from the beginning taken a pessimistic view of the French Revolution—it was impossible, he said, to make a republic out of twenty million atheists—and he had endorsed Jay's Treaty. Jefferson, on the other hand, was eminently acceptable to the French: once he was installed in the Presidency, the Directors expected, the foreign policy of the United States would be oriented radically in their favor.

And in truth, Jefferson's conviction that Great Britain was the real enemy of the United States was as strong as ever. That nation, he declared in 1797, was in the process of monopolizing American commerce, banking, and public securities; and it had made great strides through the agency of Alexander Hamilton toward bringing the government itself into vassalage. At this time, the Vice-President's advice to his countrymen was to stand up for their neutral rights regardless of any injury that might be visited thereby upon Great Britain. He shared to the full Madison's eagerness to retaliate upon British commerce: in his opinion, it was like "turning a strumpet out of doors. It is saying, 'we have sinned, but we repent and amend: we begin by banishing the tempter.'" As regards the outcome of the European war, Jefferson assumed that the issue was already decided: Great Britain was doomed to defeat and revolution. While he was not a little surprised by the stubbornness with which the British resisted their fate, the spectacle of a people heroically struggling against the decrees of destiny did not evoke his admiration. As late as 1816, he was still predicting that a revolution in Great Britain was as "inevitable as death." "I would not wonder," he observed, "to see the deportation of their king to Hindostan, and of the Prince Regent to Botany Bay." In 1797–98 he awaited with growing impatience the French conquest of Great Britain; he confessed in 1795 that he yearned for the day when he could drink tea with the French generals in London. He was prepared to celebrate that occasion as marking the deliverance of mankind from the yoke of British sea power and the dawn of a new era of peace and good will among nations.[32]

Eager to install this good friend of France in the Presidency, Adet decided to appeal to the American people in the newspapers to vote

[32] Boyd, *Jefferson Papers,* VIII, 398–399; Ford, *Jefferson,* VII, May 13, 1797.

for Thomas Jefferson and thereby restore themselves to the good graces of the French Republic. To this end, in November, 1796, he published four proclamations announcing the suspension of full diplomatic relations, the inauguration of the toughened French policy toward neutral shipping, and a review of Franco-American relations in which he cast all blame for the breakdown upon the Federalist administration. By thus making public his exchanges with the State Department, Adet sought to convert supposedly "secret" diplomatic notes into manifestoes against the government to which he was accredited. While his letters were ostensibly addressed to Secretary of State Timothy Pickering, in reality they were intended to serve the purposes of campaign propaganda.

With Washington's approval, Secretary of State Pickering published the government's answer to Adet in the newspapers. Hamilton was dismayed by this turn of events: fearful that the government would lose dignity and respect if it fought Adet with his own weapons, he wished to keep the controversy on a diplomatic plane.[33]

Adet's attacks upon the Washington administration were timed to influence the voting in Pennsylvania, the state which Jefferson expected would determine the outcome of the presidential election. Nevertheless, the voters remained singularly apathetic: less that 25,000 Pennsylvanians cast a ballot in the election of 1796 for presidential electors pledged to Adams or Jefferson. The Republicans won control of the state by a margin of less than two hundred votes. Elsewhere, Adet's intervention recoiled upon the Republicans. Coming hard upon Washington's Farewell Address, the conduct of the French minister left no doubt that "foreign influence" was at work in the Republic and that American independence could not be preserved unless it was supported by an "American character."[34]

Despite this advantage, the Federalists almost lost the Presidency to Thomas Jefferson. The election made clear that the Federalists had to fear not only foreign intrigue but intrigue within their own party. A caucus of Federalist members of Congress had resolved to give equal support to John Adams, the candidate for the Presidency, and Thomas Pinckney, the candidate for the Vice-Presidency. This action was justi-

[33] DeConde, *Entangling Alliance,* p. 441; Lodge, *Hamilton,* X, November 5, 1796.
[34] Kurtz, *Presidency of John Adams,* pp. 127–132; Rives, *Madison,* III, 586–587; M. E. Clarke, *Peter Porcupine in America* (Philadelphia, 1939), p. 85.

fied on the ground that since each elector voted for two candidates without specifying a preference for President or Vice-President, the party could not afford to scatter its votes if it were to elect its candidates to the two highest offices. Of course, if this pledge were faithfully executed, the Federalist candidates would receive equal votes in the electoral college—in which event the election of the President and Vice-President would be decided by the House of Representatives.

Unwilling to elevate Adams—whom he could not hope to control —to the Presidency, Alexander Hamilton attempted by stratagem to seat Thomas Pinckney, a far more pliable man, in the President's chair.[35] Hamilton's plan called for the Federalist electors in the North to cast their ballots for Adams and Pinckney, while the South Carolina electors voted unanimously for Pinckney but withheld a few votes from Adams. Thus Pinckney would stand first in the poll and John Adams would be relegated to the Vice-Presidency. Adams had repeatedly complained that this office was, politically speaking, like being buried alive, but Hamilton felt no compunction over keeping the New Englander underground permanently.[36]

Hamilton's political intrigues always turned out badly—he was too indiscreet and impulsive to make a successful Machiavellian—but this one almost ended in disaster. In effect, he risked the breakup of the Federalist party in the face of mounting evidence that Jefferson, "the Friend of the People," might steal the prize. Getting wind of Hamilton's "plot," the New England electors deliberately scratched Pinckney in order to ensure that he would not nose out Adams. Most shocking of all, South Carolina gave eight votes to Pinckney and eight to Jefferson. The outcome was that while Adams stood highest on the poll, with seventy-one votes, Jefferson was second, with sixty-eight votes, Pinckney ran third, with fifty-nine votes, and Burr came in a poor fourth, with thirty votes. The wonder was that Jefferson had not been elected President—"a single voice in Virginia and one in North Carolina," it was remarked, "prompted by the lingering memory of

[35] Adams was far from sharing Hamilton's views of the benefits conferred upon the community by banks and bankers. While Adams approved banks of deposit, he held "every bank of discount, every bank by which interest is to be paid or profit of any kind made by the deponent, as downright corruption. It is taxing the public for the benefit and profit of individuals." Dauer, *Adams Federalists*, pp. 69–70.

[36] *Political Science Quarterly*, LVI, 1941, 567–568; *Men and Times of the Revolution, or Memoirs of Elkanah Watson* (New York, 1856), pp. 397–398; Charles, *American Party System*, pp. 56–57.

revolutionary services, had turned the scale." It was a sectional victory: Adams received two votes south of the Potomac; Jefferson garnered eighteen votes (thirteen of them from Pennsylvania) from states north of it.[37]

The election of 1796 left scars upon both parties. John Adams hotly resented the attempt to steal the Presidency from him; and Aaron Burr complained that he had been played a scurvy trick by the Virginians, who had given him only one electoral vote. (Sam Adams received fifteen electoral votes from Virginia.) In the hope of widening the breach between Adams and Hamilton, Jefferson wrote a letter to Adams in which he contrasted his own "solid esteem" for the New Englander with the conduct of the treacherous and malignant West Indian. Madison, to whom the delivery of this letter was entrusted, did not transmit it to Adams because, as he told Jefferson, the President-elect was already aware of Hamilton's double-dealing and therefore the soundest strategy was to let the Federalists fall out among themselves—then honest men under the banner of the Republican party would come into their own.[38]

This happy consummation was set back by Jefferson's indiscretion in putting down in writing his views of President Washington and the leaders of the Federalist party. In May, 1797, a letter written by Jefferson to his Italian friend, Philip Mazzei, was published in the American newspapers. Written in 1796, this letter surveyed the progress of the "monarchical and aristocratical party" toward its objective of establishing a British form of government in the United States. Although Jefferson believed that the great mass of the people, particularly the farmers, remained true to republicanism, he declared that the monarchists were firmly entrenched in the executive, judiciary, and the Senate, and that the funding system and the Bank of the United States continued to provide an inexhaustible source of corruption. "It would give you a fever," he told Mazzei, "were I to name to you the apostates who have gone over to these heresies, men who were Samsons in the field and Solomons in the council, but who have

---

[37] J. D. Hammond, *The History of Political Parties in the State of New York* (New York, 1852), I, 101–103; DeConde, *Entangling Alliance*, pp. 201–202; C. F. Adams, *John Adams*, II, 205–206; Gibbs, *Memoirs*, I, 408; Channing, *History*, IV, 173; Dauer, *Adams Federalists*, pp. 92–111.

[38] Adams, *Gallatin*, p. 178; Gibbs, *Memoirs*, I, 411; Hunt, *Madison*, VI, 303; Ford, *Jefferson*, VII, January 1, 1797; Dauer, *Adams Federalists*, pp. 112–119; *American Historical Review*, XIV (1909), 785.

had their heads shorn by the harlot England." Jefferson complained that in the translation his letter had been garbled and that, anyway, his reference to Samsons and Solomons had been intended only for the members of the Society of the Cincinnati. Although Washington kept his own counsel, it is probable that henceforth he included Jefferson among those who had maligned him "in such exaggerated and indecent terms as could scarcely be applied to a Nero; a notorious defaulter, or even a common pickpocket."[39]

A more serious but, happily for Jefferson, undivulged evidence of his fear of monarchism was the fact that in 1798 Jefferson informed the French minister "in great secrecy" that "Pitt's gold and intrigues have won Congress over, that the plan of campaign is to be an attack on Spanish Louisiana and the Floridas, which they expect to take without resistance."[40]

While Jefferson was suffering the consequences of his indiscretion in committing his political views to paper, Hamilton was paying the price for an offense against morality. In 1796, the prospect—remote as it was—that Hamilton would be designated as Washington's heir apparent was so terrible to Republicans that John Beckley, one of the most active organizers in the party, a shrewd and unscrupulous politician who had recently lost his post as clerk of the House of Representatives, made public the sorry tale of Hamilton's misadventures with Mr. and Mrs. Reynolds.[41]

In 1791, Hamilton had fallen into the hands of James Reynolds, a professional sharper who picked up a meager living by preying upon hard-up ex-soldiers whom he persuaded to sell their government certificates for a pittance. It was Hamilton's folly alone that had landed him in this predicament. He had stumbled into the trap—Mrs. Reynolds provided the bait—prepared for him by James Reynolds; after Hamilton had briefly enjoyed Mrs. Reynolds' favors, the outraged husband had appeared to demand balm—in the form of cash—for his wounded feelings. Hamilton paid about a thousand dollars in blackmail before Reynolds and his partner, Clingman, were arrested for

[39] Fitzpatrick, *Washington,* XXXV, 120; Ford, *Jefferson,* VII, 75–76, August 3, 1797; Madison to Jefferson, August 5, 1797, Madison MSS., LC.
[40] *American Historical Review,* XXXIX (1934), 467.
[41] Lodge, *Hamilton,* VII, 469; Pickering and Upham, *Pickering,* III, 422; *Report of the American Historical Association for 1912* (Washington, 1913), p. 356; James T. Callender, *The History of the United States for 1796* (Philadelphia, 1797), p. 117.

defrauding the government. While confined to jail, Reynolds told his version of the story of his relations with the Secretary of the Treasury to a self-constituted committee of three members of Congress. Reynolds swore that he could prove that Hamilton was using his official position to swindle the government to the tune of hundreds of thousands of dollars.

The three congressmen confronted Hamilton with the evidence placed in their hands by Reynolds and his wife. Hamilton had no difficulty—or so it seemed at the time—in convincing his interlocutors that he was guilty of nothing worse than an illicit affair with Mrs. Reynolds. The congressmen swore themselves to secrecy and here the matter seemingly ended.[42]

But the secret was not kept inviolate. James Monroe, one of the congressmen present at the interview with Hamilton, was not wholly convinced of the Secretary's innocence of financial wrongdoing—and he told the story, together with his own suspicions, to his good friend Thomas Jefferson. These suspicions were shared by John Beckley, the secretary of the committee, who kept a record of the letters that had passed between Hamilton and the Reynoldses. If Beckley kept these documents under cover, it was only because he was waiting an opportune moment for blazoning Hamilton's guilt to the world. In 1796, this moment seemed to have arrived. Beckley accordingly turned the letters over to James Callender, a journalist who had escaped punishment in England for seditious libel only by fleeing to the United States. Callender published the documents, together with highly spiced editorial comment, in a pamphlet entitled *The History of the United States for 1796*. Here it was made to appear that Hamilton was guilty not only of transgressing the Seventh Commandment but, more to the point, of stealing from the Treasury.[43]

Unaware of Beckley's part in this affair, Hamilton concluded that James Monroe had broken his promise of secrecy and given the incriminating documents to Callender. For several weeks, Monroe and Hamilton were on the point of settling their differences with a brace of pistols, but, thanks in part to Aaron Burr's timely intervention, a

[42] Paul A. W. Wallace, *The Muhlenbergs of Pennsylvania* (Philadelphia, 1950), p. 282; Lodge, *Hamilton*, VII, 388–389, 398–399, 406–407, 413–414.
[43] Ford, *Jefferson*, I, 212; Callender, *History of the United States for 1796*, p. 206; John Beckley to James Morrow, June 22, 1793, Hamilton MSS., NYPL (photostat); *Pennsylvania Magazine of History and Biography*, LX (1936), 382.

duel was averted. Against the better judgment of his friends, Hamilton thereupon published a pamphlet in which he confessed his adultery with Mrs. Reynolds in order to exculpate himself from the graver charge that he had mishandled public money. Thereafter Hamilton's reputation was delivered over to Republican journalists, to whom taking pot shots at the "Colossus of Monocrats" was a rare and exhilarating sport. After they had finished with him, it was improbable that Hamilton could have been elected to any high office in the United States; to his unpopularity as a "monarchist" and leader of a "corrupt squadron" in Congress was now added an unforgivable offense against the moral code.[44]

In the eyes of the French, the United States compounded its crime of ratifying Jay's Treaty by electing John Adams President. The Directory was not accustomed to having its orders flouted by second-rate powers; apparently Americans had not heard what had happened to Holland, Geneva, and the Italian states when they had made so bold as to resist French dictation. To drive home the salutary lesson that when the "terrible republic" spoke the smaller nations fell obediently into line, the Directory stepped up the seizure of American vessels and the confiscation of neutral cargoes. In March, 1797, American citizens impressed by the British were ordered by the French government to be hung whenever captured.[45] Late in 1797, a French decree asserted that if so much as a handkerchief of British origin were found aboard an American ship, the vessel and cargo were liable to confiscation without compensation. At the same time, Charles Cotesworth Pinckney, the newly appointed American minister to France, was ordered to leave the country and the Directory declared that it would not receive another minister from the United States until French grievances had been redressed. Hitherto, France had attempted to divide Americans and to inflame relations between the United States and Great Britain by preserving at least a token regard for neutral rights; now, it was clear, an attempt was to be made to dragoon Americans to support France's plan of destroying Great Brit-

[44] *John P. Branch Historical Papers*, II (Richmond, 1905), 283, 460; *Mississippi Valley Historical Review* (December, 1947), pp. 460, 466, 467; J. C. Hamilton, *Hamilton*, VI, 261; *Collections of the Massachusetts Historical Society*, Seventh Series, I (Boston, 1900), 59; Noah Webster, *A Letter to General Hamilton* (Philadelphia, 1800), p. 6.
[45] G. W. Allen, *Our Naval War with France* (Boston, 1909), pp. 29–30.

ain by cutting off her trade and markets. If the Continent and the United States could be sealed against British goods and neutral shipping prevented from carrying British goods, the French believed that the days of the "great sea-serpent" would be numbered. Of course, in its final death agonies, neutral powers such as the United States were liable to be injured, but this was a risk the Directory, if not the neutrals, was willing to take.[46]

Subjected to the same kind of provocation that they had experienced at the hands of Great Britain in 1793–94, the Federalists, after much searching of conscience, decided to send a mission to France. In this decision Adams and Hamilton concurred; both men were convinced that the moment was not ripe for war, that France had justifiable grievances against the United States, and that diplomacy might heal the breach between the two countries. In order to give proper weight and solemnity to this peace effort, the mission dispatched to France consisted of three distinguished public men: Charles Cotesworth Pinckney of South Carolina, John Marshall of Virginia, and Elbridge Gerry of Massachusetts.[47]

Toward Gerry, however, the Federalist leaders felt serious reservations. William Vans Murray, a diplomat experienced in the ways of European courts, said that, of all the men he knew, Gerry was "the least qualified to play a part in Paris, either among the men or the women. He is too virtuous for the last, too little acquainted with the world and with himself for the first." Gerry prided himself upon belonging to no party, but he had already begun to suspect that the Federalists were plotting "to disgrace republicanism." Nevertheless, President Adams declared that Gerry was "an honest and firm man, on whom French art could have no effect," and, although his nomination was opposed by the cabinet—the Secretary of War was willing to wager ten to one that Gerry would make trouble—he was confirmed, albeit reluctantly, by the Senate.[48]

---

[46] Ford, *John Quincy Adams*, II, February 1, 1797; Lodge, *George Cabot*, p. 121.

[47] Hamilton favored the appointment of either Jefferson or Madison to this commission, but here he signally failed to win the support of his party. Much to the Federalists' relief, Madison and Jefferson declined to serve. Ford, *Jefferson*, I, 272–273; Dauer, *Adams Federalists*, pp. 124–130. See also J. C. Hamilton, *History of the Republic of the United States* (New York, 1857–64), VII, 21–23; Robert Liston to Lord Grenville, July 13, 1797, Liston MSS., LC.

[48] Lodge, *George Cabot*, pp. 129, 131–133, 204–205; Ford, *John Quincy Adams*, II, 277, 283 (footnote).

The instructions given the American envoys were intended to resolve the dispute with France before it erupted into outright war. They were directed to seek compensation for the losses inflicted upon American commerce (this, however, was not made a *sine qua non*) and to secure a release of the United States' obligation to defend the French West Indies stipulated in the Treaty of Alliance of 1778. In exchange, they were authorized to adjust the Franco-American commercial treaty of 1778 to accord with the provisions of Jay's Treaty, thereby tacitly admitting that it had placed France in a less favorable position than Great Britain.

These instructions reflected Hamilton's conviction that, as between Great Britain and France, the United States should show no favoritism when its sovereign rights were threatened. Far from welcoming every opportunity, as Jefferson supposed, of prostrating the country at the feet of George III, Hamilton acted upon the principle that the United States ought "to depend as little as possible upon European caprice, and to exert ourselves to the utmost to uphold and improve every domestic resource" and to resist aggression regardless of its origin. While he believed that the United States had a heavy stake in a British victory over France, he did not at any time favor a yielding to British depredations upon the commerce of this country. If necessary, he was prepared to go to war with Great Britain and France simultaneously. "One of them," he predicted, "will quickly court us, and by this course of conduct our citizens will be enthusiastically united to the government."[49]

As in 1794, when the country had been confronted by British aggression, the Federalists sought to negotiate from a position of strength. Experience had amply demonstrated to Hamilton and his followers that "the most equitable and sincere neutrality is not sufficient to exempt a state from the depredations of other nations at war with each other. It is essential to induce them to respect that neutrality, that there shall be an organized force ready to vindicate the national flag." To that end, bills were introduced into Congress in the spring of 1797 calling for the strengthening of the regular army and the creation of a provisional army of 15,000 men; the construction of three frigates (the six frigates authorized in 1794 had been reduced to three); the imposition of new taxes for revenue; and the granting

[49] Lodge, *Hamilton*, IX, 484–485; X, 294–295; Charles, *American Party System*, pp. 124–128.

of large discretionary powers to the Chief Executive. The Republicans, as was their wont, resisted every effort to arm the country. Gallatin declared that "there was a much more effective way of securing the respect of foreign nations than by building a Navy: applying our resources to the payment of our Public Debt." To keep aggressors at bay he advocated reducing the army and suspending work on the frigates. For who would dare attack a country with a balanced budget and a small national debt? Jefferson, who at one time had favored the creation of a navy, was now convinced that it was far more likely to make a war than to prevent one. He felt certain that this country's wars would occur upon the sea and would arise from naval and commercial rivalry; if the United States stood with respect to Europe "precisely on the footing of China," he said, "we should thus avoid wars."[50]

As a result, the Federalists had to be content, insofar as the country's defenses were concerned, with considerably less than half a loaf. The three frigates were launched in 1797; 80,000 militia were ordered to be held in readiness; and the government was authorized to contract loans totaling $800,000. Nevertheless, only merchant ships engaged in the Indian and Mediterranean trade were permitted to arm; in other areas, American ships were obliged to take their chances with French cruisers and privateers. Plainly, the United States government was resolved to avoid any acts of provocation that would impede the progress of negotiations.

While foreign relations and national defense were being debated in Congress, political acrimony reached the explosive stage. Late in 1797, Congressman Matthew Lyon of Vermont responded to an insult from Congressman Roger Griswold of Connecticut by spitting in Griswold's eye. A few days later, Griswold attacked the Vermonter with a cane while he sat at his desk in the House. Lyon defended himself with a pair of fire tongs and had succeeded in wrestling Griswold to the floor when the two men were forcibly parted by other members of the House. Griswold had to be pulled by his legs to induce him to let go of his adversary; and Lyon "expressed disapprobation at being parted, and said, as he was rising, 'I wish I had been left alone awhile.'"

As the custodians of the proprieties and all the graces, the Federalists could not tolerate the presence in Congress of the "Spitting Lyon" from Vermont. They disdained him as a "nasty," "brutish," "spitting animal"; Representative Dana of Massachusetts declared that this "kennel of filth" ought to be expelled from Congress as citizens removed *impurities* and *filth* from their docks and wharves." This was strong language for one New Englander to use against another Yankee, but in actuality Lyon had been born in Ireland and had come to America as a young man. This rendered his offense even more reprehensible in the eyes of true-born New Englanders: "I feel grieved," said a Bostonian, "that the saliva of an Irishman should be left upon the face of an American & he, a New Englandman."[51]

Notwithstanding the Federalists' lament that Lyon's career, from his birth onward, had been an offense against all that was good and wise and virtuous, they failed to expel him from Congress. Having married the daughter of Governor Chittenden of Vermont, Lyon was a political power in his own state and his record as a Republican was unimpeachable, although a bit on the rough-and-tumble side. In consequence, the Republicans rallied to his defense and the vote fell short of the two-thirds majority required for expulsion. The Federalists took this defeat much in the manner of the Romans when they saw the barbarians at the gates; the time had come to make a final stand against the enemy or to perish ignobly at the hands of "wild Irishmen."

[51] Morison, *Otis,* I, February 19, 1798; *Porcupine's Gazette,* January 10, 1799; Morison, *Jeremiah Smith,* 135; *Gazette of the United States,* July 23, 1798; *Salem Gazette,* June 12, 1798.

CHAPTER 12

Foreign Affairs and Domestic Politics

HAVING been conceived in crisis, the Federalist party depended for its continuance in power upon some compelling public emergency. After 1792, its dominance was threatened by the rise of the Republican party; and during most of the period from 1793 to 1798, Republicans constituted a majority of the House of Representatives. In the presidential election of 1796, the Federalists had barely succeeded in carrying off the prize—John Adams was never permitted to forget that he was "President by three votes." From this unpromising state of affairs the Federalists were delivered by a sudden deterioration in Franco-American relations. In 1798–99, thanks largely to Talleyrand and the Directory, President Adams and the Federalist party were raised to the pinnacle of their popularity with the American people.

Despite Hamilton's prediction that the Directory would not refuse to receive the three American plenipotentiaries, they encountered only rebuffs and humiliations in Paris. For several weeks they waited patiently in the anterooms of the Directors, occasionally spoken to by a subordinate clerk and granted unofficial interviews with Talleyrand, the Minister of Foreign Affairs. Finally, when they were prepared to write off their mission as a failure, they were approached by Talleyrand's agents, later designated in President Adams's report to Congress as X, Y, and Z. These men—there was also a mysterious lady involved—delicately suggested that the envoys could smooth the way for negotiations if they agreed to pay a bribe of $250,000 to Talleyrand and the Directors, advance the government a loan of $12 million, and offer suitable apologies for the harsh remarks against France made by President Adams in his message to Congress of May 15, 1797. Compliance with these demands was made a prerequisite to the American commissioners' official reception by the Directory.[1]

This approach was in the best traditions of French foreign policy as conducted by Talleyrand, onetime Bishop of Autun and ironically called "The Incorruptible." Having lost his fortune during the Revolution, Talleyrand deliberately set out to recoup; a master of the art of speculation, he amassed about thirty million francs during his tenure of office under the Directory. He charged Austria one million francs for the insertion of secret articles in the Treaty of Campo Formio; from Prussia he received another million francs for having informed that kingdom of these same secret articles and for having prevented their execution. In like manner, he had shaken down Portugal, the Elector of Bavaria, the Grand Duke of Tuscany, the Batavian Republic, and the Grand Vizier. Nevertheless, Talleyrand was brazen enough to allege that the Directory could not treat with the administration of John Adams because it was corrupt! Elbridge Gerry succinctly summed up the situation when he said that "a small cargo of Mexican Dollars would be more efficient in the Negotiation at present than two Cargoes of Ambassadors."[2]

While the American envoys were willing to consider paying a bribe to Talleyrand and his colleagues after the treaty had been consummated, they declined to pay before the goods had been delivered. They therefore ceased to hold talks with X, Y, and Z and asked for their passports. But Talleyrand, whose policy was to spin out the negotiations, discredit the Federalist administration, and force the United States to repudiate Jay's Treaty, succeeded at this point in dividing the American envoys. By dint of playing upon Gerry's vanity, apprehensions, and devotion to peace, and by withholding his passport, Talleyrand succeeded in detaining him in Paris after Marshall and

[1] Channing, *History*, IV, 183–184; *American Historical Review*, XLIII (1938), 522–523; Gerry to William Vans Murray, October 31, 1797, Gerry MSS., LC; John Marshall to King, December 24, 1797, Rufus King MSS., NYHS.

[2] *Proceedings of the Massachusetts Historical Society*, XLIV (1911), 398; King, *Rufus King*, II, 459, November 24, December 23, 1797; Duc de Broglie (ed.), *Memoirs of Talleyrand* (London, 1897), I, xlviii; Ford, *John Quincy Adams*, II, 298–299.

Pinckney had left the country.[3] Despite orders from the State Department, Gerry did not take his departure until July, 1798.[4]

In the meantime, the American envoys reported back to their government, and in April, 1798, the entire correspondence was printed and laid before the American people by order of the United States Senate. The publication of the X, Y, Z dispatches electrified the country as had no other event since the Revolutionary War. A newspaperman put the words "Millions for defense but not one cent for Tribute" (Pinckney actually said: "it is no, no, not a sixpence!") in the mouths of the American envoys, and the slogan became the watchword of American patriots. The champions of national rights against foreign aggression, the Federalists now reaped the reward for their long crusade against revolutionary France; they were acclaimed as patriots and heroes while their opponents, in the words of Fisher Ames, "were confounded, and the trimmers dropt off from the party like windfalls from an apple-tree in September." Small boys fought in the streets under the name of Frenchmen and Americans, and the cry was frequently heard: "Huzza! Huzza! for the AMERICANS, we have beat the FRENCHMEN!" A few months before, the British minister reported that President Adams entered and left the theater in Philadelphia "without receiving the slightest mark of attention"; now, however, he brought down the house as audiences cheered themselves hoarse at the sight of the portly little man. "Adams and Liberty" and

[3] Even before Pinckney and Marshall broke off negotiations, Gerry had carried on secret conversations with Talleyrand under an injunction not to disclose them to his colleagues. It was for this reason that Pinckney exploded: "I never met with a man of less candor and as much duplicity as Mr. Gerry." Yet Gerry never admitted to being anti-British. "In regard to the War between France & Great Britain," he said, "I considered the United States in so many respects as being embarked with the latter, that I conceived the overthrow of her government as involving that of our own." He believed that a loan made by the United States during the war would immediately involve this country in war with Great Britain. According to his own account, he remained in Paris after the departure of his colleagues solely to prevent a rupture between France and the United States. He always maintained that had he not been in Paris when the X, Y, Z dispatches were published, war would have occurred. Gerry to John Adams, July 5, 1799; to Rufus King, March 26, 1798, to Miss Helen Thompson, January 30, 1798; to Miss Gerry, November 28, 1797; to Jefferson, January 15, 1801, Gerry MSS., LC.

[4] S. E. Morison, "Elbridge Gerry, Gentleman-Democrat," *New England Quarterly*, II (1929), 25–27; Gerry to John Adams, July 5, 1799; to Rufus King, March 20, 1798; to ? April 23, 1798, Gerry MSS., LC.

"The President's March" became the popular songs of the day.[5] Anyone who dared call for a French tune was likely to be "thrown out of the windows, or from the gallery into the pit, and that too by the friends of order and good government." The President was kept so busy writing replies to the complimentary addresses that poured in upon him that Mrs. Adams feared his health would be undermined. And when "the eagle-eyed and undaunted Adams" reviewed a great military parade on July 4, 1798, many Americans were ready to believe that the American eagle would have little difficulty in taking "the Gallic cock by the Gills."[6]

But, at the moment, the American eagle was barely able to get off the ground. Except for the three frigates the United States Navy was nonexistent; and the army was composed of about 3,500 officers and men occupied in garrisoning the frontier posts. The French took full advantage of these weaknesses: in 1798, the Atlantic coast was infested with French "picaroons"—small privateers operating out of the French West Indies. Scores of unarmed American merchantmen were captured, many within American territorial waters. It was estimated that within two months, Philadelphia lost half a million dollars in shipping to French corsairs.

French insults and depredations galvanized Congress to gird the country for war. In the spring of 1798, money was appropriated for completing the frigates and for the purchase or construction of over forty additional ships, the acquisition of arms and ammunition, and the fortification of harbors. In July, 1798, the regular army was ordered to be trebled in numbers. Commercial intercourse with France was suspended and the Franco-American treaties of commerce and alliance of 1778 were declared suspended.

[5] Joseph Hopkinson, the composer of "Hail Columbia" cited as proof of the revolutionary change that had occurred in the American mind the fact that "American tunes and American sentiments have driven off those execrable french murder shouts which not long since tortured our ears in all places of public amusement, and in every lane and alley in the United States." Joseph Hopkinson to Washington, 1798 (n.d.), Washington MSS., LC; Mitchell, *Abigail Adams,* p. 164.

[6] *Salem Gazette,* July 17, 1798; Adams, *John Adams,* IX, 194, 203; X, 10–11; Adams, *John Adams,* II, 239; J. C. Hamilton, *History of the Republic,* VIII, 168; Hunt, *Madison,* VI, 315; Ames, *Fisher Ames,* I, 227; Gibbs, *Memoirs,* II, 71; Albert J. Beveridge, *The Life of John Marshall* (Boston, 1916–19), I, 349; Lodge, *George Cabot,* 154; J. C. Hamilton, *Hamilton,* VI, 277–279; Mitchell, *Abigail Adams,* 154, 164; Robert Liston to Lord Grenville, April 12, May 21, 1798, Liston MSS., LC.

All this pointed toward war—and yet the Federalists hesitated to take the plunge. A party caucus held in June, 1798, concluded that a declaration of war was inexpedient in view of the certain opposition of the Republicans (who commanded almost half the votes of the House of Representatives). The Republicans, complained a Federalist, seemed bent upon playing the part of "a weak dupe who finds himself compelled to turn an unfaithful wench out of doors, stopping her at the threshold to whine over their former loves, and to remind her of past joys." The Federalists therefore looked to President Adams to mobilize public opinion for war. And, indeed, in the President the warhawks seemed to have found a resolute and militant leader prepared to lead a crusade against the "monster" spawned by the French Revolution. In his answers to the addresses that converged upon him from his admirers in all parts of the country, he declared that there was "no alternative between war and submission to the Executive of France"; he condemned further efforts at negotiations as "not only nugatory but disgraceful and ruinous"; and he asserted that the United States was "on the point of being drawn into the vortex of European war."[7]

Yet when it came to recommending that Congress declare war, the President fell strangely silent. There could be little doubt that when the American people expressed their determination to spend millions for defense they meant defensive, not offensive, war. Moreover, hope of peace sprang eternal in Americans' breasts as long as Gerry remained in Paris. Secretary of State Pickering suggested (it was his idea of humor) that if the French would guillotine Gerry it would be a favor to the United States, but, he lugubriously admitted, it was more probable they would "keep him alive to write, a la Monroe, a book."[8] Even more disquieting to the war faction was the fact that in the spring of 1798 a French army under the command of Napoleon Bonaparte was preparing to invade England. Few Americans had any stomach for war if they were obliged to fight without the protection

[7] Adams, *John Adams*, IX, 194, 203, 304–305; Hunt, *Madison*, VI, 325, 328; Ford, *Jefferson*, I, 282–283; Gibbs, *Memoirs*, II, 118; *Report of the American Historical Association for 1896* (Washington, 1897), I, 811; *What Is Our Situation? By an American*, pp. 35–36; William A. Robinson, *Jeffersonian Democracy in New England* (Cambridge, Mass., 1916), pp. 14, 19, 26; Dauer, *Adams Federalists*, pp. 142–144.

[8] Pickering to Marshall, October 19, 1798, Marshall MSS., LC; Gibbs, *Memoirs*, II, 70.

of the British navy. And so it seemed much the safer course to leave the declaration of war to the French: if it came as a result of the Directory's action, Americans would be far more united than if the Federalists succeeded by a small majority in ramming through Congress a declaration of war against France. Both Marshall and Pinckney assured the party leaders that sooner or later the French would embark upon full-scale war. "If we would have peace with France," Pinckney declared, "it must be obtained, not by negotiation, but by the sword . . . I am convinced we must fight for its preservation." And John Marshall predicted that the Directory would "sacrifice one Hundred Thousand men sooner than recede one Step."[9]

Even without a declaration of war, hostilities occurred on the high seas. Talleyrand had said that "the United States merited no more consideration than Genoa or Geneva" and he did not expect more resistance from the United States than from those city-states. Having spent several years in the United States, Talleyrand expected that the Republicans, being friends of France, would effectively tie the hands of the administration. In 1798–99, the French learned how grossly they had miscalculated.[10]

In March, 1798, except for a few revenue cutters, the United States did not have a single ship ready for action. The three frigates whose construction had been authorized in March, 1797, had been launched in the autumn of that year, but much work remained to be done before they could put to sea. Even though the Republicans in Congress did not cease to declaim against a navy after the X, Y, Z crisis, the depredations of the French privateers left Americans little choice between building a navy or tying up their merchant ships and abandoning the sea to their enemies. Congress therefore appropriated the money necessary to complete the frigates, and in the summer of 1798 these three vessels—the *Constitution*, the *United States*, and the *Constellation*—carried the flag of the United States Navy into the Atlantic for the first time since the War of Independence.[11]

[9] Adams, *John Adams*, IX, 304–305; Ford, *Jefferson*, I, 282; Lodge, *George Cabot*, p. 168; *American Historical Review*, XLIII (1938), 527–528; Gerry to Jefferson, January 15, 1801, Jefferson MSS., LC; Dauer, *Adams Federalists*, pp. 169–170; Ames, *Fisher Ames*, I, 233; Adams, *John Adams*, II, 239; Gibbs, *Memoirs*, II, 169.

[10] Marshall to Rufus King, Pinckney to Rufus King, December 24, 1797, King MSS., NYHS.

[11] Allen, *Our Naval War With France*, p. 42.

Formidable as were these warships—they were considerably larger than their counterparts in the British and French navies—no one supposed that they were capable of coping with the multitude of French picaroons that infested the Caribbean and the coastal waters of the United States. Accordingly, in July, 1798, Congress authorized the President to construct or purchase twenty-four additional ships for the navy. To strengthen further the naval forces of the United States, Congress enacted a law providing that any individual who advanced money to the government for the purpose of building ships was to receive 6 per cent government bonds to the full amount contributed. Under this law, subscriptions were opened in the principal seaports. The response left no doubt that the businessmen were prepared to support the government to the hilt. In Boston, for example, $72,000 was subscribed during the first hour the lists were open; and in 1799 the frigate *Boston* left the ways.[12]

At the beginning of the crisis in Franco-American relations, the administration of naval affairs was assigned to the Secretaries of War and of the Treasury. But in April, 1798, Congress established a separate Department of the Navy, and President Adams appointed Benjamin Stoddert as its first Secretary. Stoddert, a Virginian, frankly confessed his ignorance of the duties of his office: "It was unfortunate," he said, "that in conferring the Appointment of Secretary of the Navy upon me, the President cou'd not also confer the knowledge necessary for the Secretary of the Navy to possess, to make him most useful to his Country." Even so, Stoddert was eager to learn, and none of the shortcomings of the Navy were owing to any lack of energy or enthusiasm on the part of the Secretary.[13]

Not the least of Stoddert's difficulties consisted in procuring trained men to man the ships of the Navy. Unwilling to deplete the merchant marine, the Navy was obliged to take some very indifferent specimens aboard its ships. Captain Thomas Truxton complained that "after discharging a Number of Rotten and inanimate Animals that found their Way into the Ship [the U.S.S. *Constellation*] by imposing on the recruiting Officers and Surgeon's Vigilance," few able hands re-

[12] *Naval Documents Related to the Quasi-War Between the United States and France. Naval Operations from February 1797 to October, 1798* (Washington, 1935), p. 168; Morison, *Maritime History of Massachusetts*, p. 175; James D. Phillips, "Salem's Part in the Naval War with France," *New England Quarterly* (XVI), (1943), 558.
[13] *Naval Documents, February, 1797–October, 1798*, p. 199.

mained. One of the peculiarities of these "animals," he complained, was that they imagined that "a democratic System" prevailed aboard the ships of the United States Navy. Truxton met this situation by literally whipping the material allotted him into shape: a marine guilty of insubordination received a dozen stripes with the cat-o'-nine-tails. A brief tour of duty under Truxton left no doubt that democracy, together with wives and sweethearts, had been left ashore.[14]

By 1800, fourteen American men of war were at sea and special commissions had been given to the owners of hundreds of private ships, authorizing them to capture French armed vessels. As a result, the coastal waters of the United States were quickly cleared of French picaroons and early in 1799 the fight was carried to the French in the West Indies. Patrolling the Caribbean were four American squadrons, one of which was commanded by Truxton, who, as the skipper of a privateer during the War of Independence, had captured so many enemy ships that Washington declared his services to be worth a regiment in the field. Early in 1799, Truxton met in battle the French frigate *L'Insurgente* and the Frenchman struck the tricolor; and in February, 1800, he so heavily damaged the *Vengeance* that it was put permanently out of action.[15]

Still, this being a quasi-war, both the United States Navy and the American privateers fought under wraps: neither the ships of the Navy nor the armed merchantmen were permitted to capture un-armed French vessels; only armed cruisers, privateers, and ships of war were declared to be lawful prey. As a result, the bag of French ships was disappointingly small: only about eighty ships, most of them of modest size, were taken by the Navy. The proceeds of the sale of these prizes were divided between the officers of the captor ship and the government. No one grew rich from these operations: the unde-clared war with France yielded little plunder and no territory, and the Navy devoured revenue faster and in greater quantities than even the Republicans had predicted.[16]

It was the United States Army, however, which really suffered the

---

[14] *Ibid.*, pp. 134–135.

[15] Allen, *Naval War with France*, pp. 58–59; Morison, *Maritime History of Massachusetts*, p. 175; *Naval Documents, February, 1797–October, 1798*, p. 168.

[16] Kurtz, *Presidency of John Adams*, p. 321; Allen, *Naval War with France*, pp. 58–59; King, *Rufus King*, II, March 19, 1797; J. C. Hamilton, *History of the Republic*, VIII, 23.

frustrations of this abortive war. During the summer of 1798, without waiting for a recommendation from the President—it was enough that Alexander Hamilton called for action—Congress ordered the immediate enlistment of an "Additional Army" of ten thousand men and the creation of a "Provisional Army" of fifty thousand men. The Additional Army was to serve during the continuance of the dispute with France; the Provisional Army was to be raised in case of war or when, in the opinion of the President, the national security required it. To encourage enlistment, the pay of privates was raised from $4 to $6 a month despite the dire prediction of one representative that "high pay would only serve to make the soldiers get drunk."[17]

Washington was called out of retirement to head this greatly enlarged military force, but he stipulated that he would assume active command only if the situation became critical. The question of who was to be second in command therefore became of capital importance. President Adams's candidate was General Henry Knox, the leading artillerist of the American army during the War of Independence and, more recently, Secretary of War in Washington's cabinet. But the President was overruled by Washington; under the threat of resignation, Washington compelled Adams to appoint Alexander Hamilton Major General, Adjutant General, and second in command. The result was catastrophic for party harmony: "You crammed him [Hamilton] down my throat," the President cried out in anguish.[18]

In June, 1798, President Adams had seemed so carried away by his ardor for war that Alexander Hamilton had feared that the old fire-eater would plunge the country prematurely into open hostilities with France. But after it had become apparent that the war would furnish Hamilton with a vehicle for riding to glory and possibly to the Presidency, the President began to drag his feet. The enlistment of the Additional Army was delayed until the spring of 1799—a season of the year when young men's fancies are not usually turned toward soldiering. By neglecting to take advantage of the patriotic fervor that swept the country after the publication of the X, Y, Z papers, the

[17] *Naval Documents, February, 1797–October, 1798*, pp. 33, 193, 195; Carlos E. Godfrey, "Organization of the Provisional Army," *Pennsylvania Magazine of History and Biography*, XXXVIII (1914), 130–132.

[18] Fitzpatrick, *Washington*, XXXVI, July 4, 1798; Charles, *American Party System*, pp. 48–49, 60–61; Dauer, *Adams Federalists*, p. 218; Carroll and Ashworth, *Washington*, VII, 517–524.

administration missed its opportunity of filling the ranks with prime military material. Instead, Washington disconsolately observed in 1799, "none but the riff-raff of the Country, and the Scape gallows of the large Cities" would sign the articles. Irishmen—who usually could be relied upon to shoulder a musket—displayed understandable reluctance to serve in an army officered by "aristocratic," "pro-British" Federalists, despite zealous recruiting sergeants who told them that their homes and farms were threatened "with fire, plunder and pillage, and your wives and sweethearts with ravishment and assassination, by horrid outlandish sans-culotte Frenchmen!" and who held out as a reward for enlistment the delectable prospect of plenty of food and drink, a handsome bounty, an elegant suit of clothes, and "rations that might tempt an epicure."[19] On the other hand, so many Federalist gentlemen applied for commissions for themselves or their relatives—even President Adams tried to secure a command for his son-in-law—that in the Additional Army (which never attained more than a third of its authorized strength of ten thousand men) the ratio of privates and noncoms to officers was seven to one. Had it come to war with France, an inordinate amount of blue blood might have been shed on the American side.[20]

The Federalists' justification for strengthening the United States army was the imminent danger in which the country presumably stood of a French invasion. If the French came, it was believed that they would strike at the southern states, where a large slave population might be expected to rise in support of an army that marched under the banner of Liberty, Equality, and Fraternity. But events in Europe and the Near East in 1798 put an end to any immediate peril from this quarter. The French failed to carry out their threat of invading England, and in October Nelson won a smashing victory over the French fleet at the Battle of the Nile and thereby immured Napoleon and a French army in Egypt. Although Hamilton and other Federalist leaders continued to beat the alarm that the French were coming, there were few to heed them. The British navy seemed to have the situation well in hand.[21]

[19] *Porcupine's Gazette,* July 27, 1798.
[20] Fitzpatrick, *Washington,* XXXVI, 474; XXXVII, 138, 159, 160–161, February 25, 1799; Dauer, *Adams Federalists,* pp. 213–215; *Pennsylvania Magazine of History and Biography,* XXXVIII (1914), 130–132; Adams, *John Adams,* X, 119.
[21] Lodge, *Hamilton,* VII, 94; *Gazette of the United States,* November 19, 1798.

With invasion no longer a serious threat, Hamilton began to contemplate offensive operations against the French and their allies, the
Spaniards. Knowing that the Directory was attempting to secure from
Spain the retrocession of Louisiana, Hamilton determined to antici-
pate them by leading the American army into Louisiana and the
Floridas. His ambition was truly imperial in scope: "We ought," he
said, "to squint at South America." Influenced by Francisco Miranda,
the Venezuelan patriot and liberator, the British government was already looking in that direction. The vast Spanish empire, closed by
mercantilist laws to the commerce of other nations, offered illimitable
prospects to the merchants and manufacturers of Great Britain and
the United States. Hamilton therefore conceived of the projected
operations in Latin America as a joint Anglo-American enterprise:
the British were to furnish the fleet, the Americans the army, and
Hamilton himself would supply the generalship. Here, however, the
British ministry parted company with the American statesman-gen-
eral: according to William Pitt's plans, the Americans were to furnish
only sailors for His Majesty's ships of war and the enterprise was to
be under the command of a British general and admiral. But nothing
came of these grandiose schemes, partly for the reason that President
Adams was unwilling to embark upon an adventure that promised to
involve the United States more deeply in European affairs, to produce
a British alliance, and to expend American lives and money in behalf
of a people who, in his opinion, were not prepared to receive the blessings of liberty.[22]

Even though Englishmen and Americans did not fight side by side
for the liberation of Latin America, the two countries were inevitably
drawn closer together by their common hostility to revolutionary
France. In the Caribbean, they co-operated in aiding the Touissant
L'Ouverture, "the Black Napoleon of the Antilles" who had established
a Negro republic on the former French island of Santo Domingo. This
spirit was not confined to the two governments: an increasing number
of Englishmen and Americans began to act upon the maxim that
blood is thicker than water. In Englishmen's eyes, Americans had
never appeared more like the descendants of "true-born Britons" than
when they defied France and prepared to go to war in defense of
their national rights and honor. To Americans, particularly those of

[22] Charles, *American Party System*, pp. 132–135; Dauer, *Adams Federalists*,
pp. 175, 181, 196–197; Perkins, *First Rapprochement*, pp. 111–115.

the Federalist persuasion, Great Britain never seemed to be more like
St. George than when the teeth of the French "dragon" began to nip
uncomfortably close to the United States.[23]

In order that Americans should not lack implements of war against
the French, the British government loaned (later it was made a gift)
the United States cannon and ammunition for harbor defense and
sold the Republic small arms, naval supplies, and naval cannon. Probably most of the shot and shell fired during the undeclared war with
France came from the mouths of cannon provided by the British. The
British navy convoyed American merchant ships in dangerous waters
in the Caribbean, off the coast of Europe, and even, for a time, in
American territorial waters. And it was the British navy that enabled
the fledgling United States Navy to concentrate its forces in the Caribbean. In December, 1798, with one exception, every ship of the Navy
was in West India waters; and in the summer of 1800, twenty out
of twenty-two ships were patrolling that theater of war—thanks to
the fact that the British navy controlled the Atlantic sea lanes.[24]

The rapprochement with Great Britain which began with Jay's
Treaty and reached its climax during the undeclared war with France
was never so entire as to remove all causes of friction between the
two countries. The French were not alone in molesting American
shipping; in this regard, the British were quite the equals of the
French. A British admiralty judge in the West Indies, for example,
was said to condemn "with the rapacity of a shark every vessel that is
brought in; a single contraband article, however trifling in value, is
held by the Judge in all cases to be efficient cause for condemning the
whole vessel and cargo." In sending its armed ships to sea, the United
States therefore ran the risk of precipitating an unwanted war with
Great Britain. For it could be foreseen that high-spirited American
ship captains, instead of standing by quietly while the British seized
defenseless American merchantmen, would try to protect their coun-

[23] Pickering and Upham, *Timothy Pickering,* III, 382; *Report of the American Historical Association for 1896* (Washington, 1897), I, 807; Robert Liston
to Lord Grenville, May 2, September 27, November 7, 1798, Robert Liston
MSS., LC; Adams, *John Adams,* IX, 211–216; J. C. Hamilton, *Hamilton,* VI,
307; Brown, *Northern Confederacy,* p. 23; King, *Rufus King,* III, March 21,
August 3, 1798; Perkins, *First Rapprochement,* pp. 106–111.

[24] Perkins, *First Rapprochement,* pp. 95–98; *Naval Documents, February,
1797–October, 1798,* pp. 255–258; Mayo, *Instructions to British Ministers,* p.
129.

trymen against all depredators regardless of whether they flew the tricolor or the Union Jack.[25]

Aware of the danger that the Navy might make two wars where only one existed before, the administration put American naval officers under strict orders not to interfere with the capture of American merchant vessels by the warships of any nation except those of France. Even if American commanders witnessed the act of capture, they were forbidden to intervene. Nor were they permitted to recapture an American vessel taken by the armed vessels of any nation but France. In these cases, the administration informed American commanders, it was to be presumed, pending proof to the contrary, that the admiralty courts of the offending nation would do justice to the ships and cargoes brought before them for adjudication.[26]

Impressment likewise became an increasingly sore point after 1796, when the British navy began to experience a critical shortage of man power. Press gangs delivered hundreds of men to the British navy, but they disappeared almost as fast as they were clapped into service. The British Admiralty thought it knew where they went: disgusted by the low pay, poor food, and harsh treatment they met with aboard British men of war, they deserted to the American mercantile marine where they were sure of a good berth, better food, and higher pay.

The only way the British navy could recover these absconders was to remove them bodily from American ships. At first, the British confined their practice of boarding and searching American ships to those moored in British ports, but after 1796 they began to extend their activities to the high seas. As Rufus King, the American minister to the Court of St. James's, observed, the British naval officers entrusted with the delicate operation of boarding and searching American vessels were "men of more nautical than political skill." In their eyes, any likely looking seaman was an English deserter and, unless he could prove otherwise, he found himself in the King's Navee. It was not an experience calculated to make a man do the hornpipe.[27]

[25] King, *Rufus King*, III, September 2, 1799; John Jay to Pickering, July 5, 1799, Pickering MSS., MHS.

[26] *Naval Documents, February, 1797–October, 1798*, pp. 193, 195, 455; *November, 1798–March, 1799*, p. 33.

[27] Robert Liston to Lord Grenville, May 2, 1798, Liston MSS., LC; John Temple to Lord Grenville, April 21, 1798, PRO, FO; *Report of the American Historical Association for 1897* (Washington, 1898), pp. 463–464, 525–526; Mayo, *Instructions to British Ministers*, p. 135; James F. Zimmerman, *Impressment of British Seamen* (New York, 1925) pp. 18, 20–21.

The impressment controversy was an example of how a common language helped create misunderstanding and ultimately war between the two English-speaking peoples. It was next to impossible for a British naval captain to determine whether the individual in question was an Englishman or, as he invariably claimed to be, an American citizen. The British never asserted the right to impress Americans—Heaven forbid, Grenville told Jay in 1794, that such an untoward event should occur! But how was an Englishman to be distinguished from an American? The United States government tried giving certificates of citizenship to American crews, and American consuls abroad were empowered to grant these documents to bona fide citizens; and in 1796 Congress passed an Act for the Relief and Protection of American Seamen which the Republican majority in Congress, although not the Federalist administration, regarded as the final word on the controversy. But fraud soon vitiated the whole system; Lord St. Vincent of the British Admiralty asserted that for one dollar any Englishman might become an American citizen. As a result, his Lordship declared, the American merchant marine was manned largely by English subjects—to which Gouverneur Morris replied: "I believe, my Lord, this is the only instance in which we are not treated as aliens."[28]

The best-known "American" to suffer impressment was not an American at all. Thomas Nash was a deserter and mutineer from the British frigate *Hermione,* the officers of which had been killed by the crew. Nash claimed to be Jonathan Robbins of Connecticut and asserted that he had been impressed by the captain of the *Hermione* before the mutiny, in which, incidentally, he denied having taken part. Even though Nash had an affidavit purporting to prove that he was really Jonathan Robbins, the British demanded that he be surrendered for trial as a mutineer under the extradition clause of Jay's Treaty. At the request of the British minister, President Adams gave his personal attention to the case and decided, upon the basis of the evidence, that Nash was not an American citizen. The President thereupon directed Judge Bee of the Federal District Court of South Carolina to turn Nash over to the British authorities, by whom he was

[28] Johnston, *Jay,* IV, 210, 221; Bemis, *American Secretaries of State,* II, 211; *An Examination of the Conduct of the Executive of the United States* (Philadelphia, 1797), pp. 66–67; Perkins, *First Rapprochement,* p. 62; Zimmerman, *Impressment,* 18, 20–21; Robert Liston to Lord Grenville, July 3, 1796, Liston MSS., LC.

tried, found guilty, and executed. Despite the evidence to the contrary, the Republicans continued to portray Nash as an American citizen delivered up to "bloodthirsty Britons" by a weak and cowardly President. But a Republican effort to censure the Chief Executive was defeated in the House of Representatives in March, 1800, partly as a result of John Marshall's powerful speech in support of President Adams.[29]

The United States was not spared the final indignity—the forcible removal of seamen aboard a ship of the United States Navy. In November, 1798, with the shortage of man power growing increasingly acute, an overzealous British officer, Captain John Loring of H.M.S. *Carnatic,* stopped the American sloop of war *Baltimore,* Captain Isaac Phillips commanding, engaged in convoying American ships to Havana. Captain Loring ordered Phillips to stop, call all hands, and furnish a list of the crew. While Captain Phillips's orders did not permit him to resist, he displayed unseemly alacrity in obeying Loring's orders, even to the extent of consenting to go aboard the *Carnatic.* When he showed his instructions to Loring, that sea dog insolently asked: "Who is Ben Stoddert?" and he appeared incredulous when he was informed that the United States had a navy and that Benjamin Stoddert was the Secretary of the Navy. He removed fifty-five men whom he suspected of being British subjects from the *Baltimore;* but when Phillips protested that he did not have enough men left properly to man his ship, the British captain returned fifty of the men.[30]

This crass violation of American sovereignty produced a vigorous protest by Secretary of State Pickering to the British government, but it was Captain Phillips who paid the penalty. Admitting that Phillips had no right to protect the ships under his convoy, the Secretary of the Navy took the position that the American officer was guilty of dereliction of duty in permitting himself "to be made instrumental in assisting the Outrage." For this offense, Captain Phillips was relieved of his command and dismissed from the service, and American commanders were instructed not to permit impressment from their vessels unless compelled by force. Unwilling to appear to condone Captain

[29] Charles Pinckney, *Three Letters* (Philadelphia, 1799), pp. 10–13; Perkins, *First Rapprochement,* pp. 124–125.

[30] *Naval Documents, November, 1798–March, 1799,* pp. 26–34; Ames, *Fisher Ames,* I, 263–264; Perkins, *First Rapprochement,* pp. 99–100.

Loring's highhanded behavior, the Admiralty transferred him to another station. The *"Baltimore* affair" made a sensation in the news, but it was the only instance of a clash between the Royal Navy and the United States Navy during the two and a half years of the undeclared war with France; and it was more than counterbalanced by the many instances of co-operation between the two forces.[31]

The sailors secured for the British navy by means of impressment cost the British government heavily in the form of American resentment and ill will. The enemies of Great Britain made the most of "British atrocities." They magnified a few hundred cases of British impressment of American citizens into thousands, and they accused the administration of having no more concern for the welfare of these unfortunates "than if they were inhabitants of California."[32]

Although President Adams declared that the British had no right to remove any American foreigners or even Englishmen from American ships and this continued to be the official American attitude, in practice the administration adopted a much more flexible attitude toward the issues raised by impressment. While the government sought to secure the release of individual American citizens impressed into British service, it did nothing that would embarrass the British government or weaken the British navy. The leaders of the Federalist party were not likely to forget that the Royal Navy was the first line of defense of the United States against France and that British men of war could not hold the seas unless they were adequately manned. "The little finger of *France*, in maritime depredations," said Secretary of State Pickering, "is thicker than the loins of *Britain*."[33]

Although there was some doubt how many American citizens were suffering involuntary servitude in His Britannic Majesty's Navy, there was no uncertainty how many American ships were seized by British men of war and privateers. A Boston newspaper regularly printed a column, listing British seizures and confiscations, entitled "Evidences of British Amity." Much as Jay's Treaty had done to regularize the

[31] Perkins, *First Rapprochement*, pp. 14–15, 99; *Naval Documents, November, 1798–March, 1799*, pp. 31, 33.

[32] Adams, *John Adams*, IX, 294; Robert Liston to Lord Grenville, January 29, 1799, Liston MSS., LC; James Wilkinson, *Memoirs of My Own Times* (Philadelphia, 1816), I, 464–465.

[33] Pickering and Upham, *Timothy Pickering*, III, 341; Adams, *John Adams*, VIII, 656; Ford, *John Quincy Adams*, II, 259 (footnote); Perkins, *First Rapprochement*, 68–69; Brown, *Northern Confederacy*, p. 23.

commercial relations between the two countries, it had not defined contraband, nor had it laid down rules governing American trade with the French West Indies. These omissions were deliberate: there was no possibility of achieving a meeting of minds between Englishmen and Americans upon these crucial matters.[34]

The British were not waging war with France for the benefit of American merchants and shipmasters, and they had no intention of permitting them to protract the war by carrying supplies to France under a neutral flag. If American claims were upheld, France would have been in a position to continue its normal trades simply by consigning its goods to neutral carriers. For this purpose, the French, early in the war, opened their West India islands to American vessels, hoping thereby to nullify British superiority at sea. The British government countered by invoking the Rule of 1756, according to which a trade closed to neutrals in time of peace could not be opened to them in time of war.

The Rule of 1756 was not recognized by the United States; but American ships were compelled to recognize its force by the British navy. Hundreds of American vessels attempting to carry French colonial produce to Europe were seized and condemned in British admiralty courts in Bermuda and the West Indies. However, the British did permit indirect trade between the French islands and Europe via the United States, provided that the cargo became American property. This leniency was grossly abused by Americans: often the ships merely touched at a United States port and the cargo was only nominally American-owned. In 1799, Sir William Scott, the leading maritime lawyer of England, attempted to resolve this difficulty by laying down the doctrine of continuous voyage: when the cargo was landed and duties paid in a United States port, it was presumed to be neutral property unless proved otherwise by the captor. This decision made possible a vast increase in American re-export trade and contributed

[34] Bradford Perkins contends that "the complete elimination of impressment as a source of controversy was an almost impossible task in wartime. To push the subject temporarily into the background might well be considered a success. This cost the freedom of a large number of American seamen. Yet it can easily be argued that the policy of the Adams administration was every bit as successful as the one of bluster and recrimination later adopted by Thomas Jefferson. Even war was not enough to make the British government promise to end impressment." Perkins, *First Rapprochement*, p. 69.

materially to cementing the good relations between the United States
and Great Britain.[35]

For the United States, the way to wealth obviously lay in co-operation with Great Britain. France, its navy bottled up in port or dis-
abled in action, could not give American shipping effective protection
against British naval power. Great Britain, on the other hand, not
only protected American shipping but by relaxing the laws of Trade
and Navigation opened up much of the Empire to American trade.
The price exacted from the United States for this boon was the surrender or suspension of American claims to neutral rights that would
have interfered with Great Britain's prosecution of the war against
France. In Jay's Treaty, the Washington administration had made
this sacrifice in order to preserve peace. In effect, Jay's Treaty laid
the foundations of American prosperity and of a decade of good relations between the two English-speaking countries. But, at best, it
was a precarious settlement, and a continuation of peaceful relations
depended upon the restraint shown by Great Britain in the assertion
of its rights as a belligerent and moderation on the part of the United
States in its claims to rights as a neutral.[36]

[35] Morison, *Maritime History*, pp. 178, 184; Perkins, *First Rapprochement*,
pp. 13, 80, 87–89; King, *Rufus King*, II, November 10, 1796; Bemis, *John
Quincy Adams and the Foundations of American Foreign Policy*, p. 135; Ames,
Fisher Ames, II, 169.

[36] King, *Rufus King*, II, May 30, 1797, August 18, 1798; III, January 28,
1801; *Parliamentary History*, XXX, 2; Fauchet, *A Sketch*, p. 28; Gibbs,
Memoirs, II, 283; Lodge, *George Cabot*, pp. 125–126; W. B. Smith and A. H.
Cole, *Fluctuations in American Business, 1790–1860* (Cambridge, Mass., 1935),
pp. 13–15; Bemis, *Jay's Treaty*, p. 40.

CHAPTER 13

The Federalist Reaction

EVEN though the war with France stubbornly refused to burst into open flame, the domestic caldron was seething ominously. For, in their efforts to suppress "Jacobinism" at home, the Federalists kindled a fire which gravely menaced freedom of speech and of the press.

The so-called American Reign of Terror, unlike that of France, was the work of conservatives bent upon upholding the established order. One of the principal benefits the Federalists expected to derive from all-out war with France was the proscription of the "internal enemies" of the government—in which category they placed most of the leaders of the Republican party. It was these "servile minions of France," they asserted, who had encouraged the Directory to believe that Americans were alienated from their own government, who fomented discord between the United States and Great Britain, and who strove "to immolate the independence and welfare of their country at the shrine of France."[1] Under the name of liberty, the Federalists complained, these "democrats, mobocrats & all other kinds of rats" opposed the war effort and heaped obloquy and contempt upon the highest officers of the government. "Even the Nursery is not exempt from the unremitting efforts of these disturbers of the human race," exclaimed an agitated Federalist. Through the medium of children's books, the Jacobins were making "a truly diabolical effort to corrupt the minds of the Rising Generation, to make them imbibe, with their

[1] *Gazette of the United States,* November 7, 1795; Lodge, *Hamilton,* VI, April 19, 1798; Fitzpatrick, *Washington,* XXXVII, 67.

228

very milk, as it were, the poison of atheism and disaffection."[2]

In the event of war with France, the Federalists did not doubt that the "gallic devotees" in the United States would support the enemy against their own country. The State Department was informed that in the West the French had "a party of mad Americans ready to join them at a given Signal." In May, 1798, it was reported that French agents, aided by Americans, were planning to set fire to Philadelphia and massacre the inhabitants.[3]

When havoc came to be wreaked upon innocent Americans, Federalists believed, foreign-born residents would be foremost in the work. The American people were told in Federalist newspapers that the United Irishmen—"so many serpents within your bosom"—commanded forty thousand men in the Republic, "a force sufficient to form an imperium in imperio." Even worse, in conservatives' opinion, by taking advantage of the leniency of the state naturalization laws, many aliens became citizens and voters. As such, they swelled the ranks of the Republican party and contested the Federalists' control of the eastern seaboard cities.[4]

So eager were the Federalists to take action against their political enemies that during June–July, 1798, without waiting for a formal declaration of war, they pushed through Congress four acts which imposed curbs upon freedom of speech and of the press and curtailed the liberty of foreigners in the United States. These acts were the Naturalization Act (June 18, 1798); the Act Concerning Aliens (June 27, 1798); the Act Respecting Alien Enemies (July 6, 1798); and the Act for the Punishment of Certain Crimes (July 14, 1798). None of these laws represented administration policy: although they approved of them, neither President Adams nor Alexander Hamilton inspired them. It was the Federalist leaders of Congress, especially Senator James Lloyd of Maryland and Representative Robert G. Harper of South Carolina, who initiated and drafted the legislation

[2] *Gazette of the United States,* June 4, 1800.

[3] Major Awandi to Pickering, November 29, 1797, Pickering MSS., MHS; Alexander Addison to Pickering, November 22, 1798; Alexander Campbell to Pickering, December 4, 1798, Pickering MSS., MHS; *Albany Centinel,* June 8, 1798; *Salem Gazette,* December 29, 1798; *Gazette of the United States,* June 20, November 22, 1798.

[4] James Kent, *Commentaries on American Law* (14th ed., Boston, 1896), I, 424–425; *Porcupine's Gazette,* February 12, 1799; *Gazette of the United States,* June 20, November 22, 23, 1798; *Albany Centinel,* January 24, 29, 1799; Fenno, *Desultory Reflections,* p. 17; Ames, *Fisher Ames,* II, 113.

known in American history as the Alien and Sedition Acts.[5]

The Alien Enemies Act gave power to the President to order imprisonment or deportation of suspected aliens, but because its operation was contingent upon a declaration of war it never went into effect. The Alien Act, which gave similar powers over aliens to the President in time of peace, likewise was never enforced. Even so, as a threat hanging over the heads of aliens in the United States, it was probably responsible for the decision of some French citizens resident in the United States to return to France, and it certainly prompted several foreign-born Republican journalists to take out citizenship papers.[6] It was the Naturalization Act which worked the greatest hardship upon aliens. The Federalists, whose aristocratic bias attracted few foreigners, demanded a long period of residence prior to naturalization or, better still, to admit only native-born to the rights of citizenship. Harrison Gray Otis declared that it was a mistake to permit immigrants to enter the country; he "considered the native American germ to be amply sufficient for the production of such scions as were worth cultivation." With such potent native-born citizens engaged in peopling the country there was no necessity, Otis exclaimed, "to invite hordes of wild Irishmen, nor the turbulent and disorderly of all parts of the world, to come here with a view to distract our tranquillity, after having succeeded in the overthrow of their own Governments."[7] Lest immigrants "contaminate the purity and simplicity of the American character," the Massachusetts General Court proposed in 1798 that the Federal Constitution be amended to disqualify all naturalized citizens from holding office. Five other states concurred. Compared with this draconic measure, the Naturalization Act passed by a Federalist-controlled Congress in 1798 was mild. It raised the term of probationary residence from five to fourteen years and required from aliens reports and certificates proving compliance with the law.[8]

[5] James Morton Smith, *Freedom's Fetters* (Ithaca, 1956), pp. 150–151; Adams, *John Adams*, IX, 291; Lodge, *George Cabot*, p. 169; King, *Rufus King*, III, January 20, 1799; Nevins, *American Press Opinion*, pp. 27–28; *Report of the American Historical Association, 1896*, I, 808; Dauer, *Adams Federalists*, pp. 199–200.

[6] *William and Mary Quarterly*, Third Series, XI (1954), 617–618.

[7] *Annals of Congress*, III, 1023; *General Advertiser*, May 11, 1798; *Albany Centinel*, April 12, 1799.

[8] Dauer, *Adams Federalists*, pp. 165–167; *The Proceedings of the House of Representatives* (Philadelphia, 1799), pp. 20–21; Frank George Franklin,

The Act for the Punishment of Certain Crimes, popularly known as the Sedition Act, passed the House of Representatives by a narrow sectional majority; the vote was forty-four to forty-one and only two members from south of the Potomac voted aye. In the bill originally introduced by Senator Lloyd the people and government of France were declared to be enemies of the United States and the death penalty was to be meted out to any citizen found guilty of adhering to them by giving them aid and comfort. This bill was shorn of some of its more repressive features by the House and Senate. While the act in its final form prescribed heavy fines and imprisonment for those judged guilty of writing, publishing, or speaking anything of "a false, scandalous and malicious" nature against the government or any offi-cer of the government, it actually ameliorated several of the oppressive rules established by the common law. Under the common law, truth was not a defense, malicious intent need not be proved, and it was given to the judge to decide whether the matter was libelous. The Sedition Act made truth a defense, made the jury judge of the fact of libel, and required proof of malicious intent.[9]

The Sedition Act was not as harsh as the British Treasonable Prac-tices Act passed in 1795 immediately after the King had been attacked on his way to Parliament. By that law, drastic restrictions were im-posed upon the press and the right of assemblage and even legitimate forms of party activity were proscribed. Instead, the Federalist law-makers sought to eliminate from the Sedition Act "those elements in English law to which objections had been persistently made on both sides of the Atlantic during the eighteenth century." For this reason, it was asserted that the Sedition Act was "remarkable for its lenity and humanity: No honest man need to dread such laws as these."[10]

In July, 1798, when the Sedition Act was adopted, few Federalists doubted that the country would soon be involved in a declared war with France. In that sense, it was a war measure designed to supple-

The Legislative History of Naturalization in the United States (Chicago, 1906), pp. 70–71; Zechariah Chafee, Free Speech in the United States (Boston, 1948), p. 240.

[9] William and Mary Quarterly, Third Series, XIII (1956), 573–576; Smith, Freedom's Fetters, p. 145; Dauer, Adams Federalists, pp. 152–164; Columbian Centinel, January 1, 1799; March 15, 1800; New Jersey Journal, March 12, 26, 1799.

[10] William and Mary Quarterly, Third Series (XIII), (1956), 573–576; Parliamentary History, XXXII, 261–262; Massachusetts Mercury, June 15, 1798.

ment the acts for strengthening the armed forces of the country. No Federalist leader questioned the constitutionality of the act; and, indeed, the authority of the Federal government to punish seditious speech and writing is firmly established at the present time. Every government is obliged to preserve itself against foreign and domestic enemies; in the Alien and Sedition Acts, as viewed by Federalists, the national government was doing no more than self-preservation required. Because of this overriding necessity, the Bill of Rights, by the Federalists' reckoning, could not debar the Federal government from imposing restraints upon freedom of speech and of the press. Harrison Gray Otis succinctly defined the attitude of his party when he declared in Congress that "to punish licentiousness and sedition is not a restraint or abridgment of the freedom of speech or of the press"; there was no absolute right, he observed, to publish whatever one pleased.[11] Certainly it was never intended, a Federalist newspaper pointed out, that freedom of speech should cover "the most groundless and malignant lies, striking at the safety and existence of the nation. . . . It never was intended that the right to side with the enemies of one's country in slandering and vilifying the government, and dividing the people should be protected under the name of the Liberty of the Press." When the country was beset by enemies, said Judge Addison of the Pennsylvania Supreme Court, Americans could not afford the luxury of discussing both sides of a question: "Truth," he remarked, "has but one side, and listening to error and falsehood is indeed a strange way to discover truth." In the opinion of this Federalist jurist, "all truths are not useful or proper for publication: therefore all truths are not to be written, printed or published."[12]

Even without the sanction of a wartime emergency, the Sedition Act was constitutional because, according to Federalist theory, the Federal Constitution endowed the national government with cognizance over all cases arising under the common law. Seditious and defamatory speaking or writing being a crime at common law, it followed that in the Sedition Act the Federal government was not overstepping its constitutional mandate. In every state of the Union the government and its officials were protected by statute or common law against the practices which the Sedition Act laid under duress. No

[11] *General Advertiser,* February 28, 1800; *Annals of Congress,* X, 413.
[12] *Columbian Centinel,* July 7, 1798; *Greenleaf's New Daily Advertiser,* February 21, 1799.

Federalist was willing to admit that in this regard the states possessed larger powers than did the Federal government.[13]

In their efforts to turn the Washington and Adams administrations out of office, Republican journalists had freely used lies, canards, and misrepresentations; nothing was too scurrilous to serve as grist for their propaganda mills. President Washington had been called "the scourge and the misfortune of our country" whose name gave "a currency to political iniquity and to legalized corruption." It was asserted that during the War of Independence he had been a secret traitor. President Adams appeared in Republican newspapers as "the blind, bald, toothless, querulous ADAMS," "the blasted tyrant of America," "a ruffian deserving of the curses of mankind," and "foremost in whatever is detestable."[14] One of the most virulent libelers of Federalist leaders was Benjamin Bache, publisher of the *General Advertiser*, or *Aurora*. Bache's newspaper was regarded as "the heart, the seat of life" of the French faction, and Bache himself was denounced in Congress as an agent of the French Directory.[15]

No doubt Republican journalists confounded opposition to administration policies with the vilification of the men at the head of the government. Even so, the Federalists could hardly claim to be innocent, unoffending victims of Republican calumny. For the Federalists gave as well as they received and they fought the Republicans with their own weapons. It was a question which party, in its efforts to gain partisan advantage, gave the lowest blows. Federalists made no distinction between "Jacobins" and Republicans: the entire party was condemned as traitorous conspirators who were prepared to use every device "that the craft of devils or the malice of the damned can invent, to paralyze our right arm, and to sap the very foundation of our existence." Noah Webster declared that "such a pack of scoundrels as our opposition & their creatures was never before collected

[13] *William and Mary Quarterly,* Third Series, XIII (1956), 573–576.

[14] *Gazette of the United States,* March 18, 1801; Pickering, *Review of the Adams-Cunningham Correspondence,* pp. 128–129; *Columbian Centinel,* July 7, 1798; James Callender, *The Prospect Before Us,* II, 81.

[15] In June, 1798, before the enactment of the Sedition Act, Bache was brought before Judge Richard Peters charged with having libeled President Adams and the Federalist administration "in a manner tending to create sedition and opposition to the law." This action was brought under the state law. Bache died from yellow fever before his trial could take place. *Massachusetts Mercury,* August 20, 1800; *Columbian Centinel,* July 7, 1798; Benjamin Bache, *Truth Will Out* (Philadelphia, 1798), pp. 1–3.

into one country. Indeed they are the refuse, the sweepings of the most depraved part of mankind from the most corrupt nations on earth."[16] Truly, on both sides, politics was an ordeal by slander.

Despite their zeal to uphold the dignity and prestige of Federal government and its chief officers against "Jacobins," the Federalists never attempted to cast the protective mantle of the Sedition Act over Vice-President Thomas Jefferson. Jefferson was a Republican and, in the eyes of the Federalists, the most rancorous fomenter of sedition in the country, the man who had been hand-picked by the Directory to serve as its proconsul when it succeeded in overthrowing the government of the United States. Had Jefferson's vilifiers been made amenable to the Sedition Act, most of the leaders of the Federalist party, including Alexander Hamilton, would have been haled before the courts. As Jefferson said, he was "a fair mark for every man's dirt." With good reason, he feared that even his high station would not save him from falling victim to the Sedition Act.[17]

Because of the Federalists' state of panic over "Jacobinism" and their eagerness to strike down their political enemies, they did not carefully study the question whether reasonable grounds existed for concluding that there was clear and present danger to the government and that immediate violence could be expected.[18] Instead, they acted precipitately and out of fear and vindictiveness. In actuality, the Republicans were a loyal opposition insofar as the Federal Constitution was concerned; their avowed purpose was to prevent the Federalists from creating an all-powerful "consolidated government." Nor was Jefferson guilty of "plotting some diabolical plan against the Federal Government." A French observer saw Jefferson in a very different light than did the Federalists: "His speeches," the Duc de la Rochefoucauld-Liancourt noted, "are those of a man firmly attached to the

[16] *Gazette of the United States,* July 3, 1798; Noah Webster to Pickering, July 7, 1797, Pickering MSS., MHS; *Russell's Gazette,* June 11, 1798; *Porcupine's Gazette,* July 9, 1798; *Remarks on the Jacobiniad* (Boston, 1798), II, vi–xi; *What Is Our Situation? By an American* [Joseph Hopkinson] (Philadelphia, 1798), pp. 8, 35.

[17] Ford, *Jefferson,* VII, February 21, 1798; Mott, *Jefferson and the Press,* pp. 38–40; Lodge, *Hamilton,* VI, April 21, 1798; Koch and Ammon, "The Virginia and Kentucky Resolutions," *William and Mary Quarterly,* Third Series (1948), pp. 174–175; Manning J. Dauer, "The Two John Nicholases," *American Historical Review,* XLV (1940), 352.

[18] Felix Frankfurter (ed.), *Mr. Justice Brandeis* (New Haven, 1932), pp. 109–110; *The Alarm* (New York, 1799), pp. 11–12.

maintenance of the Union, of the present constitution, and of the independence of the United States." True, there were British and French factions in the United States, but, as a French traveler remarked in 1797, "there is a middle party, much larger, composed of the most estimable men of the other two parties . . . which loves its country above all and for whom preferences either for France or England are only accessory and often passing affections."[19]

Acting upon the maxim that "Government should be a terror to evil doers," the Federalist administration brought fifteen indictments under the Sedition Act. Of these only ten resulted in conviction and punishment. The four leading Republican newspapers—the *General Advertiser,* the New York *Argus,* the Richmond *Examiner,* and the Boston *Independent Chronicle*—were attacked and three of the most prominent Republican editors—Thomas Cooper, James Callender, and William Duane—were convicted of violating the law. The moving spirit behind many of these prosecutions was Secretary of State Timothy Pickering, vigorously abetted by Justice Samuel Chase of the United States Supreme Court. Chase's grossly partisan conduct as a presiding judge served as the basis for the impeachment proceedings later brought against him by the Jeffersonian Republicans.[20] Truth did not prove to be an effective defense to Republican journalists accused of violating the Sedition Act because their charges were for the most part palpable falsehoods.

Among the most conspicuous victims of the Sedition Act was Matthew Lyon, the "Spitting Lyon" from Vermont. As a result of his encounter with Roger Griswold, Lyon had won the distinction of being the most hated "Jacobin" in the United States. During the summer of 1798, an English comedian on an American tour brought down the house with his inimitable portrayal of "the Beast of Vermont," or, "Ragged Mat, the Democrat." At this time, to be known as a demo-

---

[19] King, *Rufus King,* II, December 13, 1798; Rochefoucauld-Liancourt, *Travels,* II, 78–79; E. Wilson Lyon, "The Directory and the United States," *American Historical Review,* XLIII (1937–38), 520; Perkins, *First Rapprochement,* p. 28.

[20] F. M. Anderson, "Enforcement of the Alien and Sedition Laws," *Report of the American Historical Association for 1912,* pp. 115–126; Smith, *Freedom's Fetters,* pp. 324–327, 352–356; Thomas F. Carroll, "Freedom of Speech and of the Press in the Federalist Period," *Michigan Law Review,* XVIII (1920), 615–651.

crat was to invite investigation as a subversive.[21]

In July, 1798, at the instigation of his political enemies in Vermont, Lyon was indicted on the charge of having published in the Vermont *Journal* libelous statements against President John Adams (a rehash of the strictures he had passed upon Adams from the floor of Congress), together with a letter from Joel Barlow, a Connecticut Yankee who had gone to Paris and turned revolutionist. At his trial, held in Rutland, Vermont, in the summer of 1798, Lyon based his defense upon the unconstitutionality of the Sedition Act. But Justice Paterson of the United States Supreme Court refused to admit this line of argument and the jury found Lyon guilty as charged. In imposing sentence, Judge Paterson dwelt upon the peculiar clemency of the Sedition Act which debarred judges from inflicting as heavy punishment as was permitted by the common law. Having delivered this peroration, the judge sentenced Lyon to four months' imprisonment and imposed a fine of $1,000. The leniency of the law was matched by its celerity: without being given an opportunity to arrange his affairs, Lyon was hustled off to jail and thrown into a cell used for horse thieves, counterfeiters, runaway Negroes, and felons.[22]

The Federalists hailed Lyon's downfall as a memorable victory of government over "the licentiousness of the press" and the "unbridled spirit of opposition to government." In actuality, however, they had succeeded only in making Lyon a Republican martyr to the cause of freedom of the press. From his cell, Lyon wrote letters and articles which were widely reprinted in Republican newspapers and thereby drew national attention to the kind of rough justice meted out by Federalist-dominated courts. As a result, in December, 1798, he was re-elected to Congress even though he was still serving a prison term under a Federal offense. He took his seat in Congress, where, it was observed, he looked "remarkably well for a gentleman just out of jail." A few years later, he had his revenge upon his persecutors: in the election of 1801 he cast the decisive vote which made Thomas Jefferson President of the United States.[23]

[21] *Salem Gazette,* June 12, 1798; *Gazette of the United States,* July 23, 1798; Smith, *One Hundred Years of Hartford's Courant,* pp. 68, 73.

[22] *Greenleaf's New Daily Advertiser,* November 12, 13, 1798; February 11, 1799; McLaughlin, *Matthew Lyon,* pp. 334, 352.

[23] *Independent Chronicle,* July 5, 1798; *Albany Centinel,* March 26, May 17, 1799; *Porcupine's Gazette, February* 21, 1799.

The Alien and Sedition Acts were denounced as "the most diabolical laws that were ever attempted to be imposed on a free and enlightened people" and they gave substance to the Republicans' charge that the Federalists made war upon liberty.[24] Nevertheless, while opposing the exercise of power by the Federal government, the Republicans did not question the principle that government must punish libels—they merely demanded that such prosecutions be undertaken by the states rather than by the Federal government. Accordingly, when they came into power, the Republicans transferred these trials from Federal to state courts, where the common law was enforced in all its rigor.[25]

The Alien and Sedition Acts marked an important stage in the development of political parties. Hitherto, even in the final phase of the struggle over Jay's Treaty, the Republican leaders had been unable to hold their followers firmly in line; when party caucuses had been summoned, the meetings had sometimes broken up in disagreement. But the Alien and Sedition Acts were opposed to the end by the entire Republican party; upon this issue there was no weakening of the party line or defections to the Federalists.[26]

In no part of the country was the quasi-war with France and the domestic policies to which it gave rise more unpopular than in Virginia. Virginians did not doubt that the army had been enlarged primarily to suppress discontent at home; and talk about a French invasion they dismissed as a Federalist bogey designed to screen their machinations against American liberty. So little did he fear a French invasion and so deeply did he apprehend that Hamilton would use the army to establish a monarchy that Jefferson expressed the hope that the administration would be unable to raise anything but officers. No wonder, therefore, that by the end of 1798 some Virginians were speaking of the Federal government "as an enemy infinitely more formidable and infinitely more to be guarded against than the French Directory."[27]

[24] *New Jersey Journal*, December 18, 1799.

[25] *William and Mary Quarterly*, Third Series (1948), pp. 151–152, 175; *The Bee*, March 20, 1799; *Salem Gazette*, October 23, 1798, March 20, 1799; *Gazette of the United States*, November 2, 1798.

[26] *New Jersey Journal*, December 18, 1798; Smith, *Freedom's Fetters*, pp. 145–146; Dauer, *Adams Federalists*, pp. 170–171.

[27] *A Letter to a Member of Congress* (Virginia, 1799), p. 31; Richmond

238   THE FEDERALIST ERA

Among these Virginians were Thomas Jefferson and James Madison. As early as 1797, Jefferson referred to the Federal government as a "foreign jurisdiction." As Vice-President of the United States, he urged the Virginia legislature to enact a law making liable to punishment citizens of Virginia who attempted to carry cases to the Federal courts when those courts did not have clear and uncontested jurisdiction. In Jefferson's opinion, the Alien and Sedition Acts made it imperative that the powers assumed by the Federal government must be curbed if American liberty were to survive. Jefferson and other Republican leaders feared the theory of Federal power upon which these acts were based quite as much as they did the operation of the acts themselves. For, if it were conceded that the Federal courts were authorized by the Constitution to take cognizance of all cases arising under the common law, the Republicans had no doubt that the "beautiful equilibrium" established by the Constitution between the states and the Federal government would be destroyed and that the Federal government would usurp "all the powers of the state governments and reduce the country to a single consolidated government." The common law, said Jefferson, could become law in the United States only by positive adoption and only insofar as American legislatures were authorized to adopt it.[28]

As was his habit in time of crisis, Jefferson called in Madison for consultation. As a nationalist, Madison had gone far beyond Jefferson, but he was now prepared to atone handsomely for his errors. In 1798, he characterized inherent or implied powers as "the creatures of ambition. . . . Powers extracted from such sources will be indefinitely multiplied by the aid of armies and patronage which, with the impossibility of controlling them by any demarcation, would presently terminate reasoning, and ultimately swallow up the State sovereignties."

Examiner, December 24, 1798; Albert J. Beveridge, *The Life of John Marshall* (Boston, 1916), II, 395; Ford, *Jefferson*, VII, April 22, 1799; Henry H. Simms, *The Life of John Taylor* (Richmond, 1932), pp. 76–77, 80.

[28] In 1812, the Jeffersonian majority of the Supreme Court ruled against the Federalists' claims—expounded by Chief Justice John Marshall—that the national courts enjoyed common law jurisdiction. Crosskey, *Politics and the Constitution*, I, 1346, 1357; Corwin, *Judicial Review*, pp. 55–56; *Columbia Law Review*, LIV (1938), 459, 463, 466, 468; Ford, *Jefferson*, VII, November 26, 1798; August 18, 1799; *An Enquiry Whether the Act of Congress . . . Generally Called the Sedition Bill Is Unconstitutional or Not* (Richmond, 1798), pp. 12–13; Bauer, *Commentaries on the Constitution*, p. 177; Pound, *Spirit of the Common Law*, p. 27.

Since 1790, Madison had been inclining towards the doctrine of "Dual Federalism," according to which collisions between the states and the Federal government were to be avoided by recognizing that the purposes which the general government was intended to promote were relatively few, whereas the states were entrusted with the furtherance of the principal objects of government: the public safety, morals, and the general welfare. In short, national powers should be construed in deference to the prior claims of the states.[29]

The fruit of Madison's and Jefferson's collaboration was the Virginia and Kentucky Resolutions. Jefferson was the author of the Kentucky Resolutions and Madison drew up the statement adopted by the Virginia legislature, but neither man allowed his hand to appear in the proceedings. The Kentucky Resolutions were introduced by George Nicholas, while John Taylor of Caroline proposed the Virginia resolutions.[30]

These acts of the Virginia and Kentucky legislatures marked an important stage in the progress of the theory that ultimately led to the nullification by a state of a Federal law. According to Jefferson's and Madison's reading of the Constitution, it created nothing more than a compact between sovereign states which confided certain narrowly defined powers to the general government while reserving all residual powers to the states. Being the creators of the Constitution, the states were alone capable of judging when infractions of this instrument of government occurred, and they alone were able to devise measures of redress. In effect, the states were called upon to mediate between the people and the Federal government, but it was assumed that usurpation would always come from the Federal government rather than from the states. Carried to its logical conclusion, the doctrine propounded by the Virginia and Kentucky Resolutions meant that the compact between the states was a moral rather than a legal obligation and that the preservation of the Union was left to the discretion of the parties concerned.[31]

[29] Koch and Ammon, "Virginia and Kentucky Resolutions," pp. 152, 156–157.

[30] Ibid.; Sarah Nicholas Randolph, "The Kentucky Resolutions in a New Light," The Nation, XLIV (1887), 384.

[31] Hunt, Madison, VI, 333–334, 349, 352, 355, 386–389; Edward S. Corwin, Judicial Review (Princeton, 1914), pp. 155–156; McLaughlin, Constitutional History, pp. 276–277; Selected Cases on Constitutional Law, II, 571–572; William and Mary Quarterly, Third Series (1948), p. 151; The Federalist, p.

Upon the all-important question how redress was to be procured, Jefferson and Madison were not of one mind. In his determination to resist the exercise of "unconstitutional" powers by the Federal government, Jefferson was more uncompromising and militant than was Madison.[32] Jefferson advocated nullification—whether by a single state or group of states he did not make clear—but Madison preferred to keep the question upon the safer ground of abstract right. Had Jefferson's ideas been fully embraced by the Kentucky legislature, that state would have come dangerously near to placing itself in open rebellion to the Federal government; for, among other things, he made clear that he intended to extend "unconstitutionality" to include the excise and the Bank of the United States. John Nicholas toned Jefferson's draft down before presenting it to the Kentucky legislature. Even so, the Kentucky Resolutions were more radical than were the Virginia Resolutions.[33]

The impact of the Virginia Resolutions was weakened by the fact that a considerable minority in the Virginia legislature opposed the resolutions and commissioned John Marshall to draft a protest. Alone among the Federalist leaders, Marshall disapproved of the Alien and Sedition Acts, but not, like the Republicans, upon the ground of unconstitutionality. Rather, he deemed them useless and "calculated to create unnecessary discontents and jealousies when our very existence as a nation may depend on our union." Former President George Washington likewise disapproved of the Virginia Resolutions, and it was in part owing to his appeals that Patrick Henry came out of retirement in 1799 as an avowed Federalist.[34]

174; Edward Channing, "The Virginia and Kentucky Resolutions," *American Historical Review*, XX (1915), 333–336.

[32] Madison did not wholly accept the theory that a state could declare Federal laws "null, void and of no effect" or that the state was the ultimate judge of both the violation and the mode of redress. Instead, he favored a convention of the states—and this only in the last resort. Jefferson warned against "pushing the matter to extremities." His policy, he declared, was to proclaim the principles and at the same time to remain "free to push as far as events will render prudent." Ford, *Jefferson*, VII, November 17, 1798.

[33] Koch and Ammon, "Virginia and Kentucky Resolutions," pp. 152, 156, 170–173.

[34] *Ibid.*, pp. 163–164; *Pennsylvania Magazine of History and Biography*, XXXIV (1910), 395; *Report of the American Historical Association for 1912*, p. 530; King, *Rufus King*, III, December 29, 1799, January 20, May 11, 1800; Lodge, *George Cabot*, pp. 175, 179 (footnote), 185; Charles Warren, *Jacobin and Junto* (Cambridge, Mass., 1931), pp. 117–118; Fitzpatrick, *Washington*, XXXVII, 72, 89; Carroll and Ashworth, *Washington*, VII, 541–543.

The Virginia and Kentucky legislatures urged the other states to join them in securing the repeal of the Alien and Sedition Acts, but this appeal for united action fell upon barren soil. The Massachusetts General Court pronounced the acts to be "not only constitutional, but expedient and necessary," and the Maryland legislature declared them to be "wise and politic." In their replies to the Virginia and Kentucky Resolutions, seven northern states pointed out that it was the province of the United States Supreme Court to decide ultimately upon the constitutionality of acts of Congress. This was cold comfort to the Republicans: ardent Federalists to a man, the Justices of the Supreme Court left little doubt that they would uphold the constitutionality of the Alien and Sedition laws if the question were brought before them.[35]

"Mad and rebellious" as the Virginia and Kentucky Resolutions appeared to the Federalists, they were succeeded by an even more alarming development. Early in 1799, reports began to be received from Virginia of military preparations—the arming of the militia and the construction of an armory at Richmond—presumably with a view to resisting attempts at coercion by the Federal government. Most Virginians denied that these measures were directed against the Federal government: the enemy, they declared, was the French and Indians. But William Branch Giles and John Randolph later asserted that the purpose of Virginia's warlike preparations was to resist Federal troops. And, even though the Richmond armory was projected before the passage of the Alien and Sedition laws, it is undeniable that there was much talk of disunion in Virginia and that few Virginians seriously believed that the French would attempt an invasion of the United States, particularly after the destruction in 1799 of the French fleet at the Battle of the Nile.[36]

[35] Albany *Centinel*, February 19, 27, March 14, 1799; Philadelphia *Gazette*, January 25, May 6, 1799; *Virginia Magazine of History and Biography*, XXIX (1921), 263–264; Ford, *Jefferson*, VII, March 12, 1799; Lodge, *George Cabot*, p. 218; King, *Rufus King*, II, January 14, 1799; *Report of the American Historical Association for 1912*, pp. 535–536.

[36] Philip G. Davidson, "Virginia and the Alien and Sedition Acts," *American Historical Review*, XXXVI (1931), 336, takes the view that no resistance to the Federal government was contemplated by the Virginia leaders. J. C. Hamilton, *Hamilton*, V, 460–461; Lodge, *Hamilton*, X, February 2, 1799; *Annals of Congress*, IX, 3025; XXX, 795, 802, 805; Crosskey, *Politics and the Constitution*, II, 1345; John Marshall to Pickering, October 22, 1798,

Had the Federal government, on the strength of these reports of disaffection and warlike menaces, ordered the use of troops against the Old Dominion, there is every likelihood that the Virginians would have met force with force. And yet this was the very policy advocated by Alexander Hamilton. Having long smarted under the opposition of Virginia to his policies, Hamilton was eager to see the state divided into more manageable jurisdictions. With that object in view, he urged that the United States army be moved in the direction of Virginia. "This plan," he remarked, "will give time for the fervor of the moment to subside, for reason to resume the reins, and, by dividing its enemies, will enable the government to triumph with ease."[37]

With the Union in danger, Jefferson's essential conservatism came to the fore. While he did not renounce the principles he had enunciated in the Kentucky Resolutions, he counseled his more radical followers against violence. "This," he said, "is not the kind of opposition the American people will permit. But keep away all show of force, and they will bear down the evil propensities of the government, by the constitutional means of election & petition."[38] When John Taylor broached the idea of disunion, Jefferson assured him that "the reign of witches" would soon be over: the mass of the people were suffering only a temporary distemper and the doctor—in the form of a tax collector—was already on his way. And indeed, the legislation that had inspired the Virginia and Kentucky Resolutions was removed from the statute book without the necessity of calling upon the states to interpose their authority. The Alien Act expired quietly, unhonored and unsung, on June 25, 1800. The Sedition Act came within four votes of being repealed in January, 1800. In January, 1801, the Federalists attempted to re-enact the Sedition Law, and in the House of Representatives it received more votes than had the original act of July 14, 1798. But the move failed, and on March 3, 1801, the Sedition Act too expired. The Naturalization Act was repealed after Jefferson and the Republican party came into power.[39]

In June, 1798, at the height of the excitement engendered by the

Marshall MSS., LC; Anderson, *Giles*, pp. 69–70; Ford, *Jefferson*, VII, February 13, 1799; King, *Rufus King*, II, March 20, 1799.

[37] Lodge, *Hamilton*, X, February 2, 1799; Uriah Tracy to Trumbull, January 2, 1795, Trumbull MSS., CHS.

[38] Ford, *Jefferson*, VII, February 13, 1799.

[39] *Collections of the Massachusetts Historical Society*, Seventh Series, I, 82; *Annals of Congress*, X, 919, 969, 975–976.

X, Y, Z papers, President Adams had informed Congress that he would never send another minister to France "without assurances that he will be received, respected and honored, as the representative of a great, free, powerful and independent nation." By early 1799, Adams was convinced that France was prepared to meet these conditions. There was ample evidence to support such an opinion. The Directory ordered the release of embargoed American ships, the West Indian privateers were put under restraints, the admiralty courts were directed to halt the wholesale condemnation of American ships and cargoes, and the demand for a disavowal of the President's uncomplimentary allusions to France in his address to Congress was dropped. In his anxiety to patch up the quarrel, Talleyrand went to the length of repudiating his own agents and denouncing his own brain child as an "odious intrigue." Moreover, in the autumn of 1798, Elbridge Gerry returned from France bringing peace overtures from the Directory. Through Pichon, the Secretary to the French legation at The Hague, Talleyrand sent assurances of France's pacific disposition to William Vans Murray, the American minister to the Netherlands. And finally, in 1798, Dr. George Logan, a Philadelphia Quaker, journeyed to Paris on an unofficial and unaccredited (except for a letter of introduction from Thomas Jefferson) peace mission. Early in 1799, Logan returned to the United States with the good news that the Directory was eager to call off hostilities. To the Republicans, Logan's report was another straw indicating that peace was in the wind, but in the opinion of the Federalist members of Congress it merely demonstrated the necessity of preventing private citizens from interfering in the foreign affairs of the government. The Logan Act, passed in 1799 and still on the statute books, inflicts fine and imprisonment upon any citizen found guilty of holding correspondence with foreign governments or their agents, in relation to the United States.[40]

The fact remained, however, that the Directory was sincere in its professions of peace; indeed, nothing could have been more injurious than war to its plans of regaining possession of Louisiana and using American shipping to break the stranglehold of British naval suprem-

[40] DeConde, *Entangling Alliance*, p. 342; *Proceedings of the Massachusetts Historical Society*, XLIX (1916), 65–66; *New England Quarterly*, II, 1929, 23–28; Charles Burr Todd, *Life and Letters of Joel Barlow* (New York, 1886), pp. 158–159, 161; *Correspondence Between John Adams and William Cunningham* (Boston, 1823), pp. 45, 164; Bemis, *John Quincy Adams and the Foundations of American Foreign Policy*, pp. 98–101; Dauer, *Adams Federalists*, p. 228.

acy. John Quincy Adams correctly divined French policy when he observed that the Directors wished to maintain "a mongrel condition between peace and war, in which they plunder us as enemies and we continue defenceless as friends." But the United States did not remain either defenseless or friendly and the Directory was made to realize that it would be obliged to pay an inordinate price for the plunder it derived from American commerce. Elsewhere, revolutionary France had succeeded in making war lucrative, but the struggle with the United States proved costly beyond all calculation.[41]

Under these circumstances, Adams saw no reason to continue the war: "The end of war is peace," he said, "—and peace was offered me." Accordingly, on February 18, 1799, he sent to the Senate the nomination of William Vans Murray as minister plenipotentiary to the French Republic.

When John Adams assumed the Presidency he took over Washington's cabinet intact. This action—one of the most costly errors of Adams's political career—was owing to the President's reluctance to disturb the arrangements of his predecessors, to his satisfaction with the incumbent heads of the departments—two of them, Pickering and Wolcott, were New Englanders—and to his conviction that because of the low pay and heavy duties prevailing in the higher offices of the government, it was improbable that equally competent men could be induced to serve it. What Adams did not know, and what he was uncommonly slow to discover, was that most of the members of his administration looked to Alexander Hamilton rather than to the President for leadership.[42]

But by February, 1799, it had finally dawned upon the President that he did not have the allegiance of his cabinet.[43] Accordingly, Adams acted without prior consultations with his advisers—an omission he justified on the ground that the heads of the departments were so completely subservient to Alexander Hamilton that they were

[41] Adams, *John Adams,* IX, 19–20, 242, 270–271; X, 113, 122; *Correspondence Between John Adams and William Cunningham,* pp. 94–95, 101; Ford, *John Quincy Adams,* II, August 31, 1798; *Report of the American Historical Association for 1912,* p. 445; Gibbs, *Memoirs,* II, 321; Todd, *Joel Barlow,* pp. 157–158, 161; Dauer, *Adams Federalists,* 121–124; Samuel Eliot Morison, "DuPont, Talleyrand, and the French Spoliations," *Massachusetts Historical Society Proceedings,* XLIX (1916), 63–78.

[42] Adams, *John Adams,* VIII, 523; Bemis, *John Quincy Adams and the Foundations of American Foreign Policy,* pp. 100–103.

[43] A. Biddle (ed.), *Old Family Letters,* pp. 172–173; Perkins, *First Rapprochement,* p. 26

certain to conform to the wishes of the onetime Secretary of the Treasury.[44] Before he could emancipate himself from Hamilton, Adams believed that he must throw off the trammels imposed by his cabinet. But the Federalist senators were not inclined to applaud Adams's break for freedom: "Surprise, indignation, grief & disgust followed each other in quick succession," said George Cabot, "in the breasts of the true friends of our Country." A delegation of senators informed the President that they would never consent to Murray's appointment; whereupon the President threatened to resign and to leave the government in the hands of Vice-President Jefferson. Sobered by this prospect, the senators agreed to open negotiations with France provided that a commission of three Federalists was appointed. The President, on his part, promised that the envoys would not be sent until unqualified assurances had been received from France that they would be properly received.[45]

Despite this compromise, the proposed mission to France created a deep rift within the Federalist party. The Hamiltonian wing of the party—which comprised most of the leaders—continued to fight tooth and nail against opening negotiations with France; they would consent to talk peace only if France sent an envoy to the United States. John Adams was given to understand that he had committed the "unpardonable sin" against party orthodoxy; but Adams insisted that he was faithfully following Washington's policy of "a system of eternal neutrality, if possible, in all the wars of Europe." As a man of peace, Adams was almost as popular among the rank and file of the Federalist party as he had been as a man of war in the piping days of 1798. His warmest admirers were found among the southern Federalists led by John Marshall. Even more remarkable, in view of Hamilton's pervasive influence in the higher councils of the government, two members of the cabinet, Attorney General Charles Lee and Secretary of the Navy Benjamin Stoddert, favored sending a mission to France.[46]

[44] Oliver Wolcott, the Secretary of the Treasury, was informed, but his protests were not heeded by the President. Lodge, *George Cabot*, 293; Adams, *John Adams*, IX, 270–271.

[45] Kurtz, *Presidency of John Adams*, p. 342; *Report of the American Historical Association for 1896*, I, 820; Adams, *John Adams*, VIII, 629; IX, 24–25, 247; Adams, *Gallatin*, p. 221; Morison, *Otis*, I, February 18, 1799; Lodge, *George Cabot*, 236–237, 240–241; Pickering and Upham, *Timothy Pickering*, III, 440–443.

[46] King, *Rufus King*, III, June 2, November 9, December 12, 1799; *Report of the American Historical Association for 1896*, I, 819–820, 822, 823.

In November, 1799, the three United States ministers plenipotentiary—Chief Justice Ellsworth, William Vans Murray, and W. R. Davie (Patrick Henry's replacement)—departed for France with the earnest wishes of most of the leaders of the Federalist party that their mission would end in failure and disgrace. And indeed, had the envoys strictly adhered to their instructions, by which they were required to secure an indemnity for spoliations and the invalidation of the Franco-American treaty of alliance, they would certainly have returned home empty-handed. For the United States had delayed too long in opening negotiations with France: Napoleon was now First Consul and France was victorious in all theaters of the war. Late in 1800, aware of the hopelessness of making demands upon France, the American envoys disregarded their instructions and made the best terms they could, leaving the matter of spoliations and the alliance to future negotiations. This arrangement was not acceptable to the Senate, but after modifications had been agreed to by Napoleon, the United States and France signed in 1801 a Convention by which the quasi-war was brought to a close. In effect, the United States bought its release from the alliance with France by abandoning its claims of indemnity for depredations committed by French privateers and ships of war. Unsatisfactory as were these terms to many Federalists, the Convention of 1801 terminated an unpopular war and smoothed the way for the purchase of Louisiana by the United States three years later. With considerable justice, therefore, John Adams claimed that his action in sending a mission to France was "the most disinterested, the most determined and the most successful of my whole life."[47]

Jefferson's confidence that the tax collectors would drive out the

[47] *Correspondence Between John Adams and William Cunningham,* p. 101; J. C. Hamilton, *Hamilton,* VI, 448, 491–492, 511, 519; Pickering and Upham, *Timothy Pickering,* III, 475–476; Ford, *John Quincy Adams,* II, November 25, 1800; March 21, 1801; Louis Madelin, *The Consulate and the Empire* (London, 1934–36), I, 64; Morison, *Otis,* I, 103; Ford, *Jefferson,* VII, November 26, 1798; Bemis, *John Quincy Adams and the Foundations of American Foreign Policy,* pp. 104–106; Charles J. Bullock, "The Growth of Federal Expenditures," *Political Science Quarterly,* XVIII (1903), 48–49; *Collections of the Massachusetts Historical Society,* Seventh Series (Boston, 1900), I, 62; Ward and Gooch, *Cambridge History of British Foreign Policy,* I, 285–286, 294–296; Brooks Adams, "The Convention of 1800 with France," *Proceedings of the Massachusetts Historical Society,* XLIV (1911), 377–428; E. Wilson Lyon, "The Franco-American Convention of 1800," *Journal of Modern History,* XII (1940), 305–333.

"witches" who controlled the government was borne out by events. Even more than the Alien and Sedition Acts, the direct tax imposed by the Federal government in 1798 upon houses, land, and slaves served to discredit the Federalist party with the electorate.[48] The Alien and Sedition Acts, after all, were ostensibly directed against "intriguing and discontented foreigners," "Jacobins and vagabonds," "spies and incendiaries," but the tax affected every landowner, householder, and slaveowner in the country.

Pennsylvania, rapidly acquiring the distinction of being the most rebellious of the states, became the scene of armed resistance to the direct tax. In this instance, however, the seat of disaffection was in the eastern counties—Montgomery, Bucks, and Northampton; and the participants were largely Pennsylvania Dutch who had been led to believe that President Adams, among other enormities, planned to marry his daughter to the son of King George of England and to establish an American dynasty. When a United States marshal arrested two tax dodgers, John Fries, an auctioneer who had hitherto voted the Federalist ticket, led a party of armed men to Bethlehem and released the culprits from prison.[49]

Without waiting to ascertain the nature or extent of this "insurrection," President Adams ordered regular troops and militia into Northampton County. Major General Hamilton applauded the President's use of force: "Whenever the government appears in arms," he remarked, "it ought to appear like a *Hercules.*" But in Pennsylvania there was nothing for Hercules to do but to flex his muscles: there was no enemy in sight and the worst that the Army encountered was black looks from the country people. The cavalry scoured the country for three weeks and the only casualty was a bull. John Fries, the cause of all this uproar, was arrested while he was engaged in knocking down an article to the highest bidder.[50]

Fries and two others involved in the riot at Bethlehem were tried for treason. The government contended that taking a prisoner from

[48] This tax on dwelling houses, lands, and slaves (each slave was taxed fifty cents) was expected to raise two million dollars. In conformity with the provisions laid down by the Constitution, the total sum was apportioned among the states. But evasions were common: at the end of three years, one-fifth of the tax remained to be collected. Dewey, *Financial History*, p. 109.

[49] DeConde, *Entangling Alliance*, p. 352; Adams, *John Adams*, VIII, 644; Dewey, *Financial History*, pp. 109–110; Steiner, *McHenry*, pp. 432–435.

[50] Steiner, *McHenry*, pp. 432–435; Rich, *Presidents and Civil Disorder*, pp. 24–26, 30; Dauer, *Adams Federalists*, pp. 207–209.

the custody of a peace officer by armed force constituted treason; the defense relied upon the English common law which held that such action was no more than a high misdemeanor. Judges Iredell and Peters upheld the government's definition and charged the jury to the effect that to resist a law by force with intent to defeat its execution amounts to levying war—or, in other words, to treason. The judges' decision deprived Fries's counsel of their only possible line of defense; they therefore refused to proceed. Fries's trial continued without the aid of legal advice. He and his two companions were found guilty of treason and sentenced to be hanged.

This verdict was appealed and Fries was granted a new trial. In April, 1800, he came before Justice Samuel Chase, a rabid Federalist and a "hanging judge" if such ever sat on the bench of the Supreme Court of the United States. Chase's charge to the jury did not differ from that of Peters and Iredell; Fries was again found guilty and sentenced to be hanged.

With two convictions against him, Fries's case seemed hopeless. Nevertheless, an appeal was carried to President Adams. Adams consulted the cabinet, the members of which agreed that Fries ought to suffer the extreme penalty; the only difference of opinion was whether his two companions, also convicted of treason, ought to die with him. Ignoring the advice of the heads of departments and without consulting the Federal judges, Adams decided that Fries was not guilty of treason. He thereupon pardoned Fries and his two companions and issued a general pardon to all concerned in the uprising.

The President's humanitarianism struck consternation among the Hamiltonian Federalists, who had promised themselves that the "exemplary rigor" meted out by the Federal judges would go far toward ensuring Pennsylvania's future obedience to the laws: "The *principle of insurrection must be eradicated,*" they exclaimed, "or anarchy must ensue." Hamilton pronounced the President's action to be the greatest error of his career; and Secretary of State Pickering declared that he experienced "astonishment, indignation & horror" when he saw the President's proclamation. Another outraged Federalist protested that "undue mercy to villains, is cruelty to all the good and virtuous." But what the Chief Executive lost in the estimation of the Federalist leaders he gained in the esteem of the rank and file of the party: it proved impossible to convince the people of the United States that President Adams had done wrong by pardoning men whose guilt depended upon a strained interpretation of treason unsanctioned by the common law.[51]

The spectacle of the United States Army resting on its arms—except when it was chasing terrified farmers across eastern Pennsylvania —confirmed Republicans' suspicions that the army had been strengthened in 1798 not to fight Frenchmen but to suppress opposition to Federalist policies, particularly the Alien and Sedition Acts, and to perform other *"domestic* employment."[52] In truth, however, the Army had been augmented in 1798 for the purpose of defending the country against France or, had Hamilton's plans materialized, of invading Louisiana and the Floridas. But when the French failed to invade the United States and Hamilton's dream of foreign adventures went glimmering, the most compelling reason for maintaining a large military establishment was to back up Federal tax collectors, district attorneys, and judges in the enforcement of unpopular laws.[53]

As a result, the Army was exposed to jealousy of the military power on the part of civilians, to the wrath of taxpayers, and to the resentment of the champions of civil rights. In the Republican newspapers, the Army was portrayed as "a ferocious wild beast let loose upon the nation to devour it." "Our citizens can no longer walk the streets in safety," it was reported, "but are exposed to the insolence and impudence of every wretch who has sufficient interest to procure a commission." A newspaper called *Cannibals' Progress* was established by some Philadelphia Republicans to record the atrocities committed by Federal troops.[54] Speaking from the floor of the House of Representatives, John Randolph called the troops "a handful of ragamuffins" and he declared that he disdained the protection of such "hirelings" and "mercenaries." On the evening following this speech, Randolph was accosted at the theater by two marine officers who jostled him

[51] *Porcupine's Gazette,* March 30, April 8, 1799; Steiner, *McHenry,* p. 436; Adams, *John Adams,* VIII, 644; Lodge, *Hamilton,* VIII, 352–355.

[52] Henry Adams contended that the Army was raised for the express purpose of crushing democracy at home. This view has been effectively challenged by Samuel Eliot Morison. Adams, *Gallatin,* pp. 170, 199, 211; Morison, *Otis,* I, 102.

[53] J. C. Hamilton, *Hamilton,* VI, 393–394; Lodge, *Hamilton,* VIII, 219; Adams, *John Adams,* IX, 290–292; X, 127; Callender, *Prospect Before Us,* II, 84.

[54] Kurtz, *Presidency of John Adams,* p. 364; *General Advertiser,* July 10, 1799; July 11, 1800.

and pulled his coattails. Whereupon Randolph screamed—even his ordinary tone was a high falsetto—that the majesty of the people had been impugned. But the House, exhibiting more charity toward the Army than it usually manifested, declared that no breach of privilege had occurred.[55]

Nevertheless, even the Federalists saw that the days of the "Additional Army" were numbered; and it was only too clear that the party responsible for keeping up this unemployed military force would become as unpopular as the Army itself. And so, rather than permit the Republicans to gain the honor of taking the Army and Navy off the taxpayers' backs, the Federalists themselves introduced bills in 1800 that reduced the Army to its pre-quasi-war basis and laid up most of the fighting ships (which now included thirteen frigates) of the United States Navy. Even in the midst of the quasi-war with France, Americans succeeded in getting the boys out of uniform.[56]

[55] *Annals of Congress,* X, 298–300, 304–306, 325–326, 367–368; Adams, *John Adams,* X, 118; Carlos E. Godfrey, "The Organization of the Provisional Army," *Pennsylvania Magazine of History and Biography,* XXXVIII (1914), 132; Morison, *Otis,* I, 178; Lodge, *George Cabot,* 265; William Cabell Bruce, *John Randolph of Roanoke* (New York, 1922), I, 163–165.

[56] The Act of March 3, 1801, authorized the President to sell all the vessels of the Navy except the thirteen frigates. Seven of these frigates, however, were to be laid up and most of the officers of the Navy to be dismissed. President Jefferson carried out this directive. Gibbs, *Memoirs,* II, 320–321; Philadelphia *Gazette,* May 20, 1800.

CHAPTER 14

The Election of 1800

THE ISSUES that divided Americans—foreign policy, "moneyed wealth" versus agrarianism, centralized government as opposed to states' rights—were expected to be resolved in the presidential and congressional elections of 1800. The two parties had long been pointing toward this event: the Virginia and Kentucky Resolutions were the opening gun of the campaign; and the Federalists' willingness to reduce the Army to peacetime size, even before the war with France had been concluded, revealed that they, too, were looking forward to the day when they would be judged by the electorate.

While Republicans and Federalists girded themselves for the contest for possession of the government, the government itself was engaged in moving to a clearing in the wilderness along the Potomac. It was now incumbent upon Northerners to pay the price for the assumption of state debts from which they had handsomely profited in 1790. But in 1800, as Philadelphians watched the government's preparations for departure, many repented of the bargain Hamilton had struck with Jefferson. If this were true of those who remained behind, how much more true it was of the unfortunates who were obliged to exchange the amenities of Philadelphia for the mud, mosquitoes, and over-crowded boardinghouses of the new Federal City.[1]

They might have been spared this ordeal had not President Washington, Jefferson, and Madison made the removal to the Potomac

---

[1] Congress decided to continue the United States Mint temporarily at Philadelphia, from whence it never moved. Nor did the Bank of the United States make the journey to the Potomac.

one of the first orders of business. As early as October, 1790, Washington personally chose the site of the future "Grand Columbian Federal City" and in 1791 he appointed commissioners to survey the Federal District, purchase land, and arrange for the construction of buildings for the accommodation of Congress, the President, and the executive departments.[2]

From the beginning, the commissioners were beset by difficulties. Unwilling to hasten its own exile to the Potomac, Congress refused to make a direct appropriation for defraying the cost of purchasing land and constructing buildings; instead, it merely authorized the President to accept grants of money for these purposes. As a result, the initial cost was borne chiefly by the states of Virginia and Maryland, Virginia contributing $120,000 and Maryland donating $72,000. In 1795, when these funds were exhausted, the commissioners applied to Congress for permission to float a loan. So powerful was the opposition in Congress to doing anything toward helping the struggling Federal City that the petition was left unattended upon the table of the House for many weeks. Finally the commissioners were authorized to borrow money—whereupon Maryland loaned the city $100,000 in United States government bonds.[3]

Timely as was this aid, the main resource of the commissioners continued to be the sale of lots to speculators. Among the largest purchasers of land was Robert Morris, the most daring real estate plunger in the United States, and his partner John Nicholson. In 1796, Morris and Nicholson began the erection of twenty two-story houses covering the entire front of a square—"the greatest effort of private enterprise of any in the city and for the time in which they were building the greatest in the United States."[4] But in June, 1797, the speculative empire built by Morris and Nicholson collapsed. Nicholson died in prison in December, 1800, while Morris, after over three years in the Philadelphia debtors' prison, regained his liberty in 1801. For many years the buildings remained unfinished, and this eyesore was not removed until they had fallen into ruin.[5]

[2] Fitzpatrick, *Washington,* XXXI, 438; W. B. Bryan, *A History of the National Capital* (New York, 1914–16), I, 270–272; Lodge, *Hamilton,* IX, 442–443.

[3] Lodge, *Hamilton,* VIII, 232.

[4] Bryan, *National Capital,* I, 175, 181.

[5] Isaac Weld, Jr., *Travels Through the States of North America* (London, 1807), pp. 84, 87.

THE ELECTION OF 1800

Despite this setback, the construction of the Federal City proceeded apace. In 1792, the cornerstone of the President's house was laid and two years later construction was begun on the national capitol. By 1794, three large buildings were going up—the President's house, the capitol itself, and a tavern. The first manufacturing plant erected in the area was a brewery.

President Washington, who watched the progress of this little settlement with loving care, had set his heart upon creating a capital worthy of a great and populous country. Among other things, Washington wished to see a national university established in the Federal City, and for that purpose he donated fifty shares of stock in the Potomac Company.[6] The President's plan envisaged a city four times as large as Secretary of State Jefferson considered sufficient to the country's needs. In Major Pierre L'Enfant, a French engineer and one of the most imaginative city planners of his or any other time, Washington found a kindred spirit. But L'Enfant's grand design struck the commissioners, bedeviled as they were by financial stringencies, as wholly beyond the resources of the Republic. Moreover, L'Enfant soon demonstrated that he was sadly lacking in organizational and administrative ability. In consequence, construction on the Federal City stood still while the commissioners and L'Enfant wrangled. L'Enfant demanded the dismissal of the commissioners, but it was the Frenchman who was discharged. After L'Enfant's departure a much modified plan was followed; but it still remained a city of magnificent distances.[7]

By erecting the national capital and, as Washington hoped, a large and flourishing commercial city in a remote part of the country, the United States government was emulating Peter the Great, who had built and transferred the capital of Russia to St. Petersburg. The analogy was apposite in at least one other respect: both capitals were originally built largely by unfree labor. Where Peter used Russian serfs, American republicans depended for unskilled labor upon the services of slaves whose masters let them out to hire. Skilled artisans were difficult to procure. The commissioners advertised widely in Europe, offering, among other inducements, to advance passage money

[6] Bryan, *National Capital*, I, 152, 251–252.

[7] Fitzpatrick, *Washington*, XXXI, 498–499, 505–508; Saul K. Padover, *Jefferson and the National Capital* (Washington, 1946), p. 121.

(to be deducted from wages), but the War of the French Revolution kept European workmen at home.[8]

It fell to the lot of President Adams to act the part of the Moses who led the government into the wilderness. According to the law enacted in July, 1790, the seat of government was to be transferred to the new capital on the Potomac by the first Monday in December, 1800, at which time Congress was scheduled to convene. In June, 1800, President Adams visited the Federal City—although to call the collection of huts and unfinished buildings a city seemed to be a wholly unwarranted compliment—and later that same month the executive departments moved from Philadelphia. On November 1, 1800, Adams took up residence in the President's house. Not a single apartment was finished; the East Room was used to hang the family wash; and as late as 1803 the plastering had not been completed. When it was reported in the Philadelphia newspapers, not wholly without satisfaction, that the President had an attack of chills and fever, the *Federal City Gazette* indignantly denied the report. But if the President escaped illness in such surroundings, it was less a tribute to the salubrity of the capital than to the robust constitution he had inherited from his New England ancestors.[9]

As for the congressmen themselves, the manner in which they accepted the hardships of life in the new capital was largely determined by their political point of view. Federalists were appalled by the raw desolation they saw about them: workmen still engaged in felling trees on Pennsylvania Avenue, the absence of sidewalks, the mud and mire, and the unfinished state of the capitol. Gouverneur Morris reported that nothing was lacking except "houses, cellars, kitchens, well informed men, amiable women, and other little trifles of this kind, to make our city perfect." While conceding that it was "the very best city in the world for a *future* residence," he pointed out that he was not one of "those good people whom we call posterity."[10] Republicans, on the other hand, rejoiced that the seat of government had been removed from the baneful contagion of bankers, speculators, and businessmen. Having found it impossible to drive the moneychangers

---

[8] Fitzpatrick, *Washington*, XXXII, 268–269, 272.

[9] Bryan, *National Capital*, I, 357–376; John Davis, *Travels of Four Years and a Half in the United States of America* (Bristol, Eng., 1803), pp. 174, 176, 185, 208.

[10] Sparks, *Gouverneur Morris*, III, December 14, 1800.

from the temple, the Republicans did the next best thing—they moved the temple away from the moneychangers.

The Federalists went into the election of 1800 fresh from a decisive triumph in the congressional elections of 1799. Revitalized by President Adams's peace policy, the unpopularity of the Virginia and Kentucky Resolutions, and the prosperity which the European war brought in its train, Federalism suddenly came alive in states where it had long been thought dead and buried: almost half of the congressional delegation from Virginia consisted of Federalists; five out of six from South Carolina, seven out of ten from North Carolina, and both congressmen from Georgia professed to be supporters of President Adams. Few of these recruits, however, were Hamiltonians: compared with the genuine, rock-ribbed New England Federalists, they hardly seemed to be of the same breed. In many instances, the party label covered a multitude of diversities and incompatibilities.[11]

The Federalists' joy over the outcome of the election was considerably dampened, however, by the fact that Pennsylvania returned a majority of Republicans to Congress and elected as governor Thomas McKean, the Republican candidate. High taxes; the unpopularity of the Army, especially after the suppression of Fries's "rebellion"; the odium incurred by the administration as a result of its efforts to suppress freedom of the press—all these things told heavily against the Federalists in the autumn of 1799. As governor, McKean earned the distinction of introducing the spoils system into American politics: he threw out the Federalist incumbents and, in the words of one of those unfortunates, "brought forward every scoundrel who can read and write into office."[12] After McKean had finished his work, some Federalists were prepared to abandon all hope of redeeming Pennsylvania: that benighted state, it was said, was given over to "United Irishmen, Free Masons, and the most God-provoking Democrats on this side of Hell." But Jefferson did not spurn these allies: "With Pennsylvania," he declared, "we can defy the universe."[13]

[11] Ford, *Jefferson*, VII, October 27, 1799; May 12, 1800; Adams, *Gallatin*, I, 18; Dauer, *Adams Federalists*, pp. 234–237; Cunningham, *Jeffersonian Republicans*, pp. 177–178.

[12] Harry Marlin Tinkcom, *The Republicans and Federalists in Pennsylvania, 1790–1801* (Harrisburg, 1950), pp. 263–268.

[13] Kurtz, *Presidency of John Adams*, p. 366; Gibbs, *Memoirs, II*, 231, 399; Ford, *John Quincy Adams*, II, July 11, 1800.

Despite its impressive show of strength at the polls outside Pennsylvania, grave weaknesses had begun to manifest themselves within the Federalist party. True, the Federalists gained the support of Patrick Henry and of Gouverneur Morris. Henry, now a wealthy man, actively campaigned as a Federalist in 1799. In 1798, Gouverneur Morris, wearing his hair "buckled up in about one hundred Papillottes" and accompanied by an entourage consisting of two French valets and a French traveling companion, returned to the United States and was promptly elected to the United States Senate from New York. Nevertheless, in general the Federalist leaders tended to sink into opulent apathy or to take refuge in the comparative tranquillity of the diplomatic service.[14] Less fortunate than these pillars of the party, William Duer and Robert Morris languished in a debtors' prison, and James Wilson, a Justice of the United States Supreme Court, died in 1798 an insolvent debtor, a victim of alcohol, disease, and unwise investments in real estate.[15]

With the old Federalist leaders slipping into limbo, few new recruits came forward to fill the gaps. The youth, the vigor, and the optimism of the country seemed to be drawn into the Republican fold. In 1795–96, President Washington offered the post of Secretary of State to six men before he found one willing to accept. The office of Secretary of War went begging while the men qualified for the job weighed the advantages of public versus private life. Usually the decision was in favor of private life: "No man of any feeling," said John Adams, "is willing to renounce his home, forsake his property and profession for the sake of removing to Philadelphia, where he is almost sure of disgrace and ruin." This reluctance of gentlemen of the Federalist persuasion to engage in the rough-and-tumble of political life created some strange anomalies: in May, 1800, the Federalist candidates for the New York legislature from New York City included a ship chandler, a baker, a potter, a bookseller, two grocers, a bankrupt, a shoemaker, and a mason.[16]

[14] Morison, *Otis*, I, 278; Channing, *History*, IV, 167.

[15] Adams, *John Adams*, II, 191, 194; E. K. Bauer, *Commentaries on the Constitution, 1790–1860* (New York, 1952), pp. 57–58; Charles Page Smith, *James Wilson, Founding Father* (Chapel Hill, 1956), pp. 387–388.

[16] Adams, *John Adams*, II, 191, 194; Robert Troup to Rufus King, March 29, 1800, King MSS., NYHS; M. L. Davis to Gallatin, April 15, 1800, Gallatin MSS., NYHS; Perkins, *First Rapprochement*, p. 37; King, *Rufus King*, III, March 9, 1800; Gibbs, *Memoirs*, II, 379.

This despite the unmistakable signs that the Federalists would be hard pressed in the coming election. The heavy expense of waging the undeclared war with France, the new taxes the war had made necessary, the large increase in the national debt, the precipitate use of military force in eastern Pennsylvania, the fear of "monarchism," and the unpopularity of the Alien and Sedition Acts played into the hands of the Republicans. Above all, the Federalists were handicapped by the fact that the war with France had failed to erupt into open war. By election time, peace was in the air, and the men who had been hailed in 1798 as the vindicators of American rights and honor were now regarded by many of their countrymen as warmongers. Not for the last time in American political history, the party that had fought the war was rewarded with obloquy for its success.[17]

By way of preparation for the presidential election of 1800, the Federalists and Republicans altered, for partisan purposes, the method of electing electors. Eight states entrusted the choice of electors to one or both houses of the state legislature; the remainder of the states used the method of state-wide or district elections. In 1799, when the congressional elections demonstrated that at least five districts in Virginia would choose Federalist electors, the Republican majority in the legislature abolished the district system and provided for election by a general ticket—a method certain to favor the Republican candidates. In Massachusetts, on the eve of the election, the Federalist-controlled legislature decided to abolish the district system, certain to give the Republican candidates at least two votes, in favor of election by the legislature. And in Pennsylvania, where the Republicans expected to profit from a general election and the Federalists from the district system in force, a deadlock was produced which almost prevented the state from casting any vote whatever. The Maryland Federalists attempted to take the election from the people and bestow it upon the Federalist-controlled legislature. They failed to effect the change— with the result that the electoral vote of the state was divided between the two parties.[18]

[17] King, *Rufus King,* III, June 4, 1800; *Political Science Quarterly,* XVIII (1902), 98–99; Benjamin U. Ratchford, "History of the Federal Debt in the United States," *American Economic Review,* XXXVIII (May, 1947), 131–132.

[18] Robert Liston to Lord Grenville, July 5, November 6, 1800, Liston MSS., LC; Gibbs, *Memoirs,* II, 388; King, *Rufus King,* III, July 15, August 19, 1800; Morison, *Otis,* I, 186; Cunningham, *Jeffersonian Republicans,* pp. 144–147.

New York permitted the legislature to choose the electors. In the autumn of 1799, Aaron Burr, smarting under the defeat administered his party in the state and congressional elections, proposed that the district system be instituted in New York. But the Federalists, priding themselves upon their acumen in divining Burr's strategy, insisted upon retaining the established method. Seldom have politicians been given greater cause to regret their perspicacity.

In the presidential election of 1800, the outcome in New York promised to be decisive. John Adams had carried New York in the election of 1796—and his margin of victory in the electoral college was exactly three votes. If, therefore, the Federalists lost New York it seemed probable that they would forfeit the Presidency unless, of course, they could pick up enough electoral votes elsewhere to make good the deficit. It was for this reason that the Federalists refused to change a system of choosing electors that in every previous election had worked in their favor.

What the New York Federalists failed to take sufficiently into account was that the farmers and town artisans were growing progressively more Republican and that even the business community no longer presented a united front to the enemy: many of the more energetic and progressive merchants were beginning to feel that Federalism deliberately throttled enterprise in the interests of a small minority of wealthy and powerful merchants—a sentiment that was assiduously fostered by the Bank of Manhattan, a Republican institution which had been created by Aaron Burr in 1799 and which now liberally extended credit in order to capture the businessmen's vote.[19] It was now the Federalists' turn to complain that banks were a source of "political poison": "By loaning money to the people," it was said, "they create dependence, and increase their influence." Nor did Burr overlook the laboring man's vote: he worked tirelessly to bring every qualified citizen to the polls and he succeeded in uniting the two dominant factions of the Republican party—the Livingstonians and the Clintonians. Even fortune was on Burr's side: on the eve of the election, a British cruiser arrived in New York Harbor escorting several captured American merchantmen. As the friends of Great Britain, the Federalists incurred the full brunt of the resentment engendered by this ill-timed display of British sea power.[20]

[19] Bray Hammond, *Banks and Politics*, p. 160; Mathew L. Davis to Gallatin, March 29, 1800, Gallatin MSS., NYHS.
[20] Robert Liston to Lord Grenville, August 18, October 8, 1800, Liston

All these circumstances combined to give the Republicans victory in the election and control of the New York legislature, thereby ensuring that the state's electoral votes would go to the Republican candidates. Arguing that Jefferson must be kept out of the Presidency at all costs, Alexander Hamilton suggested to Governor John Jay that the right of choosing electors be taken from the legislature and given to the people (as Burr had proposed in 1799), but Jay declined to sanction a move that could be defended only on the ground that the end justified the means. After all, the Federalists had deliberately chosen the method of electing electors that had led to their downfall, and they could not legitimately change the rules after they had lost the game.[21]

The reverse suffered by the Federalists in New York meant that the party would need every electoral vote it could muster if the Presidency were to be saved. Accordingly, in May, 1800, a caucus of Federalist representatives and senators selected John Adams and Charles Cotesworth Pinckney as the party's standard-bearers. As a South Carolinian, Pinckney was expected to strengthen the ticket in the South, especially in his home state, where a Federalist victory would do much to offset the loss of New York. Lest Federalist electors throw away votes in order to ensure John Adams's re-election to the Presidency, the caucus pledged the party's equal support to both candidates. "By union," said John Marshall, "we can scarcely maintain our ground—without it we must sink and with us all sound, correct American principles." The Republican caucus entered into a similar compact with regard to its candidates, Thomas Jefferson and Aaron Burr. If these promises were faithfully observed, the election of President and Vice-President

---

MSS., LC; Lodge, *Hamilton*, VI, 435; X, May 4, 1800; Hammond, *Banks and Politics*, p. 160; Mathew L. Davis to Gallatin, May 1, 1800, Gallatin MSS., NYHS; Adams, *Gallatin*, 234–235, 241–242; James Parton, *The Life and Times of Aaron Burr* (New York, 1863), p. 243; Jay to King, June 16, 1800, King MSS., NYHS; Spaulding E. Wilder, *His Excellency Governor George Clinton* (New York, 1938), pp. 238–239; Hammond, *Political Parties*, I, 134–136; Mathew L. Davis, *Memoirs of Aaron Burr* (New York, 1837), I, 434; James Cheetham, *A View of the Political Conduct of Aaron Burr* (New York, 1802), p. 39; John Nicholson to Gallatin, March 29, May 6, 1800, Gallatin MSS., NYHS.

[21] Lodge, *Hamilton*, X, 371–374; Johnson, *Jay*, IV, 275; Gibbs, *Memoirs*, II, 347, 375, 407; Hammond, *Political Parties*, I, 144–145; Monaghan, *Jay*, 417; Pickering and Upham, *Timothy Pickering*, III, 327; John Dawson to Madison, May 4, 1800, Madison MSS., LC; Cunningham, *Jeffersonian Republicans*, pp. 184–185.

would be transferred to the House of Representatives. But both parties preferred to take this risk rather than impair their chances of victory in the election.[22]

The semblance of party unity achieved by the Federalist caucus was of short duration. President Adams ascribed the defeat in New York to the lukewarmness of the party leaders, especially Alexander Hamilton, toward his own re-election. The President's suspicions were well founded: since 1799, when Adams announced his intention of sending a peace mission to France, Hamilton and his friends had been seeking to rid themselves of the troublesome old man.[23]

They tried to draft Washington for a third term, but the former President refused again to expose himself to the calumny and malice which he had experienced in that office. His advice to Hamilton and his friends was to depend upon the purity of their principles rather than upon the evanescent popularity of one man to bring them victory in the election. A few months later, in December, 1799, Washington died of streptococci laryngitis and the complications that followed upon the ministrations—which included bloodletting, emetics, and blistering—of his physicians.[24]

Washington's death not only deprived the Hamiltonians of a presidential candidate; it removed the one restraint upon Hamilton that might have kept him from breaking up the Federalist party. For Hamilton still refused to resign himself to suffering Adams for another four years; instead, as in 1796, he undertook to elevate Pinckney to the Presidency and to relegate John Adams to the Vice-Presidency by manipulating the vote in the electoral college. The plot was the same as in 1796, the only difference being a slight change in characters.[25]

[22] Collections of the Massachusetts Historical Society, Seventh Series, I, 77; Gibbs, Memoirs, II, 347; Dauer, Adams Federalists, pp. 246–247; Ames, Fisher Ames, I, 280–281; J. C. Hamilton, Hamilton, VI, 464; Morison, Otis, I, 184–185.

[23] Pickering to Timothy Williams, May 19, 1800, Pickering MSS., MHS; Brown, Northern Confederacy, pp. 18–19.

[24] Fitzpatrick, Washington, XXXVII, 348–349; Dr. Rudolph Marx, "A Medical Profile of George Washington," The American Heritage Reader (New York, 1956), pp. 33–38; King, Rufus King, III, September 24, 1800; Adams, Documents Relating to New England Federalism, pp. 149–150; Morris, Gouverneur Morris, II, 380–381; Carroll and Ashworth, Washington, VII, 637–647.

[25] Lodge, George Cabot, pp. 291–292, 295; Robert Liston to Lord Grenville, May 29, 1800, Liston MSS., LC; King, Rufus King, III, March 9, September

In May, 1800, well aware that he walked a slippery quarter-deck and that half his crew were ready to pitch him overboard, President Adams struck first by removing two of the leading Hamiltonians— Secretary of State Pickering and Secretary of War McHenry—from the cabinet. Both men had counterworked the President's policies and had gloried in their obstructionism: Pickering, in particular, felt that he deserved the gratitude of the country for his efforts to thwart the objectives of a doddering, wrongheaded Chief Executive "influenced by the vilest passions." McHenry resigned his office at Adams's demand, but Pickering had to be dismissed. Unfortunately for the President, he retained Oliver Wolcott as Secretary of the Treasury. Wolcott was not less devoted to Hamilton than were McHenry and Pickering; and for the remainder of President Adams's term of office, Wolcott served as Hamilton's spy within the administration.[26]

In the offices vacated by McHenry and Pickering, the President placed two Virginians—thereby demonstrating his awareness of the importance of cultivating the Federalist vote in the Old Dominion. (In 1796, a single electoral vote from Virginia had helped give Adams his narrow margin over Jefferson.) Samuel Dexter was appointed Secretary of War and John Marshall assumed the duties of Secretary of State. Marshall was the leader of the southern Federalists in Congress, but he was not highly esteemed by the party elders of the North. He had incurred their displeasure by voting in favor of the repeal of the Sedition Act (even though he defended its constitutionality) and by approving John Adams's efforts to make peace with France. For these offenses against party orthodoxy he had damned himself in the eyes of the Essex Junto, the archconservative New Englanders who looked to Hamilton to save the country from "Jacobinism."[27] Fisher

---

24, 1800; Brown, *Northern Confederacy*, p. 18; Gibbs, *Memoirs*, II, 367–368, 371, 384, 398; *Report of the American Historical Association for 1896* (Washington, 1897), I, 833–834; J. C. Hamilton, *Hamilton*, VI, 957.

[26] Pickering and Upham, *Timothy Pickering*, III, 301, 484–488; Pickering to Herman Stamp, May 30, 1800, Pickering MSS., MHS; Pickering, *Review of the Adams-Cunningham Correspondence* (Boston, 1829), p. 124; Bemis, *American Secretaries of State*, II, 170–171; Mitchell, *Abigail Adams*, p. 221; *William and Mary Quarterly*, XI (1954), 631; Lodge, *George Cabot*, p. 272; Brown, *Northern Confederacy*, p. 19; *Correspondence Between John Adams and William Cunningham* (Boston, 1823), pp. 34–40; Morison, *Otis*, I, 99; Lodge, *Hamilton*, VII, 349–351; Adams, *John Adams*, X, 6–7; Gibbs, *Memoirs*, II, 348, 384.

[27] The name Essex Junto first appeared during the period of the Articles

Ames declared that Marshall's character was "done for"; and Oliver Wolcott thought him "too much disposed to govern the world according to the rules of Virginia."[28] Hamilton campaigned covertly against Adams in New England where he found that the great majority of Federalists were firmly attached to the President. Adams himself denounced Hamilton as the leader of a "pro-British" faction, "a bastard, and as much an alien as Gallatin." Hamilton thereupon wrote two letters to Adams demanding an explanation; when no reply was forthcoming, the Federalist leader determined to denounce Adams publicly. Aided by Pickering, McHenry, Wolcott, and other enemies of the President who had enjoyed his confidence, he began in the summer of 1800 to collect evidence purporting to prove that Adams was unfit to hold the Presidency. These spicy details, together with Hamilton's own reminiscences of Adams's vagaries, were incorporated in the "Letter from Alexander Hamilton Concerning the Public Conduct and Character of John Adams."[29]

Hamilton's pamphlet purported to be the case history of a personality the distinguishing features of which were "disgusting egotism," "distempered jealousy," "ungovernable indiscretion," and "vanity without bounds." No wonder, therefore, Hamilton exclaimed, that the President's policies were fatal to the best interests of the country: they were conceived not in wisdom and rectitude but in passion, spite, envy, and malice. The President did not lack for good advice—the cabinet was always ready to set him straight—but, Hamilton lamented, Adams was bent upon going his own way even though it led to national dishonor. Nevertheless, Hamilton conceded that Adams was a man of

of Confederation, when John Hancock attached this label to his opponents in Essex County, Massachusetts. John Adams used it to designate the supporters of Alexander Hamilton and Jefferson applied it to the most virulent of his enemies in New England. The members of the Essex Junto were Theophilus Parsons, John Lowell, and Jonathan Jackson of Newburyport; George Cabot and Nathan Dane of Beverley; Timothy Pickering and Benjamin Goodhue of Salem; and Fisher Ames, Theodore Sedgwick, Tristram Dalton, John Lowell, Jr., Stephen Higginson, Josiah Quincy, Caleb Strong, Harrison Gray Otis, Francis Dana, and Robert Treat Paine, most of whom resided in Boston.

28 Sedgwick to Rufus King, May 11, 1800, King MSS., NYHS; Gibbs, Memoirs, II, December 29, 1799; Perkins, First Rapprochement, pp. 122–123.

29 Brown, Northern Confederacy, p. 20; J. C. Hamilton, Hamilton, VI, 957; King, Rufus King, III, August 19, 1800; Gibbs, Memoirs, II, 315, 395; Adams, John Adams, IX, 620; Lodge, George Cabot, pp. 281–282, 297; Mitchell, Abigail Adams, pp. 255, 258; Lodge, Hamilton, VII, 309–310, 357, 361–362; Correspondence Between John Adams and William Cunningham, pp. 159–160; Ames, Fisher Ames, II, 153.

patriotism and integrity and that he even possessed "talents of a certain kind"—unfortunately, not of the kind required by the Presidency. Even so, he concluded that Adams must be supported equally with Pinckney in accord with the agreement reached by the Federalist caucus. Few could fail to see, however, that Hamilton's purpose in writing this diatribe was not to reinforce the pledge of equal support but to steal the election from Adams.

This letter was intended for circulation only among the leaders of the Federalist party. To this restriction Hamilton had reluctantly consented, complaining that it was foreign to his blunt, plain-speaking character and unfair to the people of the United States, who had a right to know the worst about their President. But at this point, Aaron Burr took an unexpected hand in the proceedings: having procured a copy of Hamilton's "Letter," he gave it to the newspapers. Hamilton accepted this development with more aplomb than he usually displayed toward Burr's political manipulations: he declared that he "had no doubt it would be productive of good"—the good, of course, being the defeat of John Adams in the presidential election.[30]

Hamilton's philippic had little effect upon the outcome of the election. In the eyes of the people, Adams appeared to be a firm and upright patriot devoted to Washington's policy of peace. Even many of the party leaders came to Adams's defense. John Marshall, John Jay, and Harrison Gray Otis aligned themselves with the President; and Noah Webster, hitherto one of Hamilton's admirers—Hamilton had helped him to establish a Federalist newspaper in New York—published a pamphlet accusing the Federalist leader of being cankered by ambition and jealousy and overmastered by an ungovernable temper—in short, of possessing all the infirmities which Hamilton had attributed to Adams. Thomas Cooper, a Republican editor who had just served a six months' sentence for libeling President Adams, attempted to bring Hamilton within the purview of the Sedition Act. But the American people were denied the truly extraordinary spectacle of Alexander Hamilton, the great exponent of executive powers, in jail for libeling a President of the United States. John Adams was sick of the Sedition Act and wanted nothing further to do with a law that seemed to make two antiadministration newspapers sprout where only one had existed before and proscribed "under imputations of democracy, some of the ablest, most influential, and best characters in the Union."[31]

The breach between Adams and Hamilton was now irreparable and the Federalist party was divided at a time when only unity could have prevented the triumph of the Jeffersonian Republicans. Adams's supporters attempted to create a third party, called the Constitutionalists, leaving the Hamiltonians in possession of the tarnished name of Federalist, but the attempt did not prosper. Clearly, the Federalist Babylon was tottering, and some of the stanchest members of the party rushed for the exits: Theodore Sedgwick, Robert Goodloe Harper, and Harrison Gray Otis announced their intention to retire from politics.[32]

Despite the quarrels of their leaders, the Federalists did not concede the election. Recovering from the shock of the loss of New York, they rallied their forces and vigorously contested other states. In New Jersey they took advantage of a law dating from the colonial period by which women were not expressly barred from voting; the Federalists marched their wives, daughters, and other qualified "females" to the polls and, thanks to this unexpected support, they made a clean sweep of the state's seven electoral votes.[33]

But it was chiefly upon propaganda that the Federalists relied to bar the Virginia "Jacobin" from the Presidency. All the forces of bigotry and intolerance were recruited in this cause. When Jefferson was elected to the Vice-Presidency in 1796, a Federalist divine prayed: "O Lord! wilt Thou bestow upon the Vice President a double portion

[31] Noah Webster, *A Letter to General Hamilton* (Philadelphia, 1800), pp. 1, 6–7; Gibbs, *Memoirs*, II, 407; Morison, *Otis*, I, 184; *Report of the American Historical Association for 1912* (Washington, 1913), p. 675; Bernard C. Steiner, *Life and Correspondence of James McHenry* (Cleveland, 1907), p. 476; Pickering to Higginson, December 23, 1799; John Jay to Pickering, June 19, 1800, Pickering MSS., MHS; Adams, *John Adams*, IX, 87, 291; *Pennsylvania Magazine of History and Biography*, XLIV (1920), 17–18; King, *Rufus King*, III, December 4, 31, 1800; Channing, *History*, IV, 218 (footnote); Lodge, *George Cabot*, p. 299.
[32] Noah Webster, *A Letter to General Hamilton* (Philadelphia, 1800), p. 1; *A Solemn Address to Christians and Patriots* (New York, 1800), p. 32; *Answer to Alexander Hamilton's Letter* (New York, 1800), p. 5; Cunningham, *Jeffersonian Republicans*, p. 230.
[33] Robert Liston to Lord Grenville, November 6, 1800, Liston MSS., LC; *Collections of the Massachusetts Historical Society*, Seventh Series, I (1900), 78–79; King, *Rufus King*, III, August 6, 1800.

of Thy grace, *for Thou knowest he needs it.*" But this prayer seems not to have been answered, for by 1800 he was being denounced from Federalist pulpits as an atheist, an "intellectual voluptuary," and the progenitor of the mulatto children upon his plantation. At Monticello, the Goddess of Reason was reputed to be the tutelary divinity; in place of the altars of the Most High, Jefferson set up his philosophical apparatus and practiced, among other enormities, vivisection. (With some justification, Monticello was called "Dogs' Misery.") A vote for Jefferson, the voters were told, was a vote against God; if he were elected to the Presidency, the people of the United States must expect "the just vengeance of insulted heaven" which, presumably, would take the form of "dwellings in flames, hoary hairs bathed in blood, female chastity violated . . . children writhing on the pike and halberd." Little as the Federalists were disposed to put their trust in the wisdom of the people, they took comfort in the hope that God would not "permit a howling atheist to sit at the head of the nation"—unless, of course, He had utterly forsaken the United States.[34]

Unfortunately for the Federalists' efforts to make religion a buttress of the established order, the rapidly growing Methodist and Presbyterian churches, particularly in the West, were predominantly composed of Republicans. Even in New England, Unitarianism began to undermine Congregationalism, with results far more destructive to orthodoxy than any of the anti-Christian arguments advanced by Tom Paine in *The Age of Reason.* It was an age in which "men of information were . . . nearly as free from vulgar superstition or the Christian religion as they were in the time of Cicero from pagan superstition." In this respect, the Federalist leaders were no less emancipated than were their Republican counterparts. Nevertheless, partly as a result of the French Revolution, a definite revival of the old-time religion occurred in the United States during the 1790's. Jefferson declared

[34] A campaign placard put the issue succinctly before the electorate:
"GOD—AND A RELIGIOUS PRESIDENT;
or impiously declare for
JEFFERSON—AND NO GOD!!!"
Charles Warren, *Odd Byways in American History* (Cambridge, 1942), pp. 127–128; Morison, *Otis,* I, 196; J. E. Smith, *One Hundred Years of Hartford's Courant* (New York, 1947), p. 78; J. C. Hamilton, *Hamilton,* VI. 435, 501–502, 514; Mott, *American Journalism,* p. 169, and *Jefferson and the Press,* pp. 38, 169; Vernon Stauffer, *New England and the Bavarian Illuminati* (New York, 1918), pp. 94–97; Fisher Ames to Rufus King, September 24, 1800, King MSS., NYHS; Gibbs, *Memoirs,* II, 367–370.

that Connecticut was "so priest-ridden, that nothing is expected from them, but the most bigotted passive obedience." At Yale in 1790, a hotbed of infidelity where not a single member of the sophomore class was a professing Christian and where the student body in general ridiculed the idea of divine revelation and sneered at "priestcraft," President Timothy Dwight succeeded in restoring piety on the campus. Dwight's lectures on "The Evidences of Divine Revelation" confounded the skeptics and brought the students in droves to the chapel to offer up prayers for Grace to descend, among other places, upon Harvard.[35]

Jefferson did not deign to answer his vilifiers; he knew that once they found they had drawn blood, a host of new assailants would descend upon him and that every lie uttered against him would be multiplied twentyfold. Jefferson preferred to conduct the campaign from his study at Monticello: through his friends, he kept his finger upon the public pulse; he advised Republican state leaders as to stragegy; and he laid down the propaganda line followed by his party. The platform, if it can be called such, was essentially Jefferson's: support of the Constitution; preservation of states' rights; "a government rigorously frugal and simple"; the prompt liquidation of the public debt; a small army and navy; freedom of religion and of the press; "commerce with all nations; political connection with none; and little or no diplomatic establishment."[36]

While Jefferson was presented to the electorate chiefly in the guise of the farmer's friend—his theory that those who tilled the earth were the chosen people of God was frequently quoted in campaign literature—in the seaboard cities he figured as the apostle of commerce and neutral rights. Yet everywhere—in town and country alike—the Republicans rung the changes upon peace and economy. As for John Adams, having written a book and spoken his mind freely on all occasions, he had in effect delivered himself into the hands of his enemies. From his own words, sometimes garbled and quoted out of

[35] James T. Horton, *James Kent, A Study in Conservatism* (New York, 1934), p. 115; F. J. C. Hearnshaw, *Social and Political Ideas of Some Representative Thinkers of the Revolutionary Era* (London, 1931), pp. 128–129; G. Adolph Koch, *Republican Religion* (New York, 1935), pp. 268–270, 275, 282, 294–295; Johnston, *Jay*, III, 404; *Report of the Trial of Justice Samuel Chase* (Baltimore, 1805), Appendix, 59.

[36] Ford, *Jefferson*, VII, January 26, 1799.

context, he was convicted of being an advocate of monarchy, life tenure for senators, an alliance with Great Britain, and a fighting Navy. Even so, the President fared better than did his party: he had proved that he was a friend of peace, whereas the Hamiltonian Federalists had done everything in their power to produce war except declare it.[37]

In 1800, the states voted for presidential electors at various times from October to December. As the returns came in, the Federalists began to take heart: Rhode Island, which had been expected to go Republican, voted for the Federalist candidates; the vote of Maryland was evenly divided; and in Pennsylvania, a strongly Republican state, the House and Senate remained deadlocked. As a result, by the end of November the Republican and Federalist candidates were running virtually a dead heat. Only one doubtful state remained to be heard from. South Carolina had failed to support Adams in 1796, but in 1800 Republicans admitted that "the Weight of Talent, Wealth, and personal and family interest" in the state was arrayed against them. Upon this circumstance Federalists pinned their hope that South Carolina would make good the loss of New York and thereby would carry Adams and Pinckney to victory.

But the Federalists reckoned without Charles Pinckney, the leader of the Republican branch of the Pinckney family, who, with Aaron Burr, shared the honor of being the President-maker of the election of 1800. By dint of liberal promises of patronage (which Jefferson later duly honored) to the members of the South Carolina legislature in whose hands the choice of electors lay, Pinckney succeeded in swinging the eight electoral votes of South Carolina to Jefferson and Burr. As a reward for this signal contribution to the Republican triumph, Pinckney was appointed minister to Spain by President Jefferson.[38]

[37] Bemis, *John Quincy Adams and the Foundations of American Foreign Policy*, pp. 106–107.

[38] *American Historical Review*, IV (1899), 113–116, 128; Charles Biddle, *Autobiography* (Philadelphia, 1883), p. 289; Channing, *History*, IV, 233–234; *Proceedings of the Massachusetts Historical Society*, LIX (1926), 259; Ford, *Jefferson*, VII, December 18, 1800; J. C. Hamilton, *Hamilton*, VI, 457, 483, 492; King, *Rufus King*, III, December 27, 1800; *Collections of the Massachusetts Historical Society*, Seventh Series, I, 78–79; *John Steele Papers*, Publications of the North Carolina Historical Commission (Raleigh, 1924), I, 192–193; Cunningham, *Jeffersonian Republicans*, pp. 231–239; Charles O. Lerche, Jr., "Jefferson and the Election of 1800," *William and Mary Quarterly*, Third Series, V (1948), 467–491.

In the final tabulation, the vote in the electoral college stood: Jefferson and Burr were tied with seventy-three votes each, Adams placed third with sixty-five, Pinckney occupied fourth place with sixty-four, and Jay came in fifth with one vote. (Rhode Island gave one vote to Jay in order to ensure that Pinckney would not be elected President over John Adams.) Delaware gave three votes to Adams and Pinckney; Pennsylvania (where a compromise was reached in December, 1800) split its vote eight to seven between the Republican and Federalist candidates; Maryland divided its electoral votes evenly between the two parties; North Carolina gave eight electoral votes to Jefferson and Burr, four to Adams and Pinckney. The New England states went solidly Federalist; Virginia, Georgia, Kentucky, and Tennessee were equally solid in the Republican cause.[39]

On both sides, it was a remarkable display of party discipline: in 1796, the electoral vote had been scattered among thirteen candidates; in 1800, only five names were considered by the electoral college. For the Republicans, however, the agreement to support each candidate equally had been observed too literally for the party's good; as a result of the tie in the electoral college, the election of the President and Vice-President was transferred to the House of Representatives. This eventuality had not been anticipated by the party leaders. While Jefferson had urged the Virginia electors to vote unanimously for Burr, he had expected that somewhere along the line—either in Georgia or South Carolina—a vote or two would be deducted from Burr. But the Republican electors, resolved to demonstrate the solidarity of the party and the sanctity of its promises and to erase the bad impression created by the vote of 1796, voted to the last man for Jefferson and Burr.[40]

[39]Had it not been for the loss of New York, Adams would have received more electoral votes in 1800 than in 1796. And the outcome in New York had been decided by about 250 votes in the New York City elections. But the ultimate responsibility for the Republican victory in 1800 was properly attributed to South Carolina: if that state had gone Federalist, Adams would have been elected. Channing, *History*, IV, 219, 236, 239; Robert Liston to Lord Grenville, November 6, 1800, Liston MSS., LC.

[40] Morris, *Gouverneur Morris*, II, 396; Gibbs, *Memoirs*, II, 379; Adams, *Gallatin*, pp. 239–243; Hunt, *Madison*, VI, 411–412; Morison, *Otis*, I, 211; J. C. Hamilton, *Hamilton*, VI, 437; *American Historical Review*, IV (1899), 115; Cunningham, *Jeffersonian Republicans*, pp. 239–241; Ulrich B. Phillips (ed.), "South Carolina Federalist Correspondence, 1789–1797," *American Historical Review*, XIV (1909), 780.

For such a contingency, the Constitution provided that the voting in the House of Representatives should be by states, a majority being necessary to elect. While the Federalists were numerically in the majority—the new Congress did not assemble until March 4, 1801— they disposed of the vote of only six states and divided control of two states. Thus, although they could not elect a President, they were in a position, provided they held firm, to prevent a choice.[41]

What the Republicans had most to fear was a contest in the House of Representatives between Burr and Jefferson for the Presidency. Despite the fact that Jefferson knew himself to be the choice of the people, he was not without apprehensions that Burr would make a bid for the first office. But Burr seemed resigned to take the second place: in December, 1800, he assured Jefferson that he would not be "instrumental in counteracting the wishes and expectations of the United States."[42]

The Federalists had no intention, however, of letting Burr bow out of a contest with Jefferson. Looking to Burr to save them from "the fangs of Jefferson," they credited him with being ambitious, subtle, unscrupulous, and fond of playing a double game—qualities which for the Federalists' purposes might be accounted virtues. Indeed, they loved Burr for his vices. Moreover, after the worst had been said of Burr, he was still preferable to Jefferson. This elegant, urbane, dissolute, and aristocratic New Yorker was not a democrat, a critic of the funding system, an inveterate enemy of executive powers, a revolutionist, an atheist, or a "visionary philosopher"; whereas Jefferson was pronounced guilty on all these counts. Finally, if Burr were elected President by their votes, many Federalists flattered themselves that the Republican party would be divided, the "preponderance of the state of Virginia in the national Councils" would be averted, and the country would be spared the horrors of a "Jacobin" revolution.[43]

Not all Federalists were willing to elevate to the Presidency a man they regarded as a reprobate and a blackguard in order to keep out

[41] Ford, *Jefferson*, I, 304; Aaron Burr to Gallatin, January 16, 1801, Gallatin MSS., NYHS; Hunt, *Madison*, VI, 410.

[42] Adams, *Life of Gallatin*, pp. 255–257; Adams, *Gallatin, Works*, I, 18–19; Ford, *Jefferson*, I, 283.

[43] Theodore Sedgwick to Theodore Sedgwick, Jr., January 11, 1801, Sedgwick MSS., MHS; Morris, *Gouverneur Morris*, II, 398, 401–403; King, *Rufus King*, III, January 18, May 24, 1801; J. C. Hamilton, *Hamilton*, VI, 454, 501–502, 512.

Jefferson. Indeed, most of the leaders of the party—Alexander Hamilton, Gouverneur Morris, John Jay, and William Bingham—thought that Burr was quite dangerous enough in the Vice-Presidency without raising him to the highest office in the land. Hamilton, in particular, exerted himself to prevent his party from lashing itself to Burr's chariot. To his friends in Congress, Hamilton wrote letters denouncing Burr as "the most unfit and dangerous man of the community"—a demagogue who pandered to the worst passions of the populace in the hope of making himself Caesar. From Burr's elevation to the Presidency, Hamilton predicted a host of evils: war with Great Britain, the overthrow of the fiscal system, and the establishment of a "Jacobin system" by which Burr would "employ the rogues of all parties to overrule the good men of all parties, and to prosecute projects which wise men of every description will disapprove." "Adieu to the Federal Troy," Hamilton exclaimed, "if they once introduce this Grecian horse into their citadel."[44]

In comparison with this "Catiline," Jefferson appeared to Hamilton to have some "pretensions to character." Not that Hamilton was in any danger of erring on the side of charity in assessing the Virginian's worth: he reminded his partisans that Jefferson was "a contemptible hypocrite" who was "tinctured with fanaticism . . . crafty and persevering in his objects . . . not scrupulous about the means of success, nor even mindful of truth." Still, Hamilton was willing to concede that Jefferson possessed a certain amount of integrity and devotion to principle, and that he had been partly cured of his excessive partiality for all things French, including French revolutionary principles. Finally, Hamilton ventured to hope that Jefferson as President would not uproot the executive authority—"viewing himself as the reversioner, he was solicitous to come into the possession of a good estate."[45]

Hamilton's advice to his party was to give the Presidency to Jefferson in exchange for a promise to uphold the fiscal system established by the Federalists, make no removals from office below cabinet rank, maintain the Army and Navy, and continue the policy of neutrality

[44] Gibbs, *Memoirs*, II, 375; A. M. Hamilton, *Intimate Life*, pp. 385–388; Lodge, *Hamilton*, X, December 16, August 6, 1800; J. C. Hamilton, *Hamilton*, VI, 493–494; Adams, *Gallatin*, p. 254; Ford, *John Quincy Adams*, II, March 17, 1801.
[45] Lodge, *Hamilton*, X, December 16, 1800; January 16, 1801; Robert Troup to King, June 24, 1800, King MSS., NYHS.

laid down by Washington and Adams. But upon most of the Federalist members of Congress, Hamilton's adjurations had little effect. Come what would, they were resolved to stick with Burr. As a result, Hamilton was left in "the awkward situation of a man who continues sober after the company are drunk."[46]

Meeting in the unfinished capitol in the new Federal City, the House of Representatives began balloting on February 10. The vote stood eight states for Jefferson, six for Burr, and two divided. The concurrence of nine states was necessary to elect. On both sides, spirit ran high. Congressman Nicholson of Maryland "left his sick-bed—came through a snow storm—brought his bed and prevented the vote of Maryland from being given to Burr." The wife of Congressman Craik of Maryland threatened to divorce him if he did not vote for Jefferson.[47]

The Federalists stood firm for Burr as though their lives, as well as their wives, depended upon it. And yet, to their astonishment, Burr refused to lift his finger to attain the Presidency. During the election, he remained in Albany, quietly attending to his legal practice and refusing the Federalists' pleas that he come to Washington and rally his devoted followers in Congress. To the end, he declined to give his new-found allies "any assurances respecting his future intentions and conduct, saying that to do it might injure him with his friends, and prevent their co-operation." Seemingly, at the critical moment, Burr had lost his nerve or—what few Federalists believed—had become an honest man.[48]

The truth is, Burr was a far shrewder politician than the Federalist congressmen who presumed to instruct him how to carry off the Presidency. Burr saw no reason to open negotiations with the Federalists—they were already, so to speak, in his bag. He knew that by

[46] Sparks, *Morris*, III, December 19, 1800; J. C. Hamilton, *Hamilton*, VI, 493–494; Lodge, *George Cabot*, p. 284; King, *Rufus King*, III, December 31, 1800.

[47] *William and Mary Quarterly*, I (1892), 103; St. George Tucker to Madison, January 7, 23, 1801, Madison MSS., LC; William Cabell Bruce, *John Randolph of Roanoke* (New York, 1922), I, 168.

[48] *New York History*, XXVI (1945), 449–450; *Documents Relating to the Presidential Election in the Year 1801* (Philadelphia, 1831), p. 4; Lodge, *Hamilton*, X, January, 1801; J. C. Hamilton, *Hamilton*, VI, 524; Gallatin to James Nicholson, February 14, 1801; Aaron Burr to Gallatin, February 25, 1801, Gallatin MSS., NYHS; Davis, *Memoirs of Aaron Burr*, II, 94, 96–97, 100; Adams, *Gallatin*, p. 254; Ford, *Jefferson*, VII, January 4, 1801.

openly aligning himself with the Federalists he would forfeit all hope of support from the Republicans—and it was only with Republican aid that he would hope to nose out Jefferson. Nor was Burr so desperate as to accept the purple from a praetorian band of politicians who had just been repudiated by the voters of the United States. Accordingly, Burr played a waiting game. The one thing which would have eliminated him from consideration and put an end to the deadlock in Congress—an announcement that he would not serve as President if elected—was not forthcoming from Burr. It was not his practice to burn bridges either before or after him.[49]

There were present in Congress six men, the vote of any one of whom would have decided the election in a moment. Among these six congressmen, the least resolute in support of Burr was James A. Bayard. The sole representative of the state of Delaware, Bayard had it in his power to shift the vote of his state from Burr to Jefferson, thereby giving Jefferson the nine states requisite to election. Although Bayard preferred Burr to Jefferson, the New Yorker's refusal to secure the Presidency "by deceiving one man (a great blockhead) and tempting two (not incorruptible)" left Bayard with "but a humble opinion of the talents of an unprincipled man."[50]

Since the Federalists could get nowhere with Burr, Bayard tried to strike a bargain with Jefferson whereby, in exchange for Federalist votes, the Virginian would bind himself to observe the conditions laid down by Hamilton. But Jefferson, like Burr, was unwilling to make a deal with the Federalists. Just when Bayard was on the point of despairing of doing business with anyone, he was told by Senator Samuel Smith of Maryland, a confidant of Jefferson's, that the Virginian had given all the assurances required by the Federalists.[51] This welcome

[49] Steiner, *Life and Correspondence of James McHenry*, p. 483; *Documents Relating to the Presidential Election in the Year 1801* (Philadelphia, 1831), pp. 7, 9–10; Irving Brant, *James Madison, Secretary of State* (Indianapolis, 1953), pp. 23–24; Elbridge Gerry to Jefferson, January 15, 1801, Jefferson MSS., LC; Edward Thornton to Lord Grenville, February 28, 1801, Thornton MSS., LC; Elbridge Gerry to Jefferson, January 15, 1801, Jefferson MSS., LC; Cunningham, *Jeffersonian Republicans*, p. 243; John S. Pancake, "Aaron Burr: Would-Be Usurper," *William and Mary Quarterly*, Third Series, VIII (1951), 205–209.

[50] Morton Borden, *The Federalism of James A. Bayard* (New York, 1954), pp. 80–81, 90–93; *John P. Branch Historical Papers*, III (Richmond, 1909), 32–33; *Documents Relating to the Presidential Election in the Year 1801*, p. 6; J. C. Hamilton, *Hamilton*, VI, 506, 524.

[51] Jefferson later denied that he had given such assurances. When he spoke

news, together with the hopelessness of Burr's position, determined Bayard's decision to abandon the struggle.[52] On February 16, 1801, after thirty-five ballots had failed to break the impasse, Bayard informed his Federalist colleagues that he had decided to vote for Jefferson. "The clamor," he later reported, "was prodigious, the reproaches vehement." The meeting broke up in confusion, some diehards swearing that they would "go without a constitution & take the risk of civil war" rather than vote for "such a wretch as Jefferson." Finally, an arrangement was worked out whereby Jefferson was elected President without a single Federalist vote being cast in his favor.[53] In this way, the Federalists absolved themselves of all responsibility for the horrors they confidently expected would occur in the United States.[54]

From the standpoint of the Federalist Old Guard, the worst had happened: a "Jacobin" was in the Presidency and the country was under the heel of Virginia and its satellites. The sun of Federalism had sunk forever, exclaimed a distraught New Englander, and a long night of "blood and ashes" seemed about to descend upon the country. "Our only consolation," the Federalists lamented, "is that the Lord reigns." Jefferson called it the "revolution of 1800"—"as real a revolution in the principles of our government as that of 1776 was in form"

to Senator Smith, Jefferson said, he had no idea that he was committing himself to certain policies in exchange for Federalist votes; he was simply outlining to a friend the general policies which would govern his administration in the event he was elected President. *William and Mary Quarterly,* Third Series, VII (1951), 211; Adams, *Gallatin,* II, 663; Aaron Burr to Gallatin, February 25, 1801, Gallatin MSS., NYHS; Ford, *Jefferson,* VII, 491, 494; Cunningham, *Jeffersonian Republicans,* pp. 245–246.

[52] On February 12, 1801, Burr wrote a letter to Gallatin declaring that he was "utterly surprized" by the voting in the House of Representatives. The report spread among the Federalists on February 15, 1801, that Burr had "explicitly renounced" his pretensions to the first office. Aaron Burr to Gallatin, February 12, 1801, Gallatin MSS., NYHS; Theodore Sedgwick to Theodore Sedgwick, Jr., February 16, 1801, Sedgwick MSS., MHS.

[53] This was accomplished by permitting Matthew Lyon to cast the vote of Vermont for Jefferson, The four Federalist representatives from Maryland put in blank pieces of paper. Delaware and South Carolina likewise voted blank. The final ballot gave ten states for Jefferson, four for Burr, and two blank.

[54] A. J. Dallas to Gallatin, February 15, 1801; William Eustis to Gallatin, March 6, 1801; John Beckley to Gallatin, February 15, 1801; Gallatin to John Nicholson, February 16, 1801, Gallatin MSS., NYHS; J. A. Bayard to Samuel Bayard, February 22, 1801, Gratz MSS., PHS; J. C. Hamilton, *Hamilton,* VI, 523; Adams, *Gallatin,* II, 663.

—and there was hardly a Federalist who did not agree that for once the President-elect spoke the truth.[55]

Even though no "mighty revolution in opinion" was discernible in the vote of the electoral college, the result of the congressional elections of 1800 left no doubt that the Republicans had won a sweeping triumph. The Federalists suffered a loss of approximately forty seats: the incoming House was composed of sixty-six Republicans and forty Federalists. New Jersey, Georgia, Kentucky, and Tennessee sent full Republican delegations to Congress; out of nineteen members elected from Virginia, only one was a Federalist; Republicans were in a majority in the New York and Pennsylvania contingents; and even the Massachusetts delegation was evenly divided between the two parties. Even the Senate, hitherto impregnably Federalist, passed under Republican control by virtue of the vote of Vice-President Burr. "Compare the situation of the Federalists in 1798 with their present situation," said A. J. Dallas in May, 1801, "and we find a party can never be too high, to fall. Compare the situation of the Republicans at the same periods, and we find a party can never be too low, to rise."[56]

John Adams could justly claim that the election had revealed that he was more popular than his party. This was disclosed not only by the vote in the electoral college but by the fact that candidates favorable to John Adams often ran ahead of their party. For example, presenting himself to the electorate as "the friend of Peace and as . . . the personal & confidential friend of the President," Elbridge Gerry, now a Republican, almost succeeded in snatching the governorship of Massachusetts away from Strong, the Federalist candidate. Gerry polled 17,000 votes in a strongly Federalist state, only about 200 less than Strong.[57]

[55] *William and Mary Quarterly,* Third Series, VII (1951), 211; J. C. Hamilton, *Hamilton,* VI, 523; *Documents Relating to the Presidential Election in the Year 1801,* pp. 5–6, 9–10; A. J. Dallas to Gallatin, February 15, 1801; John Beckley to Gallatin, February 15, 1801, Gallatin MSS., LC; Sedgwick to Theodore Sedgwick, Jr., February 16, 1801, Sedgwick MSS., MHS; Adams, *Gallatin,* p. 267.

[56] Bemis, *John Quincy Adams and the Foundations of American Foreign Policy,* pp. 106–107; A. J. Dallas to Gallatin, May 21, 1801, Gallatin MSS., NYHS; Adams, *Gallatin,* p. 260; Morrison, *Otis,* I, 177–178; Channing, *History,* IV, 233–237; Cunningham, *Jeffersonian Republicans,* 246–248.

[57] King, *Rufus King,* III, May 7, 1800; Stephen Higginson to Pickering, April 16, 1800, Pickering MSS., MHS; *Report of the American Historical Association for 1896,* I, 836.

The Federalists were not wholly unprepared for the impending ordeal. In January, 1801, they had succeeded in converting the national judiciary, the only branch of the government that would remain in Federalist hands after March 4, 1801, into a bastion of defense against the victorious democrats. The Judiciary Act of 1801, passed in the closing weeks of the session, created twenty-three new judicial officers and completely reorganized the judicial system. The jurisdiction of the Circuit Courts was extended to include cognizance of debts of $400 or more and three judges were appointed to each of the six Circuit Courts, except one which had only one judge. The Supreme Court was reduced to five members and the Justices were relieved of the necessity of riding circuit the length and breadth of the United States: they could now settle down in Washington where a small chamber in a basement had been allotted them.[58]

President Adams barely had time before surrendering the seals of office to sign the commissions of these and other newly created judicial officers—hence the name bestowed upon them of "Midnight Judges."[59] But the most important appointment made by Adams at the end of his administration was the designation of John Marshall as Chief Justice of the Supreme Court. Adams did not list this action among the great achievements of his career, but it deserved to rank as the most signal service he rendered to the eventual triumph of the Federalist concept of sacrosanct property rights protected by a powerful central government.[60]

Early in the morning of March 4, 1801, without tarrying for the inauguration of Thomas Jefferson, John Adams left Washington "car-

[58] Warren, *Supreme Court*, I, 185–186, 193, 205; Wright, *Growth of American Constitutional Law*, p. 33; Gibbs, *Memoirs*, II, 316; Lodge, *Hamilton*, VIII, 331–332; *Journal of Economic History*, III (November, 1946), p. 212.

[59] Contrary to popular belief, Adams did not stay up until midnight in order to sign these commissions. If he remained at his desk until that hour, it was because he planned to make an early start the next morning for Massachusetts. There was no difficulty in signing the commissions of the newly created Justices; much more time-consuming were the commissions of the justices of the peace created by the Act of 1801. Jefferson later complained that these appointments placed before him the alternative "either to execute the government by my enemies, whose study it would be to thwart and defeat all my measures, or to incur the odium of such numerous removals from office, as might bear me down." Warren, *Supreme Court*, I, 188; *Journal of Economic History* (November, 1946), p. 212; Ford, *Jefferson*, VII, February 14, 1801; IX, 297.

[60] Morison, *Otis*, I, 202; J. C. Hamilton, *Hamilton*, VI, 510–511; Warren, *Supreme Court*, I, 185–186, 188; Crosskey, *Politics and the Constitution*, II, 759; Morris, *Gouverneur Morris*, II, 405.

rying with him, as the only acknowledgment of his past services, the privilege of receiving his letters free of postage for the remainder of his life." Later in the day he was seen passing through New York "like a shot" on his way to Boston. Although Adams could plead the serious illness of his wife in justification of this haste, his conduct left no doubt that the wounds he had suffered in the political wars had not healed. He never forgave Hamilton; and not until thirteen years later did he resume his correspondence with Thomas Jefferson.[61]

In one respect, the Federalist prophets of doom were proved right: no member of that party ever again offered serious contention for the Presidency. The election of 1800 forged the Virginia-New York axis under which the "Virginia dynasty" of Presidents dominated American politics. Nor was the Federalists' distrust of the people and their ideal of government by the wise, the rich, and the good ever again openly espoused by an American political party. The fate of the Federalists served as a warning to all politicians who came after them. John Marshall praised "those few real patriots who love the people well enough to tell them the truth," but the Federalists demonstrated that the shortest way to political oblivion was to tell the people "truths" that they did not want to hear.

The Federalists' downfall was owing primarily to their self-defeating political philosophy, to their ineptness as politicians, and to the vindictiveness with which, in their hour of triumph, they pursued their political enemies. By scorning the popular intelligence and behaving as though politics was a matter of preaching wisdom to the untutored masses, the Federalists condemned themselves not only to defeat in the election of 1800 but to extinction as a party. As Noah Webster said, "they have attempted to resist the force of current public opinion, instead of falling into the current with a view to direct it. In this they have manifested more integrity than address." Confronted by an opposition which extolled the wisdom of the people, appealed to the dominant economic and social groups of the population, and exerted itself to organize the forces of resistance on a national scale, the Federalists were helpless.[62]

[61] Pickering, *Review of the Adams-Cunningham Correspondence*, p. 51; Robert Troup to Rufus King, March 23, 1801, King MSS., NYHS; McRee, *James Iredell*, II, 547.

[62] Warfel, *Noah Webster*, p. 263; Bassett, *Federalist System*, pp. 295–296.

After 1800, the remnants of the party took refuge in the states, where they continued to wage a rearguard action against the enemy. But even in New England, Federalism stood upon steadily contracting ground: New Hampshire and Rhode Island fell to the Republicans and they made heavy inroads in Massachusetts and Connecticut. Thus the peril of two sectional parties looking down each other's throats across Mason and Dixon's line was averted. The Republican party became a national party; only the Federalists upheld the cause of sectionalism. But in the end the Federalists became a party in search of a section.

From the viewpoint of the defeated Federalists, the American experiment in free government, after ten years of trial, had ended in tragedy. It was a tragedy because "the education, the talents, the virtues, and the property of the country" had been laid prostrate before ignorance and demagoguery.[63] And yet this dispirited little band of gentlemen had wrought better than they knew. They had made a parchment into a workable instrument of government; they had proved themselves to be conscientious, honest, and efficient administrators; they had proved that republicanism was compatible with stability; they had established procedures that even their enemies adopted; and they had demonstrated that the powers of the Federal government could be made to promote the general welfare. Nor did the heritage of Federalism wholly disappear: devotion to the Union, respect for property rights, and the attitude of mind that distrusts those who promise too much too soon became integral parts of the American philosophy. The measure of Federalism's achievement was best summed up in its epitaph: "It found America disunited, poor, insolvent, weak, discontented and wretched. It hath left her united, wealthy, respectable, strong, happy and prosperous."[64]

---

[63] Adams, *John Adams*, IX, 582.

[64] A. B. Hart (ed.), *American History Told by Contemporaries* (New York, 1906), III, 343; John A. Krout, "Alexander Hamilton's Place in the Founding of the Nation," *Proceedings of the American Philosophical Society*, Vol. 102, No. 2 (April, 1958), pp. 124–128.

Bibliography

Bibliographies

The *Harvard Guide to American History,* compiled by Paul H. Buck, Oscar Handlin, Frederick Merk, Samuel Eliot Morison, Arthur M. Schlesinger, and Arthur M. Schlesinger, Jr. (Cambridge, Mass., 1954), has superseded all previous publications of this kind. *Writings on American History,* edited since 1906 by Grace G. Griffin, contains an annual survey of printed articles, books, and documents. A guide to printed diaries and journals is found in William Matthews (ed.), *American Diaries: an Annotated Bibliography . . . to the Year 1861* (Berkeley, 1945). The most useful guide to diplomatic history is Samuel F. Bemis and Grace Gardner Griffin, *Guide to the Diplomatic History of the United States, 1775–1921* (Washington, 1935).

Manuscripts

The period 1789 to 1801 is particularly rich in manuscript materials. While most of the letters written by Washington have been printed by John C. Fitzpatrick, *The Writings of George Washington* (39 vols., Washington, 1931–44), the bulk of the letters written to Washington, except for the selection published by Jared Sparks (ed.), *Correspondence of the American Revolution: Being Letters of Eminent Men to George Washington* (4 vols., Boston, 1853), is available only in manuscript form. The principal depository of these letters is the Library of Congress, which also houses the Hamilton, Madison, and Jefferson MSS. among many other notable collections.

MANUSCRIPT SOURCES

Adams, Henry. Transcripts of Correspondence of the British Ministers in the United States, 1789–1901. Library of Congress.

Adams, John. Massachusetts Historical Society.

Brackenridge, Hugh Henry. Library of Congress.

Clinton, De Witt. Columbia University.

Craigie, Andrew. American Antiquarian Society.

280 THE FEDERALIST ERA

Duer, William. New-York Historical Society.
Emmet. New York Public Library.
Etting. Historical Society of Pennsylvania.
Gallatin, Albert. New-York Historical Society.
Gerry, Elbridge. Library of Congress.
Hamilton, Alexander. Library of Congress; Columbia University.
Harper, Robert Goodloe. Library of Congress.
Irvine, William. Historical Society of Pennsylvania.
Jay, John. Columbia University.
Jefferson, Thomas. Library of Congress; Massachusetts Historical Society; University of Virginia.
King, Rufus. New York Public Library.
Knox, Henry. Massachusetts Historical Society.
Livingston, Edward. New-York Historical Society.
Livingston, R. R. New-York Historical Society.
McHenry, James. Library of Congress.
Madison, James. Library of Congress.
Marshall, John. Library of Congress.
Monroe, James. Library of Congress.
Morris, Gouverneur. Columbia University; Library of Congress.
Nicholson, Joseph N. Library of Congress.
Peters, Richard. Historical Society of Pennsylvania.
Pickering, Timothy. Massachusetts Historical Society.
Plumer, William. Autobiography, Library of Congress.
Rush, Benjamin. Library Company of Pennsylvania.
Sedgwick, Theodore. Massachusetts Historical Society.
Smith, William L. Library of Congress.
Trumbull, Jonathan. Connecticut Historical Society.
Wadsworth, Jeremiah. Connecticut Historical Society.
Wallace. Historical Society of Pennsylvania.
Washington, George. Library of Congress.
Wayne, Anthony. Historical Society of Pennsylvania.
Wilson, James. Historical Society of Pennsylvania.
Wolcott, Oliver. Connecticut Historical Society.

Collections of Documents

Henry Adams (ed.), *Documents Relating to New England Federalism, 1800–1815* (Boston, 1877), consists largely of letters written by New England Federalists. This collection affords insights into the minds of the leaders of New England Federalism after the party had begun the decline which ended in the Hartford Convention. Important official documents are found in *American State Papers: Foreign Affairs, Indian Affairs, and Finance* (Washington, 1832–34); Clarence E. Carter (ed.), *The Territorial Papers of the* *United States* (20 vols., Washington, 1934); Miller Hunter (ed.), *Treaties* *and Other International Acts of the United States* (8 vols., Washington, 1931); and J. D. Richardson (ed.), *Compilation of the Messages and Papers* *of the Presidents, 1789–1897* (10 vols., Washington, 1907). Legal and constitutional cases are best studied in A. J. Dallas (ed.), *Reports of Cases in* *the Courts of the United States and Pennsylvania, 1790–1800* (3 vols., numerous editions); and Francis Wharton (ed.), *State Trials of the United States* *During the Administrations of Washington and Adams* (Philadelphia, 1849). The debates in Congress are reported by Joseph Gales (comp.), *Debates and* *Proceedings in the Congress of the United States, 1789–1824* (42 vols., Washington, 1834–56).

Newspapers

Early in the period 1789–1801, the newspapers assumed a partisan tone. On the Federalist side, the most important newspaper was the *Gazette of* *the United States,* edited by John Fenno. The New York *Minerva,* edited by Noah Webster, and *Porcupine's Gazette,* edited by William Cobbett, were stanchly Federalist. The Republican point of view is exemplified in the *National Gazette,* edited by Philip Freneau, and the *General Advertiser,* edited by Benjamin Bache.

The most complete collections of newspapers are found in the Library of Congress, the New York Historical Society, the Historical Society of Pennsylvania, the Massachusetts Historical Society, the Library Company of Philadelphia, the New York Public Library, and the American Antiquarian Society.

Clarence L. Brigham, *History and Bibliography of American Newspapers,* *1690–1820* (2 vols., Worcester, Mass., 1947), is indispensable for determining the location of the various newspapers.

Travelers' Accounts

A considerable number of travelers, mostly French and British, visited the United States during the Federalist Era and published books recounting their journeys and their impressions of the new Republic. Of the British travelers, the most important are John Davis, *Travels of Four Years and a Half in* *the United States of America during 1798, 1799, 1800, 1801, and 1802* (Bristol, 1803); Henry Wansey, *An Excursion in the United States of North* *America in 1794* (Salisbury, 1798); and Isaac Weld, Jr., *Travels Through the* *States of North America* (2 vols., London, 1807). Allan Nevins has edited *American Social History as Recorded by British Travelers* (New York, 1948), which contains excerpts from the books of these and other British observers of the American scene. French travelers are represented by Kenneth and Anna M. Roberts (trans.), *Moreau de St. Méry's American Journal* (Boston,

1948); the Duc de la Rochefoucauld-Liancourt, *Travels Through the United States of North America* (2 vols., London, 1799); and C. F. Volney, *A View of the Soil and Climate of the United States* (Philadelphia, 1804).

Not a few Americans left records of their travels, the most important of whom are John Drayton, *Letters Written During a Tour of America* (Charleston, 1794), and Timothy Dwight, *Travels in New England and New York* (4 vols., New Haven, 1821–22).

General Histories Relating to the Federalist Era

Most of the historical and biographical writing about this period is distinguished by extreme partisanship. Claude G. Bowers, *Jefferson and Hamilton: The Struggle for Democracy in America* (Boston, 1925), reads like a campaign document for Jefferson and for all subsequent Democratic candidates for the Presidency. Edward Channing, *History of the United States* (6 vols., New York, 1905–25), is a well-balanced account, full of the insights for which Channing is famous. The American Whig historians of the nineteenth century found much to praise in Federalism and much to condemn in Jeffersonianism. Richard Hildreth, *The History of the United States* (6 vols., 1849–56), is a good example of the neo-Federalist school of historical writing; it is also an example of sound scholarship. John A. Krout and Dixon Ryan Fox, *The Completion of Independence, 1790–1830* (New York, 1944), is excellent for social and intellectual developments during this period. John B. McMaster, *A History of the Republic of the United States* (8 vols., New York, 1883–1913), is valuable chiefly for the numerous quotations from contemporary newspapers. John Dos Passos, *The Men Who Made the Nation* (New York, 1957), contains nothing fresh or original. Nathan Schachner, *The Founding Fathers* (New York, 1954), while more fair to the Federalists than is Bowers or Dos Passos, is based largely upon the debates in Congress, most of which are reported in overwhelming detail.

Collected Works

With some notable exceptions, the collected works of the statesmen of the Federalist Era leave much to be desired upon the score of inclusiveness. Better days are in store, however, for students of this period. The letters and official papers of Alexander Hamilton are in the process of being edited by a staff of experts at Columbia University. New editions of the writings of John Adams, John Quincy Adams, John Jay, and James Madison are in progress, and the magnificent edition of Jefferson's writings by Julian C. Boyd is well advanced.

Charles Francis Adams has edited the *Memoirs of John Quincy Adams* (12 vols., Philadelphia, 1874–77), to which it is essential to add Worthington C. Ford (ed.), *The Writings of John Quincy Adams* (7 vols., New York,

1917). For John Adams, several collections must be consulted: Charles Francis Adams (ed.), *The Works of John Adams* (10 vols., Boston, 1850–56); Charles Francis Adams (ed.), *Letters of John Adams Addressed to His Wife* (2 vols., Boston, 1841); *Correspondence Between the Honorable John Adams . . . and William Cunningham* (Boston, 1823); Worthington C. Ford (ed.), *Statesman and Friend: Correspondence of John Adams with Benjamin Waterhouse, 1784–1822* (Boston, 1927); Alexander Biddle (ed.), *Old Family Letters* (Philadelphia, 1892); Lester J. Cappon (ed.), *The Adams-Jefferson Letters* (2 vols., Chapel Hill, 1959); and Worthington C. Ford (ed.), *Warren-Adams Letters,* Collections of the Massachusetts Historical Society, LXXII–LXXIII (2 vols., Boston, 1917–25). Among the most interesting of the letters written during this period are those found in Charles Francis Adams (ed.), *Letters of Mrs. Adams, Wife of John Adams* (Boston, 1848), and Stewart Mitchell, *New Letters of Abigail Adams* (Boston, 1947). Since Seth Adams edited *The Works of Fisher Ames* (2 vols., Boston, 1854), few new Ames letters have come to light. Elizabeth Donnan has edited the *Papers of James A. Bayard, 1796–1815,* Report of the American Historical Association for 1913, II (Washington, 1914), which contain important material relating to the election of Thomas Jefferson to the Presidency. There is no collection of Burr's correspondence, but Worthington C. Ford made a start in that direction by editing *Some Papers of Aaron Burr* in the Proceedings of the Massachusetts Historical Series, New Series, 29 (Boston, 1919).

Henry Adams (ed.), *The Writings of Albert Gallatin* (3 vols., Philadelphia, 1879), contains only a fraction of the Gallatin MSS. in the New-York Historical Society. Henry Cabot Lodge (ed.), *The Works of Alexander Hamilton* (12 vols., New York, 1904), and John C. Hamilton (ed.), *The Works of Alexander Hamilton* (7 vols., New York, 1850–51), are not complete; Lodge even omitted documents printed by John C. Hamilton. Richard B. Morris (ed.), *Alexander Hamilton and the Founding of the Nation* (New York, 1957), incorporates new as well as old material and contains an excellent summary of Hamilton's thought and career. J. Franklin Jameson (ed.), *Letters of Stephen Higginson, 1783–1804,* Report of the American Historical Association for 1897 (Washington, 1898), conveys the full flavor of the New England Federalist mind. Henry P. Johnston (ed.), *The Correspondence and Public Papers of John Jay* (4 vols., New York, 1890–93), is good as far as it goes, but the accession of the Jay Papers by Columbia University, supplemented by photocopies of correspondence in other repositories both here and abroad, makes a new edition of Jay's writings imperative.

Thomas Jefferson has been well served by Julian Boyd (ed.), *Papers of Thomas Jefferson* (Princeton, 1950–58). Of this monumental work, fifteen volumes have been issued, reaching to 1789. In time, this edition of Jefferson's writings (which has the added merit of containing the letters written to Jefferson) will entirely supersede the earlier collections of Jefferson's works, notably Paul Leicester Ford (ed.), *Writings of Thomas Jefferson* (10 vols., New York, 1892–99); C. F. Jenkins (ed.), *Jefferson's Germantown Letters* (Philadelphia, 1906); and the *Jefferson Papers* in the Collections of the Massachusetts Historical Society, Seventh Series, I (1900). Charles R. King, *The Life and Correspondence of Rufus King* (6 vols., New York, 1895), contains many letters written to King by Federalist leaders, but it is not wholly satisfactory as an edition of King's writings. James C. Ballach has edited an excellent edition of *The Letters of Richard Henry Lee* (2 vols., New York, 1911–14). The *James McHenry Letters* in the Publications of the Southern History Association, 9 (1905) ought to be supplemented by Bernard C. Steiner, *The Life and Correspondence of James McHenry* (Cleveland, 1907). Gaillard Hunt (ed.), *The Writings of James Madison* (9 vols., New York, 1900–1910), needs to be supplemented by new Madison material, much of which is still unavailable in print. This shortcoming is likewise apparent in Stanislaus Murray Hamilton, *The Writings of James Monroe* (9 vols., New York, 1900–1910), although Worthington C. Ford (ed.) has filled part of this gap in the *Letters of James Monroe,* Proceedings of the Massachusetts Historical Society, 42 (Boston, 1909). Anne C. Morris, *Diary and Letters of Gouverneur Morris* (2 vols., New York, 1888), prints only part of the materials found in the Gouverneur Morris MSS. in the Library of Congress. Worthington C. Ford (ed.), *Letters of William Vans Murray to John Quincy Adams, 1797–1803,* Annual Report of the American Historical Association for 1912 (Washington, 1913), while incomplete as regards Murray's whole correspondence, is essential for an understanding of John Adams's efforts to make peace with France in 1799–1800. Philip S. Foner (ed.), *The Complete Writings of Thomas Paine* (2 vols., New York, 1945), is eminently satisfactory.

Lyman H. Butterfield (ed.), *The Letters of Benjamin Rush* (2 vols., Princeton, 1951), is a model of editorship. William H. Smith (ed.), *The St. Clair Papers: Life and Public Services of Arthur St. Clair* (2 vols., Cincinnati, 1882), is particularly important for the light it casts upon western affairs. Henry M. Wagstaff (ed.), *The Papers of John Steele* (2 vols., Raleigh, 1924), contains valuable letters relating to the struggle between Federalists and Republicans in the South, a subject to which Ulrich B. Phillips (ed.), "South Carolina Federalist Correspondence, 1789–1797," *American Historical Review,* XIV (1909), makes a contribution of the first order. An important western leader is given merited attention by Beverly Bond (ed.), *The Correspondence of John Cleves Symmes* (New York, 1926). There is no edition of the complete writings of John Taylor; the most extensive collection is William E. Dodd (ed.), *Letters of John Taylor,* John P. Branch Historical

Papers of Randolph-Macon College, II (Richmond, 1903). By far the best edition of George Washington's writings is John C. Fitzpatrick (ed.), *The Writings of George Washington* (39 vols., Washington, 1931–44). Worthington C. Ford (ed.), *The Correspondence and Journals of Samuel Blackley Webb* (3 vols., New York, 1892), is an interesting collection of political correspondence of the period. For Noah Webster, several sources must be consulted: Noah Webster, *A Collection of Papers on Political, Literary and Moral Subjects* (New York, 1943); Emily Skeel and Emily Ford (eds.), *Notes on the Life of Noah Webster* (2 vols., New York, 1912); and Grenville H. Norcross, *Letters of Noah Webster, 1796–1840,* Proceedings of the Massachusetts Historical Society, 43 (1909). The great collection of documents relating to the Federalist period, and which serves as the starting point of any political study, is George Gibbs (ed.), *Memoirs of the Administrations of Washington and John Adams, Edited from the Papers of Oliver Wolcott* (2 vols., New York, 1846).

Memoirs and Journals

Charles Biddle, *Autobiography* (Philadelphia, 1883), and Alexander Graydon, *Memoirs of a Life Chiefly Passed in Pennsylvania Within the Last Sixty Years* (Harrisburg, 1811), complement each other inasmuch as both deal largely with the Philadelphia scene during the Federalist Era. Edward S. Maclay (ed.), *The Journal of William Maclay* (New York, 1890), must be used with caution; Maclay was bitterly hostile to Hamilton and the Federalist party in general. Douglass Adair (ed.), *James Madison's Autobiography,* William and Mary Quarterly, Third Series, II (1945), is an essential supplement to Madison's letters. Stuart Gerry Brown (ed.), *The Autobiography of James Monroe* (Syracuse, 1959), is a dull book which is mostly concerned with Monroe's diplomatic missions to France. Timothy Pickering, *A Review of the Correspondence Between John Adams and William Cunningham* (Salem, 1824), provides a running commentary upon events as seen through the eyes of President Adams's waspish-tempered Secretary of State. G. W. Corner (ed.), *The Autobiography of Benjamin Rush* (Princeton, 1948), reveals the many-sided interests of this stalwart Republican politician, physician, and social reformer. Franklin B. Dexter (ed.), *The Literary Diary of Ezra Stiles* (3 vols., New York, 1901), is required reading for a comprehension of the intellectual life of the period; Theodore Sizer (ed.), *The Autobiography of Colonel John Trumbull* (New Haven, 1953), deals in part with the same intellectual milieu in which Stiles flourished. Winslow C. Watson (ed.), *Men and Times of the Revolution: or Memoirs of Elkanah Watson* (New York, 1856), contains interesting sidelights upon the public men of the Federalist Era. James Wilkinson, *Memoirs of My Own Times* (3 vols.,

Philadelphia, 1816), ought to be approached with skepticism; Wilkinson was
a past master of chicanery and duplicity.

Biography

The best biography of John Adams is Gilbert Chinard, *Honest John Adams*
(Boston, 1933). The *Life of John Adams*, by Charles Francis Adams (Boston,
1856), reflects the filial devotion of the grandson, but is based upon his
edition of the *Works* of John Adams. Essential to an understanding of Adams's
philosophy is Zoltan Haraszti, *John Adams and the Prophets of Progress*
(Cambridge, Mass., 1952).

Aaron Burr has been made the subject of several biographies, most of
which are highly partisan in tone. The best and most balanced of the lot is
Nathan Schachner, *Aaron Burr* (New York, 1937). Matthew L. Davis, author
of *Memoirs of Aaron Burr with Miscellaneous Selections from His Correspondence* (2 vols., New York, 1836–37), was a friend of Burr. His book
contains many interesting sidelights upon Burr's career, but no biographer has
wholly succeeded in penetrating the mask Burr habitually presented to the
world. James Parton, *The Life and Times of Aaron Burr* (New York, 1858),
was one of the ablest practitioners of the art of biography in the United
States. Less satisfactory, partly because of its journalistic flavor, is S. H.
Wandell and Meade Minnigerode, *Aaron Burr* (2 vols., New York, 1925).

Henry Cabot Lodge's *Alexander Hamilton* (Boston, 1882) represents the
Republican apotheosis of Hamilton as an apostle of strong government, sound
finance, and big business. Nathan Schachner, *Alexander Hamilton* (New
York, 1946), presents a more balanced appraisal of Hamilton, but the book
is marred by frequent errors of fact. The definitive study, of which the first
volume, *Alexander Hamilton: Youth to Maturity* (New York, 1957), has
already appeared, is by Broadus Mitchell. John C. Miller, *Alexander Hamilton, Portrait in Paradox* (New York, 1959), presents Hamilton as a man
bent upon creating an active, efficient, and all-pervasive national government.

Dumas Malone, *Jefferson and the Rights of Man* (Boston, 1951), is the
second volume of a projected definitive biography of Jefferson. Although it
brings Jefferson only to 1793, it makes abundantly clear the reasons for his
breach with Hamilton and the founding of a party in opposition to the
policies of the Secretary of the Treasury. Francis W. Hirst, *Life and Letters
of Thomas Jefferson* (New York, 1926), is valuable for the many insights
it offers to Jefferson's character. Nathan Schachner, *Thomas Jefferson: A
Biography* (2 vols., New York, 1951), emphasizes Jefferson's political career
rather than his philosophy. Of the shorter biographies, the best is Gilbert
Chinard, *Thomas Jefferson: The Apostle of Americanism* (Boston, 1929).

James Madison has inspired several multivolume biographies, but there is
no brief biography that does him justice. William C. Rives, *History of the*

Life and Times of James Madison (3 vols., Boston, 1859–68), has been displaced as the authoritative life by Irving Brant, *James Madison* (5 vols., Indianapolis, 1948–56). This is a "life-and-times" biography and sometimes the times tend to take precedence over the life. Mr. Brant so vigorously champions Madison against his critics that the reader is left with the impression that Madison could do no wrong.

Albert J. Beveridge, *The Life of John Marshall* (4 vols., Boston, 1916–19), is one of the classics of American biography. There is no short biography that adequately covers all the aspects of Marshall's career; Edward S. Corwin, *John Marshall and the Constitution* (New York, 1919), is largely devoted to a study of his constitutional opinions.

Douglas Southall Freeman did not live to complete his monumental biography of Washington. The seventh and concluding volume, *George Washington: First in Peace* (New York, 1957), which deals with the period 1793–99, has been ably written in the Freeman manner by two of his research assistants, John Alexander Carroll and Mary Wells Ashworth. It was awarded the Pulitzer Prize in 1958. G. W. Stephenson and W. H. Dunn, *George Washington* (2 vols., New York, 1940), brings Washington into sharper focus than does the discursive, life-and-times method of Freeman. Paul Leicester Ford, *The True George Washington* (Philadelphia, 1896), and J. C. Fitzpatrick, *George Washington Himself* (Indianapolis, 1933), attempt to present Washington as a human being. The best study of this kind is Samuel Eliot Morison, "The Young Man Washington," in *By Land and By Sea* (New York, 1953). Marcus Cunliffe, *George Washington: Man and Monument* (Boston, 1958), is more concerned in demolishing the monument than in creating the image of the man.

Of the figures of the second rank who played a part in the events treated in this book, the following biographies are particularly noteworthy. Although Jane J. Boudinot, *The Life, Public Services, Addresses and Letters of Elias Boudinot* (Boston, 1896), contains important source material, as a biographical study it has been superseded by G. A. Boyd, *Elias Boudinot* (Princeton, 1952). Claude M. Newlin, *The Life and Writings of Hugh Henry Brackenridge* (Princeton, 1932), is scholarly and judicious. Henry Cabot Lodge, *Life and Letters of George Cabot* (Boston, 1877), is vigorously Federalist in tone and is chiefly valuable for the letters to and from Cabot which it contains. Harold Hutcheson, *Tench Coxe* (Baltimore, 1938), suffers from the fact that Mr. Hutcheson was unable to gain access to the Tench Coxe MSS. James Alton James, *The Life of George Rogers Clark* (Chicago, 1928), is a sympathetic portrayal of that tragic hero. The career of Alexander J. Dallas, one of the leading Pennsylvania Republicans, has been treated by George M. Dallas in the *Life and Writings of Alexander J. Dallas* (Philadelphia, 1871). This partisan work has been superseded by Raymond

Walters, Jr.'s excellent book, *Alexander James Dallas* (Philadelphia, 1943). William Garrett Brown, *The Life of Oliver Ellsworth* (New York, 1905), is a barely satisfactory account of this Federalist judge and diplomat. Bernard Fay in *The Two Franklins* (Boston, 1933) has written the best study we have of Benjamin Bache, Benjamin Franklin's grandson. Philip Freneau is given lively treatment by Lewis Leary in *That Rascal Freneau* (New Brunswick, 1941). James T. Austin, *The Life of Elbridge Gerry* (2 vols., Boston, 1827–29), offers important source material relating to Gerry, but the reader in search of a readable account of that worthy can do no better than Samuel Eliot Morison's brief but delightful sketch, "Elbridge Gerry, Gentleman-Democrat," in *By Land and By Sea* (New York, 1953). William Wirt Henry's *Patrick Henry, Life, Correspondence and Speeches* (3 vols., New York, 1891) has long remained the standard account. Important letters are found in Thomas Wentworth Higginson, *Life and Times of Stephen Higginson* (Boston, 1907); Francis L. Humphreys, *Life and Times of David Humphreys* (2 vols., New York, 1917); and Griffith J. McRee, *Life and Correspondence of James Iredell* (2 vols., New York, 1852). William Jay, *The Life of John Jay* (New York, 1833), has been superseded by Frank Monaghan's excellent study, *John Jay: Defender of Liberty* (New York, 1935). Charles R. King, *The Life and Correspondence of Rufus King* (6 vols., New York, 1895), contains a vast store of letters relating to the Federalist Era. Noah Brooks's biography, *Henry Knox* (New York, 1900), does not make full use of the Knox MSS.; Francis Frake, *Life and Correspondence of Henry Knox* (Boston, 1873), suffers from the same shortcoming. Charles Haven Hunt, *Life of Edward Livingston* (New York, 1864), has been displaced as the standard life by W. B. Hatcher, *Edward Livingston* (University, La., 1940). William E. Dodd, *Life of Nathaniel Macon* (Raleigh, 1903), is one of the better biographies of the Republican leaders of the South. Bernard C. Steiner, *The Life and Correspondence of James McHenry* (Cleveland, 1907), is essential for an understanding of Alexander Hamilton's relations with members of President Adams's cabinet and for the conduct of the quasi-war with France. William S. Robertson, *The Life of Miranda* (2 vols., Chapel Hill, 1929), sheds light upon the plans of the Federalist war party in 1798–99. Monroe is adequately treated in W. P. Cresson, *James Monroe* (Chapel Hill, 1946). Paul A. Wallace has added materially to our knowledge of Pennsylvania politics in *The Muhlenbergs of Pennsylvania* (Philadelphia, 1943). Samuel Eliot Morison, *The Life and Letters of Harrison Gray Otis, Federalist* (2 vols., Boston, 1913), is the best biography we have of a New England Federalist leader. Octavius Pickering and Charles W. Upham, *The Life of Timothy Pickering* (4 vols., Boston, 1867–73), is more valuable as a compilation of letters than as a contribution to biography. M. D. Conway, *Omitted Chapters of History, Disclosed in the*

Life and Papers of Edmund Randolph (New York, 1888), contains important source material, but leaves many questions concerning Randolph unanswered. William Cabell Bruce, *John Randolph of Roanoke* (2 vols., New York, 1922), is scholarly but fails to bring Randolph's singular personality into sharp relief. Richard Barry, *Mr. Rutledge of South Carolina* (New York, 1942), is indispensable for an understanding of South Carolina politics. H. H. Simms, *Life of John Taylor* (Richmond, 1932), provides a good introduction to the "Philosopher of Jeffersonian Republicanism." Henry T. Wildes, *Anthony Wayne* (New York, 1941); James R. Jacobs, *Tarnished Warrior: Major General James Wilkinson* (New York, 1938); and Thomas R. Hay and Morris R. Werner, *The Admirable Trumpeter: A Biography of General James Wilkinson* (New York, 1941), are good studies of military leaders. The best biography of James Wilson is Charles Page Smith, *James Wilson, Founding Father: 1742–98* (Raleigh, 1956).

The Rise of Political Parties

Within recent years, the emergence of the first national political parties has attracted the attention of historians and political scientists. Wilfred E. Binkley, *American Political Parties* (New York, 1943), ably surveys the entire period of American history. Stuart Gerry Brown, *The First Republicans* (New York, 1943), is a penetrating study of the philosophy of the leaders of the Republican-Democratic party. Edward Channing, *Washington and Parties, 1789–97,* in Proceedings of the Massachusetts Historical Society, 47 (Boston, 1914), provides an excellent introduction to the subject. Joseph Charles, *The Origins of the American Party System* (Williamsburg, 1956), is so hostile to the Federalists that it reads like a political tract of the 1790's. The best study of the early history of the Republican party is Noble E. Cunningham, Jr., *The Jeffersonian Republicans: The Formation of Party Organization, 1789–1801* (Chapel Hill, 1957). Essential to an understanding of the Federalist party is Manning J. Dauer, *The Adams Federalists* (Baltimore, 1953). Louise B. Dunbar, *A Study of 'Monarchical Tendencies' in the United States from 1776 to 1801* (Urbana, Ill., 1922), effectively disposes of the charge that the Federalists were monarchists. Bernard Fay, "Early Party Machinery in the United States in the Election of 1796," *Pennsylvania Magazine of History and Biography,* LX (1936), brings to light the activities of one of the most successful of the Republican party managers, John Beckley, who is the subject of Noble E. Cunningham's essay, "John Beckley: An Early American Party Manager," *William and Mary Quarterly,* III Series, XIII (1956), and who is also treated by Philip M. Marsh in "John Beckley, Mystery Man of the Early Jeffersonians," *Pennsylvania Magazine of History and Biography,* LXIII (1939). Gilbert L. Lycan, "Alexander Hamilton and the North Carolina Federalists," *North Carolina Historical Re-*

view, XXV (1948), reveals the causes of the breakdown of the Federalist party in the South. Richard P. McCormick, *The History of Voting in New Jersey: A Study of the Development of Election Machinery, 1664–1911* (New Brunswick, 1953), is an important contribution to the history of electioneering. William Miller, "First Fruits of Republican Organization: Political Aspects of the Congressional Elections of 1794," *Pennsylvania Magazine of History and Biography,* LXII (1938), while chiefly concerned with the congressional elections of 1794 in New York City, identifies the Democratic Societies with the Republican party. Edgar Eugene Robinson, *The Evolution of American Political Parties* (New York, 1924), is good for political parties as a whole. The political quarrels of the 1790's sometimes divided families: Charles Warren, *Jacobin and Junto: or Early American Politics as Viewed in the Diary of Dr. Nathaniel Ames, 1758–1822* (Cambridge, Mass., 1931), presents the case of two brothers, Nathaniel and Fisher Ames, who took wholly opposite positions upon every important political question of the decade. Finally, Leonard D. White, in *The Federalists: A Study in Administrative History* (New York, 1948), and *The Republicans* (New York, 1950), has made a contribution of fundamental importance to the administrative side of political history.

Relations with Foreign Powers, 1789–1801

No aspect of this period has been treated more fully than have the foreign relations of the United States. Because of the large amount of material relating to this subject, it is necessary to divide the bibliography into three sections.

RELATIONS WITH GREAT BRITAIN

Ephraim D. Adams, *The Influence of Grenville on Pitt's Foreign Policy, 1789–1798* (Washington, 1904), is an important study based upon source material in British archives. The authoritative book on Jay's Treaty is Samuel F. Bemis, *Jay's Treaty: A Study in Commerce and Diplomacy* (New York, 1923). Professor Bemis's conclusion that Hamilton's indiscretion was responsible for some of the more onerous features of Jay's Treaty does not stand up under close scrutiny. His *John Quincy Adams and the Foundations of American Foreign Policy* (New York, 1949) is one of the best books dealing with the career of an American diplomat; and "The London Mission of Thomas Pinckney, 1792–96," *American Historical Review,* XXVII (1923), is excellent for this period of Anglo-American relations. Herbert W. Briggs, *The Doctrine of Continuous Voyage* (Baltimore, 1926), explores the intricacies of this technical subject. For a survey of the period, Alfred L. Burt, *The United States, Great Britain and British North America, 1783–1812* (New Haven, 1940), is useful. Anna C. Clauder, *American Commerce as Affected by the Wars of the French Revolution, 1793–1810* (Philadelphia,

1932), contains relevant statistical information. W. C. Ford (ed.), "Edmund Randolph on the British Treaty, 1795," *American Historical Review,* XII (1907), consists of documents relating to Jay's Treaty. Holden Furber, "The Beginnings of American Trade with India, 1784–1812," *New England Quarterly,* XI (1938), reveals how this trade contributed to American prosperity and why it was condoned by the British. Gerald S. Graham, *Sea Power and British North America, 1783–1820* (Cambridge, Mass., 1941), relates British policy toward the United States with imperial concerns. Ralston Hayden, *The Senate and Treaties, 1789–1817* (New York, 1920), is particularly valuable for its discussion of the struggle over Jay's Treaty in the House of Representatives. J. Franklin Jameson (ed.), *Letters of Phineas Bond, British Consul at Philadelphia to the Foreign Office of Great Britain, 1790–94,* Report of the American Historical Association for 1897 (Washington, 1898), contains a running commentary upon Anglo-American relations and important information on developments in the United States, particularly those relating to commerce and manufacturing. Louise P. Kellogg, *The British Regime in Wisconsin and the Northwest* (Madison, Wis., 1935), treats of an area where relations between the United States and Great Britain were strained almost to the breaking point. Bernard Mayo (ed.), *Instructions to the British Ministers to the United States,* Annual Report of the American Historical Association for 1936, III (Washington, 1941), is indispensable for an understanding of British policy toward the United States. Samuel Eliot Morison, *The Maritime History of Massachusetts, 1783–1860* (Cambridge, Mass., 1921), is a classic of American historiography. Bradford Perkins, *The First Rapprochement: England and the United States, 1795–1805* (Philadelphia, 1953), is temperate, judicious, and well written; it is by far the best account we have of Anglo-American relations during this period and it will stand comparison with any book dealing with American foreign policy. Archibald Primrose (ed.), *The Windham Papers: Life and Correspondence of the Right Honorable William Windham, 1750–1810* (London, 1913), is important for the light it sheds upon the climate of opinion prevailing in the British Foreign Office. Nelson V. Russell, *The British Regime in Michigan and the Old Northwest, 1760–1796* (Northfield, Minn., 1939), supplements the work of Louise B. Kellogg. Beckles Willson, *America's Ambassadors to England, 1783–1928* (London, 1928), and *Friendly Relations* (Boston, 1934), are designed for a wider audience than are most of the books enumerated herein. James F. Zimmerman, *Impressment of American Seamen* (New York, 1925), is a detailed account, fair to both sides.

RELATIONS WITH FRANCE

Brooks Adams, *The Convention of 1800 with France,* Proceedings of the Massachusetts Historical Society, XLIV (1911), spiritedly defends President

John Adams's policy of peaceful coexistence with Revolutionary France. Beverly W. Bond, Jr., *The Monroe Mission to France, 1794–1796* (Baltimore, 1907), is fair both to Monroe and the Washington administration. Francis C. Childs, *French Refugee Life in the United States, 1790–1800* (Baltimore, 1940), is an excellent study of the problems created for the United States by refugees, many of them destitute, from France and Santo Domingo, and of the difficulties encountered by these foreigners in adapting themselves to American conditions. On General Collot, a French spy in the United States, there are three scholarly articles: Heloise H. Cruzat, "General Collot's Reconnoitering Trip Down the Mississippi," *Louisiana Historical Quarterly,* I (1918); Durand Echeverria (ed.), "General Collot's Plan for a Reconnaissance of the Ohio and Mississippi Valleys in 1796," *William and Mary Quarterly,* Third Series, X (1952); and George W. Kyte, "A Spy on the Western Waters: The Military Intelligence Mission of General Collot in 1796," *Mississippi Valley Historical Review,* XXIV (1947). Alexander De-Conde, *Entangling Alliance: Diplomacy and Politics under George Washington* (Durham, N.C., 1958), is sympathetic toward the Franco-American alliance and toward those who upheld it against the assaults of the Hamiltonian Federalists. Joseph Fauchet, the French minister to the United States during 1794–95, published *A Sketch of the Present State of our Political Relations with the United States* (Philadelphia, 1797), in which he held up the "pro-British" policy of the Washington administration to the execration of all "true Republicans." Mildred S. Fletcher, "The Policy of France toward the Mississippi Valley in the Period of Washington and Adams," *American Historical Review,* X (1905), reveals that the Federalists' distrust of French ambitions was well founded. Added evidence of the danger to which the United States was exposed by French designs upon the North American continent is supplied by E. Wilson Lyon, "The Directory and the United States," *American Historical Review,* XLIII (1938); *Louisiana in French Diplomacy, 1759–1804* (Norman, Okla., 1934); and "The Franco-American Convention of 1800," *Journal of Modern History,* XII (1940). Frederick Jackson Turner has edited the *Correspondence of the French Ministers to the United States, 1791–97,* Report of the American Historical Association for 1903 (2 vols., Washington, 1904), an indispensable source for the study of French policy toward the United States. Turner has also edited "Carondelet on the Defense of Louisiana," *American Historical Review,* II (1897); "Documents on the Relation of France to Louisiana, 1792–95," *American Historical Review,* III (1898); *The Mangourit Correspondence in Respect to Genêt's Projected Attack on the Floridas, 1793–94,* Annual Report of the American Historical Association for 1897 (Washington, 1898); and *Selections from the Draper Collection . . . to elucidate the proposed French expedition under George Rogers Clark against Louisiana in the years*

1793–1794, Annual Report of the American Historical Association for 1896, I (Washington, 1897). Charles D. Hazen, *Contemporary American Opinion of the French Revolution* (Baltimore, 1897), is a pioneering study of public opinion, to which should be added James Alton James, "French Opinion as a Factor in Preventing War Between France and the United States, 1795–1800," *American Historical Review,* XXX (1924), and *French Diplomacy and American Politics, 1794–1795,* Annual Report of the American Historical Association for 1911, I (Washington, 1912). There are two excellent books relating to American neutrality during the Federalist period: Charles S. Hyneman, *The First American Neutrality: A Study of the American Understanding of Neutral Obligations During the Years 1792–1815* (Urbana, Ill., 1934) and Charles M. Thomas, *American Neutrality in 1793: A Study in Cabinet Government* (New York, 1931). Frederick A. Tolles has written an excellent account of the man who inspired the Logan Act: "Unofficial Ambassador: George Logan's Mission to France, 1798," *William and Mary Quarterly,* Third Series, VII (1950).

RELATIONS WITH SPAIN

Samuel F. Bemis, *Pinckney's Treaty: A Study of America's Advantage from Europe's Distress, 1783–1800* (New York, 1926), is one of the best accounts we have of any treaty made by the United States government; it should be supplemented, however, by Arthur P. Whitaker, "New Light on the Treaty of San Lorenzo," *Mississippi Valley Historical Review,* XV (1929), and "Godoy's Knowledge of the Terms of Jay's Treaty," *American Historical Review,* XXXV (1930). Jane M. Berry, "The Indian Policy of Spain in the Southwest, 1783–95," *Mississippi Valley Historical Review,* III (1917), is based upon research in original documents; Caroline M. Burson, *The Stewardship of Don Esteban Mero, 1782–1792* (New Orleans, 1940), examines Spanish policy through a biographical approach. Myrna Boyce, "The Diplomatic Career of William Short," *Journal of Modern History,* XV (1943), is a good account of an American diplomat who has been undeservedly neglected by historians. John W. Caughey has written a fascinating account of a remarkable Indian leader, *McGillivray of the Creeks* (Norman, Okla., 1938). Thomas R. Hay, "Some Reflections on the Career of General James Wilkinson," *Mississippi Valley Historical Review,* XXI (1935), provides a good introduction to a man whose career was a long record of duplicity. William R. Manning, *The Nootka Sound Controversy,* Annual Report of the American Historical Association for 1904 (Washington, 1905), is an authoritative treatment of a dispute between Great Britain and Spain which vitally affected the United States. Frederick Austin Ogg, *The Opening of the Mississippi: A Struggle for Supremacy in the American Interior* (New York, 1904), is an older account which has been superseded by Arthur P. Whitaker's masterly studies:

The Spanish American Frontier, 1783–1795 (Boston, 1927, and *The Mississippi Question, 1796–1803* (New York, 1934).

The West: 1789–1801

Thomas B. Abernethy, *From Frontier to Plantation in Tennessee* (Chapel Hill, 1932), and Beverly E. Bond, Jr., *The Civilization of the Old Northwest: A Study of Political, Social and Economic Development, 1788–1812* (New York, 1934), are excellent accounts of the changes wrought by advancing civilization in the West. Randolph C. Downes has written an engrossing study of Indian affairs, *Council Fires on the Upper Ohio: A Narrative of Indian Affairs in the Upper Ohio Valley until 1795* (Pittsburgh, 1940), but Max Farrand, "The Indian Boundary Line," *American Historical Review,* X (1905), is still valuable. Important biographies of western leaders are Carl S. Driver, *John Sevier, Pioneer of the Old Southwest* (Chapel Hill, 1932), and William H. Masterson, *William Blount* (Baton Rouge, 1954). Russell J. Ferguson, *Early Western Pennsylvania Politics* (Pittsburgh, 1938), is detailed and scholarly, while Charles Homer Haskins presents an illuminating picture of rampant land speculation in *The Yazoo Land Companies,* American Historical Association Papers, V, 1891 (Washington, 1892). Military events are adequately covered by Milo M. Quaife (ed.), "General Wilkinson's Narrative of the Fallen Timbers Campaign," *Mississippi Valley Historical Review,* XVI (1930); William Clark, "Journal of General Wayne's Campaign," *Mississippi Valley Historical Review,* I (1915); and Frazwe E. Wilson, *The Peace of Mad Anthony* (Greenville, Ohio, 1905).

The Whisky Rebellion

The best account of the Whisky Rebellion is Leland D. Baldwin, *Whisky Rebels: The Story of a Frontier Uprising* (Pittsburgh, 1939). Hugh H. Brackenridge, *Incidents of the Insurrection in the Western Parts of Pennsylvania in the Year 1794* (Philadelphia, 1795), and William Findley, *History of the Insurrection in the Four Western Counties of Pennsylvania in the Year 1794* (Philadelphia, 1796), are contemporary accounts of the insurrection and its causes by Republican leaders of western Pennsylvania. William Miller, "Democratic Societies and the Whiskey Insurrection," *Pennsylvania Magazine of History and Biography,* LXII (1938), presents the evidence against the theory that the insurrection was inspired by the Democratic Societies.

Economics and Finance: 1789–1801

Charles A. Beard, *An Economic Interpretation of the Constitution of the United States* (New York, 1913), despite its unflattering views of the motives of the Founding Fathers, long remained almost uncontested as a work of

scholarship and penetrating insight. On both scores, Beard has been subjected to devastating criticism by Robert Brown, *Charles Beard and the
Constitution* (Princeton, 1956), and Forrest McDonald, *We the People*
(Chicago, 1958). Even so, Beard's thesis that the Constitution was molded
'to a great degree by the economic ideas of the framers has not been suc-
cessfully refuted. Beard, *Economic Origins of Jeffersonian Democracy* (New
York, 1915), treats of the political contests of the period as manifestations of
a basic conflict between "agrarian" and "capitalistic" interests. Albert Sydney
Bolles, *The Financial History of the United States from 1789 to 1860* (New
York, 1894), has been superseded by D. R. Dewey, *Financial History of the
United States* (New York, 1931), and, more recently, by Paul Studenski and
Herman E. Krooss, *Financial History of the United States* (New York, 1952).
Victor S. Clark, *History of Manufactures in the United States* (3 vols.,
Washington, 1916–28), is unrivaled as an exhaustive study of the subject—
a dictum which is equally applicable to Lewis Cecil Gray, *History of Agriculture in the Southern United States* (2 vols., Washington, 1933). Tench
Coxe, *A View of the United States of America* (Philadelphia, 1794), is a
contemporary examination of the state of American commerce and manufacturing which has served many historians as a rich source of economic
data. Joseph Dorfman has written a brilliant four-volume study of economic
thought, *The Economic Mind in American Civilization* (New York, 1946–
59); the chapters relating to the Federalist period ought not to be missed.
Charles Franklin Dunbar has several chapters in his *Economic Essays* (New
York, 1904) which bear upon the Federalist period and in "Some Precedents
Followed by Alexander Hamilton," *Quarterly Journal of Economics,* III
(1888), he has delved into the origin of Hamilton's ideas on finance. Bray
Hammond, *Banks and Politics in Early America* (Princeton, 1957), is a
stimulating study, replete with fresh insights. It was awarded the Pulitzer
prize for History in 1958. On the Bank of the United States, J. T. Holdsworth
and D. R. Dewey, *The First and Second Banks of the United States* (Washington, 1910), is required reading, but it ought to be supplemented by James
O. Wetterau, "New Light on the First Bank of the United States," *Pennsylvania Magazine of History and Biography,* LXI (1937). Edward C. Kirk-
land, *A History of American Economic Life* (New York, 1933), is one of
the best economic histories in print and it is particularly good on the Federalist period. Samuel McKee has compiled a selection from the official
papers of Alexander Hamilton, *Papers on Public Credit, Commerce and
Finance* (New York, 1957), to which James O. Wetterau has added some
significant documentation in "Letters from Two Business Men to Alexander
Hamilton on Federal Fiscal Policy," *Journal of Economics and Business History,* III (1946). Allan Nevins and Jeannette Mirsky, *Eli Whitney* (New
York, 1952), presents Whitney as one of the most significant figures in the

296   THE FEDERALIST ERA

history of American invention. James D. Phillips, *Salem and the Indies* (Boston, 1947), is the work of an assiduous chronicler of Salem's rise to commercial greatness; besides, Mr. Phillips is uncompromisingly Federalist in his political sympathies. Fritz Redlich, *The Molding of American Banking* (2 vols., New York, 1951), and E. R. Taus, *Central Banking Functions of the United States Treasury* (New York, 1943), are excellent studies of early banking practices. On the significance of Hamilton's achievement, the best short account is Rexford Guy Tugwell and Joseph Dorfman, "Alexander Hamilton, Nation-Maker," *Columbia University Quarterly*, XXIX, XXX (1937–38).

Constitutional Developments: 1789–1801

Lord Acton, *Essays on Freedom and Power* (Boston, 1948), helps provide the necessary background for an understanding of American constitutionalism. E. K. Bauer, *Commentaries on the Constitution, 1790–1860* (New York, 1952), is a valuable compilation of selections from the principal authorities upon the United States Constitution, one of the most important of whom is Joseph Story, *Commentaries on the Constitution of the United States* (2 vols., Boston, 1858). Charles A. Beard has set forth his views of constitutional questions in *The Supreme Court and the Constitution* (New York, 1922); *The Republic: Conversations on Fundamentals* (New York, 1945); and *The Enduring Federalist* (New York, 1948). James Bryce, *The American Commonwealth* (2 vols., New York, 1888), contains several chapters of much interest to students of the Federalist era. Of the many books exploring the entire field of American political thought, the best are W. S. Carpenter, *The Development of American Political Thought* (Princeton, 1930); Percy T. Finn, *The Development of the Constitution* (New York, 1940); Andrew C. McLaughlin, *A Constitutional History of the United States* (New York, 1935); Benjamin Wright, *The Growth of American Constitutional Law* (New York, 1946); and Louis Harz, *The Liberal Tradition in America: An Interpretation of American Political Thought Since the Revolution* (New York, 1955). Among the many books written by Edwin S. Corwin, a leading authority on the Constitution, three have particular relevance for the Federalist period, *Court over Constitution* (Princeton, 1938); *The Twilight of the Supreme Court* (New Haven, 1934); and *The President's Removal Power* (New York, 1927). William Crosskey, a professor of law at the University of Chicago, is the author of *Politics and the Constitution* (2 vols., Chicago, 1952), the thesis of which is that the framers of the Constitution actually intended to create a unitary form of government. Few students of the Federalist period endorse Professor Crosskey's conclusions. Significant studies of various aspects of the Constitution are found in Charles G. Haines, *The American Doctrine of Judicial Supremacy* (New York, 1914); Walton Hamilton and Douglass Adair, *The Power to Govern* (New York, 1937); Learned Hand, *The Bill of Rights* (Cambridge, Mass., 1958); Benjamin Wright, *The Contract Clause of the Constitution* (Cambridge, Mass., 1938); and *Selected Essays on Constitutional Law* (5 vols., Chicago, 1938). The best account of the formation of the Federal Constitution is A. N. Holcombe, *Our More Perfect Union* (Cambridge, Mass., 1950); A. H. Kelly and W. A. Harbison, *The American Constitution, Its Origins and Development* (New York, 1948), covers the history of the Constitution from its inception to World War II with clarity and thoroughness. Russell Kirk, *The Conservative Mind* (Chicago, 1953), is good on John Adams but disappointing on Alexander Hamilton. Roscoe Pound, *Federalism as a Democratic Process* (New Brunswick, 1942), and *The Spirit of the Common Law* (Boston, 1921), add depth to our understanding of the constitutional issues of 1789–1801. Conyers Read (ed.), *The Constitution Reconsidered* (New York, 1938), assembles the opinions of some of the leading authorities of the present day. Fred Rodell, *Nine Men: A Political History of the Supreme Court* (New York, 1955), is a popular account written in an almost comically "jazzed up" style; much sounder and more readable is Charles Warren, *The Supreme Court in United States History* (2 vols., Boston, 1937). R. A. Rutland, *The Birth of the Bill of Rights* (Chapel Hill, 1955), fills a gap in our knowledge of this important sector of constitutional history. Of federal government as a whole, the best study is by an English scholar, K. C. Wheare, *Federal Government* (Oxford, 1953).

The Alien and Sedition Acts

The pioneering study was made by Frank Maloy Anderson, *The Enforcement of the Alien and Sedition Laws,* Annual Report of the American Historical Association for 1912 (Washington, 1913). In 1951, John C. Miller published *Crisis in Freedom: The Alien and Sedition Laws* (Boston, 1951), which, the author hoped, would help restore Americans to sanity during the McCarthy Era by reminding them of their heritage of freedom. James Morton Smith, *Freedom's Fetters: The Alien and Sedition Laws and American Civil Liberties* (Ithaca, 1956), is a definitive study, as scholarly and detailed as the most exacting student could require. Mr. Smith writes under the assumption that the Sedition Act was unconstitutional—a premise which has been ably refuted by Mark De Wolfe Howe in the *William and Mary Quarterly,* Series 3, XIII (1956), 573–576. Of the many articles dealing with the Alien and Sedition Acts, two are worthy of special mention: Marshall Smelser, "The Jacobin Phrenzy: Federalism and the Menace of Liberty, Equality and Fraternity," *Review of Politics,* XIII (1951), and "George Washington and the Alien and Sedition Laws," *American Historical Review,* LIX (1954). Accounts of the trials held under the Sedition Act will be found in Francis Wharton, *State Trials of the United States during the Administration of Washington and Adams* (Philadelphia, 1849).

Developments in the States: 1789–1801

To understand fully the political, economic, and social changes which took place in the United States during this period it is necessary to study the states individually. For the New England states, James Truslow Adams, *New England in the Republic, 1776–1850* (Boston, 1926); Oscar Handlin, *Commonwealth: A Study of the Role of Government in the American Economy, Massachusetts, 1774–1861* (New York, 1947); David Ludlum, *Social Ferment in Vermont, 1791–1850* (New York, 1939); Anson E. Morse, *The Federalist Party in Massachusetts to the Year 1800* (Princeton, 1909); Richard J. Purcell, *Connecticut in Transition, 1775–1800* (Washington, 1918); and William A. Robinson, *Jeffersonian Democracy in New England* (New Haven, 1916), make important contributions to our knowledge of social, economic, and political change in this area. For New Jersey and New York, Walter R. Fee, *The Transition from Aristocracy to Democracy in New Jersey, 1789–1829* (Somerville, N.J., 1933); and Dixon Ryan Fox, *The Decline of Aristocracy in the Politics of New York* (New York, 1919), demonstrate that the victory of democracy in these states occurred prior to the election of Jackson to the Presidency. Pennsylvania has been made the subject of two excellent studies: Early Bruce Thomas, *Political Tendencies in Pennsylvania, 1783–1794* (Philadelphia, 1939); and Harry M. Tinkcom, *The Republicans and Federalists in Pennsylvania, 1790–1801: A Study in National Stimulus and Local Response* (Harrisburg, 1950). For the South, three studies merit mention: Charles A. Ambler, *Sectionalism in Virginia from 1776 to 1861* (Chicago, 1910); Delbert H. Gilpatrick, *Jeffersonian Democracy in North Carolina, 1789–1816* (New York, 1931); and John Harold Wolfe, *Jeffersonian Democracy in South Carolina* (Chapel Hill), 1940.

Index